Third Edition

MAX WEBER

The Protestant Ethic and the Spirit of Capitalism

New Introduction and Translation by
Stephen Kalberg
Boston University

Includes Weber's Essays
'The Protestant Sects and the Spirit of Capitalism'
and
'Prefatory Remarks' to Collected Essays in the Sociology of Religion

BLACKWELL
Publishers

Roxbury Publishing Company
Los Angeles, California

First published 2002

2 4 6 8 10 9 7 5 3 1

Blackwell Publishers Ltd
108 Cowley Road
Oxford OX4 1 JF
UK

British Library Cataloguing in Publication Data

A CIP catalogue record for this book is available from the British Library.

ISBN 0631230815 (pbk)

Typeset in Times and Adobe Garamond
by Roxbury Publishing Company
Printed in Great Britain by TJ International, Padstow, Cornwall

This book is printed on acid-free paper.

CONTENTS

THE PROTESTANT ETHIC AND THE SPIRIT OF CAPITALISM

Part I: The Problem

Chapter I.

Chapter II.

Chapter III.

Part II: The Vocational Ethic of Ascetic Protestantism

Chapter IV.

Chapter V.

Advance Praise for *The Protestant Ethic and the Spirit of Capitalism* *Third Roxbury Edition*

"Stephen Kalberg has produced a book that teachers and students will find invaluable. What an excellent idea, to combine a new translation of Max Weber's *The Protestant Ethic and the Spirit of Capitalism* with other closely related writings of Weber's, including a detailed and accessible introduction and supporting background information on Weber the man, on the book, and on its place in contemporary social science. Kalberg's comprehensive introduction manages to be informative and scholarly while remaining a clear and intelligible guide to the book. The introduction offers an accurate and refined statement of Weber's important and influential (if often misunderstood) thesis, placing it in the context of its era and to Weber's general idea of sociology. This new version of *The Protestant Ethic* should greatly improve upon its predecessor and clear up misunderstandings of Weber's meaning which the earlier translation may have engendered."

—*Wes Sharrock, University of Manchester*

"This new translation of Weber's *The Protestant Ethic*, one of the most important social science works of the twentieth century, is a welcome and worthwhile enterprise. It carefully presents the numerous and important nuances of Weber's text, giving a clear idea of the place of this text in the intellectual framework of his time. Professor Kalberg's introduction provides a very interesting commentary on this text as well as the place of Weber's work in the history of sociology and its relevance to the central problems of contemporary sociology theory. [The book] is a distinct contribution—and a tool for students of sociological theory and its history."

—*S. N. Eisenstadt, The Hebrew University of Jerusalem*

About the Translator

Stephen Kalberg is the author of *Max Weber's Comparative-Historical Sociology* (1994), *Max Weber's Sociology of Civilizations* (forthcoming), and numerous articles on Weber. He is the editor of *Max Weber: The Confrontation with Modernity* (2002). He teaches at Boston University, where he is Associate Professor of Sociology. He is also co-chair of the German Study Group at Harvard University's Center for European Studies.

INTRODUCTION TO THE TRANSLATION

Stephen Kalberg

The only heretofore existing translation into English of Max Weber's renowned study, *The Protestant Ethic and the Spirit of Capitalism*[1] (*PE*), is now over seventy years old. Ideally, classic works should be retranslated every generation. As translations age, they become less accessible to younger audiences. Languages changed especially rapidly in the twentieth century and many terms and expressions quickly acquired a hollow ring. Moreover, whereas the 1930 translation of *PE* was oriented mainly to scholars and students steeped in a liberal arts canon, today's readership is more general and less acquainted with the great works of the past. This new translation is long overdue.

It has been guided by two goals. First, I have sought to render Weber's text more accessible to the many audiences it has now acquired: scholars, students, undergraduate instructors, and not least, the general reader. Second, I have attempted to retain the integrity of Weber's study by offering a close-to-the-text translation. The full substance of his thought must be conveyed and his nuanced, complex reasoning must be captured accurately. Indeed, I have sought to provide a translation that offers the reliability of meaning and precision of intention, especially in respect to Weber's fine-grained causal lines of argument, indispensable to scholars of his works. In sum, I have placed a premium upon *both* readability and accuracy. For many texts, fulfillment of both of these goals would not present a large challenge to a translator. Unfortunately, in this respect, *PE* deviates from the norm and strays far afield from the "user-friendly" ideal.

Published in two parts in a social science journal in 1904–05,[2] Weber knew that his audience of scholars would be conversant with the entire landscape of Western history. As difficult as it may be for us to imagine today, his readers were quite capable of tracing the ebb and flow of Western civilization's unfolding since the ancient Greeks. All had attended elite schools (Gymnasien) that emphasized philosophy, literature, and languages, and all had benefited from three cycles of instruction, over a nine-year period, on the entire history of the West. Weber was well aware that his short-hand references—whether to ancient

Greek mythology, medieval monastic orders, or civil wars in England—would be readily understood.[3] Moreover, in keeping with the format of scholarly writing in Germany at the time, he knew that "matters of presentation" required little attention. Unfortunately, publishers in Weber's time in Germany did not employ copyeditors.[4]

Weber's study not only lapses occasionally into abbreviated formulations and fails to provide identifying cues to obscure persons and places, it also confronts the reader frequently with sentences one-half page in length and paragraphs two or three pages long. Multiple clauses reside within each sentence, as Weber continuously struggles to lay out his theme in all its complexity. Yet even when he succeeds in doing so in a nuanced fashion, he frequently calls attention to qualifications and emphasizes the milieu-specific contingency of his statements.

Any attempt by a translator to render Weber's text in a way that exactly captures his own manner of writing will stand opposed to the first goal mentioned above: readability and accessibility. This aim has required conformity to a practice frequently followed in German-English translations, namely, the radical shortening of sentences and paragraphs. In addition, in order to designate more clearly major and minor emphases, I have occasionally inserted parentheses into long sentences that proved impossible to shorten.

However, it soon became apparent that my goal of readability and accessibility would not be adequately achieved through these measures alone. Hence, several propaedeutic aids became indispensable:

- Persons, places, groups, and documents have been identified in short bracketed phrases inserted into the text.

- Some persons, places, groups, and documents have been further identified in new endnotes; [sk] follows these endnotes.

- Occasional endnotes that clarify Weber's argument have been added; [sk] follows these endnotes.

- Short supplementary phrases have occasionally been added into the text, in brackets, on those occasions where Weber's shorthand formulations require clarification.[5]

- Translations, in brackets, of foreign language passages have been added. *All passages in brackets in the text and endnotes are mine.*

- Terms that are key to Weber's argument, as well as several historical terms, have been defined in a glossary; their first usage in each chapter has been set in bold type.
- With only a few exceptions as required by context, the translation of all key terms has been standardized throughout the book. In this manner, Weber's forceful call for terminological precision in the social sciences has been respected and the major threads of his argument can more easily be followed.
- Innumerable partial bibliographical entries have been adjusted and completed.

In two important ways Weber *did* assist his audience. First, through regular italicization. Although italicization at the level he practiced is generally not permitted today in English publications, Weber's frequent italicization is retained. He regularly orients and guides his reader to concepts, themes, and distinctions central to his argument through this mode of emphasis. Second, Weber inserts nuance through regular use of inverted commas ("national character"). This practice has also been retained, as it indicates his unwillingness to accept fully a number of commonly used concepts and his awareness of their problematic and controversial character.

Finally, this translation designates the paragraphs and endnotes that Weber added in 1920 when he prepared *PE* for publication in his three-volume series, Collected Essays in the Sociology of Religion.[6] All such paragraphs and endnotes are followed by [1920].[7] These additions mainly involved: (a) responses to criticism of *PE* published in journals and newspapers from 1907–10;[8] (b) responses to books by his colleagues Sombart and Brentano; (c) independent clarifications of his argument;[9] (d) comparisons of ascetic Protestantism to Islam, Hinduism, Buddhism, and Confucianism; (e) reference to an overarching process in the developmental history of Western religions according to which magic became eliminated (*Entzauberung*) as a viable mechanism to assist the search for salvation; and (f) extensions of bibliographical sources.

This new edition also includes a new translation of Weber's introduction to his Collected Essays in the Sociology of Religion series (1920; see pp. 149–164). His essay on the Protestant sects and churches in America, written shortly after his visit in the United States and translated by Hans H. Gerth and C. Wright Mills, is reprinted (1906; see pp. 127–

147). Only slight alterations of their translation, on behalf of terminological consistency, have been undertaken.

***

Throughout my work on this new translation I have been the fortunate recipient of a completely unexpected outpouring of generosity from friends, colleagues, and specialists. It has far exceeded any claims for assistance that a translator might reasonably expect, and it has sustained me—even through several hundred long endnotes.

I am very pleased to acknowledge the vital assistance of Susan Converse Winslow and Jim Ballinger of Roxbury Publishing Company. The entire Roxbury staff mobilized behind this book in a extraordinarily impressive fashion. I am especially grateful to Roxbury's president, Claude Teweles, for having the vision to see the importance of this new translation and the patience to see the project through to its proper conclusion.

A number of persons offered specialized assistance at various points along my journey: Juliane Brandt, Josef Chytry, Jeff Coulter, Lewis A. Coser, John Heecht, Charles Lindholm, Sandro Segre, Guenther Roth, David N. Smith, Paul Windolf, and Kurt H. Wolff. Their helpfulness has been a source of inspiration to me.

Robert J. Antonio, Ira J. Cohen, Lyn Macgregor, and Michael Moody read an entire early draft of the text and offered comments that altered the direction of my work. My bicultural assistant, Jessica Horst, tirelessly tracked down dozens of references in Boston-area libraries and on the internet. Ulrich Nanko, a theologian in Stuttgart, located innumerable obscure persons and documents in the best German encyclopedias. John Drysdale, a native speaker of English, closely evaluated the entire translation; his suggestions were always beneficial and almost always accepted. Finally, I owe my greatest debt to Michael Kaern, a native speaker of German who checked the translation line by line. He unfailingly answered my many questions, large and small, and counseled on a daily basis with patience, insight, and high generosity of spirit. He did so, as we debated the merits of various English translations for technical terms, on the basis of an intimate knowledge of the world inhabited by German scholars 100 years ago.

I am more grateful to all than a person with a "this-worldly" Protestant upbringing could ever find words to express. They have improved this translation far beyond what it otherwise would have been.

Endnotes

1. Max Weber, *The Protestant Ethic and the Spirit of Capitalism.* Translated by Talcott Parsons. New York: Scribner's, 1930. Various publishers have reissued this translation over the last twenty years.
2. As I note in my introduction, Weber revised the text in 1920. This translation, as was the earlier translation by Parsons, is based upon the 1920 version. See *Gesammelte Aufsätze zur Religionssoziologie*, vol. 1, pp. 17–206 (Tübingen: Mohr, 1920). I have consulted throughout the later German paperback edition of 1979 edited by Johannes Winckelmann (Gütersloh: Gütersloher Verlagshaus).
3. Approximately 1 percent of youth attended these elite schools. Graduation from this type of school alone allowed admission to a university. Fritz Ringer has referred to this closed, highly educated circle as "German mandarins." See *The Decline of the German Mandarins* (Cambridge, MA: Harvard University Press, 1969).
4. In any case, owing to the extremely high social prestige of professors in Weber's Germany, editing of manuscripts by publishers, as is common today, would have been impossible.
5. Explanatory passages have been added in particular whenever Weber uses phrases such as "of interest to us *here*" and "for *our* theme" without identifying clearly his point of reference.
6. Single sentences and words altered or added in 1920 are *not* designated. However, Weber's major additions were in full paragraph form. Weber deleted or altered 1904–05 passages and words only extremely rarely.
7. A recent German edition has distinguished the 1904–05 and 1920 versions. See Max Weber, *Die protestantische Ethik und der 'Geist' des Kapitalismus*, edited by Klaus Lichtblau and Johannes Weiß (Bodenheim: Athenäum-Hain-Hanstein, 1993).
8. Most of these criticisms, and Weber's answers, have been collected now in two separate volumes. See Peter Baehr and Gordon C. Wells, eds., *Max Weber—The Protestant Ethic and the 'Spirit' of Capitalism—The Version of 1905, Together with Weber's Rebuttals of Fischer and Rachfahl and Other Essays on Protestantism and Society* (New York: Penguin Books, 2002), and David Chalcraft and Austin Harrington, eds., *'The Protestant Ethic Debate': Max Weber's Replies to his Critics, 1907–10* (Liverpool: Liverpool University Press, 2001).
9. These are fairly rare (for example, the contrast between asceticism and mysticism). ✦

INTRODUCTION TO *THE PROTESTANT ETHIC*

Stephen Kalberg

For certain, even with the best will, the modern person seems generally unable to imagine how *large a significance those components of our consciousness rooted in religious beliefs have actually had upon culture . . . and the organization of life. (p. 125*)*

First published in 1904–05, revised in 1920, and translated into English in 1930, Max Weber's famous study, *The Protestant Ethic and the Spirit of Capitalism* (*PE*), is one of the most enduring books of the twentieth century and a major classic in the social sciences. Its focus on values and ideas as sources of social change set off an intense discussion. The controversy has continued to this day almost unabated.

Although *PE* has often been understood as providing an explanation for the rise of **modern capitalism****, and even for the origin of our secular, urban, and industrial world today, its aim was actually far more modest. Weber wished to demonstrate that one important source of the modern work ethic and orientation to material success, which he calls the "spirit of capitalism," is located *outside* the realm of "this-worldly" utilitarian concerns and business astuteness. Even human avarice, the evolutionary course of progress, or the economic interests of heroic capitalists cannot explain its origin. Rather, this spirit, he contends, to a significant extent grew out of "the Protestant ethic" of sixteenth- and seventeenth-century **Puritan** churches and sects: Calvinists (today known as Presbyterians), Methodists, Congregationalists, Baptists, Quakers, Independents, and Mennonites. These sincere believers forcefully placed work and material success in the middle of their lives; little else seemed to matter greatly to them, not even family, friendship, leisure, or hobbies. Any discussion of the spirit of capitalism's origins, Weber insists, must acknowledge this *central* religious source.

He freely admits that this argument may appear today quite unorthodox. "We moderns" only infrequently explain human behavior, let alone economic activity, by reference to religion. In our epoch dominated by a

* Otherwise unidentified page numbers in parentheses refer to the text below.

** Terms defined in the Glossary, when first used in each chapter, have been set in bold type.

worldview anchored in the social and natural sciences, belief in the supernatural is seldom viewed as a causal force. Instead, we generally award priority to structural factors (such as social class and level of education), economic and political interests, psychological and biological forces, power and external constraint, and unencumbered, rational choices. Yet Weber insists that social scientists must seek to understand the activities of others contextually by reference to the world in which *they* lived and the nature of *their* motives for acting. Scholars must do so especially when investigating groups living in distant epochs and foreign lands, however difficult it may be to perform the indispensable leap of imagination into an unfamiliar universe. In times past, Weber speculates, religious belief possessed a greater influence on daily life than today. Moreover, if **carried** along by powerful social groups, many patterns of religion-oriented action formulated centuries ago, he contends, cast long and wide shadows. Indeed, their impact in some cases may endure into the present, even though these patterns of action may today be underpinned by entirely nonreligious motives.

Although the question grounded in "other-worldly" religious concerns that, Weber believes, ultimately directed the Puritan faithful toward work and material success—Am I among the few who are saved?—is no longer of burning urgency in the nation most influenced by Puritanism, the United States, Americans' dedication to work and success is still influenced by the **ascetic Protestant** tradition. This nation is frequently described today as a work-obsessed society. In 1999 the United States replaced Japan as the worldwide leader in number of hours worked per person per year; Europeans, in contrast, work approximately two-thirds as many hours per year as Americans. Americans read daily on the one hand of people who are exhausted and deprived of sleep and on the other of people who "love their work." Expressions that reflect the centrality of work in our lives are pervasive: we arrange "working lunches," we "work out" daily, we "work" on love, our relationships, our personalities, and our tans. We praise the work ethic of our peers and "hard workers" are generally assumed to be people of good character. A salary increase is awarded often to the "most dedicated" employee—a person who works, with pride, not only days but also nights and weekends. If we take naps, they must be "power naps." "Workaholics" take "working vacations." Many people define self-worth, and even their own identity, according to their success in a profession.[1] A steady orientation to career goals and the disciplined organization of one's life to that end are praised.[2]

Were he alive today, Weber would see these pivotal features of American society as secularized legacies of ascetic Protestantism. However, and although fascinated by the enduring impact of the Puritan heritage in the United States (see p. 246 [note 53]; see also "The Protestant Sects" essay [pp. 127–147]; 1985), his quest in *PE* was primarily that of an historical sociologist: (1) to discover the *sources* in the past of the idea that life should be organized around systematic work and material success, and (2) to argue that this manner of organizing life played a significant part in calling forth the spirit of capitalism. To him, this particular focusing of life appeared originally in a specific historical epoch and in identifiable groups. These were religious groups, he contends, and they introduced the Protestant ethic. As first manifest in the spirit of capitalism and visible even today in the ways in which Americans conduct their lives, the legacies of this ethic have proved long-lasting. In the end, as we shall see, both the Protestant ethic and the spirit of capitalism placed into motion significant thrusts that facilitated the rise of modern capitalism.

Max Weber: The Man and His Central Concerns

Shortly after his birth in Erfurt, Germany, in 1864, Max Weber moved with his family to Berlin. His ambitious father, soon elected to seats in the Prussian state government and the Reichstag, became a key figure in the Berlin city government. The social conscience of Max's well-educated mother, who descended from a long line of distinguished scholars and successful businessmen, was highly influenced by mid-century American Unitarian and English Progressive theology. After raising seven children, she became an activist in progressive religious circles. While the father's intense engagement in the political issues of the time followed an ethos of pragmatism and realism, the mother's example conveyed to young Max a heightened sensitivity to moral questions, an appreciation of the ways in which a life of dignity must be guided by ethical standards, and a respect for the worth and uniqueness of every person.

A precocious child, Weber early on developed a strong love of learning. His rigorous, elite high school (*Gymnasium*) in Berlin emphasized a classical curriculum—history, philosophy, literature, and languages—and the regular writing of interpretive essays. Upon graduation he studied law and economic history at the universities in Heidelberg, Berlin, and Göttingen. At the unusually young age of 30, Weber was appointed to a full professorship at the University of Freiburg. Called to a chair in economics two years later, he moved to the University of Heidelberg, where he remained until his death in 1920.

A significant incident occurred during a visit by his mother to his home in Heidelberg in the summer of 1897. Unexpectedly, Weber's father appeared and commenced a heated argument with his mother. The young Weber, who had passively witnessed his mother's mistreatment for years, then evicted his father from his home. The father's death seven weeks later seems to have served as the catalyst for a paralyzing mental illness that afflicted Weber for more than five years. By 1903 he had regained much of his strength, and a three-month journey with his wife in the fall of 1904 throughout the American East, Midwest,[3] and South further raised his spirits. Nonetheless, he did not teach again until the last two years of his life.

***

Weber's generation stood between two worlds and thus found the "past" and "future" starkly demarcated. The German agrarian countryside of feudal manors and small, self-contained villages had remained basically unchanged for centuries, while industrialization proceeded rapidly in Europe's cities throughout the latter half of the nineteenth century. The pulsating pace of change left Weber and many of his colleagues with a deep sense of foreboding. Fully uncharted waters seemed ahead. Urbanization,[4] bureaucratization, secularization, and a massive expansion of capitalism took place on such a vast scale that a clear continuity between past and present appeared to have vanished forever.

Seeing vividly before them a new era in opposition to familiar traditions and values extending back over 2,000 years of Western history, Weber's contemporaries began to ask a series of fundamental questions. What will be left to guide our lives in this new epoch? How can we live under capitalism, which gives priority to the laws of the market over long-standing traditions, ethical values, and personal relationships? Does the new order rest upon a stable foundation? As the philosopher Wilhelm Dilthey asked: "Where are to be found the instruments for surmounting the spiritual chaos which threatens to engulf us?"

Among scholars, these urgent concerns led naturally to questions regarding the *origin* of this new "cosmos." What were its early sources? What *causal forces* drove the making and unfolding of the industrialized world? What were the origins of modern capitalism? If these questions could be answered, the nature of this new universe would be better understood. Not least, the parameters would be charted within which possible change could realistically take place.

Weber did not share the extremely bleak "cultural pessimism" of many of his contemporaries, especially Georg Simmel and Friedrich Nietzsche (Kalberg, 1987, 2001). And he refused to lend support to the many Romantic movements of his time, all of which sought, in one way or another, to retreat into the "simpler" world of the past. Indeed, he welcomed emphatically the freedoms and rights the modern world bestowed on the individual, arguing that "it is a gross deception to believe that without the achievements of the [Enlightenment] Age of the Rights of Man any one of us, including the most conservative, can go on living his life" (1968, p. 1403). He spoke and wrote tirelessly on behalf of strong and contending political parties and advocated an "ethic of responsibility" for politicians, constitutional guarantees for civil liberties, an extension of suffrage, and strong parliaments. In addition, he sought to erect mechanisms that would sustain pluralistic, competing interest groupings in order to check the power of bureaucracies, for "we 'individualists' and supporters of 'democratic' institutions are swimming 'against the stream' of material developments" (1978, p. 282).[5]

Nevertheless, and despite indefatigable political activism, Weber's view of the twentieth century is pervaded by skepticism and ambivalence. His scholarship arose out of questions similar to those asked by his more fatalistic colleagues. What "type of person" will inhabit this new universe? How, amidst the overwhelmingly material and pragmatic character of everyday life in industrialized societies, will persons be able to orient their lives to *ethical values*? Especially now that religion has been weakened, will not the sheer instrumental-rational calculations typical of the modern capitalist economy push aside *all* ethical values?

A "practical rational" way of life grounded in utilitarian considerations, juxtaposed with a rigidly bureaucratized workplace, Weber feared, would eventually call forth a society of highly conforming persons lacking noble ideals and individualism. If this occurred, a sense of ethical responsibility for one's actions would not be cultivated and the autonomy of individuals would gradually fade. Finally, without ethical values how could compassion, charity, and the ethos of brotherhood survive (see 1946a)? Although ascetic Protestantism had introduced onto the stage of history a "type of person" firmly oriented to ethical values, today only remnants of this mode of organizing life remain. Has the Puritan "devotion to a cause" disappeared, supplanted by pleasure-seekers on the one hand and the utilitarian calculations of "organization men" on the other (pp. 122–24)?

***

These broad-ranging questions and dilemmas stand behind *PE*. They capture Weber's overarching concerns, ones he will explore in roughly 15 volumes of sociological writings. *PE* constitutes his first major investigation of these themes. It analyzes how methodical work becomes endowed with significant meaning and moves to the very center of the lives of a specific group of people. *PE* can even be seen as Weber's earliest, and partial, attempt to define clearly the uniqueness of the modern West and to identify the major causal forces that drove its development (see "Prefatory Remarks" below, pp. 149–164). These themes continued to dominate his scholarship until the end of his life.

The first part of *PE* (pp. 3–50) was written in Heidelberg in the summer of 1904. It was printed a few months later in a journal when Weber and his wife were traveling in the United States. Finished in early 1905 upon his return to Germany, the second part (pp. 53–125) appeared in June, 1905, in the same journal.[6] Although Weber noted that the libraries at Colgate and Columbia universities, as well as the libraries of small colleges "scattered all over the country," would be of use for his "cultural history" study, he managed to conduct very little research during his visit. As he reported in a letter, "I did not see much more than where the things are that I ought to see" (Marianne Weber, 1988, p. 304; see also p. 253).[7]

PE is a difficult text. An understanding of its complex analysis can be facilitated by, first, a brief overview of the axes around which it is organized and the intellectual context within which Weber wrote. The next section turns to these themes. The subsequent two sections summarize and comment upon *PE*'s frequently misunderstood argument. Although lengthy, these sections offer more so highlights of Weber's analysis; they fail to capture its extreme subtlety and cannot substitute for a reading of the text. *PE* is then examined by reference to central axes in Weber's sociology as a whole. This introduction concludes with brief comments on two famous essays by Weber included in this volume ("The Protestant Sects and the Spirit of Capitalism" and " 'Prefatory Remarks' to Collected Essays in the Sociology of Religion), a few tips on reading this classic study, short descriptions of an array of interesting *PE* endnotes, and a listing of suggested further reading. A glossary of key terms follows this introduction.

The Protestant Ethic and the Spirit of Capitalism: Organizational Axes and the Intellectual Context

Organizational Axes

The distinction between "capitalism" and "modern capitalism" stands at the foundation of Weber's entire analysis in *PE*. Capitalism, as involving the exchange of goods and calculations of profit and loss balances in terms of money, has existed in civilizations in all corners of the globe, from ancient times to the present. The assessment of balances has been more efficient in some epochs and societies than in others, where it remained primitive and approximated guesswork. However, a calculation of income and expenses, or "capital accounting," has been found universally, as has "the expectation of profit based upon the utilization of opportunities for exchange" (p. 152). Moneylenders, merchants engaged in trade, entrepreneurs investing in slaves, and promoters and speculators of every sort have calculated profits and losses in every epoch (pp. 16–17, 152–156; 1927, p. 334; 1968, p. 91).[8]

Weber turns quickly away from such "adventure capitalism" and "political capitalism" to a discussion of the distinguishing features of *modern* capitalism: a relatively free exchange of goods in markets, the separation of business activity from household activity, sophisticated bookkeeping methods, and the rational, or systematic, organization of work and the workplace in general. Workers are legally free in modern capitalism rather than enslaved. Profit is pursued in a regular and continuous fashion, as is the maximization of profit in organized, productive businesses (see pp. 152–157; 275, note 9; 1927, pp. 275–351; 1968, pp. 164–66; Kalberg, 1983, pp. 269–276).

Nevertheless, Weber insists that this definition of modern capitalism is incomplete, for it refers to formal aspects only (the "economic form"). It is important to recognize, he argues, that modern capitalism *also* involves the organization of economic activity in terms of an "economic ethic." This *ethos* legitimates and provides the motivation for the rigorous organization of work, the methodical approach to labor, and the systematic pursuit of profit typical of modern capitalism. It implies: "the idea of the *duty* of the individual to increase his wealth, which is assumed to be a self-defined interest in itself" (p. 16; emph. in original); the notion that "labor [is] an absolute end in itself" (p. 24); the desirability of "the acquisition of money, and more and more money, [combined with] the strictest avoidance of all spontaneous enjoyment of it" (p. 17); the view that the "acquisition of money . . . is . . . the result and manifestation of competence and proficiency in a vocational calling" (p. 18); and a "particular **frame of mind** that . . . strives systematically and rationally *in a* ***calling*** for legitimate profit" (p. 26).

Weber called this "modern economic ethic" the "spirit of capitalism."[9] Its violation, he asserts, involves not merely foolishness but "forgetfulness of *duty*" (p. 16; emph. orig.). The eighteenth-century American printer, inventor, entrepreneur, businessman, and statesman Benjamin Franklin, according to Weber, embodied the essence of this *ethos*, as apparent from his attitudes toward work, profit, and life in general (pp. 14–15). As Weber notes in his "Prefatory Remarks" essay below:

> The origin of economic rationalism [of the type which, since the sixteenth and seventeenth centuries, has come to dominate the West] depends not only on an advanced development of technology and law but also on the capacity and disposition of persons to organize their lives in a practical-rational manner. (p. 160; see 1946c, p. 293)

Typically, Weber isolates the distinctive qualities of the spirit of capitalism through comparisons, above all to the economic ethic of "traditionalism." He does so mainly along two axes: attitudes toward work and the business practices of employers.

Wherever the spirit of capitalism reigned, work was perceived as a noble and virtuous endeavor; one who engaged in it was respected throughout the community and believed to be of good character. Work played a central role in the formulation even of a person's sense of dignity and self-worth. This "elevation" of work to a special position in one's life resulted, Weber contends, from an array of modern historical conditions; work never held such importance for adherents to the **traditional economic ethic**. They regarded work as involving drudgery and exertion; it was a necessary evil to be avoided as soon as customary and constant economic needs were met. Thus, such people approached labor in an unfocused and lackadaisical manner. Moreover, they understood work as only one arena of life, deserving of no more attention, concentration, or time than other important arenas, such as the family, hobbies, friendship, and leisure in general. Not surprisingly, those who understood work in this way could not be induced to increase productivity even if employers introduced a piece-rate system that provided monetary incentives for faster and more efficient labor. On the contrary, because employees viewed work negatively and other activities positively, a higher piece-rate led to less work: employees could earn the amount of money necessary to fulfill their accustomed needs in a shorter period of time. They would then have more time to pursue leisure activities. As Weber notes:

> The opportunity of earning more appealed to him less than the idea of working less. . . . People do not wish 'by nature' to earn more and more money. Instead, they wish simply to live, and to live as they have been accustomed and to earn as much as is required to do so. (pp. 22–23; see pp. 21–25; 1927, pp. 355–56)

The traditional economic "spirit" also held sway over persons engaged in business until relatively recently in human history. Whereas employers imbued with the spirit of capitalism sought profit systematically, organized their entire workforce according to the rules of productive and efficient management, reinvested profits in their companies, and saw themselves as engaged in harsh, competitive struggles, economic traditionalism implied a more comfortable and slow-paced manner of conducting business. Set by long-standing custom rather than by the laws of the market, prices and profits generally remained constant. The circle of customers did not vary, and relations between workers and owners were regulated largely by tradition. There was always time for friends and long meals, for the workday lasted generally only five to six hours. Although capitalistic in terms of the use of capital and the calculation of income and expense, a leisurely ethos characterized the entire approach to moneymaking and to business (pp. 24–29).

Weber is proposing that these differences between the traditional and modern orientations toward work and business management are not insignificant. Moreover, although economic forms and economic ethics "exist generally in . . . a relationship . . . of 'adequacy' to each other," there is no " 'lawful' dependency," and they may exist separately (pp. 26–28; 1946c, pp. 267–68). On the one hand, even though the spirit of capitalism strongly infused Benjamin Franklin's habits and general way of life, the operations of his printing business followed those typical in handicraft enterprises (pp. 26–27). On the other hand, the traditional economic ethic might combine with a highly developed capitalist economy (e.g., Italian capitalism before the Reformation). After comparing the widespread capitalism in Florence in the fourteenth and fifteen centuries (where activity directed toward profit for its own sake was viewed as ethically unjustifiable) with the economic backwardness of eighteenth-century Pennsylvania (where a spirit of capitalism was "understood as the essence of a morally acceptable, even praiseworthy way of organizing and directing life"), Weber concludes that capitalism itself did not produce the spirit of capitalism (pp. 34–37).

***

How did the "revolution" (p. 27) that brought economic traditionalism to an end take place? What are the sources of this monumental shift to a modern economic ethic? And how did it happen that work moved to the center of life? To Weber, the approach to work "as if [it] were an absolute end in itself . . . is not inherently given in the nature of the species. Nor can it be directly called forth by high or low wages. Rather, it is the product of a long and continuous process of education and socialization" (pp. 24–25; see p. 176, note 17). In light of the extreme immutability and endurance of the traditional economic ethic, Weber is convinced that only persons of unusually strong character were capable of banishing it (p. 29). Yet such an orientation of activity toward hard work appears fully "irrational" and unnatural viewed from the perspective of the spontaneous enjoyment of life (pp. 24, 30–31, 33, 37).

This is Weber's modest concern in this "essay in cultural history." Rather than investigating the origins of modern capitalism, the rise of the West, or capitalism as such, this case study seeks to discover the specific "ancestry" of the *spirit* of capitalism (pp. 37, 49–50, 54–55). In defining this task, Weber was responding critically to a heated discussion in German scholarship. The unorthodox focus of "the Weber thesis" on the importance of a spirit of capitalism separated *PE* clearly from the major orientation of this debate toward capitalism as an economic form. In fact, the explorations by his colleagues into the origins of modern capitalism usually denied the salience of an economic ethic. By explicitly seeking to broaden the boundaries of this controversy in an unwelcome direction, *PE* immediately set off a furor. Before turning to Weber's analysis of "the Protestant ethic's" religious origins, a glance at the main contours of this debate is indispensable. Doing so will situate *PE* within the intellectual currents of its time and demarcate its uniqueness.[10]

The Intellectual Context: The Controversy Over the Origins of Capitalism and Industrialism

Nearly all participants in the debate on the origins of modern capitalism and industrialism 100 years ago in Germany offered explanations that neglected cultural forces. The six explanations that dominated this controversy can be mentioned only briefly.

The intensification of avarice. A number of German scholars at the end of the nineteenth century argued that, in earlier times, the "acquisitive instinct" (p. 20) was less developed or even nonexistent. In the eighteenth and nineteenth centuries, however, they saw avarice and greed as becoming stronger. They believed that modern capitalism resulted from an intensification of the "acquisitive instinct" [and the] pursuit of gain" (p. 152).

This characterization of more recent centuries as ones in which the "striving for . . . the greatest profit" (p. 152) has been more widespread, Weber contends, does not bear up once experimental comparisons are undertaken. The "greed for gain" can be found among "all sorts and conditions of men at all times and in all countries of the earth, wherever the objective possibility of it is or has been given" (p. 152). To him, the "*greed* of mandarins in China, of the aristocrats in ancient Rome, or the modern peasant is second to none" (p. 20). Because such an *auri sacra fames* (greed for gold) has existed universally and is "as old as the history of man," it fails to offer a causal explanation for his *specific* problem: the rise of a spirit of capitalism in the sixteenth and seventeenth centuries in the West. Finally, Weber will argue that the rise of modern capitalism involves a "tempering" of all acquisitive desires; indeed, such a "restraining" of avarice—and its channeling into a methodical orientation toward work—is indispensable for the systematic organization of work and production in permanent businesses (pp. 19–21, 152; 1927, pp. 355–56).

The adventure and political capitalism of charismatic entrepreneurs. Other scholars in Germany were convinced that the desire of great charismatic entrepreneurs for riches pushed economic development past the agrarian and feudal stages to mercantilism and modern capitalism. Typically engaged in gigantic commercial ventures often involving the continent-spanning trade of luxury items, these unscrupulous and egocentric promoters, financiers, bankers, merchants, and speculators ushered in the modern epoch simply on the basis of their extraordinary energy (pp. 16–17, 19–20).

Again, however, Weber discovered this adventure and political capitalism universally. Yet these types of capitalism never called forth *modern* capitalism. Furthermore, he refused to view the exceptional commercial daring of these sporadically appearing "economic supermen" as implying the continuity of disciplined action requisite for shattering the traditional economic ethic. Isolated individuals alone could never call forth this monumental transformation; rather, an organizing of life common to whole "*groups* of persons," all *intensively* oriented toward profit and the rational organization of labor and capital, would be necessary (pp. 19, 21).

Evolution and progress. In *Der moderne Kapitalismus* (1902), Werner Sombart, Weber's colleague and friend, held that the expansion of production, trade, banking, and commerce could best be understood as clear manifestations of a society-wide unfolding of "rationalism" and progress in general. In this view, the spirit of capitalism constituted simply further, and not unusual, evidence of a general evolution. To Sombart, societal progress as a whole deserved explanation rather than the separate component elements in this broad-ranging evolutionary process.

Weber opposed Sombart vehemently. "Society" was too global a level of analysis, Weber claimed. Instead, the separate societal "realms" (*Lebensbereiche*), "orders" (*Lebensordnungen*), or "spheres" (*Lebenssphären*), which together comprise a "society," must be examined. If one proceeds in this manner, a *nonparallel* development in the various realms becomes evident, Weber insists, rather than a general evolutionary process. For example, a systematization, or "**rationalization**," in the sphere of law (in the sense of increasing conceptual clarity and the refinement of the content of the law based upon a fundamental written source, such as a constitution) reached its highest point in the Roman law of later antiquity. On the one hand, however, this type of law remained far less developed in a number of countries where a rationalization of the *economy* advanced farthest. In England, for example, a less rationalized form of law—Common law—prevailed. On the other hand, Roman law remained strong throughout southern Europe, an area where modern capitalism developed quite late (pp. 34–37). In neither region did the law and economy realms develop in a parallel fashion.

These and similar observations persuaded Weber to reject the notion of "general evolutionary progress" and to focus his attention on a variety of societal orders rather than "society" as an organic whole. He investigated the realm of religion in *PE* and later, in his three-volume analytic treatise, *Economy and Society* (1968), the domains of law, rulership (*Herrschaft*), economy, status groups, and "universal organizations" (the family, the clan) (see Kalberg, 1994b, pp. 53–54, 103–117; 1996, pp. 50–51; 1998, pp. 221–25).

The Jews as the carriers of modern capitalism. Sombart's book, *The Jews and Modern Capitalism* (1913), argued that the Jews as a group were the major social carriers of modern capitalism. He viewed the putatively typical business dealings of Jews as decisive: the loaning of money for interest, continuous speculation, and the financing of wars, construction projects, and political activities. In addition, Sombart argued that an "abstract rationalism," which allegedly characterized Jewish thinking, was identical with the "spirit of capitalism" of English Puritans. The wish to make money dominated in both groups.

Weber disagreed forcefully on all points both in *PE* and in later writings (see p. 111, pp. 247–48, notes 66 and 67; 1968, pp. 611–23, 1202–04; 1927, pp. 358–59).[11] He viewed the innovation-averse economic ethos of the Jews as "traditional" and noted their absence among the heroic entrepreneurs in the early stages of Western European capitalism. Furthermore, he saw the capitalism of the Jews as a form of the speculative capitalism that had existed universally rather than as involving a systematic organization of production, labor, and the workplace in general (pp. 110–112; 247–49, note 67). Finally, Weber argued, the outcaste position of the Jews kept them outside the pivotal craft and guild organizations of the medieval period, and their double ethical standard, which followed from this outcaste position (strong ethical obligations to other Jews, yet quite different practices in economic relationships with non-Jews), hindered the unfolding of measures of economic efficiency across the economy.

Historical materialism, economic interests, and the power of the dominant class. Although the "internal contradictions" of capitalism constituted the major concern of Karl Marx, his writings clearly yield an analysis of its origin. For him, the rise of modern capitalism can be equated with the overthrow of the feudal aristocracy and the hegemonic rule of a new class: the bourgeoisie. Ownership of the means of production (property, factories, technology, tools, etc.) by this class, as well as its economic interests, were believed to be crucial; they stood as foundational ingredients in the quest of capitalists to acquire more and more wealth. Moreover, the desire of the bourgeoisie to pursue profit and sheer greed served this class well. As it became larger and more powerful, trade, banking, production, and commerce expanded. Eventually, factory-based capitalism came into being.

A "spirit of capitalism" could play no part in the historical materialism of Marx. Had he been alive to address the Weber thesis, Marx surely would have viewed this ethos as arising directly out of the economic interests of the bourgeoisie; the set of values it implied would be understood as nothing more than an expression, in abstract form, of their economic interests. Such an "ideology" served, Marx argued frequently, following Jean Jacques-Rousseau (1712–78), to justify the hegemony of the dominant class and to sedate workers into accepting their misery and exploitation.

Despite his agreement on certain points with Marx, in *PE* Weber rejected this analysis completely. He insists that economic interests did not give birth to the spirit of capitalism. Franklin himself offers evidence against this position: his economic ethos far preceded the formation of a bourgeoisie (pp. 19, 32–33). Moreover, Weber doubted in general the capacity of social groupings to call forth uniform action:

> The assumption is . . . by no means justified *a priori* . . . that, on the one hand, the technique of the capitalist enterprise and, on the other, the spirit of 'work as a vocational calling,' which endows capitalism with its expansive energy, must have had their *original* sustaining roots in the same social groupings. (p. 177, note 24; emph. in original; see, e.g., 1946c, pp. 268–71, 292; 1968, pp. 341, 577)

As noted, even those members of the bourgeoisie who proved to be economic supermen were incapable, Weber contended, of the sustained effort necessary for a rupturing of **economic traditionalism**. Finally, Weber found that the spirit of capitalism was formulated and cultivated not by the entrepreneurs of a commercial elite (the "Patricians merchants") but above all by self-made parvenus from the modest circumstances of the **middle classes** (pp. 26–27, *passim*). To him, the "youth of the 'capitalist' spirit is altogether more thorny than was assumed by the 'superstructure' theorists" (p. 19, *passim*).[12]

Miscellaneous forces. Many historians and economists emphasized the importance for economic development of technological innovations, geographical forces, the influx of precious metals from the New World, population increases, and the growth of cities and science. Weber examined all of these arguments. Through scrutiny of comparative cases, he deduced that favorable technological and scientific inventions, population changes, and climatological and other factors had existed in the Middle Ages in the West, in the ancient world, and in a number of epochs in China and India—yet modern capitalism had failed to appear first in these civilizations.[13]

***

In these ways,[14] *PE* seeks fundamentally to recast the ongoing debate toward an exploration of the origins of a "rational" economic ethic, or spirit of capitalism (pp. 19–35). Weber laments the exclusion of this factor, and thus the inadequacy of the major explanations for the rise of modern capitalism; all these explanations attend to modern capitalism mainly as an "**economic form**." By insisting that a modern economic ethic must be acknowledged as a sociologically significant causal force in modern capitalism's early development and that an exploration of its origins must take place, Weber seeks (1) to bring values and ideas unequivocally into the debate, and (2) to legitimize an investigation of their causal origins.

Weber is attempting to persuade his readers that cultural values must not be left out of the equation. However complicated it may be to investigate their origins and to assess their influence, to him values should not be regarded as passive forces generally subordinate to social structures, power, classes, evolution and progress, and economic and political interests. Weber insists that the spirit of capitalism had significant noneconomic and nonpolitical roots.

Empirical Observations, the Turn Toward Religion, and the Aim of *PE*

In searching for the sources of the spirit of capitalism, Weber never pursued a trial-and-error pathway. Rather, he took the view, not uncommon in the Germany of his time, at the outset that *religious belief* influenced work habits and approaches to business, as well as life in general.[15] Hence, an exploration of differences between Protestants and Catholics appeared to him a quite plausible and natural orientation for his research. Indeed, he had been reading theological literature, including the American Unitarians William Ellery Channing and Theodore Parker, since his teenage years.[16]

Although a relationship between occupational status and educational attainment on the one hand and Catholicism and Protestantism on the other was acknowledged among journalists and the educated public in Germany in the 1890s, as well as earlier,[17] very little social science research had addressed this theme. As he pondered English and American Puritanism in the mid-1890s, Weber read the massive study by the economic historian Eberhard Gothein, *Wirtschaftsgeschichte des Schwarzwalds* (1892) (Economic History of the Black Forest), which called attention to Calvinism's strong role in spreading capitalism (pp. 9–10). He praised Gothein, but was even more struck by Georg Jellinek's *Die Erklärung der Menschen- und Bürgerrechte* (1901) (The Declaration of the Rights of Man and Citizens), which "stimulated [me] to study Puritanism again."[18] Jellinek's documentation of how devout Dissenters in seventeenth-century England had been central in the emergence of the notion of fundamental political rights and liberties impressed Weber and aroused his curiosity:

> [Jellinek's] proof of religious traces in the genesis of the Rights of Man . . . gave me a crucial stimulus . . . to investigate the impact of religion in areas where one might not look at first. (Marianne Weber, 1988, p. 476)

In the late 1890s, Weber encouraged his student Martin Offenbacher to examine the influence of religion on social stratification in the southwest German state of Baden. Offenbacher's statistical investigation concluded that distinct differences existed between Protestants and Catholics in regard to occupational choices and levels of education: Protestants dominated as owners of industrial concerns, while Catholics were more often farmers and owners of businesses utilizing skilled labor. Protestants' generally higher levels of education accounted for their disproportionately high employment as state civil servants and their unusually high earnings if they remained in the working class (1900, pp. 63–64).[19] Weber used his student's "facts and figures" in order to outline his research agenda and central questions (see ch. 1).

Despite his crippling mental illness, he had completed his research on the economic ethic of the Quakers by the late 1890s.[20] The publication in 1902 of Sombart's two-volume work, *Der moderne Kapitalismus*, appears to have motivated Weber to intensify his own research. In his chapter on the origin of the capitalist spirit, Sombart had dismissed the role of Protestantism, especially Calvinism and Quakerism, as "too well-known to require further explanation." Instead, he discovered "empirical proof" of capitalism's origins in the high esteem accorded to the possession of money, indeed the addiction to "sparkling gold" (*auri sacre fames*) that appeared in the European Middle Ages. To Sombart, "the Protestant religion was not the cause but the result of modern capitalist thinking." He provoked his readers to discover "empirical proof of *concrete-historical contexts* to the contrary" (1902, vol. 1, pp. 380–81; emph. in original; see vom Brocke, 1987; Lehmann, 1993, pp. 196–98).[21]

Weber took up the challenge, completing the research for *PE* in 1903.[22] His response to Sombart is vigorous. Even external social structures of extreme rigidity, such as those typical of religious sects, Weber asserts, should not be viewed as themselves calling forth homogeneous patterns of action.[23] How then could capitalism do so? The studies he had read in the 1890s pointed in a different direction. As well, Weber noted the unusually methodical and conscientious work habits of young women from Pietistic families in Baden (pp. 24–25). Even this:

> Analysis derived from [early twentieth century] capitalism has indicated to us yet again that it would be worthwhile simply to *ask* how these connections between people's capacity to adapt to [modern] capitalism, on the one hand, and their religious beliefs, on the other, could have been formulated during the youth of [modern] capitalism. (p. 25; emph. in original)

He then explicitly states his aim in *PE*:

> It should here be ascertained only whether, and to what extent, religious influences *co*-participated in the qualitative formation and quantitative expansion of this 'spirit' across the globe. (p. 49; emph. in original)

Whether religious beliefs constitute the "specific ancestry" of the spirit of capitalism must be investigated.[24]

Weber responds to Sombart's provocation even more directly when he describes his step-by-step procedure. He will first investigate whether an "elective affinity" (*Wahlverwandtschaft*) exists between certain religious beliefs of the Reformation and a vocational ethic (*Berufsethik*). If this "meaningful connection" (*sinnhaften Zusammenhang*) can be established, he will then be able to clarify the "way" and "general direction" in which religious movements, as a result of this elective affinity, influenced the development of *material culture*, or practical, workaday life.[25] Only then will it be possible to assess "to what degree the historical origin of the values and ideas of our modern life . . . can be attributed to religious forces stemming from the Reformation, and to what degree to other forces" (p. 50). Weber's complex and multidimensional analysis in *PE* can be broken down into two major stages: (1) his investigation of the origins of the Protestant ethic and (2) his linkage of the Protestant ethic to the spirit of capitalism.

The Origins of the Protestant Ethic: Weber's Analysis

In searching for the spirit of capitalism's ancestry, Weber scrutinizes medieval Catholicism, Lutheranism, and the ascetic Protestant churches and sects from two perspectives: the extent to which religious belief calls forth motivations that give rise to a *methodical-rational organization of life*, and the degree to which religious belief places **psychological rewards** directly upon systematic economic activity. He is convinced, as discussed, that only methodical activity of extreme rigor and continuity in large *groups* of people had the capacity to call forth a "revolution" against the traditional economic ethic (pp. 27–30). Instrumental action on behalf of a goal to accumulate wealth does not possess the indispensable sustaining power to do so.

The lay Catholicism of the Middle Ages never linked the important question—am I among the saved?—to economic activity. On the contrary, the faithful believed themselves to be saved if they regularly prayed, confessed their sins, sought to uphold the commandments, and engaged in "good works." Moreover, Weber emphasizes, the church acknowledged human imperfection and provided a mechanism to ameliorate the sinner's anxiety: the sacrament of confession. By unburdening their conscience to a priest and performing the penance he imposed, the devout were enabled to conduct their lives in an "accounting" fashion: sinful behavior, however reprehensible, could be balanced out over the long run by repentance and the more frequent practice of charitable good works as penance. A cycle of sin, atonement, and forgiveness—a "series of *isolated* actions" (p. 69)—characterized lay Catholicism rather than the placing of uninterrupted psychological rewards upon a systematized, rigorously directed way of life. Only the "religious 'virtuosi' "—monks and nuns—organized their lives in a methodical rational manner, yet they remained in monasteries "outside the world" (pp. 69–70).

Finally, Catholicism maintained a highly negative image of merchants and businessmen in general. Their perceived lust for gain placed riches above the kingdom of God and thereby endangered the soul, and their exploitation of persons on behalf of economic gain opposed the Christian ethic of brotherhood and group solidarity. An unequivocal axiom prevailed: *homo mercator vix aut numquam potest Deo placere* (the merchant may conduct himself without sin but cannot be pleasing to God) (p. 33; 1927, pp. 357–58; 1946a, pp. 331–32; 1968, pp. 583–87, 1189–91). To Weber, a traditional economic ethic prevailed in Catholicism.

In banishing the Catholic confessional and the parallel salvation paths for lay and virtuoso believers, Lutheranism distanced itself from medieval Catholicism. In doing so, and in introducing the idea of salvation through faith—penitent humility, an inward-oriented mood of piety, and trust in God—as its doctrinal fulcrum, Lutheranism placed qualitatively different psychological rewards on the believer's action (pp. 58, 66–67). Moreover, and salient to Weber, Luther introduced the idea that work in a "calling" (*Beruf*) was given by God. Believers, in essence, had been *called* by God into a vocation, or specific line of work, and hence were duty-bound to it.

Nevertheless, Weber failed to discover the religious origins of the spirit of capitalism here (pp. 39–40). Because all callings for Luther were of equal value (p. 41), there were no psychological rewards for occupational mobility. In addition, Luther never extolled "success" in a vocation or an intensification of labor beyond the standards set by each calling. Instead, one's religious duty involved a reliable, punctual, and efficient performance of the tasks and obligations required by the vocation itself. Indeed, a "moral legitimation of vocational life" now appeared (p. 41), and the mundane work-life of all believers became penetrated by a religious dimension. Thus a dramatic step away from Catholicism had been taken. A systematization of life as a whole, however, did not occur in Lutheranism. Finally, because God firmly defines the boundaries for each vocation and station in life (*Stand*), Luther saw the acquisition of goods beyond this level as morally suspect and sinful (pp. 42–43). Weber concludes that the economic ethic of Lutheranism in the end remained basically traditional, all the more because it retained the Catholic ethic of brotherhood and thus opposed the impersonal exchange characteristic of relationships in the marketplace (pp. 43–45; see 1968, pp. 514, 570, 600, 1198)

Weber then turned to *ascetic* Protestantism: the Puritan sects and churches of the seventeenth century, most prominently Calvinism, Pietism, Methodism, and the adult baptizing denominations (the Baptists, the Quakers, and the Mennonites). He believed that the Protestant ethic of Calvinism most clearly expressed the origins of the spirit of capitalism. How did this *Protestant ethic* originate? Only a sketch of Weber's argument can be offered here.

Calvinism and Puritanism

In the sixteenth century John Calvin formulated a religious doctrine built on two pillars. First, in opposition to Catholicism and Lutheranism, he accepted the Old Testament's view of God as an all-powerful and omniscient deity, far superior to all previous gods and separated from earthly mortals by an unbridgeable chasm. This "fully transcendent," majestic God was also a wrathful and vindictive deity, prepared at any moment to express his anger against sinful human beings. Because he was a distant being, His motives for doing so could never be understood by lowly humans (pp. 57–60). Second, Calvin argued that this inscrutable God had "predestined" for all time, and unalterably, only a tiny minority to be saved; everyone else was condemned to eternal damnation. The activities of believers, whether they confessed sins, performed good works, or donated to charity, would not change this "double decree" (i.e., saving a few, damning all others). One's salvation status had been preordained. The confession of sins and the sinner's absolution by a priest were no longer possible, for Calvin had abolished the sacrament of confession (pp. 60–61).

Weber saw that the doctrine of predestination, especially when combined with the concept of an omnipotent and vengeful yet unknowable God, led logically to massive fatalism, loneliness, and anxiety among the faithful. In an epoch in which an overriding question—"am I among the saved?"—dominated the lives of believers to a degree scarcely comprehensible today, the despair of the devout became unbearable (pp. 57–60).

Ascetic Protestants after Calvin, the Puritans, with whom Weber was concerned, sought to address the doctrine of predestination's bleak outcome in a variety of ways.[26] Undoubtedly, if congregations hoped to retain their membership, revisions had to be undertaken. Weber sees that, remarkably and unexpectedly, reformulations of Calvin's teachings in the seventeenth century led believers eventually to uphold an ethos of "world mastery" and to orient their entire lives toward work and material success. Puritanism gave birth to a "Protestant ethic." Weber's explanation of how this took place can best be examined by scrutiny of two themes: (1) the strict organization by believers of their conduct with the result that they came to lead tightly controlled, methodical-rational lives; and (2) the *directing* of these systematically organized lives toward work in a vocational calling, wealth, and profit.[27]

How the Ascetic Protestant Faithful Came to Lead Methodically Organized Lives

According to Weber, despite God's incomprehensible decree of predestination, Puritan believers felt compelled, in order to alleviate their overwhelming anxiety, to seek signs of their membership among the chosen few. Although His motives could not be known, God obviously desired action in strict conformity with His commandments and laws. Yet virtuous conduct, in light of the sinful character of the human species, proved difficult. Indeed, taming all wants and physical desires, and then orienting life in a consistent fashion to His laws, required heroic efforts of discipline. Nevertheless, according to Puritan doctrine, righteous conduct must be undertaken and an overcoming of impulsive and spontaneous human nature—the **status naturae**—must be achieved, for this vain and angry Puritan God demanded that His will be honored and His standards upheld. The purpose given to God's terrestrial creatures—to honor and glorify Him—could be fulfilled *only* in this manner. Thus, despite the double decree, believers were expected as an absolute duty to consider themselves among the chosen, and as such to conduct their lives according to this divinity's commandments. Indeed, an inability to muster the requisite self-confidence to do so or to combat doubts was believed to indicate "insufficient faith," a condition that surely would not characterize one of the saved (pp. 65–66).

Of course, the concentration of their entire energies on behalf of God's laws did not guarantee the salvation of the devout. The predestination decree could not be changed by the actions of mere mortals, even if pleasing to this vindictive deity. However, the revisions of Calvin's doctrines by Richard Baxter and other seventeenth-century "Puritan Divines"[28] persuaded the faithful that, *if they proved capable* of mastering their selfish desires and leading righteous, dignified lives oriented unequivocally to God's commandments, *then* they could assume that the *capacity* to do so had been in fact bestowed upon them by their deity, who after all was omniscient and all-powerful. The devout knew that their energy derived from the very strength of their belief, and they were further convinced that unusually intense belief emanated from God, whose will was operating within them (pp. 67–69). They could then conclude that God, naturally, would convey powerful belief and energy only to those He had "favored," that is, predestined for salvation.

Hence, the faithful now knew what was necessary in order to answer the crucial question regarding the "certainty of salvation" (*certitudo salutis*): they must **strive to** live the "sanctified," or holy life. A continuous "monitoring of their own pulse," to insure that actions remained consistent with God's laws, became necessary. Although even the most dutiful and disciplined believers could never know *with certainty* that they belonged among the elect few, they could still comprehend their own devout and organized conduct as a *sign* of their saved status. *God's* hand, acting within the predestined by bestowing intense belief, had rendered them capable (as His "tools" on earth) of obeying His laws (pp. 64–65, 67, 77–78, 85; see 1968, p. 572).

In sum, by virtue of this nonlogical, psychological dynamic,[29] believers created for themselves, as a consequence of their conduct in conformity with the good Christian ideals that serve God's glory, "*evidence* of their own salvation" (pp. 68, 85). By **organizing their lives** on behalf of God's laws, the faithful were able to "bear witness" through this methodical conduct, or **testify** to their membership among the elect "saints." In this way, believers could *convince themselves* of their favorable salvation status. Moreover, their upright conduct could be recognized by others as a sign of their membership among the chosen few.

This achievement answered the crucial question—"am I among the saved?"—affirmatively and thus held in check the tremendous anxiety and fatalism that resulted logically from the doctrine of predestination. Simultaneously, and of pivotal concern to Weber, this accomplishment gave birth to a frame of mind that he saw as specifically Puritan: the tempered, dispassionate, and restrained disposition that completely tamed the *status naturae*. A systematic rationalization of life now took place. The rigorous and focused conduct of these ascetic saints contrasted dramatically with the unsystematized lives of Catholics and Lutherans.

> The believer could receive and above all recognize his call to salvation only through consciousness of a central and unitary relation of this short life toward the supra-mundane God and His will; in other words, through striving toward 'sanctification.' In turn, sanctification could testify to itself only through God-ordained activities and, as in all active asceticism, through ethical conduct blessed by God. Thus, the individual could gain certainty of salvation only in being God's tool. The strongest inner reward imaginable was thereby placed upon a rational and moral systematization of life. Only the life that abided by firm principles and was controlled at a unitary center could be considered a life willed by God. (1951, pp. 239–40; translation altered)

Yet the Puritan's organization of life as a whole proved fragile. A perpetual danger remained: temptations might threaten the commitment of the devout to God's laws and the modes of taming the *status naturae* might prove ineffective. Even the sincere faithful might still draw the logical conclusions from the predestination decree: fatalism and despair.[30] In fact, Weber saw that a more solid foundation for the methodical-rational organization of life crystallized once the writings of the Puritan Divines connected the all-important *certitudo salutis* question directly to methodical work in a vocation and the systematic pursuit of wealth and profit. This connection stood at the center of Weber's interests and at the core of his argument regarding both the overcoming of economic traditionalism and the birth of the Protestant ethic.

How the Ascetic Protestant Faithful Came to Direct Their Methodically Organized Lives Toward Work in a Vocation, Wealth, and Profit

The orientation toward work. Ascetic Protestant theologians of the sixteenth and seventeenth centuries emphasized that the world exists in order to serve God's glory (p. 63). The purpose of this short life was to render a contribution toward the creation of His kingdom on earth. God's goodness and justice would surely be served if His earthly cosmos became one of wealth, abundance, and the common good. The exemplary "city on the hill" must be built by believers *in majorem Dei gloriam*, or for God's glory; a kingdom of poverty and destitution would only dishonor this majestic deity. As a crucial means of creating His prosperous kingdom and the common good, work acquired a special dignity. It served to increase God's magnificence (pp. 63, 104–105).

Baxter and the Puritan Divines also emphasized that God ordained the faithful to work. He "willed" and desired them to work (pp. 105–06). Even methodical work in a vocational calling "is commanded to all," for sustained work not only enables a focusing on the "impersonal societal usefulness" that promotes God's glory but also keeps in check all egocentric wishes (pp. 63, 106–08). In other words, rigorous work in a calling provides regularity to the believer's life and combats confusion (p. 107). God decrees that even the wealthy must work, and St. Paul's maxim—"He who will not work shall not eat"—is understood by the Puritans as God's law (pp. 105–06). And God is pleased by the active execution of His will by believers in vocational callings: "The entire corpus of literature on asceticism . . . is permeated with the point of view that loyal work is highly pleasing to God" (p. 121; see pp. 104–06).

This focusing, through continuous and systematic work, of the energies of the devout upon God and His plan serves the further purpose of taming creaturely desires. As a mechanism opposing the "unclean life" and all sexual temptation, work provides moderation to life, thereby further assisting the concentration upon God and the soul's "uplifting" (pp. 105–06). Not least, "intense worldly activity" dispels the overwhelming doubt, anxiety, and sense of moral unworthiness that follows from the doctrine of predestination. Finally, restless work in a calling enhances the self-confidence that enables the faithful to consider themselves among the chosen (pp. 65–66).

For all these reasons industrious work acquired an unequivocal meaningfulness to the Puritan devout of the seventeenth century. Psychological rewards, Weber emphasized, originating from the domain of religion, were bestowed on labor, even rendering it methodical. Work now directly became sanctified, or **providential**; it acquired a religious value. Nevertheless, he perceives that an even stronger linkage between systematic work and religious belief arose out of Calvinism when the idea of "testifying to belief" became interwoven securely with labor. The great capacity of this idea to organize the believer's entire life around disciplined work resulted simply from its power *to convince* the faithful of their membership among the predestined few, thereby answering the burning question: Am I among the saved? The devout, according to Weber's exploration of the subjective predicament they confronted, could acquire *evidence* of their chosen status not only by adhering strictly to God's laws, but also by methodical work in a vocation.

Methodical work as a sign of one's salvation. For all the reasons mentioned above, work had become important in the religious lives of Calvinists. Its general prominence insured its centrality in all discussions among theologians and pastors regarding the urgent question of whether signs of one's chosen status could be discovered and uncertainty regarding one's salvation could be lessened. The idea that systematic work might constitute a sign of one's salvation arose mainly out of the practical problems confronted by pastors seeking to offer, through "pastoral care," guidance to believers.

As noted, the continuous orientation to God's laws required unusual effort and the successful upholding of His decrees involved heroic faith. The devout even believed that the source of their intense belief, and their subsequent energy to maintain righteous conduct, derived solely from the presence of divine powers acting within them. They came to view the capacity to sustain a methodical orientation to work in the same way. One's energy to perform hard and continuous labor in a vocational calling must come ultimately from intense and sincere belief, and such belief originated from the favoring hand of an omnipotent God. Indeed, rigorous work *testified*, to the devout themselves as well as to others, to an inner, spiritual relationship with Him and to His assistance. Anyone capable of rejecting the confusion of irregular work, not to mention the *status naturae*, and of adopting a systematic orientation to work could do so only because of His blessing. God must be "operating within" such a person. Surely this omniscient divinity would choose to help only those he had predestined for salvation (p. 116; 1968, p. 572).

In this manner, the capacity for constant work further acquired a religious halo. If the faithful made an effort to work in a methodical manner, and discovered an ability to do so, a sign of God's favor had been given them, it could be concluded. In an epoch when anxiety about salvation dominated the lives of the faithful and threatened their mental stability, the search for a sign of God's blessing contained a mighty power to motivate believers to undertake disciplined work in a vocation. As Weber notes,

> [A] psychological *motivation* . . . arose out of the conception of work as a *calling* and as the means best suited (and in the end often as the *sole* means) for the devout to become certain of their state of salvation. (p. 121)

And:

> The religious value set on restless, continuous, and systematic work in a vocational calling was defined as absolutely the highest of all ascetic means for believers to testify to their elect status, as well as simultaneously the most certain and visible means of doing so. (p. 116)

Methodical work now became deeply hallowed, and "the view of work as a 'vocational calling' [for the modern worker] became . . . characteristic" (p. 121; see also pp. 120–21; 1968, p. 1199). Obviously, the understanding of work carried out in this manner—appropriately performed in a systematic fashion and correctly placed at the very core of the believer's life—served as a powerful lever to dislodge the traditional economic ethic.

This close linkage of religious belief and economic activity, founded on the idea that work in a vocation testified to membership among the elect few, constituted a cornerstone of Weber's explanation for the origin of the Puritan's dispassionate and restrained frame of mind. A further argument proved crucial for persons oriented to business. The connection, most evident in Calvinism, of a methodical striving for wealth and profit with a favorable answer to the *certitudo salutis* question gave these believers a subjective reassurance of salvation and thus served as an additional fundamental source for the Protestant ethic.

Wealth and profit as signs of one's salvation. A further adjustment of Calvin's doctrine of salvation by Baxter and the Puritan Divines proved significant for an understanding of the striving for wealth and profit among people oriented to business. Although believers could never know with certainty their salvation status, they could logically conclude, in light of God's desire for an earthly kingdom of abundance to serve His glory, that the actual production of great wealth by an individual for a community was a sign that God favored that individual. In effect, personal wealth became, to the faithful, actual *evidence* of their salvation status. An omnipotent and omniscient God would never allow one of the condemned to praise His glory. Surely, "the acquisition of wealth, when it was the *fruit* of work in a vocational calling, [was a sign of] God's blessing" (p. 116). Similarly, the opportunity to compete with others to make a profit did not appear by chance; rather, it constituted an opportunity given by God to acquire wealth:

> If God show you a way in which you *may*, in accord with His laws, acquire *more profit* than in another way, without wrong to your soul or to any other and if you refuse this, choosing the less profitable course, *you then cross one of the purposes of your calling. You are refusing to be God's steward, and to accept his gifts*. (p. 109; emph. in the original [this is a quote from Baxter]; see also pp. 116–17)

Weber emphasizes repeatedly that, for the Puritans, a psychological certainty of salvation was crucial. The exercise of astute business skills and the acquisition of money were not ends in themselves. On the contrary, to strive for riches in order to live well and carefree could only be considered sinful. All covetousness—the pursuit of wealth for its own sake—and frivolous indulgence must be condemned as a deification of human wants and desires. Instead, the Puritans viewed riches as an unintended consequence of their major quest, namely, to acquire the certainty of salvation. Wealth, which was received exclusively through the favor of an omnipotent God, in the eyes of the sincere faithful was important evidence of religious virtue, and it was valued in this sense alone (pp. 107–08, 114–17; 1951, p. 245; 1968, p. 1200). According to Weber:

> In no other religion was the pride of the predestined aristocracy of the saved so closely associated with the man of a vocation and with the idea that success in *rationalized* activity demonstrates God's blessing as in Puritanism. (1968, p. 575; emph. in original; see also p. 556)

Thus, business-oriented believers could now seek to produce the evidence—literally, wealth, profit, and material success generally—that would convince them of their status as among the chosen. Accordingly, riches acquired, uniquely, a *religious* significance: they constituted signs that indicated one's salvation. For this reason they lost their traditionally suspect character and became sanctified.

Three Central Aspects

In sum, Weber offers a complex and multidimensional explanation for the origins of the Protestant ethic. It has been examined here by reference mainly to, first, the question of what motivated the devout to organize their lives in a methodical manner and, second, what motivated them to direct their systematized conduct toward work, the acquisition of wealth, and material success in a vocation.[31]

Weber's many critics have often simplified (and then attacked) his analysis. Some have failed to see either the centrality of the *certitudo salutis* question or its powerful capacity—grounded in the doctrine of predestination, an Old Testament view of God, and pastoral care concerns—to give an impetus to religious development from Calvin to seventeenth-century Puritans. Others never acknowledge that, despite the logical consequences of the doctrine of predestination, conduct oriented to God's laws and disciplined work was understood by the Puritans as *testifying* to intense belief, which was believed to emanate originally from God. Many interpreters have neglected Weber's analysis of how believers seek to serve God as His "tools" and then to systematize their entire lives, to unusual degrees, around work and His laws. Still others have been unaware of the several ways that the devout discover signs of God's favoring hand and the manner in which these signs motivate the organization and direction of their activity. Weber's early critics (see Chalcraft and Harrington, 2001), as well as many later commentators (see Lehmann and Roth, 1993), refused to take cognizance of his pivotal distinction between action guided by *values* and oriented to the supernatural and other, basically utilitarian, action. Finally, Weber's emphasis on how motivations for action arise through religious belief, and the capacity of belief to call forth psychological rewards that direct action, has been often downplayed.

All of these themes will continue to capture our attention. Before turning to the urgent question that must now be addressed—How did Weber link the Protestant ethic to the spirit of capitalism?—three central aspects of his analysis of the origins of the Protestant ethic must be briefly highlighted.

(1) As carried by groups of seventeenth-century Puritans, Weber insists that the Protestant ethic involves a methodical-rational organization of

life. An unusual, and extreme, *internal* systematization of energies is apparent, and the impulsive and spontaneous *status naturae* is overcome and replaced by a tempered, restrained, and dispassionate frame of mind. Weber calls this taming a "reversal" of the "natural" life and argues that it rests on a firm orientation by sincere believers to the supernatural realm, without which such an implausible reversal would be meaningless (pp. 16–17, 30–31, 77–78). Now as tools of God's will and His commandments, the faithful have become ascetic saints.

> Puritan asceticism . . . worked to render the devout capable of calling forth and then acting upon their 'constant motives,' especially those motives that the believer, through the practice of asceticism itself, 'trained' against the 'emotions.' . . . The goal was to be able to lead an alert, conscious, and self-aware life. Hence, the destruction of the spontaneity of the instinct-driven enjoyment of life constituted the most urgent task. (p. 72; see also 1951, p. 248; 1968, pp. 572–73)

The entire existence of the devout now became radically penetrated by religious values. A "meaningful total relationship of the organization of life to the goal of religious salvation" came into existence (1968, p. 478). For Puritan believers, labor in a calling existed only as an expression of their striving for other-worldly salvation. This methodical-rational organization of life must be qualitatively distinguished from the frame of mind of the lay Catholic rooted in a "series of isolated actions," the Lutheran's penitent humility and inward-oriented mood of piety, and the common "affirmation of the world" typical of all utilitarian, means-end rational action (pp. 15–17, 78–80).

(2) Although in an earlier epoch work had been elevated to the center of life and had become capable of internally rationalizing the believer's entire conduct, these developments took place in the seventeenth century in a qualitatively new fashion. Weber stresses that a comprehensive organization of life also characterized medieval monks. Yet these *other-worldly* ascetics lived "outside the world" in monasteries, while the Puritans were engaged in **earning a living** in commerce, trade, and all the endeavors of the workaday world; they lived "*in* the world." Nevertheless, owing to their ultimate focus on God's laws and salvation in the next life, the values of the Puritans belonged "beyond" the workaday world, namely, to the religious realm. Ascetic Protestants, Weber contends, acted *in* the world, but their lives neither emanated from this world nor were lived *for* it (pp. 70–71, 101; 1968, p. 549).[32] Still, as instruments of an eth-

ical and commanding deity, believers were expected to carry God's laws *into* the routine and practical activities of everyday life, and as His tools to transform, even revolutionize, its haphazard events on His behalf. God's glory—the mastery of the world (*Weltbeherrschung*) for His sacred aims—deserved nothing less. Moreover, because earthly life exists as the single field for testifying to membership among the elect, a mystic flight from the world could never constitute a viable option.

Thus, although the *inner-worldly* asceticism of the Puritans devalued terrestrial life in comparison to the next life, they nonetheless oriented their lives *to* the world and acted within it in a methodical and ethical manner. Weber argues that because a psychological certainty of salvation can be found only in such a "**surpassing**" of the customs and morality of everyday routines, "perhaps there has never been a more intense form of religious valuation of moral *action* than that which Calvinism produced in its followers" (p. 69).

> The special life of the saint—fully separate from the 'natural' life of wants and desires—could no longer play itself out in monastic communities set apart from the world. Rather, the devoutly religious must now live saintly lives *in* the world and amidst its mundane affairs. This *rationalization* of the organized and directed life—now in the world yet still oriented to the supernatural—was the effect of ascetic Protestantism's *concept of the calling*. (p. 101; see also pp. 72–73; 1946c, p. 291; 1968, pp. 546, 578)

In this context Weber cites the maxim of the sixteenth-century German mystic Sebastian Franck: *Every* Christian must now be a monk for an entire lifetime (p. 74).

(3) Closely related is his emphasis on how a whole series of heretofore mundane activities become, as the Protestant ethic spread, sanctified, or "providential." In the traditional economic cosmos, work, wealth, profit, and competition, for example, were all closely tied to utilitarian action. Now, with the Puritans, all acquired, remarkably, a religious significance. To the same extent they became severed from the "worldly" realm of pragmatic considerations. In other words, from the vantage point of the all-important *certitudo salutis* question, these practical activities became, to the devout, endowed with **subjective meaning**. Even an unwillingness to work and a lapse into begging assumed a providential meaning.[33] People engaged in business and oriented to profit were no longer scorned as calculating, self-interested actors; rather, a good conscience was now bestowed upon them and they became perceived by others as honest employers engaged in

a task given by God (pp. 109–10, 120). Similarly, the reinvestment of profit indicated loyalty to God's grand design, and because all income and profit came from His grace, the devout practiced frugality and avoided ostentation (pp. 114–15). Indeed, because "this world" constituted the field for impersonal service to God's glory and for testifying to one's elect salvation status, routine conduct in general acquired a greater focus and intensity (p. 77–78).[34] It became enveloped in a religious halo.

These three central aspects of Weber's analysis—the taming of the *status naturae* and the appearance of inner-worldly asceticism, the Protestant ethic's *this*-worldly orientation, and the providential rendering of heretofore mundane, utilitarian activities—are central to his study of the origins of the Protestant ethic. Moreover, all contribute mightily to the capacity of this ethic, on the one hand, to confront and banish the traditional economic ethic and, on the other hand, to give a positive thrust to the development of modern capitalism.

In *PE*, this thrust flows into the "spirit of capitalism." Weber maintains that the Protestant ethic, as noted, "co-participated" in the formation of the spirit of capitalism.

From the Protestant Ethic to the Spirit of Capitalism

That 'objective' formulae for determining points of demarcation do not exist in the attribution of historical cause is not of my doing. (1972, p. 325)

This section will first acknowledge the unusual capacity of the Protestant ethic to displace economic traditionalism, which is always highly resistant to change. Then it will quickly recapitulate the way the Protestant ethic offered a "push" to modern capitalism. Finally, it will sketch the pathway from the Protestant ethic to the spirit of capitalism.

The Protestant Ethic, the Traditional Economic Ethic, and the Push to Modern Capitalism

As noted, the banishment of age-old, obdurate economic traditionalism required patterns of action qualitatively more systematic and intense than means-end rational action oriented to economic interests and profit-making. After all, Weber reasoned, as discussed above, trade, commerce, and the pursuit of wealth have existed universally. Entrepreneurial astuteness and "business savvy," as well as all intelligent modes of making one's way in the world (*Lebensklugheit*), can be found in every epoch and civilization (pp. 16, 20–21, 152). Nonetheless, the traditional economic ethic was only rarely uprooted. Even charismatic adventure capitalists, who can be found universally also, failed to weaken economic traditionalism.

Weber insists that the extreme methodicalness of the Puritan's orientation toward work, wealth, and profit, anchored ultimately outside the mundane world in the salvation question, proved decisive in bringing about change. Action motivated by religious values, and the concerted bestowing of religion-based psychological rewards on economic activity in a vocation, alone managed to uproot the traditional economic ethic. Unified and focused ethical action, which characterized this *coherent group* of persons, had to be clearly distinguished, he argues, even from intensified means-end rational action. The tenacity and "lasting resilience" (p. 30) of Puritan employers and workers who succeeded in replacing economic traditionalism with the Protestant ethic was anchored in a methodical-rational organization of life. Work motivated "from within," by an "internally binding" set of religious values, introduced the "life organized around ethical principles" that banished the traditional economic ethic (p. 76, see pp. 76–80). As Weber notes elsewhere:

> The true Christian . . . wished to be nothing more than a tool of his God; in this he sought his dignity. Since this is what he wished to be, he was a useful instrument for rationally transforming and mastering the world. (1951, p. 248)

The ethical dimension that penetrated the Puritan's economic activity not only constituted a "revolutionary" force against economic traditionalism; it also pushed forward the development of modern capitalism. Weber sees the Protestant ethic as doing so for all the reasons discussed above. In particular, he emphasizes, of course, the methodical organization of the lives of ascetic believers and the vigorous direction of focused energies, in a vocational calling, toward work, wealth, and profit. He repeatedly notes the necessity of testifying to belief through conduct, the search for signs of one's salvation status, the providential rendering of heretofore purely utilitarian activities, and the new-found clear conscience of the capitalist in search of profit.

Weber calls attention as well to the Puritan's preference to live modestly and frugally, to restrict consumption (especially of luxury goods), to save, and to invest surplus income, which, the faithful knew, came from the hand of an omnipotent deity and must be utilized on behalf of His purposes only (pp. 114–17). To indulge desires and to pursue an ostentatious mode of living would distract the devout from their exclusive orientation to God's will and from their task, as His instruments, to create the righteous kingdom on earth. Believers viewed themselves as the earthly trustees of goods that came from God and hence the enjoyment of wealth became "morally reprehensible" (p. 104). Only activity, not leisure and enjoyment, serves to increase the majesty of God (pp. 104–06, 115).[35]

Moreover, owing to the Puritan perception of the feudal aristocracy as lacking an orientation to God and as decadent, the purchase of titles of nobility and imitation of the feudal lord's lifestyle, as commonly occurred among the *nouveaux riches* in Europe, could not appeal to these social carriers of the Protestant ethic (pp. 117–18). They disapproved of this "feudalization of wealth" because the acquisition of a country estate and the building of a mansion would preclude the reinvestment of wealth in business. Property, they knew, must be used for purposes of production and to increase wealth (p. 109).

Weber emphasizes also that the Protestant ethic called forth an unusually industrious labor force. Because they were convinced that diligent labor served God's design, devout workers were not only disciplined and reliable but also willing. Their "*exclusive* striving for the kingdom of God . . . through fulfillment of the duty to work in a vocational calling . . . must have promoted the 'productivity' of work" (p. 121). The Puritans "took pride in their own superior business ethics" (p. 122).

In sum, and although the Puritans' radical rationalization of world-oriented action was eventually "routinized," or weakened, this ascetic Protestantism called forth an organized, directed life that, Weber contends, stands at the very root of today's "economic man" (p. 118). As the "only consistent carrier" of this methodical-rational orientation to life, the Puritans "created the suitable 'soul' for capitalism, the soul of the 'specialist in a vocation' " (1972, p. 168). An inner **affinity** between the ethically-rigorous devoutness of ascetic Protestantism on the one hand and "the modern culture of capitalism" and "economic rationalism" on the other hand can be said to exist (p. 11; see 1968, pp. 479–80). To Weber, the rational work ethic of the Puritans gave a strong boost to the development of modern capitalism, and the "significance [of the Protestant ethic] for the development of [modern] capitalism is obvious" (p. 115; see 1968, pp. 1200, 1206).

That being said, *PE* never attempts to establish either the precise impact of the Protestant ethic or its exact causal weight compared to "external" factors, such as economic, political, or technological forces. To do so would require, Weber knew well, a multicausal and comparative theoretical framework beyond the scope of this "essay in cultural history" (see pp. 149–64; Kalberg 1994a, 1994b, pp. 50–78, 143–92; 1999). He defines his aim in *PE* in more modest terms, seeking to assess, as noted, only the extent to which *religious* beliefs stand at the origin of the spirit of capitalism,[36] which encompasses far larger groupings of people than does the Protestant ethic. In studying the rise of modern capitalism, reference to utilitarian calculations, adventure capitalists, material interests, avarice, the business transactions of Jews, or general evolution will not tell the whole story. To Weber, the Protestant ethic also played a significant role.

The Religious Ancestry of the Spirit of Capitalism

The Protestant ethic spread throughout several New England, Dutch, and English communities in the seventeenth century. Disciplined, hard labor in a calling and the wealth that followed from a steadfast adherence to Puritan values marked a person as among the chosen elect. By Franklin's time, one century later, the Protestant ethic was cultivated not only in churches and sects but also throughout entire communities. Its expansion, however, had weakened and transformed its religion-based ethical component into an ethos with a utilitarian accent (pp. 16, 119–20, 122–23). Weber refers to this ethos as the spirit of capitalism: a configuration of values that implied the individual's duty to increase his capital, to view work as an end in itself to be performed rationally and systematically in a calling, to earn money perpetually (without enjoying it), and to view material wealth as a manifestation of "competence and proficiency in a vocational calling" (p. 18). Adherents to this spirit, like Franklin, rather than viewed by others as among the saved, were believed to be simply community-oriented citizens of good moral character. Their stalwart demeanor, which was immediately recognizable, no longer served to testify to firm belief; it indicated instead respectability, dignity, honesty, and self-confidence.[37]

Rather than being a believer, Franklin, the embodiment of this spirit, was a "bland deist" (p. 18). Weber contends that the *origins* of Franklin's conduct, however, were not located only in pragmatic considerations, business astuteness, utilitarian calculations, or greed; ascetic Protestantism also played a part. Indeed, the ethical element in Franklin's manner of organizing and directing his life, Weber argues, confirms such an interpretation (pp. 16–18). Yet here a conundrum appears. How had the ethical dimension in the Protestant ethic, now shorn of its legitimating certainty-of-salvation component and lacking a sustaining *religious* community, survived into the eighteenth century?

Long before the religious roots of ethical action had become weakened, the Puritan's ethical values had expanded beyond their original social carriers—ascetic Protestant churches and sects—to another carrier grouping: Protestant families. For this reason, these values remained central in childhood socialization *even* as a gradual secularization occurred. Parents taught children to set goals and organize their lives methodically, to be self-reliant and shape their own destinies, to behave in accord with ethical standards, and to work diligently. They encouraged children to pursue careers in business and see virtue in capitalism's open markets, to seek material success, to become upwardly mobile, to live modestly and frugally, to reinvest their wealth, to look toward the future and the "opportunities" it offers, and to budget their time wisely—just as Franklin admonished in his writings (pp. 14–15). Families stressed, as well, the importance of individual achievement, honesty and fair play in business transactions, ascetic personal habits, systematic work in a vocation, and hard competition. Children were socialized, through intimate, personal relationships,[38] to conduct themselves in a restrained, dispassionate manner, and to do so by reference to a configuration of guiding values.

In this way, an entire array of ethical values and modes of conduct were passed on from generation to generation. Sects and churches were no longer the exclusive social carriers of this organized life; families, and even constellations of community organizations, including schools, also cultivated its typical values and conduct. Hence, new generations continued to be influenced. Indeed, action oriented toward a configuration of values originally carried by ascetic Protestant sects and churches endured long after these religious organizations had become weakened. Protestantism's "sect spirit," now routinized into maxims, community norms and values, and familiar customs and traditions, remained integral in Franklin's colonial America. Yet the ancestry of this spirit of capitalism, Weber contends, was not "this-worldly" but "other-worldly," namely, the Protestant ethic: "The Puritan's sincerity of belief must have been the most powerful lever conceivable working to expand the view of life that we are here designating as the spirit of capitalism" (p. 116).

> One of the constitutive components of the modern capitalist spirit, and, moreover, generally of modern civilization, was the rational organization of life on the basis of the *idea of the calling*. It was born out of the spirit of *Christian asceticism*. (p. 122; emph. in original)

***

At this point, Weber rests his case regarding "the way in which 'ideas' become generally effective in history" (p. 48). He has traced the lineage of the spirit of capitalism and discovered that the Protestant ethic, indeed, "co-participated" in its formation. Yet Weber moves a step further. He contends also that he has, in *PE*, discovered the "ethical style of life 'adequate' to the new capitalism" (1972, p. 286) and he is convinced that the spirit of capitalism accelerated, albeit in a nonquantifiable manner, the growth of modern capitalism.[39] It did so in a manner parallel to that of the Protestant ethic, although now on a broader scale. He speaks of a relationship of "adequacy" (p. 26) between the spirit of capitalism and modern capitalism as an economic form. This spirit, in other words, provided the "economic culture" that served as a legitimating foundation for modern capitalism:

> [The] spirit of (modern) *capitalism* . . . finds its most adequate form in the modern capitalist company and, on the other hand, . . . the capitalist company discovers in this frame of mind the motivating force—or spirit—most adequate to it. (pp. 26–27)

***

The final pages of *PE* diverge from the main task of this study. Weber here leaps across the centuries in order to quickly survey, in broad strokes and unforgettable passages, modern capitalism two centuries after Franklin's birth. Firmly entrenched after the massive industrialization of the nineteenth century, "victorious capitalism" now sustains itself on the basis of *means-end* rational action alone, he argues. In this present-day urban, secular, and bureaucratic milieu, neither Franklin's spirit nor Baxter's this-worldly asceticism endows methodical work with subjective meaning. These supporting religious roots for modern capitalism have faded. Activity originally motivated by values and ideas has "collapsed" and become "routinized." The means-end rational action characteristic of sheer utilitarian calculations "surreptitiously shoved itself under" (p. 120) the original constellation of ideas and **value-rationalization**, and now alone carries methodical work. Today, an inescapable network of pragmatic necessities overwhelms the individual.

People born into this "powerful cosmos" are coerced to adapt to the impersonal laws of the market in order to survive. In this "steel-hard casing" of "mechanized ossification," the motivation to work—its *subjective meaning*—is rooted exclusively in constraint and means-end rational calculations. A "mechanical foundation" is in place and "the idea of a 'duty in one's calling' stalks around in our lives like a ghost of past religious beliefs." In one of his most famous passages, Weber succinctly captures the significant transformation that has occurred at the level of motives: the Puritan "*wanted* to be a person with a vocational calling; today we *are forced* to be" (p. 123; see pp. 123–24; 1972, pp. 319–20).

If this brief commentary upon advanced capitalist societies is acknowledged, four stages to Weber's analysis in *PE* now become apparent (see chart on next page).

PE as an Example of Weber's Sociology

The discipline of sociology was in its infancy when *PE* was written. Trained as an economic and legal historian, Weber began to call his own research sociological only about 1911. The term *sociology* is never used in *PE*. In other writings he refers to this volume as an "essay in cultural history" or simply as a "sketch" on the relationship between religious belief and conduct. Nevertheless, central aspects of Weber's sociological approach, which he designated **interpretive understanding** (*Verstehen*), are quite apparent in *PE*. In fact, among Weber's many works, *PE* is perhaps the best and most vivid example of how he combines his major methodological tool, the ***ideal type***, with his methodology of interpretive understanding designed to grasp subjective meaning (see 1949, pp. 42–45, 85–110; 1968, pp. 3–26). His entire sociology is driven by a wish to understand how social action, often viewed by observers as irrational, foolish, and strange, becomes plausible and altogether "rational" once its subjective meaningfulness is comprehended.

A brief discussion of several ways in which Weber's procedures in *PE* illustrate his general mode of conducting sociological research will assist a clearer understanding of this classic volume and of his sociology of interpretive understanding.

Frame of Mind

Throughout *PE*, as well as in his sociology as a whole, Weber demarcates, from vantage points of interest to him, "frames of mind." As they relate to economic activity, he discusses the frames of mind of adventure capitalists, medieval entrepreneurs (Jakob Fugger), feudal aristocrats, Puritan employers and workers, workers and employers immersed

***The Protestant Ethic and the Spirit of Capitalism*: Stages of Weber's Analysis**

	Period	Organization	Types of Action	Religious Devotion
I. **Calvin**: Fatalism as result of doctrine of predestination	16th cen.	small sects	value-rational	yes
II. **Baxter**: The protestant ethic	17th cen.	churches and sects	value-rational (methodical this-worldly activity)	yes
↕ "Powerful Lever" (I–II ↔ III); ↕ "Affinity" (II ↔ IV)				
III. **Franklin**: The spirit of capitalism	18th cen.	communities	value-rational[40] (methodical this-worldly activity)	no
↕ "Adequacy" (III ↔ IV)				
IV. The **"specialist"**: capitalism as a "cosmos"	20th cen.	industrial society	means-end rational	no

Adapted from Kalberg, 'On the Neglect of Weber's *Protestant Ethic* as a Theoretical Treatise' (*Sociological Theory*, 1996, p. 63), with permission from the American Sociological Association.

within economic traditionalism, and the patrician capitalists of the seventeenth century. The frames of mind of the Catholic, Lutheran, Calvinist, Pietist, Methodist, Baptist, Quaker, and Mennonite faithful capture his main attention.

Weber articulates major components of each group's subjective meaning; how it occurs, for example, that Calvinists view methodical work seriously and orient their entire lives accordingly. His concern is to understand the meaningfulness of systematic work to this group of people rather than to evaluate or judge it; he seeks to do so by investigating the motivations that underlie the rigorous work patterns of these believers. Instead of referring to the unconscious, however, as a disciple of Freud would do, Weber attempts to comprehend how work becomes meaningful by analyzing the beliefs, and the psychological rewards they imply for specific conduct, of an ideal type—or an unusually representative figure—of Calvinism, such as Baxter.

For this reason Weber studies the historical-cultural context within which the beliefs of Calvinists crystallized: the sermons they listen to, the Bible passages and doctrinal statements they read, the character of their religious community. Indeed, in seeking to convey to his reader the frame of mind of these believers, through this method of interpretive understanding, Weber avoids the domain of psychology proper. He also rejects, as explanatory concepts, national character, genetic makeup, innate disposition (greed and lust for gain), and developmental-historical laws. Economic and political interests must be considered, according to Weber, but they do not alone offer adequate explanations for the Calvinist's conduct and frame of mind. Throughout his sociology, Weber attends to the extent to which a particular frame of mind implies an uprooting of persons from the *status naturae* on the one hand and purely this-worldly, utilitarian calculations on the other, and then an organization of life around ethical values.

Owing to its focus on arrays of specific groups and the psychology of motives for their members, this procedure avoids reference to the global concepts utilized in organic holism theorizing (society, community, tradition, modernity, particularism, universalism, evolution, or progress), all of which Weber finds too diffuse. His methodology also forcefully rejects a focus on charismatic figures. Instead, he chooses an "intermediary" level of analysis between global concepts and "great men" theories of historical change: the subjective meaning of persons in groups as captured by ideal types and explored through interpretive understanding.

Case Studies

The task of sociology involves the causal explanation of specific cases, according to Weber, rather than the discovery of history's developmental tendencies or the formulation of general laws that predict future events. Even Weber's systematic treatise, *Economy and Society*, does not seek to discover general laws. Instead, it charts out empirically-based ideal types that, as heuristic tools, assist researchers to undertake causal analyses of specific cases (see 1949, pp. 56–57, 72–84; 1968, p. 10; Kalberg 1994b, pp. 81–142; 2000, pp. 157–59).

In *PE* Weber offers a causal explanation for the rise of a particular case, here the spirit of capitalism. He attempts to identify its religious sources and persuade his readers, through both empirical documentation and logical argument, that these sources are plausible causes. In his terms, he seeks to demonstrate that the Protestant ethic constitutes an "adequate cause" for the spirit of capitalism.

Weber's orientation to causal explanations of specific phenomena is often neglected, not least because of the massive scale of the cases he chooses to investigate. For example, in his Economic Ethics of the World Religions volumes he studies the origins of the caste system in India (1958), the rise of monotheism in ancient Israel (1952), the rise of Confucianism in China (1951; see Kalberg 1994a; 1994b, pp. 177–92; 1999) and even the rise of the modern West (see pp. lviii–lxiv).

The Influence of Culture

PE emphatically calls attention to the influence of cultural values on action. Weber addresses one aspect of culture, religious belief, and its impact on economic activity. Even "purely" means-end rational action in reference to the laws of the market possesses a cultural aspect. Market-oriented activity, he insists in *PE*, is played out not merely according to economic interests but also to an economic culture, and work today in a vocation "carries with it an *ascetic* imprint" (p. 123; emph. in original). Yet Weber unveils the cultural forces that underlie and legitimate everyday activity not only in *PE* but throughout his sociology. In addition to a broad array of economic cultures, he explores, for example, a variety of political cultures "behind" the exercise of power (see, for example,

1968, pp. 980–94, 1204–10, 1381–1462; 1985; Kalberg, 1997, 2001) and an array of legal cultures that legitimate the orientations of persons to laws (see 1968, pp. 809–92).

Weber's cognizance of the causal capacity of cultural forces is apparent as early as *PE*'s first chapter. The assumption that the *origins* of an economic ethic, whether traditional or modern, can be explained by reference to social structures—an "economic form"—is rejected. To him, as noted above, even identical external structures of extreme rigidity, such as those typical of religious and political sects, let alone those of the factory and the bureaucracy, fail to call forth homogeneous patterns of action. The Calvinist, Methodist, Pietist, and Baptist sects all advocated distinct doctrines, as did sects in India (1946c, p. 292), and believers oriented their lives accordingly. The same must be said, Weber is convinced, of strata and classes (pp. 34–35, 177 [note 24]; 1946c, pp. 268–70). Similarly, although he acknowledges the influence of institutions (such as schools, churches, families, the state, the military) on action, he notes repeatedly how cultural contexts, often rooted in regional religious traditions, have an independent impact upon institutions (pp. 5–12, 32–33). This impact is so prevalent that, viewed comparatively, quite different patterns of action are apparent even in institutions possessing very similar structures.

Weber's articulation of the capacity of cultural forces to shape social contexts also places his sociology in direct opposition to rational choice, neo-Marxist, and "economic man" theories. *PE*, as well as an array of Weber's other writings, argues, for example, that sustained economic development, whether occurring today in Asia, Latin America, or central Europe, is a complex process not moved along only by economic interests, market calculations, or wage incentives.

PE contends that a sociology oriented exclusively to economic and political interests, social structures, classes, power, organizations, or institutions is theoretically inadequate. The diverse ways in which cultural values form the context for conduct, albeit often obscure and scarcely visible, runs as a major thread throughout his works.

The Interpenetration of Past and Present

Weber refused in *PE* to take the immediate present as his point of reference. Indeed, his analysis rejects the idea of a disjunction between past and present and offers a host of examples that demonstrate their interwovenness. He emphasizes in *PE*, as well as in his sociological writings generally, that recognition of history's impact remains indispensable for an understanding of the present and that radical change, although possible, is rare. This holds despite his acknowledgment of the heroic capacity of charismatic leaders to sever past and present abruptly, given facilitating conditions (see 1968, pp. 1111–19). Even in those eras in which massive structural transformations have occurred (urbanization, industrialization, secularization), the past lives on into the present as an influential force: "That which has been handed down from the past becomes everywhere the immediate precursor of that taken in the present as valid" (1968, p. 29; translation altered). Cultural forces in particular often survive great structural metamorphoses, thereby linking past and present.

In general, Weber's "open" theoretical framework grounded in multitudes of specific groups (as captured by ideal types), and his position that the domains of religion, law, domination, and the economy develop at uneven rates (pp. 36–38; 1968), place his "view of society"—an array of multiple, dynamically interacting "parts," each endowed with an autonomous causal thrust and unfolding along its own pathway—in opposition to other approaches. First, approaches that elevate a single variable (such as class or the state) to a position of general causal priority are opposed, as are, second, all schools of thought that conceptualize social life by reference to sets of encompassing dichotomies (such as tradition-modernity, particularism-universalism, and *Gemeinschaft-Gesellschaft*). To Weber, these exclusive concepts focus too much on cross-epochal disjunctions and downplay the deep interlocking of past and present. Moreover, because to him very few significant developments from the past ever die out fully, he argues that a charting in the immediate present of economic and political interests on the one hand, or "system needs" and "functional prerequisites" on the other hand, can serve sociological analysis only in a preliminary, trial-and-error fashion (1968, pp. 14–18).[41] To Weber, the past always penetrates deeply into the present, even molding its core contours. His concepts "social carrier" and "legacy" illustrate how this penetration takes place.

The Linking of Past and Present: Social Carriers and Legacies

Weber's analysis of how the Protestant ethic survives, in secularized guise as a spirit of capitalism carried by families, schools, and communities rather than by churches and sects, offers a vivid illustration of the way in which cultural values and ideas from the past endure, for him, as legacies that influence the present. The crystallization of a new status group, organization, or class to cultivate and carry cultural values and ideas is crucial if these values and ideas are to remain viable. Thus, *PE* explores ideas and values *in reference to* the churches, sects, organizations, classes, and strata that bear them, rather than exclusively focussing on ideas and values. This theme also is found at a variety of places in Weber's sociology.

He especially emphasizes in *PE* how values and ideas either resonate with pastoral care practices in churches or else become transformed by pastors attentive to the "religious needs" of believers. A back-and-forth movement characterizes his analysis. Although values and ideas retain an autonomous capacity, they must become located in strong carrier groups in order to become effective. At times, just the sheer logical rigor and persuasiveness of ideas regarding salvation may *themselves* call forth values and a carrier group (see pp. 56, 74–75). If they are to endure, however, values and ideas must, even in these cases, eventually stand in a relationship of elective affinity with the religious needs of members of a carrier group (see 1946c, pp. 268–70).

In general, Weber is convinced that patterned action of every imaginable variety has arisen in every epoch and civilization. Yet, if a particular conduct is to become prominent in the social fabric, cohesive and powerful social carriers for it must crystallize. Only then can its influence range across decades and centuries. As Weber notes,

> Unless the concept 'autonomy' is to lack all precision, its definition presupposes the existence of a bounded group of persons which, though membership may fluctuate, is determinable. (1968, p. 699; translation altered)

He defines a wide variety of carrier groups in *Economy and Society.* Regularities of action in some groupings can be recognized as firm, and carriers can be seen, in some cases, as powerful; others fail to carry conduct forcefully and prove fleeting. Patterned action may fade and then, owing to an alteration of *contextual* forces, acquire carriers and become reinvigorated, influential, and long-lasting. At times coalitions of carriers are formed; at other times carriers stand clearly in a relationship of antagonism to one another. The view of society that flows out of *Economy and Society*—as constructed from numerous competing and reciprocally interacting patterns of social action "located" in carrier groups—easily takes cognizance of the survival of certain conduct from the past and its significant influence, as a legacy, upon action in the present.

Weber often charts such legacies from the religious domain. He does so not only in regard to work in a vocation. In the United States, innumerable values, customs, and practices deriving from Protestant asceticism remain integral even today (see above, p. lxv; also pp. 127–48). The "direct democratic administration" by the congregation practiced in Protestant sects, for example, left a legacy crucial for the establishment of democratic forms of government, as did the unwillingness of sect members to bestow a halo of reverence upon secular authority (1985; 1968, pp. 1204–10).[42] The Quakers in particular, by advocating freedom of conscience for others as well as for themselves, paved the way for political tolerance (pp. 219–21, note 129; see 1968, pp. 1204–10; Kalberg 1997).

The Routinization and Sublimation of Motives, the Maxim of Unforeseen Consequences, and the Aims of Interpretive Understanding

Weber depicts the transformation from Franklin's spirit of capitalism to today's "victorious capitalism" (see pp. xlvi–xlvii above) as involving a routinization of the motives behind economic activity from value-rational to means-end rational. The alteration of motives in *PE* moves in the diametrically opposite direction when Weber emphasizes that great variation exists across Catholicism, Lutheranism, and ascetic Protestantism in the extent to which they sublimated the *status naturae*. Did religious doctrines call forth the methodical-rational organization of life among the faithful that tamed impulsive and spontaneous human nature?

Both the routinization and sublimation interpretations of motives prove pivotal in *PE*. However, a focus on the way in which motives for action vary across a spectrum and the significance of this variation for the continuity of action and even for the *ethical* organization of life, as well for economic activity, stands at the foundation of Weber's entire sociology. Sociologists who wish to practice his method of interpretive understanding, he asserts, must be attuned to these distinctions.

Weber stresses in *PE*, as well as elsewhere in his works, that such shifts at the level of motivation are frequently unforeseen; they are often blatantly antagonistic to the intentions of persons at the beginning of the process. Surely Weber's Puritans, who worked methodically as a consequence of *other-worldly* considerations, would be appalled to see that their systematic labor and profit-seeking eventually led to a degree of wealth threatening to their frugal and modest style of life oriented to God (pp. 118–19; 1968, p. 1200). Moreover, their riches created a highly advanced technological cosmos anchored ultimately by laws of science based on empirical observation rather than by the laws of God and methodical *ethical* conduct oriented to Him. A scientific world view, cultivated and developed by the modern capitalism that ascetic Protestantism helped to call into existence, opposes in principle—for it refuses to provide legitimacy to a "leap of faith"—all worldviews rooted in religion (see 1946b, pp. 148–54).

Finally, Weber emphasizes in *PE*, as well as throughout his sociology, that those born into today's "powerful cosmos," where pragmatic necessities, sheer means-end calculations, and secularism reign, can scarcely imagine the actual contours of the religion-saturated world of the past. Even with the best of wills, "we moderns" can barely conceive of work in a vocation as motivated by that crucial query in the lives of the seventeenth century devout: "Am I among the saved" (p. 125; 1946b, pp. 142–43)? The dominance today of radically different assumptions regarding typical motives for action, Weber believes, obscures our capacity to comprehend how conduct was differently motivated in the distant past. Indeed, sociologists often unknowingly impose present-day assumptions on action in the past.

For this reason also Weber calls for a sociology of interpretive understanding that seeks to comprehend, "from within," the subjective meaning of persons through detailed investigation of *their* milieux of values, traditions, emotions, and interests. This procedure, he is convinced, will extend the sociologist's capacity to grasp the meaning of action. Determined to comprehend human beings as "meaning-seeking creatures" (see Salomon, 1962, p. 393) and to understand how people in various epochs and civilizations endow their actions with meaning, Weber hoped that his method of interpretive understanding would be used in this "universal-historical" manner. Furthermore, he hoped that, through comparisons, the unique features and parameters of eras, civilizations, and distinct groupings would be isolated. Important insight would be gained in the process (see 1946b, pp. 150–53).

'The Protestant Sects and the Spirit of Capitalism'[43]

The "Sects" essay reprinted in this volume (pp. 127–48) was written soon after Weber's return to Germany from the United States. Published in abbreviated form in two newspapers in 1906,[44] he now sought to reach a much broader German audience. Weber hoped, through a close-up view of the United States in 1904, to confront an array of stereotypes widespread in Germany.

"Sects" is far less scholarly than *PE*. Informal in tone, it is built around Weber's perspicacious social observations as he travels through the Midwest, the South, the Middle Atlantic states, and New England. His delightful commentary, however, should not be understood as providing merely fragmented "impressions of American life." Instead, Weber brings his audience up to date in respect to the fate of Puritan beliefs in the United States 250 years after their origin.

On the one hand, *PE* provided an historical investigation of believers' orientations to particular religious doctrines, an overview of the inner psychological dynamics and anxieties of the devout in search of salvation, and a scrutiny of the influence of belief and pastoral practices upon economic activity in the seventeenth and eighteenth centuries in the United States, England, Holland, and Germany. The "Sects" essay, on the other hand, at the dawning of the twentieth century, examines the ways in which ascetic Protestantism in America has influenced communities. Weber addresses the social psychology of group membership and the playing out, even in interaction, of the ascetic Protestant stress on work and economic activity (see Berger, 1970). The spirit of capitalism has now "entered the world" even more than in Franklin's time, and Weber wishes to summarize briefly its major impact. In this manner, "Sects" complements *PE*'s orientation to the origins of the spirit of capitalism and the differences, in regard to the connection of belief and conduct, between Catholics, Lutherans, and Puritans. For this reason, it has been selected for inclusion in this volume.

Weber retains a steady focus throughout "Sects" on the "straight derivatives, rudiments, and survivals [in American society] of those conditions which once prevailed in all ascetic sects" (p. 144; see also pp. 134–36; 1972, pp. 173–74). Multiple legacies of the "sect spirit," Weber argues, form the sociological underpinnings of, for example, social trust, skeptical attitudes toward secular authority, the practice of self-governance, and the nimble capacity of Americans to form civic associations (see also 1968, pp. 1204–10).

Only the latter residual of the sect spirit can be addressed here. Weber emphasizes that the Protestant sects were the original social carriers of the idea that membership in a social group testifies to a person's respectability, honesty, and good character. As "exclusive" organizations, the original sects allowed membership only on the basis of sincere belief. Rigorous scrutiny of candidates' moral character took place before a decision was made. Hence, membership automatically bestowed on a person a reputation of integrity. And the sect, owing to its capacity to exert immediate social pressure on those members who might be tempted to deviate from the righteous path, was quite capable of guaranteeing respectable conduct among its members.

Weber argues that the badges and lapel pins worn by Americans in 1904, all of which denoted membership in a secular club or society, involved a similar attempt by persons to establish social honor and personal integrity through group membership. An elevation of one's social status even occurred with membership in civic groups; persons were now "certified" as trustworthy and as "gentlemen." Indeed, membership proved indispensable if one hoped to be fully accepted in one's community (pp. 135–36; 1985, pp. 7–8; 1968, p. 1207). In this way, the influence of ascetic Protestantism, manifest in 1904 as community norms of "involvement" and "service," contributed to the formation of diverse civic associations "between" the distant state and the individual standing alone. This achievement of the sect spirit forms the foundation for American society's unique proclivity to create a multitude of such associations.[45] In turn, this capacity comprises a pivotal component in its political culture of participation and self-governance.

> Today, large numbers of 'orders' and clubs of all sorts have begun to assume in part the functions of the religious community. Almost every small businessman who thinks something of himself wears some kind of badge in his lapel. However, the archetype of this form, which *all* use to guarantee the 'honorableness' of the individual, is indeed the ecclesiastical community. (1985, p. 8, emph. in original; see pp. 146–47)[46]

To Weber "no one doubts the decisive role of Puritanism for the American style of life" (1972, p. 300).

In drawing out this feature of the American social landscape, he wished to confront widespread stereotypes held by Germans and, more broadly, to confront a common image of "modern society." It was widely believed in Europe that the advance of capitalism, urbanism, and industrialism severed individuals from "community" (*Gemeinschaft*), leaving them adrift and cut off from others in "society" (*Gesellschaft*). Without viable social ties, persons wandered aimlessly as unconnected "atoms." To Emile Durkheim, this situation led to anomie and high suicide rates (1951). Others spoke of the "anonymity" of modern life.

Europeans, and Germans in particular, viewed the United States, which they considered as the nation where capitalism had developed to the farthest extent, in precisely this manner—as a "sand pile" (*Sandhaufen*) of individuals lacking personal, nonmarket connections to others (see 1985, pp. 10–11). In noting the broad tendency among Americans to form associations, and the particular importance they attributed (deriving out of their unique religious traditions) to membership, Weber wished to confront this European stereotype directly. Moreover, as a sociologist oriented to cases rather than to general "developmental laws," he desired to point out how modern nations vary, despite a common experience of capitalism, urbanism, and industrialism, as a consequence of specific historical legacies anchored in religion. Case-by-case analysis would reveal, he maintained, how each developing nation followed its own pathway. To his German countrymen Weber wished to convey that the origins of the nightmare scenario they associated with the "atomized" *Gesellschaft* may have in part arisen out of constellations of historical and cultural forces specifically German.

'Prefatory Remarks' to The Economic Ethics of the World Religions (1920)

After writing *PE* and "Sects," Weber's research on the relationship between religious belief and economic activity became radically comparative. About 1911 he began a series of studies on Confucianism, Taoism, Hinduism, Buddhism, Jainism, and ancient Judaism. First published separately as articles in the *Archiv für Sozialwissenschaft und Sozialpolitik*, these investigations were later given the title Economic Ethics of the World Religions (EEWR) and prepared in 1919 and 1920 for publication in book form.[47] The complete three-volume enterprise, which placed *PE* and "Sects" at its beginning, was published after Weber's death in 1920 under the title Collected Essays in the Sociology of Religion.[48] Written late in 1919,[49] the "Prefatory Remarks" ("PR") essay included below is the general introduction to this entire set of essays.[50] It indicates to us one prominent path taken by Weber's sociology after *PE*.[51]

Weber's studies on the "world religions" in China, India, and the ancient Near East have often been understood as mirror images of *PE*. That is, they have been viewed as placing the emphasis on the "ideas" side of the causal equation—the religious doctrines and their influence on the conduct of believers—and as neglecting "interests." Interpreters of Weber then asserted that, according to him, modern capitalism failed to develop first in India or China because no "functional equivalent" of the Protestant ethic ever existed in the religions of these civilizations. On the basis of this reading, several generations of scholars sought through empirical studies to disprove (or prove) "the Weber thesis" by discovering (or failing to discover) equivalents in Asia. If to develop at all, they asserted modern capitalism required a counterpart to ascetic Protestantism. Conversely, to these scholars, the absence of such an equivalent explained "economic backwardness."

This unilinear manner of utilizing Weber, we now understand, fundamentally distorted his argument both in *PE* and in EEWR. *PE*'s unforgettable concluding passage—where Weber emphasizes the incomplete and "one-sided" nature of his analysis—rejects all such "idealist" versions of historical change (p. 125). This same disavowal thoroughly penetrates the EEWR volumes.[52] Although continuing to investigate the world religions by reference to the ways in which belief influences economic activity, Weber adds the "other side" of the causal equation: the influence of "interests" (or "external forces") on ideas ("internal forces") becomes just as apparent in EEWR as the influence of ideas on interests. Indeed, Weber's stress on the full intertwining of interests and ideas precludes any quick-and-easy formula. As he notes in *Economy and Society*:

> Religion nowhere creates certain economic conditions unless there are also present in the existing relationships and constellations of interests certain possibilities of, or even powerful drives toward, such an economic transformation. It is not possible to enunciate any general formula that will summarize the comparative substantive powers of the various factors involved in such a transformation or will summarize the manner of their accommodation to one another. (1968, p. 577; see also p. 341; 1946c, pp. 267–70)

Hence, Weber himself would be the first to question the validity of research oriented exclusively toward possible functional equivalents of ascetic Protestantism, and to criticize—as monocausal and "one-sided"—all explanations for economic development that refer to ideas alone (see also pp. 155–157). Despite a continued orientation in EEWR to the influence of belief on economic conduct, "PR" unequivocally conveys EEWR's fundamental broadening, in just this manner, of *PE*. EEWR offers complex, multidimensional causal arguments.

EEWR expands upon *PE* in a directly related manner as well: the EEWR studies explore causality also contextually. Ideas are now *situated* within complex contexts of economic, political, stratification, and legal forces; and complex contexts of economic, political, stratification, and legal forces are now *situated* within ideas. As Weber asks, in discussing the causal origins in the modern West of a type of law based upon formal rules and administered by a stratum of specially-trained jurists, hence a type of law that served the interests of businessmen owing to the stability and calculability it provided for economic transactions, "Why then did capitalist interests not call forth this stratum of jurists and this type of law in China or India" (p. 159)? Similarly, he contends that the technical application of scientific knowledge was determined by economic interests and opportunities, yet the existence of these "rewards" did not derive merely from constellations of interests; rather, "[they] flowed out of the particular character of the West's *social* order." Hence, "It must then be asked: from *which* components of this unique social order did these rewards derive" (p. 159). One of the major tasks of "PR" is to set the stage for EEWR's contextual, multicausal, and conjunctural causal analyses.[53]

***

"PR" also delineates several further ways that EEWR moves beyond *PE*. As in *PE*, Weber offers a definition of *modern Western* capitalism and vigorously contends that this type of economy, in contrast to capitalism generally (which appeared universally), arose first in the modern West and acquired aspects found only in the West. As he states in the "Social Psychology of the World Religions" essay (1946c), "We shall be interested . . . in the **economic rationalism** of the type which, since the sixteenth and seventeenth centuries, has come to dominate the West" (1946c, p. 293; transl. altered).

Unlike *PE*, however, Weber now seeks in EEWR to offer a complex analysis for the rise of modern Western capitalism, one rooted in ideas *and* interests on the one hand and the methodology of the comparative experiment on the other hand.[54] Population growth, technological innovations, and the presence of raw materials, for example, are all rejected as powerful causal forces behind economic rationalism, for these phenomena were not exclusively present in the West and absent elsewhere. Geographical factors and biological heredity are downplayed as well (pp. 163–164). Again Weber asserts that *constellations* of forces must be scrutinized rather than single factors, as well as their conjunctural interaction in delineated contexts and the ways in which, consequently, unique configurations are formulated. In EEWR he identifies in each civilization a vast array of types of domination, religion, social status, law, and forms of the economy. He found that the many clusters conducive to the unfolding of modern capitalism in China, India, and ancient Israel were in the end outweighed by a series of opposing constellations.

For example, Weber notes a variety of nonreligious obstacles to economic development in China, such as extremely strong sibling ties and an absence of a "formally guaranteed law and a rational administration and judiciary" (1951, p. 85; see also pp. 91, 99–100). Obstacles were apparent also in India: the caste system placed constraints upon migration, the recruitment of labor, and credit (1958, pp. 52–53, 102–6, 111–17). Yet he discovers also in both countries an entire host of conducive material forces that nonetheless failed to bring about modern capitalism—such as, in China, freedom of trade, an increase in precious metals, population growth, occupational mobility, and the presence of a money economy (1951, pp. 12, 54–55, 99–100, 243). However, in a pivotal passage in "PR," Weber insists that a further constellation must also be considered, namely, internal forces:

> Every attempt at explanation, recognizing the fundamental significance of economic factors, must above all take account of [economic conditions]. However, the opposite line of causation should not be neglected if only because the origin of economic rationalism depends not only on an advanced development of technology and law but also upon the capacity and disposition of persons to organize their lives in a practical-rational manner. Wherever magical and religious forces have inhibited the unfolding of this organized life, the development of an organized life oriented systematically toward *economic* activity has confronted broad-ranging internal resistance. Magical and religious powers, and the ethical notions of duty based on them, have been in the past among the most important formative influences upon the way life has been organized. (p. 160)

Weber was quite convinced that modern capitalism could be *adopted* by—and would flourish in—a number of Eastern civilizations. Indeed, he identified the forces that would allow this to occur in Japan (see 1958,

p. 275; see also pp. 270–82). Yet adoption, he insisted, involved different processes than those that concerned him in Collected Essays in the Sociology of Religion: the *origin*, in a specific region and epoch, of a *new* economic ethos and a *new* type of economy.

***

"PR," however, not only introduces the "rise of modern capitalism" theme by reference to ideas and interests and an experimental comparative methodology; it also turns to an even broader theme, one that moves the EEWR studies still further beyond *PE*. Weber now wishes, through the comparative vantage point offered by the EEWR studies, to isolate in detail that which is specific to the modern West, or in his terms, the "characteristic uniqueness of modern Western rationalism."

At the outset, "PR" forcefully addresses this theme by examining features of Western art, music, science, and architecture that are not found elsewhere. Weber then demarcates the ways in which the modern Western state, its civil service stratum, and modern capitalism are specific to the West (pp. 151–58). Impressive in its sweeping range, his definition of modern Western rationalism remains also concise and firmly anchored in historical observation.

Nonetheless, also in respect to this expansive theme, Weber is not content to offer definitions alone, however broad-ranging. The clearly formulated concept constitutes to him simply the first step in comparative-historical research. Thus, "PR" quickly alludes to a further large task. *Why* did modern Western rationalism develop when and where it did? What were the "ideas *and* interests" that caused it? Although Weber's analysis in EEWR of the origins of modern Western capitalism succeeds to a certain extent,[55] his investigation of Western rationalism's sources remains fragmented and incomplete. Unfortunately, a reconstruction cannot be attempted here.[56]

Despite Weber's underlying orientation to the uniqueness of modern Western rationalism, the EEWR studies cannot be viewed (as they often have been) simply as "contrast examples" written with the single aim of defining precisely the West's unique development. Rather, as is apparent even from "PR," EEWR provides independent portraits of "Chinese rationalism," the "rationalism of India," and the "rationalism of the ancient Near East." The uniqueness of *each* of the EEWR civilizations is rendered. On this basis Weber then seeks to formulate *both* comparisons and contrasts to modern Western rationalism *and* to provide explanations for the particular routes of development followed by *each* great civilization. EEWR conducts, from *his* particular vantage point, *civilizational* analysis. Hence, even while failing to offer an adequate level of detail in respect to the rise of modern Western rationalism, Weber's EEWR studies yield tremendous insight into the different developmental pathways followed in the East as well as in the West (see p. 278, note 26).

Precisely this insight led to worry about the West's present course of development. While pluralistic conflict between relatively independently unfolding societal spheres distinguished the Western developmental path (see pp. 36–38; 1968, pp. 1192–93), as well as a societal flexibility that facilitated gradual social change, Weber views, in 1920, Western societies as losing their dynamism and comparative openness. Conceivably, a new "Egyptianization" and societal ossification might ensue, carried along by a bureaucratization under modern industrialism pervading all societal domains. This scenario constituted a nightmare for him, for he was convinced that without the dynamism which results from competing domains and value spheres, a massive stagnation would soon follow (1968, pp. 1399–1404; 1978, pp. 281–84). If societal ossification descends, people would cease, Weber feared, to defend *ethical values*—and values alone offer dignity and a sense of self-worth (see 1946d, pp. 117–25; Kalberg, 2000, pp. 185–91).

***

Weber acquired insight, clarity, and knowledge from his EEWR studies regarding the specific "tracks" within which a number of major civilizations had developed (see 1946b, p. 150–51; 1946c, p. 280). He argued that these tracks called forth in the West in the twentieth century the dominance of an impersonal and nonethical "formal rationality" in the domains of law, politics, and the economy, and a "theoretical rationality" in the domain of science that *cannot*—and *must not*—provide people with a new set of values (1946b; 1946a, pp. 331–40, 350–57; 1949). Great consequences followed, Weber insisted repeatedly, regarding the "type of person" (*Menschentyp*) that *could* live under modern Western rationalism (see Löwith, 1970; Mommsen, 1970; Kalberg, 1980, 2001).

Finally, the EEWR volumes assisted Weber to answer three further burning questions, all of which originated from his foreboding, as expressed at the end of "Science as a Vocation," (1946b), "Politics as a Vocation" (1946d), and *PE*, regarding Western civilization's "progress." First, in light of the modern West's distinct features, what is the nature of the social change that can take place in the modern West? Second, how do persons in different social contexts, and in different civilizations, form meaning in their lives? Under what circumstances does, for example, methodical work become viewed as personally meaningful? Finally, what patterned regularities of action have become meaningful in each of the major civilizations, and how did they come into being?

Because Weber viewed the political, economic, and religious context out of which compassion, ethical action, and a reflective individualism had arisen in the West as having largely disappeared, hence endangering their viability, answers to these queries became especially urgent. Would ethical values continue to orient human action? To him, the immediacy of these questions itself served to call forth the Herculean motivation required to conduct the EEWR investigations.

Reading *The Protestant Ethic*: The Text and the Endnotes

Weber presents his major argument in *The Protestant Ethic* in Part I (chapters 1 through 3) and in Section A of chapter 4. Here he examines Calvinism, which provides the most stark example for his thesis. He then draws all the threads together in a masterful concluding chapter.

Weber offers support for his argument in his massive endnotes as well as in the body of the text. The student who wishes to acquire a higher level command of his thesis cannot avoid serious study of these notes. Moreover, they are of great interest not only as documentary materials, but also in a wider sense: in dozens of insightful and broad-ranging commentaries, Weber draws out the frame of mind of the Puritans and contrasts their mode of organizing life to that of a variety of other groups. The various ways in which ascetic Protestantism introduced new ideas and values become evident only through a detailed reading of the endnotes. This being said, many endnotes move beyond Weber's theme proper and render commentaries upon dozens of aspects of modern life in general.

A word count reveals that the endnotes are longer than the text. Thus, a short sampling of a number of their major subjects seems feasible, if only to assist the reader in locating themes of particular interest. This section conveys only a rough sketch of their contents.

Chapter 1

Endnotes 15 and 25, pages 167 and 168: On the work ethics of immigrants.

Chapter 2

Endnote 10, page 170: The "rational" and "irrational" depend upon one's vantage point.

Endnote 12, page 170–74: On the work ethic of the Middle Ages.

Endnote 17, page 174: Low wages and high profits do not call forth modern capitalism, as widely believed.

Endnote 18, page 174–75: On how industries select new areas for relocation.

Endnote 28, page 175: The quality of aesthetic design declines with mass production techniques.

Chapter 3

Endnote 32, page 188: Church membership is less central for an organizing of the believer's entire life than a religion's values and ideals.

Endnote 41, page 188: On the national pride of the English.

Chapter 4

Endnote 7, page 189: On the greater influence of salvation rewards upon action than rules for appropriate conduct.

Endnote 8, page 190: On the slowness of the inter-library loan system in Germany.

——, page 190: On the denial in the United States of its sectarian past and a consequence for scholarship: libraries have not retained documents relating to this past.

Endnote 32, page 194: On trusting friends and taking revenge.

Endnote 34, page 194–95: On the uniqueness of social organizations in those cultures with a Puritan past.

Endnote 35, page 195: On how the anti-authoritarian character of Calvinism opposed the development of the welfare state.

Endnote 39, page 195: On the intensity of community-building when Calvinism constitutes a strong influence.

——, page 195: On the suspect character of purely feeling-based relationships.

——, page 196: On the Calvinist's striving to make the world rational.

——, page 196: On the overlap of Calvinism's view of the "public good" with that of classical economics.

——, page 196: On the comparative immunity to authoritarianism of political cultures influenced by Puritanism (see also note 205.)

Endnote 43, page 197: On the ideas behind Christian missionary activity.

——, page 196: On loving one's neighbor.

Endnote 74, page 202: Goethe on how one knows oneself.

Endnote 76, page 202: On why fatalism does not follow, for the Calvinist, from the doctrine of predestination.

——, page 202: On William James' pragmatic view of religious ideas as an outgrowth of the world of ideas in his Puritan native land.

Endnotes 83 and 115, pages 204 and 207: On the checking-account manner of living (balancing out sins with good works, and vice-versa), and how this was no longer an option for the Puritans.

Endnote 95, page 205: On the emphasis on reason and the downplaying of the emotions among the Puritans.

Endnote 129, page 210: Calvinism as a social carrier of the idea of tolerance.

——, page 210: On the origins of the idea of tolerance generally and the importance of religious ideas.

Endnote 133, page 212: On the limitations of psychology, given its state of advancement, to assist Weber's research.

Endnote 138, page 213: On our indebtedness to the idea of basic human rights (one source of which is Puritanism).

Endnote 169, page 216: On the predilection of ascetic Protestants for mathematics and the natural sciences (see also ch. 5, note 83).

——, page 216: On the driving religious forces behind the scientific empiricism of the seventeenth century (see also ch. 5, note 83).

——, page 217: On the implications that follow for the educational agenda of ascetic Protestantism.

Endnote 199, page 221: On how to define a sect.

Endnote 206, page 222: On asceticism's hostility to authority.

——, page 222: On the uniqueness of democracy, even today, among peoples influenced by Puritanism (and the differences between these democracies and those that flowed out of the "Latin spirit").

——, page 222: On the "lack of respect" at the foundation of American behavior

Endnote 222, page 224: The "truthfulness," "uprightness," and candor among Americans are all legacies of Puritanism.

Chapter 5

Endnote 22, page 228: On Puritanism's view that proximity to a large city may enhance virtue.

Endnote 27, page 228–29: On the Puritan view of marriage and "the sober procreation of children," and the visible legacies of this view in Benjamin Franklin's "hygenic utilitarian" view of sexual intercourse.

——, 229page : On the part played by the baptizing churches and sects in protecting women's freedom of conscience.

Endnote 37, page 230: On Hinduism and economic traditionalism in India.

Endnote 39, page 230–31: On economic utilitarianism as deriving ultimately from an impersonal formulation of the "love thy neighbor" commandment.

Endnote 47, page 231: Milton's view that only the middle class (between the aristocracy and the destitute) can be the social carrier of virtue.

Endnote 48, page 232: Weber states his interest in how the religious orientations of believers exercise a practical effect upon their vocational ethic.

Endnote 53, page 233: On the American lack of respect for inherited wealth.

Endnote 67, page 234–35: Comparing Jewish and Puritan ethics (including economic ethics).

Endnote 77, page 236–37: On the lesser development of Protestant asceticism in Holland.

——, page 237: On the formality of the Dutch as a mixture of middle-class "respectability" and the consciousness of status among the aristocracy.

Endnote 83, page 238: On the influence of Puritanism on the development of the natural sciences.

Endnote 87, page 239: On the resistance of ascetic Protestants to culinary delights (oysters).

Endnote 89, page 239: On the two (very different) psychological sources of the wish to accumulate wealth.

Endnote 92, page 239–40: To the Quakers, all "unconscientious" use of possessions must be avoided.

Endnote 94, page 240: Economic development very importantly influences the formation of religious ideas, yet ideas for their part carry within themselves an autonomous momentum and coercive power.

Endnote 101, page 241: That the "character disposition" of the English was actually less predisposed toward penitence than the "character disposition" of other peoples.

Endnote 102, page 241: On the colonization of different New England regions by different groups of people.

Endnote 118, page 243: An example of how Protestant asceticism socialized the masses to work.

Endnote 119, page 243: On the medieval craftsman's putative enjoyment of "that which he produced himself."

——, page 244: On Puritanism's glorification of work and capitalism's capacity today to coerce a willingness to work.

Endnote 123, page 244: On the origins in England of powerful public opposition to monopolies; on the belief that monopolistic barriers to trade violated human rights.

Endnote 126, page 244: On the parallel development of the "lofty profession of spirituality" among Quakers and their "shrewdness and tact in the transaction of mundane affairs."

——, page 244: On how piety is conducive to the businessperson's success.

Suggested Further Reading

The Protestant Ethic Thesis

Eisenstadt, S. N., ed., *The Protestant Ethic and Modernization*. London: Basic Books, 1968.

Lehmann, Hartmut and Guenther Roth, eds., *Weber's Protestant Ethic: Origins, Evidence, Contexts*. Cambridge, UK: Cambridge University Press, 1987.

Marshall, Gordon, *Presbyteries and Profits: Calvinism and the Development of Capitalism in Scotland, 1560–1707*. New York: Oxford University Press, 1980.

Marshall, Gordon, *In Search of the Spirit of Capitalism: An Essay on Max Weber's Protestant Ethic Thesis*. London: Hutchinson & Co., 1982.

Troeltsch, Ernst, *The Social Teachings of the Christian Churches* (2 vols.). Translated by Olive Wyon. New York: Harper Torchbook, 1931.

Max Weber: Life and Work

Albrow, Martin, *Max Weber's Construction of Social Theory*. New York: St. Martin's Press, 1990.

Bendix, Reinhard and Guenther Roth, *Scholarship and Partisanship*. Berkeley: The University of California Press, 1971.

Heydebrand, Wolf, ed., *Max Weber: Sociological Writings*. New York: Continuum, 1994.

Kalberg, Stephen, *Max Weber's Comparative-Historical Sociology*. Chicago: The University of Chicago Press, 1994.

Kalberg, Stephen, ed., *Max Weber: The Confrontation With Modernity*. Oxford: Blackwell Publishers, 2002.

Käsler, Dirk, *Max Weber: An Introduction to His Life and Work*. Chicago: The University of Chicago Press, 1988.

Löwith, Karl, *Max Weber and Karl Marx*. Translated by Hans Fantel. London: Allen & Unwin, 1982.

Mommsen, Wolfgang J. and Jürgen Osterhammel, eds., *Max Weber and His Contemporaries*. London: Unwin Hyman, 1987.

Schroeder, Ralph, ed., *Max Weber, Democracy and Modernization*. London: Macmillan, 1998.

Weber, Marianne, *Max Weber: A Biography*. Translated by Harry Zohn. New York: John Wiley & Sons, 1975.

Whimster, Sam and Scott Lash, eds., *Max Weber, Rationality and Modernity*. London: Allen & Unwin, 1987.

Endnotes

1. Thus, as a matter of course, newly introduced persons in the United States quickly query one another regarding the type of work each does. In contrast, in most of Europe, to turn the topic of conversation to work immediately after an introduction is considered rude.

2. Schor's book (1992) illustrates the endurance of the ascetic Protestant heritage in dozens of ways. See also Hochschild (1990) and Kalberg (1992).
3. Weber journeyed as far west as the railroad could take him at the time. However, he didn't stay long at the end of the line in Guthrie, Oklahoma. Noting the guns strapped around the waist of his innkeeper, he hurried back, in panic, to the train station, arriving just in time to catch his train, now headed east. See "A German Professor's Visit at Guthrie was Suddenly Terminated," in *The Daily Oklahoman* (Guthrie, Oklahoma), September 20, 1904, p. 1.
4. Fritz Lang's classic film on the modern city, *Metropolis*, although made in 1926, vividly depicts the bleak vision of the future widespread in turn-of-the-century Germany.
5. This statement takes as it point of reference Weber's fear that the bureaucratization indigenous to industrial societies will lead to such a great concentration of power in massive organizations that, effectively, citizens will be disenfranchised and democratic governance will be curtailed.
6. This translation, however, is based on the expanded version of 1920 (see "Translator's Preface" above). For a comparison of the 1904/1905 and the 1920 texts, see Lichtblau and Weiss (1993b). A translation of the original *PE*, published in the journal Weber coedited, *Archiv für Sozialwissenschaft und Sozialpolitik* (vol. 20 [1904]: 1–54; vol. 21 [1905]: 1–110), is forthcoming (Baehr and Wells 2002).
7. *PE* does not include Weber's many insights into the workings of American society. Rather, they are summarized in the two essays he wrote shortly after his return to Germany. See "The Protestant Sects" below and its earlier version (1985). See also Marianne Weber (1988), pp. 281–304. On Weber's views of the USA generally, see Mommsen (1974), Roth (1985), Scaff (1998), Berger (1970), and Rollman (1993). On his analysis of American political culture, see Kalberg 1997; 2001.
8. In a number of further writings, Weber returns fairly frequently to arguments formulated originally in *PE*. At times his points are more clearly rendered in the later texts. References to these later relevant passages are occasionally provided.
9. Following Weber, the terms *modern economic ethic*, *rational economic ethic*, and *spirit of capitalism* will be used as synonyms. *Ethos* and *ethic* are also synonymous terms. It must be kept in mind that, *for Weber*, "rational" never evokes "better." Rather, the term merely implies a systematic, even methodical element (see Kalberg, 1980).
10. The major criticisms, and Weber's replies, have been published separately (see Weber 1972). For translations of Weber's essays in this volume, see Chalcraft and Harrington (2001) and Baehr and Wells (2002). In his 1920 revisions to *PE*, Weber added many comments (mostly in the footnotes) addressed to his critics. (His 1920 additions to the endnotes and the text are designated throughout this edition; see p. vii.)
11. In order to strengthen his argument against Sombart, Weber significantly expanded the endnotes on this theme in his 1920 revisions. These endnotes are marked. In a letter to Sombart in 1913, Weber states: " . . . *perhaps not a word* is correct [in your book] concerning Jewish religion" (see Scaff, 1989, p. 203n.). On Sombart and Weber generally, see Lehmann (1993).
12. See also, for example, 1968, pp. 70, 341, 480, 630; 1972, pp. 31, 171. Sombart supported also this Marxian analysis. Weber's rejection in *PE* of "developmental laws" or "laws of economic development," as explanations for historical change,

is directed against Marx, though also against an array of German and English scholars.

13. This theme constitutes a background theme in *PE*. It is only infrequently discussed directly. It appears, however, in numerous passages throughout Weber's other writings. See, for example, 1927, pp. 352–54; 1968, p. 1180; 1972, pp. 323–25, 344. His vehement rejection of such causal forces as sufficient constitutes a foundational point of departure for his Economic Ethics of the World Religions series (see pp. lviii–lxiv).
14. These positions were central in the debate on the origin of modern capitalism and industrialism during Weber's time. Weber also argued in *PE* against minor streams in this ongoing controversy (especially in the endnotes added in 1920), such as Lamprecht's biology-based evolutionary determinism (see p. 221, note 133), all proponents of "national character" (p. 47), the many theorists who understood social change as resulting from changes in laws, and, finally, Hegelians who viewed ideas as causal forces. (Weber insists that Hegelians neglected the crucial questions. Did social carriers crystallize to bear the ideas? Did they exist as cognitive forces only? Or did ideas also place "psychological rewards" upon action. See below.)
15. The centrality of religious affiliation was acknowledged as well by Durkheim in France. He hypothesized, at roughly the same time, that suicide rates would vary according to religious belief (see 1951).
16. On Anglo-American religious influences on the young Weber, see Roth (1997).
17. A pamphlet written in 1887 by Weber's uncle, the Reformation and Counter-Reformation historian Hermann Baumgarten, who was very close to his nephew, notes this theme in a vivid passage:

    > Where Protestants and Catholics live together, the former occupy predominantly the higher, the latter the lower rungs of society. . . . Where the Catholic population flees higher education or cannot attain it, the Protestants must inevitably gain a considerable lead in public administration, justice, commerce, industry, and science. (Marcks 1894, p. 16)

18. Weber deleted this remark when he revised *PE* in 1920. It appeared originally in the second installment of *PE* (1905, p. 43).
19. Chapter 1 of *PE* borrows its title, "Religious Affiliation and Social Stratification," from Offenbacher's book.
20. Personal communication from Guenther Roth (February 22, 1999).
21. On the background to the writing of *PE*, see Poggi (1983); Lichtblau and Weiss (1993); Lehmann and Roth (1993).
22. Personal communication from Guenther Roth (February 22, 1999).
23. For a later formulation of this point, see Weber 1946c, p. 292.
24. For Weber's restatement of this aim at the end of *PE*, see pp. 122–23. See also pp. 15–16, 19, 34–35, 37, 48–49. See further the numerous statements in the essays in response to his early critics where he restates his goal in *PE* (1972, pp. 163, 169, 173, 285–86, 302–07). Many of these passages illustrate Weber's awareness of the multiplicity of causes for historical events, as well as of the importance of viewing single factors within configurations of factors.
25. This is nearly a literal rendering of Weber's passage below at pp. 49–50.

26. Calvin himself saw no problem with the predestination double decree, for he considered himself among the elect (p. 64).
27. Of course, as will be noted later, these themes are intertwined.
28. As most succinctly brought together in the Westminster Confession (1648).
29. This conclusion—the necessity of living the holy life—did not follow logically from the predestination doctrine.
30. One might be inclined *today* to conclude that, if only a few are chosen and nothing can change God's decree, then one might as well live according to the pleasure principle. However appropriate such a conclusion might be to us now, the Puritans were denied this option—for they lived (unlike "we moderns") in a *milieu* dominated by religion and, specifically, *the* foremost question: Am I among the saved? One of *PE*'s underlying messages can be stated succinctly: Social scientists must exercise caution whenever tempted to assume that persons in the past lived according to the same values as persons in the present.
31. This analytic distinction, as we have seen, has not always held up in the course of the exposition of Weber's analysis above. These two threads of his argument interweave repeatedly.
32. Weber here refers to inner-worldly asceticism as "Janus-faced" (*Doppelgesicht*): to focus on God and the question of salvation, a turning *away* from the world and even rejection of this random, "meaningless, natural vessel of sin" (see, e.g., 1968, p. 542) was called for. On the other hand, a turning toward and mastering of the world was necessary, on behalf of ethical values and the creation on earth of God's kingdom (see 1946a, p. 327). This Janus-faced character of action in the world itself bestowed a methodicalness on this action that separated it from utilitarian worldly action motivated by sheer economic interests, as well as practical concerns generally. See below.
33. The devout could understand an "unwillingness to work [as] a sign that one is not among the saved" (p. 106, and those living in poverty could not possibly be among the saved (pp. 109; 258, note 114). Thus, being poor indicated not laziness alone but also a poor *moral* character.
34. "Only in the Protestant ethic of vocation does the world, despite all its creaturely imperfections, possess unique and religious significance as the object through which one fulfills his duties by rational behavior according to the will of an absolutely transcendental God" (1968, p. 556).
35. To Weber, "[The effect of] the stricture against consumption with this unchaining of the striving for wealth [led to] *the formation of capital* . . . [which] became used as *investment* capital . . . Of course, the strength of this effect cannot be determined exactly in quantitative terms" (p.116–17; emph. in original). See also p. 255, note 96.
36. That Weber acknowledges the existence of other origins of this spirit is apparent. See p. 49; 1972, pp. 28, 285.
37. The origins of the American emphasis on honesty toward all as a central aspect of "good character," to be manifested both in personal conduct and even in the political realm (as an ideal), must be sought here. For the Puritan, righteous conduct that testified to one's elect status emanated ultimately from God's presence *within* the believer (see above, pp. xxxii), and He could not be other than honest and candid.

38. Weber argues elsewhere that the teaching of *ethical* values, if it is to occur, necessarily involves a strong personal bond. See, for example, 1927, pp. 357–58; 1946a, p. 331; 1968, pp. 346, 585, 600, 1186–87.

39. The issue here is the same as that surrounding the impact of the Protestant ethic (see above, pp. xliii–iv). Weber is well aware that an assessment of the spirit of capitalism's precise impact would require a more ambitious investigation, one that examined multiple causal forces and provided experimental comparisons. See below (pp. lviii–lxiv) and the "Prefatory Remarks" essay in this volume.

40. Significantly, the value-rational action—the spirit of capitalism—of Franklin is oriented, as the Protestant ethic, *both* to individuals (their salvation status) *and* to a community (pp. 108–09, 115), while the means-end rational action of the individual entrapped within the "powerful cosmos" of industrial capitalism is oriented merely to the individual's survival. For recent discussions of this significant shift, see Bellah (1985), Putnam (2000), Hall and Lindholm (1999), Etzioni (1996), and Kalberg (1997, 2001).

41. The interweaving of past and present is a complex and important theme throughout Weber's writings. Unfortunately, it cannot be addressed in detail here. See Kalberg, 1994b, pp. 158–67; 1996, pp. 57–64; 2000, pp. 176–79.

42. As did Lutheranism, Weber points out, in Germany (p. 84; see 1968, pp. 1198).

43. The single existing translation of this essay, by Hans H. Gerth and C. Wright Mills, is retained here. A few terms have been altered in order to establish terminological consistency with *PE*. See the essay's first endnote (p. 263) for bibliographical information.

44. Two translations of the earlier articles are now available; see Weber (1985); Baehr and Wells (2002). The version presented here was expanded significantly by Weber in 1920. Additions were too numerous to note.

45. Of course, Tocqueville had earlier emphasized just this developed capacity of American society (1945). His explanation, however, for this proclivity to form associations (which opposes a tendency in the United States toward a "tyranny of the majority") varies distinctly from Weber's; Tocqueville refers to egalitarianism, commercial interests, and the interests of the individual whereas Weber turns to the ascetic Protestant religious heritage. See Kalberg, 1997.

46. The extreme importance, for one's social status, of admission into a community's churches and clubs (e.g., Rotary, Lions, etc.) led Weber to describe the United States as a society of "benevolent feudalism" (see 1978, p. 281).

47. Weber lived to complete revisions only on *PE*, "Sects," and *The Religion of China: Confucianism and Taoism* (1951 [1920]).

48. Two analytic essays were also included: "The Social Psychology of the World Religions" (1946c), which is the introduction to the Economic Ethics of the World Religions studies, and "Religious Rejections of the World" (1946a), which is placed after the investigation of Confucianism and Taoism and before *The Religion of India* (1958). "Religious Rejections," which mainly offers a masterly, sweeping analysis of modern Western civilization, does not fit well into this series (although it could have been placed at the end). Collected Essays remained incomplete. Weber had planned to write chapters on the religions of ancient Egypt, Phoenicia, Babylonia, and Persia, and volumes on Islam, ancient Christianity, and Talmudic Judaism.

49. This essay is believed to be the last sociological work Weber wrote.

50. This essay was given the title "Author's Introduction" in the earlier translation by Parsons. Placed in his volume before *PE*, generations of readers of *PE* have incorrectly viewed this essay as an introduction to *PE* (despite a partial explanation by Parsons).
51. His three-volume opus, *E&S* (1968), constituted the other major direction for his empirical sociology. Weber's sociology of religion also moved in a more theoretical direction. See the "Sociology of Religion" chapter in *E&S* (pp. 399–634).
52. Nonetheless, to this day nearly every introductory textbook in sociology depicts Weber as an "idealist" and contrasts his sociology to the historical materialism of Marx.
53. I will hold to this statement even though it should also be clearly noted that most chapters in the EEWR volumes treat ideas and interests separately rather than contextually and conjuncturally. These aspects of Weber's analysis are mainly apparent in innumerable paragraphs throughout EEWR and in the "Social Pscyhology of the World Religions" essay (1946c). I have systematically examined Weber's contextual and conjunctural causal methodology elsewhere. See 1994b, pp. 98–102, 155–76, 189–92.
54. The EEWR analysis must be supplemented by multiple analyses in *General Economic History* (1927), *E&S* (1968), and *The Agrarian Sociology of Ancient Civilizations* (1976).
55. See the preceding note.
56. Moreover, such a reconstruction would require frequent reference to the works mentioned in note 54 (see also Kalberg, forthcoming).

References

Baehr, Peter and Gordon C. Wells, eds. and trans. 2002. *Max Weber—The Protestant Ethic and the 'Spirit' of Capitalism—The Version of 1905*. London: Penguin, 2002.

Bellah, Robert *et al.* 1985. *Habits of the Heart*. Berkeley: California.

Berger, Stephen. 1972. "The Sects and the Breakthrough into the Modern World: On the Centrality of the Sects in Weber's 'Protestant Ethic' Thesis." *Social Forces* 42: 444–58.

Brocke, Bernhard vom, ed. 1987. *Sombart's 'Moderner Kapitalismus.'* Munich: Piper.

Chalcraft, David and Austin Harrington, eds. 2001. *The Protestant Ethic Debate: Max Weber's Replies to his Critics, 1907–1910*. Translated by Harrington and Mary Shields. Liverpool: University Press, 2001.

Durkheim, Emile. 1951. *Suicide*. New York: Free Press.

Etzioni, Amitai. 1996. *The Good Commonwealth*. New York: Basic Books.

Gothein, Eberhard. 1892. *Wirtschaftsgeschichte des Schwarzwalds*. Strasbourg: Treubner.

Hall, John and Charles Lindholm. 1999. *Is America Breaking Apart?* Princeton: University Press.

Hochschild, Arlie. 1990. *The Second Shift: Working Parents and the Revolution at Home*. London: Piatkus.

Jellinek, Georg. 1901 (1895). *The Declaration of the Rights of Man and of Citizens*. New York: Holt.

Kalberg, Stephen. 1980. "Max Weber's Types of Rationality: Cornerstones for the Analysis of Rationalization Processes in History." *American Journal of Sociology* 85, 3: 1145–79.

——. 1983. "Max Weber's Universal-Historical Architectonic of Economically-Oriented Action: A Preliminary Reconstruction." Pp. 253–88 in *Current Perspectives in Social Theory*, edited by Scott G. McNall. Greenwood, CT: JAI Press.

——. 1987. "The Origin and Expansion of *Kulturpessimismus*: The Relationship Between Public and Private Spheres in Early Twentieth Century Germany." *Sociological Theory* 5 (Fall): 150–64.

——. 1992. "Culture and the Locus of Work in Contemporary Western Germany: A Weberian Configurational Analysis." Pp. 324–65 in *Theory of Culture*, edited by Neil J. Smelser and Richard Münch. Berkeley: University of California Press.

——. 1994a. "Max Weber's Analysis of the Rise of Monotheism." *The British Journal of Sociology* 45, 4: 563–84.

——. 1994b. *Max Weber's Comparative-Historical Sociology*. Chicago: The University of Chicago Press.

——. 1996. "On the Neglect of Weber's *Protestant Ethic* as a Theoretical Treatise: Demarcating the Parameters of Post-War American Sociological Theory." *Sociological Theory* 14 (March 1996): 49–70.

——. 1997. "Tocqueville and Weber on the Sociological Origins of Citizenship: The Political Culture of American Democracy." *Citizenship Studies* 1 (July): 199–222.

——. 1998. "Max Weber's Sociology: Research Strategies and Modes of Analysis." Pp. 208–41 in *Reclaiming the Argument of the Founders*, edited by Charles Camic. Cambridge, MA: Blackwell.

——. 1999. "Max Weber's Critique of Recent Comparative-Historical Sociology and a Reconstruction of His Analysis of the Rise of Confucianism in China." Pp. 207–46 in *Current Perspectives in Social Theory* (vol. 19), edited by Jennifer Lehmann. Stamford, CT: JAI Press.

——. 2000. "Max Weber." Pp. 144–205 in *The Blackwell Companion to Major Social Theorists*, edited by George Ritzer. Oxford: Blackwell Publishers.

——. 2001. "Max Weber's Reflections on the American Political Culture Today: An 'Iron Cage'?" Forthcoming in *Max Weber Studies*.

Lehmann, Hartmut. 1993. "The Rise of Capitalism: Weber versus Sombart." Pp. 195–209 in *Weber's Protestant Ethic: Origins, Evidence, Contexts*, edited by H. Lehmann and Guenther Roth. New York: Cambridge University Press.

Lichtblau, Klaus and Johannes Weiss. 1993a. "Einleitung der Herausgeber." Pp. vii–xxxv in *Max Weber: Die protestantische Ethik und der 'Geist' des Kapitalismus*, edited by K. Lichtblau and J. Weiss. Bodenheim: Athenäum Hain Hanstein.

——, eds. 1993b. *Max Weber: Die protestantische Ethik und der 'Geist' des Kapitalismus*. Bodenheim: Athenäum Hain Hanstein.

Marcks, Erich. 1894. "Einleitung." Pp. 3–25 in Hermann Baumgarten, *Historische und politische Aufsätze und Reden*. Strasbourg: Truebner.

Mommsen, Wolfgang. 1974. "Die Vereinigten Staaten von Amerika." Pp. 72–96 in W. Mommsen, *Max Weber: Gesellschaft, Politik und Geschichte*. Frankfurt: Suhrkamp.

——. 1989. *The Political and Social Theory of Max Weber*. Chicago: The University of Chicago Press.

Offenbacher, Martin. 1900. *Konfession und soziale Schichtung*. Tübingen: Mohr.

Putnam, Robert D. 2000. *Bowling Alone*. New York: Simon and Schuster.

Rollman, Hans. 1993. " 'Meet Me in St. Louis': Troeltsch and Weber in America." Pp. 357–82 in *Weber's Protestant Ethic: Origins, Evidence, Contexts*, edited by Hartmut Lehmann and Guenther Roth. New York: Cambridge University Press.

Roth, Guenther. 1985. "Marx and Weber on the United States—Today." Pp. 215–33 in *A Weber-Marx Dialogue*, edited by Robert J. Antonio and Ronald M. Glassman. Lawrence, KS: University Press of Kansas.

——. 1997. "The Young Max Weber: Anglo-American Religious Influences and Protestant Social Reform in Germany." *International Journal of Politics, Culture, and Society* 10, 4: 659–71.

Salomon, Albert. 1935. "Max Weber's Political Ideas." *Social Research* 2 (Aug.): 368–84.

——. 1962. *In Praise of Enlightenment*. Cleveland: World Publ. Co.

Scaff, Lawrence. 1989. *Fleeing the Iron Cage*. Berkeley: The University of California Press.

——. 1998. "The 'Cool Objectivity of Sociation': Max Weber and Marianne Weber in America." *History of the Human Sciences* 11, 2: 61–82.

Schluchter, Wolfgang. 1989. *Rationalism, Religion, and Domination: A Weberian Perspective*. Berkeley: The University of California Press.

——. 1996. *Paradoxes of Modernity*. Stanford, CA: Stanford University Press.

Schor, Juliet. 1991. *The Overworked American*. New York: Basic Books.

Sombart, Werner. 1902. *Der moderne Kapitalismus*. Leipzig: Duncker & Humblot.

——. 1969 (1913). *The Jews and Modern Capitalism*. New York: Burt Franklin.

Swedberg, Richard. 1998. *Max Weber and the Idea of Economic Sociology*. Princeton: Princeton University Press.

Tocqueville, Alexis de. 1945. *Democracy in America*, two vols. New York: Vintage.

Weber, Marianne. 1975 (1926). *Max Weber*. New York: John Wiley and Sons.

Weber, Max. 1927. *General Economic History*. Translated by Frank H. Knight. Glencoe, IL: Free Press. Originally: 1923. *Wirtschaftsgeschichte*. Edited by S. Hellman and M. Palyi. Munich: Duncker & Humblot.

——. 1946a. "Religious Rejections of the World." Pp. 323–59 in *From Max Weber: Essays in Sociology* (hereafter *FMW*), edited and translated by H. H. Gerth and C. Wright Mills. New York: Oxford. Originally: (1920) 1972. "Zwischenbetrachtung." Pp. 537–73 in *Gesammelte Aufsätze zur Religionssoziologie* (hereafter *GARS*), vol. 1. Tübingen: Mohr.

——. 1946b. "Science as a Vocation." Pp. 129–56 in *FMW*. Originally: (1922) 1973. Pp. 582–613 in *Gesammelte Aufsätze zur Wissenschaftslehre*, edited by Johannes Winckelmann. Tübingen: Mohr.

——. 1946c. "The Social Psychology of the World Religions." Pp. 267–301 in *FMW*. Originally: (1920) 1972. Pp. 237–68 in *GARS*, vol. 1.

——. 1946d. "Politics as a Vocation." Pp. 77–128 in *FMW*. Originally: (1919) 1971. *Gesammelte Politische Schriften*. Edited by Johannes Winckelmann. Tübingen: Mohr.

——. 1949. *The Methodology of the Social Sciences*. Edited and translated by Edward A. Shils and Henry A. Finch. New York: Free Press. Originally: (1922) 1973. Pp. 489–540, 146–214, 215–290 in *Gesammelte Aufsätze zur Wissenschaftslehre*, edited by Johannes Winckelmann. Tübingen: Mohr.

——. 1951. *The Religion of China*. Edited and translated by Hans H. Gerth. New York: The Free Press. Originally: (1920) 1972. "Konfuzianismus und Taoismus." Pp. 276–536 in *GARS*, vol. 1.

——. 1952. *Ancient Judaism*. Edited and translated by Hans H. Gerth and Don Martindale. New York: Free Press. Originally: (1920) 1971. *Das antike Judentum*. *GARS*, vol. 3.

——. 1958. *The Religion of India*. Edited and translated by Hans H. Gerth and Don Martindale. New York: Free Press. Originally: (1920) 1972. *Hinduismus und Buddhismus*. *GARS*, vol. 2.

——. 1968. *Economy and Society*. Edited by Guenther Roth and Claus Wittich. New York: Bedminster Press. Originally: (1921) 1976. *Wirtschaft und Gesellschaft*. Edited by Johannes Winckelmann. Tübingen: Mohr.

——. 1972. *Max Weber: Die protestantische Ethik II, Kritiken und Antikritiken*, edited by Johannes Winckelmann. Hamburg: Siebenstern Verlag.

——. 1978. "The Prospects for Liberal Democracy in Tsarist Russia." Pp. 269–84 in *Weber: Selections in Translation*, edited by W. G. Runciman. Cambridge, UK: University Press. Originally: (1906) 1958. Pp. 333–68 in *Gesammelte Politische Schriften*, edited by Johannes Winckelmann. Tübingen: Mohr.

——. 1985 (1905). " 'Churches' and 'Sects' in North America: An Ecclesiastical Socio-Political Sketch." *Sociological Theory* 3, 1: 7–13. Originally: (1906) 1992. Pp. 382–97 in *Max Weber: Soziologie unversalgeschichtliche Analysen, Politik*, edited by Johannes Winckelmann. Stuttgart: Kröner. ✦

GLOSSARY

This listing includes (a) historical terms that are often forgotten today and (b) terms that are key to Weber's analysis. When first used in each chapter, all Glossary terms have been set in bold type.

Affinity (elective, inner) (*Wahlverwandtschaft, innere Verwandtschaft*). A notion taken from Goethe that implies an "internal" connection between two different phenomena rooted in a shared feature and/or a clear historical linkage (for example, between certain religious beliefs and a vocational ethic). The causal relationship is not strong enough to be designated "determining."

Ascetic Protestantism. This generic term refers to the Calvinist, Pietist, Methodist, Quaker, Baptist, and Mennonite churches and sects. Weber compares and contrasts the vocational ethics of these faiths to each other and to those of Lutheran Protestantism and Catholicism.

Calling (*Beruf*). Denotes a task given by God and the incorporation of a demarcated realm of work into the Protestant believer's life in the sixteenth and seventeenth centuries in the West. Despite a vast comparative-historical search, Weber found this definition of "calling" only in Protestantism.

Carriers. See Social Carriers.

Conventicles. Small group Bible and prayer gatherings ("house churches") of the faithful that aimed to counteract any weakening of belief. The Scriptures and devotional literature were studied and spiritual exercises performed.

Deification of Human Wants and Desires. The Puritan's loyalty must be exclusively to God. Human wants and desires (personal vanity, sexual fulfillment, the enjoyment of love, friendship, luxury, etc.) must be tamed and remain subordinate to this noble and prior allegiance.

Dispassionate (*nüchtern*). A term Weber uses repeatedly to characterize the temperate and restrained frame of mind of Puritans. This disposition implies rigorous self-control and a capacity to organize life systematically around defined goals.

Dordrecht Synod. An Assembly of the Reformed Church of the Netherlands in Dordrecht in 1618–1619. Disputes concerned Arminianism and its rejection of the doctrine of predestination.

Earning a Living (making a living; orientation toward acquisition; *Erwerbsleben*). Carried by Puritanism, a middle-class activity that is necessary in profit-oriented economies; contrasted in *PE* mainly to persons who live off rents ("rentier wealth") and to the life-style of feudal nobles .

Economic Ethic of the World Religions. This is the title Weber gave to a series of studies on the world's great religions. See pp. lviii–lxiv.

Economic Form. An economic form refers to the way in which a company is organized and managed, the relationship of employer to workers, the type of accounting, the movement of capital, etc. Contrasted by Weber in chapter 2 to an "economic spirit" or "economic ethic."

Economic Rationalism. This term refers to the modern capitalism that developed in the sixteenth and seventeenth centuries in the West. It implies the utilization of science on behalf of a systematic organization of labor and the entire production process, and hence qualitative increases in productive capacity.

Economic Traditionalism (traditional economic ethic). A frame of mind in respect to work. Work is viewed as a necessary evil and only one arena of life, no more important than the arenas of leisure, family, and friends. "Traditional needs" are implied: when fulfilled, then work ceases. This frame of mind stands in opposition to the development of modern capitalism. ("Traditionalism," in Weber's time, referred to the conduct of activities in an accustomed, habitual fashion.)

Feeling (feeling-based; *Gefühl*). The "strangely warmed heart" (Wesley) sought especially by Pietists and early Methodists that indicated the presence within of God and strengthened commitment and ethical responsibility toward Him. At the vital core of these denominations because tantamount to the subjective experiencing of salvation (and out of which emotions—exhilaration, joy, relief—flowed), feeling remained suspect to Calvinists, who viewed salvation in terms of a striving to render one's life holy (see below). In Weber's analysis, feeling provided a less firm foundation for the vocational calling than the Calvinist's striving.

Frame of Mind (*Gesinnung*). The specific temperament or disposition that Weber sees as specific to a group of people. He uses the term to refer to characteristic features (in the sense of an ideal type) of Calvinists, Catholics, Lutherans, adventure capitalists, feudal aristocrats, old commerce-oriented (patrician) families, persons in the middle class, etc. Each group has its own temper or outlook. The frame of mind in some groups may be more weighted toward values, even ethical values (the religious groups); in others it tends more toward endowing interests (adventure capitalists) or traditions (peasants) with greater meaning.

Glorification of Desires. See "Deification of Human Wants and Desires."

Ideal Type. Weber's major methodological tool. He creates in *PE* "ideal types" for an array of groups (Catholics, Lutherans, Calvinists, adventure capitalists, etc.). Each ideal type, by accentuating that which is *characteristic* from the point of view of *Weber's* theme, seeks to capture that which is essential to a group. (See pp. 13–14; ch. 4, note 78)

Interpretive Understanding (*Verstehen*). This is the term Weber uses to describe his own methodology. He wishes to understand the actions and beliefs of people in demarcated groups by reconstructing the milieu of values, traditions, interests, and emotions within which they live, and thereby to understand how "subjective meaning" (see below) is formulated.

Middle Class (*bürgerlich, das Bürgertum*). *PE* offers an analysis of the religious origins of the ethos and frame of mind of a new class that elevated steady and constant work to the center of life. Composed of both employers and workers, this middle class was the social carrier (see below) of a set of values oriented to economic activity and "earning a living" that distinguished it significantly from the destitute urban poor, feudal nobles, patrician old-family capitalists, and adventure capitalists. Weber seeks to offer an explanation for the origin of this set of values and to argue that they played a role in calling forth the spirit of capitalism.

Modern Capitalism. Weber sees capitalism as universal. He is interested in the origins of *modern* capitalism as it appeared in the West in the sixteenth and seventeenth centuries. This capitalism involved the rational organization of free labor, the systematic pursuit of profit, and a "modern economic ethos" or "spirit." He concludes that a "Protestant ethic" played a role in giving rise to modern capitalism.

Organization of Life, Organized Life. Weber's term *Lebensführung* implies a conscious directing, or leading, of life. Although for him the organized life is generally "internally" rooted in a set of values (even ethical values), this is not always the case (interests anchor the "practical rational" *Lebensführung*). This term stands as a contrast in Weber's writings generally to the undirected life that simply, like a natural event, flows on in time without guidance. Because Weber emphasizes in *PE* that the Puritans must organize and direct their lives according to their beliefs, the phrase "organization of life" appears best to capture his meaning here.

Providential (sanctifying). Rendering with religious (salvation) significance an activity heretofore purely utilitarian (work, wealth, and profit, for example).

Psychological Motivations (*Antriebe*). Weber is concerned throughout *PE* with the motivation behind action, particularly action directed toward work, making a living, and profit as it originates from religious beliefs. The important psychological motivations for religion-oriented action derive, he argues, not from the ethical theory implied by doctrines or what is officially taught in ethical manuals, but from the motivations that arise out of a combination of belief and the regular *practice* of the religious life as transmitted by the clergy to believers through pastoral care, church discipline, and preaching (see "Psychological Reward").

Psychological Reward (*psychologische Prämien*). Through belief and the practice of religion, "salvation premiums" are awarded to particular activities (such as the accumulation of wealth or the organization of life in accord with God's laws), thereby assisting the devout, as long as they perform this activity, to more easily convince themselves of their membership among the saved.

Puritanism. Weber's usage follows the everyday language of the seventeenth century. This "amorphous" term refers to the ascetic Protestant (see above) movements in Holland, England, and North America oriented toward this-worldly asceticism (including the Congregationalists and "Independents"). All Puritans organized their lives around work and a this-worldly, morally rigorous asceticism. Puritanism, Weber argues, provides a consistent foundation for the idea of a vocational calling.

Rational. A systematic, rigorous, disciplined element to action.

Rationalization. Weber is using this term in accord with the usage of his time. It implies a systematizing of one's actions (usually to accord with religious values) in the sense of an increased rigor and methodicalness and a taming of the *status naturae* (see below).

Reformed Church (*reformierte*). Although "by no means identical with Calvinism," Calvinism constituted to Weber the major theological force behind the broader Reform movement of ascetic Protestant churches and sects in Holland, England, and America (except for the Methodists). He tends in chapter 4 to use "Calvinism" when referring to ideas, doctrines, and values stemming from John Calvin, and "Reformed" when referring to the several organized churches he founded. All Reformed churches stood in stark contrast to the Lutheran "state church" in Germany.

Religious Reward. See "Psychological Reward."

Savoy Declaration (1658). A statement of faith by English Congregationalists. Advocated (unlike the Westminster Confession) the autonomy of local churches.

Sect. As opposed to a church, an exclusive, voluntary, and tightly knit group that admits new members only once specific criteria have been fulfilled. Membership implies both "good character" and a monitoring of behavior by other sect members to ensure compliance.

Social Carrier (*Träger*). Ideas are important causal forces of historical change, for Weber, but only if they are "carried" by demarcated and influential groupings, strata, and organizations (Calvinists or a middle class, for example). Weber wishes to know in *PE* what groups carried specific types of vocational ethics. A central concept in Weber's sociology (see lii–liv).

Status Naturae. The "natural status" of the human species. The spontaneous aspects of human nature are not tamed, channelled, sublimated, or organized. Puritanism, Weber argues, by systematically organizing the lives of believers according to a set of values, accomplished just this—indeed in an extremely rigorous manner.

Striving to Make Life Holy (sanctified, (*Heiligung*). Calvinists organized their entire lives around a search for psychological certainty of their salvation status. Despite the doctrine of predestination, they came to believe (especially owing to Baxter's revisions) that their capacity to adhere to specific modes of conduct approved by God *testified* to their membership among the saved. Hence, through their righteous conduct, they could "strive" for salvation. Pietists and Methodists believed that certainty of salvation came also through a feeling (see above) of being possessed by God.

Subjective Meaning. Weber seeks, throughout his sociology, to understand how persons view their own behavior and how they justify it to themselves, or lend it "meaning" (no matter how odd it may appear to the observer). He wishes in *PE* to understand, for example, why continuous hard work and a systematic search for profit and wealth constitutes a subjectively meaningful endeavor for Calvinists.

Surpassing (*Überbietung*). The Puritans, in organizing their lives according to God's laws, surpassed "this-worldly" (utilitarian) morality.

Testify (*Bewährung*). This central notion for Calvinists (and for all striving for salvation) implies both an outward demonstration visible to others (one's conduct, demeanor, and bearing) and a psychological element: the devout understand their strength to "prove" their belief through perpetual righteous conduct as emanating from God—and hence they feel an inner confidence regarding their salvation status

This-Worldly (*innerweltlich, diesseitig*). This term implies activity "in" the world in contrast to the monks activity "outside" the world (in the cloister). With Puritanism, Weber argues, asceticism moved out of the monastery and "into" the world. Remarkably, the activity of Puritans was *in* the world but not *of* the world (since its major orientation was not to this-worldly goods or interests but to salvation in the next life).

Tradition Economic Ethic. See "Economic Traditionalism."

Utilitarian Adaptation to the World. The orientation of life to the pragmatic morality of the everyday world rather than a surpassing (see above) of this morality on the basis of a rigorous orientation to God's laws and a striving for salvation.

Value-Rational Action (motives). One of Weber's "four types of social action," this term implies that a person's action is oriented to values to a significant extent, indeed even to the degree that values become obligatory, or "binding" upon action. It contrasts, in Weber's sociology to "means-end rational action."

Westminster Confession. A confession of faith by Calvinists. Approved by the Long Parliament in 1648, but denied official status after the restoration of the monarchy in 1660. Adopted later by several American and English ascetic Protestant churches. ✦

THE PROTESTANT ETHIC

AND

THE SPIRIT OF CAPITALISM

PART I

THE PROBLEM

Modern capitalism has as little use for liberum arbitrium [undisciplined] persons as laborers as it has for the businessman fully without scruples in the running of his company.

(Kalberg, p. 20)

The question of the motivating forces behind the expansion of modern capitalism is not primarily one of the source of money reserves that can be used by capitalist firms but above all a question of the development of the spirit of capitalism.

(Kalberg, p. 29)

CHAPTER I

RELIGIOUS AFFILIATION AND SOCIAL STRATIFICATION[1]

A glance at the occupational statistics for any country in which several religions coexist is revealing. They indicate that people who own capital, employers, more highly educated skilled workers, and more highly trained technical or business personnel in modern companies tend to be, with striking frequency,[2] overwhelmingly *Protestant.*[3] The variation in this regard between Catholics and Protestants has often been discussed, in a lively fashion, in Catholic newspapers and journals in Germany,[4] as well as at congresses of the Catholic Church.

According to the statistics, this variation between Catholics and Protestants is prominent where differences in religious belief and in nationality are found in the same region (and hence differences in the extent of historical development). Germans and Poles in northern central Europe come to mind.[5] Yet the numbers demonstrate as well that differences are equally apparent in nearly all areas where capitalism, in the period of its great expansion [in the eighteenth and nineteenth centuries], possessed a free hand to reorganize a population. As these transformations took place, populations then changed according to indigenous paths of development, both socially and occupationally. In the process, differences according to religious belief became all the more striking.

Of course the disproportionately high percentage of Protestants among the owners of capital,[6] the more highly educated skilled workers, and those employed in large industrial and commercial companies[7] can in part be traced back to historical forces[8] from the distant past. Moreover, religious affiliation may not appear to be the *cause* of economic activity; rather, differences in religious belief may seem, to a certain extent, to be the *result* of economic factors. After all, participation in certain economic activities assumes in part some ownership of capital to begin with, in part a costly education, and in part—most frequently—both. Today this participation is tied to ownership of inherited wealth or at least to a certain material affluence. It must also be noted that in the old German Empire, a large number of the richest and most economically developed areas—favored by nature or a geographical location that facilitated trade and commerce—turned Protestant in the sixteenth century. This held especially for the majority of the wealthy cities. The effects of this wealth benefit Protestants in the economic struggle for existence even today.

The historical question then arises, however: What reasons explain the particularly strong predilection in the most economically developed regions toward a revolution in the Catholic Church [in the sixteenth century]? The answer is by no means as simple as one might at first believe.

Certainly the shedding of the old **economic traditionalism** would seem essentially to support both the tendency to doubt, even religious belief, and the resistance to traditional authorities. Nevertheless, that which is today so often forgotten must be noted here: the Reformation of the sixteenth century not only involved the *elimination* of the Catholic Church's domination (*Herrschaft*)[9] over the believer's life in its entirety but also the substitution of one form of control by *another*. A highly agreeable domination that had become a mere formality, one that was scarcely felt in a practical manner, was replaced by an infinitely burdensome and severe regimentation of the entire **organization of the believer's life** (*Lebensführung*). Religion now penetrated all private and public spheres in the most comprehensive sense imaginable.

A classic adage succinctly characterizes the Catholic Church's domination as it was earlier even more than today: "The heretic must be punished, but the sinner must be treated leniently." This view was upheld at the beginning of the fifteenth century in the richest, most economically developed regions on earth, and it is upheld even now by groups of people with thoroughly modern orientations to economic activity. In contrast, the domination of Calvinism as it existed in the sixteenth century in Geneva and Scotland, at the end of the sixteenth and beginning of the seventeenth centuries in large parts of Holland, in the seventeenth century in New England, and even in England from time to time, would constitute for us today the most absolutely unbearable form of control by the church over the individual. Large segments of the old commercial aristocracy at that time experienced Calvinism in just this way. Yet the religious activists of the Reformation period, who arose in the most economically developed nations, complained that religion and the church exercised too little domination over life rather than too much.

How then did it happen that precisely the most economically developed nations of that period, and (as will become apparent) specifically their upwardly mobile **middle classes** (*"bürgerlichen" Mittelklassen*), not only simply allowed this heretofore unknown Puritan tyranny to encompass them but even developed a heroic defense of it? *Middle* classes *as such* had only rarely submitted to such religious tyranny prior to the sixteenth and seventeenth centuries, and they have never done so since then. Not without reason, [the Scottish writer and historian Thomas] Carlyle [1795–1881] referred to this defense as "the last of our heroisms."

But let us proceed. Could it be, as noted, that the greater ownership of capital by Protestants and their more frequent participation at the top levels of the modern economy are to be understood today in part as a consequence of their historical possession of substantial wealth and their success in passing it on to succeeding generations? Further observations, only a few of which can be mentioned here, indicate that the causal relationship surely *cannot* be formulated in this manner.

First, as is clearly demonstrable, Catholic parents in [the German states of] Baden and Bavaria, as well as in Hungary, for example, enroll their children in different *types* of programs and curricula from those chosen by Protestant parents. The percentage of Catholic students enrolled in the "accelerated" tracks and schools, and then graduating, remains significantly below the percentage of Catholics in the population as a whole.[10] Of course, one is inclined to explain this difference largely by reference to the greater transfer of wealth by Protestants across generations.

This line of reasoning, however, fails to offer an adequate explanation for a second observation. *Within* the group of Catholic graduates enrolled in the accelerated tracks and schools, the percentage of students who decided to take courses in preparation for university study in technical fields or for careers in commerce and industry (or other middle-class ways of making a living in business) lagged *far* behind the percentage of Protestant graduates who decided to do so.[11] Catholics preferred courses of instruction that emphasized languages, philosophy, and history (*humanistische Gymnasien*). Reference to varying levels of inherited wealth will not account for these differences in respect to schooling. Indeed, they must be acknowledged in any explanation for the lower rates of entry into business by Catholics.

Third, an even more remarkable observation helps us to understand the lesser representation of Catholics among skilled *workers* in modern, large industrial concerns. It is well-known that the factory takes its skilled laborers to a large degree from the younger generation of handicraft workers. Thus, the factory leaves the training of its labor force to the crafts. Once skills have been acquired, the factory pulls workers—or "journeymen"—away from the crafts. This situation holds much more for Protestant than for Catholic journeymen. That is, Catholic journeymen demonstrate a much stronger inclination to remain in their crafts and thus more often become master craftsmen. In contrast, Protestants stream into the factory at a comparatively higher rate and then acquire positions as high-level skilled workers and industrial managers.[12] In these cases the causal relationship is undoubtedly one in which a *learned inner quality* decides a person's choice of occupation and further course of occupational development. And this learned inner quality is influenced by the direction of one's upbringing and education, which in turn is influenced by the religious climate in one's native town and one's parental home.

The less frequent participation of Catholics in modern business life in Germany is indeed all the more striking because it opposes an age-old[13] (as well as present-day) empirical rule of thumb: ethnic or religious minorities, as "dominated" groups standing opposite a "dominant" group and *as a consequence of* their voluntary or involuntary exclusion from influential political positions, have been driven to an especially strong degree into the arena of business. Hence, in Germany the most talented among the minority, who might, if not oppressed, hope for the highly sought-after positions at the top levels of the state civil service, instead seek to satisfy their ambitions in the realm of business. Unmistakably, this situation holds for the undoubtedly economically advancing Poles in Russia and eastern Prussia, where, as Catholics, they were a minority (in contrast to their situation in the province of Galicia in Poland, where they were the majority population). It also holds for earlier groupings: the Huguenots in France under Louis XIV, the Nonconformists and Quakers in England, and, last but not least, the Jews for two thousand years. Catholics in Germany, however, do not today follow this pattern. There seems to be no evidence (or at least no clear evidence) of a movement of this minority into large-scale industry, commerce, and business in general. In the past as well, in Holland and England and in both periods of toleration as well as those of persecution of Catholics, in contrast to Protestants, evidence for any particular *economic* development among Catholics cannot be found.

A different situation existed for Protestants. *Both* as ruling *and* ruled strata and *both* as majority *and* minority, Protestants (especially the denominations to be discussed later [in this study]) have demonstrated a specific tendency toward ***economic rationalism***. This tendency has not been observed in the same way in the present or the past among Catholics, regardless of whether they were the dominant or dominated stratum *or* constituted a majority or minority.[14] Therefore, the cause of the different behavior must be mainly sought in the enduring inner quality of these religions and *not* only in their respective historical-political, external situations.[15] Our first task will be to investigate which of the elements in the characteristic features of each religion had, and to some extent still have, the effects described above. [1920]

On the basis of a superficial consideration of the matter and from the vantage point of certain modern impressions, one could attempt to formulate the contrast as one in which Catholicism's greater "estrangement from the world" (*Weltfremdheit*)—the ascetic features proclaimed by its highest ideals—had to socialize believers to be more indifferent to material and consumer goods. In fact, this explanation corresponds to the familiar mode of evaluating these differences popular in Germany in both religions [at the turn into the twentieth century]. German Protestants employ this view in order to criticize every (real or presumed) ascetic ideal in the Catholic way of organizing life. Catholics answer by reproaching Protestants for the "materialism" that has arisen from a secularization of the very meaning of life, holding Protestantism responsible for this development. A modern writer has attempted to capture the contrasting behavior of German Protestants and Catholics in regard to ways of making a living:

> The Catholic . . . is more calm and endowed with a weaker motivation to become engaged in business, retains as cautious and risk-averse an approach to life's journey as possible, and prefers to get by on a smaller income rather than to become engaged in more dangerous and challenging activities—even if they may lead to greater honor and wealth. It is evident, in light of a popular and humorous maxim in Germany—'one can either eat well or sleep peacefully'—that the Lutheran gladly eats well. On the other hand, the Catholic prefers to sleep undisturbed.[16]

This "wish to eat well" may indeed (at least in part and even though it remains incomplete as an explanation) correctly sum up the motivation of those Protestants in *Germany today* who remain rather indifferent believers. Matters were quite different in the past, however. As was commonly acknowledged, precisely the opposite of a natural and uncomplicated enjoyment of life's pleasures (*Weltfreude*) characterized the English, Dutch, and American **Puritans**. And, as will become evident, this approach to life is one of their traits of most importance to us. Moreover, French Protestantism,[17] for example, for centuries and to a certain extent even today, has retained the stamp imposed upon the Calvinist churches generally (although chiefly upon those "under the cross"[18] in the epoch of the religious struggles), namely, a certain severity rather than a natural enjoyment of life. Yet Protestantism was one of the most important carriers of industrial and capitalist development in France, as is well-known. This has remained so even if, owing to persecution, only on a small scale. Was this severity related to Protestantism's important role in capitalist development? This will be our query later.

One might be inclined to call this Protestant severity and the strong penetration of the believer's organization of life by religious interests "estrangement from the world." If one wished to do so, however, *then* the French *Calvinists* of the present, as well as of the past, must be viewed as at least as estranged from the world as, for example, the *Catholics* of northern Germany, whose Catholicism is undoubtedly more heartfelt than that of any other group of people. Moreover, *both* groupings are distinguished in parallel ways from the dominant religious groupings in their respective nations [Catholicism in France and Lutheran Protestantism in Germany]. Unlike French Calvinists, an immediate enjoyment of life is typical of lower-status Catholics in France, while an actual antagonism to religion characterizes French Catholics of higher status. And unlike Catholics of northern Germany, lower-status Protestants in Germany today have become immersed in mundane business activities and higher-status Protestants manifest a dominant indifference to religion.[19]

***

Hardly any examples could demonstrate more vividly than these parallels that vague ideas, such as Catholicism's (alleged!) "estrangement from the world" and Protestantism's (alleged!) materialistic "enjoyment of life's pleasures," remain at too high a level of generality to be helpful. This holds for the analysis of the present, despite the fact that exceptions can be found, but it is especially the case for the past. If one nonetheless wished to use such diffuse concepts, *then* further observations would at once become salient and unavoidable. These would lead to a question: Could not the entire contrast between estrangement from the world, asceticism, and church-based piety on the one hand, and the earning of one's living under capitalism on the other, be understood as actually implying an inner **affinity** (*innere Verwandtschaft*)?

To begin with only an external observation, a striking relationship has already become apparent to us: an unusually high number of persons affiliated with precisely the most spiritual forms of Christian piety came from business-oriented social circles. This origin was common in particular for a remarkably large number of Pietism's most devout believers. One might speculate here that the explanation involves a type of extreme reaction by more spiritually inclined people less well adapted to vocations in commerce and sales against the view that money and wealth have a vulgar, evil, and debasing influence ("mammonism"). Many of these Pietists, like St. Francis of Assisi [1181–1226, founder of the Franciscan mendicant order], have often actually depicted the course of their own "conversions" in just this manner.[20] Similarly, the conspicuous occurrence that unusually successful capitalist entrepreneurs were frequently the sons of ministers, including even Cecil Rhodes [1853–1902, the rich adventure capitalist and defender of British colonialism in Africa], could be explained as a reaction against an ascetic upbringing.

This mode of analysis, however, proves powerless to explain those cases in which a capitalist's virtuoso business sense *combines* in the same person and groups of persons with the most intense forms of piety that penetrate and order the believer's entire life. In fact, far from rare, this combination constitutes precisely the distinguishing aspect for whole groups of the historically most important Protestant **sects** and churches.

Wherever it has appeared, Calvinism in particular[21] demonstrated just this combination. Although Calvinism cannot be said to have been linked to a particular single class in the period of the expansion of the Reformation into various territories (as little as were the other Protestant faiths), it is nonetheless characteristic, and in a certain way "typical," that monks and industrialists (both retailers and craftsmen) were particularly highly represented among those, for example, proselytized into the Huguenot churches in France.[22] Indeed, groupings oriented to commerce remained in disproportionately high numbers in these churches even during the periods of persecution.[23] The Spaniards as well knew that "heresy" (that is, Calvinism from the Netherlands) "promoted the spirit of commerce." This conclusion corresponds fully to the views articulated by [the British statistician and political economist] Sir William Petty [1623–87] in his discussion of the causes for capitalism's growth in the Netherlands. [The economic historian W. Eberhard] Gothein, [1863–1923] appropriately,[24] depicts the Calvinist diaspora as the "capitalist economy's seed-bed."[25]

Of course it could be argued that the superiority itself of the French and Dutch economic cultures, out of which the Calvinist diaspora primarily arose, constituted the decisive factor. Or central significance might be attributed to the powerful effect of the exile experience and the uprooting it entailed from all of life's customary and traditional relationships.[26] This combination of a business orientation with intense piety was the situation in France in the seventeenth century, as we know from the struggles of [Jean Baptiste] Colbert [1619–83, diplomat, reformist finance minister under Louis XIV, and proponent of mercantilism and colonialism]. Even Austria, not to mention other nations, directly imported Protestant manufacturers occasionally.

Nevertheless, it should be noted that not all Protestant denominations exhibited an equally strong effect on capitalism's growth. Calvinism[27] exercised an apparently strong effect also in Germany, in the *Wuppertal* region as well as elsewhere, and the "**reformed**" faiths seem to have promoted the development of the capitalist spirit, as became especially clear in comparison to other faiths. Lutheranism, for example, in the *Wuppertal* proved less powerful in this respect. Comparisons of both large-scale situations and individual cases lead to this conclusion.[28] [The British historian Henry Thomas] Buckle [1821–62] and a number of English poets, especially [John] Keats [1795–1821], have documented similar relationships in Scotland.[29] [1920]

Even more striking is the connection (as we need only to be briefly reminded) between a religious regimentation of life and the most intensive development of a sense for business. This connection is apparent in the large number of precisely those sects whose "estrangement from life" (*Lebensfremdheit*) has become as familiar as their wealth. The *Quakers* in England and North America and the *Mennonites* in Germany and the Netherlands particularly come to mind. Even the absolute refusal of the Mennonites in East Prussia to perform military service did not prevent Frederick William I [1688–1740, king of Prussia] from declaring their indispensability as **social carriers** of industry. This example is just one, although one of the most clear in light of the particular qualities of this monarch, of the many well-known illustrations of this situation. Finally, a combination of intense piety with an equally intensely developed business sense, as well as success, likewise exists among the German *Pietists*, as is well-known in Germany. One need only think over the history of Calv, [a major center of Pietism], in southwest Germany in comparison to that of Catholicism in the Rhineland.[30]

***

An accumulation of further examples in this purely preliminary discussion is unnecessary. The few illustrations already noted all lead to the same conclusion: the "spirit of work" or "progress" (or whatever else it may be called), whose awakening one is inclined to attribute to Protestantism, should not be understood as implying a natural and uncomplicated "enjoyment of life's pleasures." Furthermore, this "spirit of work" should not be comprehended as otherwise somehow involving "enlightenment," as many today now believe. The old Protestantism of [Martin] Luther [1483–1546], [John] Calvin [1509–64], [John] Knox [1505–72], and [Gisbert] Voët [1589–1676][31] had very little to do with what is today called progress. Indeed, their Protestantism stood directly antagonistic to a number of central elements of modern life that even the most fundamentalist believer today would not wish to banish.

Hence, if an inner affinity is to be discovered at all between certain streams of the old Protestant spirit and the modern culture of capitalism, our investigation—for better or worse—must *not* attempt to find this affinity in this Protestant spirit's (allegedly) more or less materialistic, or even anti-ascetic, "enjoyment of life's pleasures." It should focus instead on Protestantism's purely *religious* features. [Charles de Secondat, baron de] Montesquieu [1689–1755, the French social philosopher, writer, and opponent of absolutism], described the English as having advanced "farther than other peoples in three important ways: in respect to piety, commerce, and freedom" (see *Spirit of the Laws*, bk. 20, ch. 7). Could it be that the superiority of the English in regard to commerce, as well as their aptitude for free political institutions (the discussion of which belongs in another context), is perhaps connected to the unusual piety Montesquieu attributes to them?

A whole multitude of possible relationships immediately, if only dimly, appear before us if we frame the question in this manner. Thus, we must take as our task to *formulate*, as clearly as possible and despite full cognizance of the inexhaustible diversity that lies within every historical case, that which now appears to us diffusely. To do so, however, we must necessarily abandon the arena of vague and general depictions heretofore our plane of reference. Instead, we must attempt to penetrate the characteristic qualities and distinctiveness of the great religious worlds of thought given to us historically in the diverse forms of Christianity.

Nevertheless, a few remarks are indispensable before proceeding in this direction. The particular features of the phenomenon for which we intend to offer an historical explanation must first be discussed. A commentary on the meaning (*Sinn*) that such an explanation can possibly have within the framework of these investigations will then follow. ✦

CHAPTER II

THE SPIRIT OF CAPITALISM

The title of this study uses a concept that sounds rather intimidating: the "*spirit* of capitalism."[1] What should be understood by it? An attempt to provide even an approximate definition immediately unveils certain difficulties that are embedded in the essence of this investigation's purpose. [1920]

If one can discover at all an object for which the phrase *spirit of capitalism* is meaningful, then it can only be a specific *historical case*. Such a singular entity is nothing more than a complex of relationships in historical reality. We join them together, from the vantage point of their *cultural significance*, into a conceptual unity.

Such a historical concept, however, cannot be defined according to how it is "demarcated" vis-à-vis other concepts (*genus proximum, differentia specifica*). This holds if only because the concept denotes a phenomenon that is of qualitative importance as a consequence of its individual *uniqueness*. Moreover, this concept must be gradually *put together* from its single component parts, each of which is taken out of historical reality. Therefore, the final formation of the concept cannot appear at the beginning of the investigation; rather, it must stand at its *conclusion*. In other words, how our understanding of a spirit of capitalism is to be best defined will have to unfold only in the course of our discussion and only as its main outcome. Only a definition formulated in this manner will be adequate to the particular vantage points of interest to us here.

In turn, it must be recognized that these vantage points (which are still to be discussed) by no means constitute the only ones possible in reference to which the historical cases under consideration can be analyzed. Other vantage points would identify other features of our historical cases as "essential," as is true with every historical case. From this premise it follows unequivocally that whatever one understands by a spirit of capitalism by no means necessarily can or must correspond to *that which we* will note as essential in our exegesis here. This must be acknowledged, namely, the central role played by the researcher's particular vantage point in identifying what is essential to each case, as it belongs to the very essence of the formation of historical concepts—an endeavor that does not aim, in terms of its methodological goals, to trap reality in abstract, general concepts (*Gattungsbegriffe*). Rather, we strive, when forming historical concepts, to achieve something different: to order reality into tangible, causal connections that are stable and, unavoidably, of a *unique* character.[2]

That being said, and even if we succeed in demarcating the case we are attempting here to analyze and explain historically, our concern now cannot be to offer a conceptual definition. Instead, our focus at the beginning should be only to provide a provisional *illustration* of the activity implied here by the term *spirit of capitalism*. Indeed, such an illustration is indispensable in order to attain our aim now of simply understanding the object of our investigation. On behalf of this purpose we turn to a document that contains the spirit of concern to us in near classical purity, and simultaneously offers the advantage of being detached from *all* direct connection to religious belief—hence, for our theme, of being "free of presuppositions."

> Remember, that *time* is money. He that can earn ten shillings a day by his labor, and goes abroad, or sits idle, one half of that day, though he spends but sixpence during his diversion or idleness, ought not to reckon *that* the only expense; he has really spent, or rather thrown away, five shillings besides.
>
> Remember, that *credit* is money. If a man lets his money lie in my hands after it is due, he gives me the interest, or so much as I can make of it during that time. This amounts to a considerable sum where a man has good and large credit, and makes good use of it.
>
> Remember, that money is of the prolific, generating nature. Money can beget money, and its offspring can beget more, and so on. Five shillings turned is six, turned again it is seven and threepence, and so on, till it becomes a hundred pounds. The more there is of it, the more it produces every turning, so that the profits rise quicker and quicker. He that kills a breeding-sow, destroys all her offspring to the thousandth generation. He that murders a crown, destroys all that it might have produced, even scores of pounds. . . .
>
> Remember this saying: *The good paymaster is lord of another man's purse*. He that is known to pay punctually and exactly to the time he promises, may at any time, and on any occasion, raise all the money his friends can spare. This is sometimes of great use. After industry and frugality, nothing contributes more to the raising of a young man in the world than punctuality and justice in all his dealings; therefore never keep borrowed

money an hour beyond the time you promised, lest a disappointment shut up your friend's purse for ever.

The most trifling actions that affect a man's credit are to be regarded. The sound of your hammer at five in the morning, or eight at night, heard by a creditor, makes him easy six months longer; but if he sees you at a billiard-table, or hears your voice at a tavern, when you should be at work, he sends for his money the next day; demands it, before he can receive it, in a lump.

It shows, besides, that you are mindful of what you owe; it makes you appear a careful as well as an honest man, and that still increases your credit.

Beware of thinking all your own that you possess, and of living accordingly. It is a mistake that many people who have credit fall into. To prevent this, keep an exact account for some time, both of your expenses and your income. If you take the pains at first to mention particulars, it will have this good effect: you will discover how wonderfully small, trifling expenses mount up to large sums, and will discern what might have been, and may for the future be saved, without occasioning any great inconvenience.

For six pounds a year you may have the use of one hundred pounds, if you are a man of known prudence and honesty.

He that spends a groat a day idly, spends idly above six pounds a year, which is the price of using one hundred pounds.

He that wastes idly a groat's worth of his time per day, one day with another, wastes the privilege of using one hundred pounds each year.

He that idly loses five shillings' worth of time, loses five shillings, and might as prudently throw five shillings in the river.

"He that loses five shillings, not only loses that sum, but all the advantage that might be made by turning it in dealing, which by the time that a young man becomes old, will amount to a comfortable bag of money.[3]

It is *Benjamin Franklin* [1706–90] who preaches to us in these sentences. As the supposed catechism of a Yankee, Ferdinand Kürnberger satirizes these axioms in his brilliantly clever and venomous *Picture of American Culture.*[4] That the spirit of capitalism is here manifest in Franklin's words, even in a manner characteristic for him, no one will doubt. It will not be argued here, however, that *all aspects* of what can be understood by this spirit is contained in them.

Let us dwell a moment upon a passage, the worldly wisdom of which is summarized thusly by Kürnberger: "They make tallow for candles out of cattle and money out of men." Remarkably, the real peculiarity in the "philosophy of avarice" contained in this maxim is the ideal of the *credit-worthy* man of honor and, above all, the idea of the *duty* of the individual to increase his wealth, which is assumed to be a self-defined interest in itself. Indeed, rather than simply a common-sense approach to life, a peculiar "ethic" is preached here: its violation is treated not simply as foolishness but as a sort of forgetfulness of *duty*. Above all, this distinction stands at the center of the matter. "Business savvy," which is found commonly enough, is here not *alone* taught; rather, an *ethos* is expressed in this maxim. Just *this* quality is of interest to us in this investigation.

A retired business partner of Jakob Fugger [1459–1525, an extremely wealthy German financier, export merchant, and philanthropist] once sought to convince him to retire. Yet his colleague's argument—that he had accumulated enough wealth and should allow others their chance—was rebuked by Fugger as "contemptible timidity." He "viewed matters differently," Fugger answered, and "wanted simply to make money as long as he could."[5]

Obviously, the spirit of this statement must be *distinguished* from Franklin's. Fugger's entrepreneurial daring and personal, morally indifferent proclivities[6] now take on the character, in Franklin, of an *ethically*-oriented maxim for the **organization of life**. The expression *spirit of capitalism* will be used here in just this specific manner[7]—naturally the spirit of ***modern*** **capitalism**. That is, in light of the formulation of our theme, it must be evident that the Western European and American capitalism of the last few centuries constitutes our concern rather than the "capitalism" that has appeared in China, India, Babylon, the ancient world, and the Middle Ages. As we will see, *just that peculiar ethic was missing in all these cases.*

Nevertheless, all of Franklin's moral admonishments are applied in a utilitarian fashion: Honesty is *useful* because it leads to the availability of credit. Punctuality, industry, and frugality are also useful, and are *therefore* virtues. It would follow from this that, for example, the *appearance* of honesty, wherever it accomplishes the same end, would suffice. Moreover, in Franklin's eyes an unnecessary surplus of this virtue must be seen as unproductive wastefulness. Indeed, whoever reads in his autobiography the story of his "conversion" to these virtues,[8] or the complete discussions on the usefulness of a strict preservation of the *appearance* of modesty and the intentional minimizing of one's own accomplishments in order to attain a general approval,[9] will necessarily come to the conclusion that all virtues, according to Franklin, become virtues *only to the extent* that they are useful to the individual. The surrogate of virtue—namely, its appearance only—is fully adequate wherever the same purpose is achieved. Indeed, this inseparability of motive and appearance is the inescapable consequence of all strict utilitarianism. The common German tendency to perceive the American virtues as "hypocrisy" appears here confirmed beyond a doubt.

***

In truth, however, matters are not so simple. Benjamin Franklin's own character demonstrates that the issue is more complex: his character appears clearly, however seldom, in his autobiography as one of candor and truthfulness. It is also evident in Franklin's tracing of his realization, that virtues can be "useful," back to a revelation from God that was designed, he believed, to guide him onto the path of righteousness. Something more is involved here than simply an embellishing of purely self-interested, egocentric maxims.

The complexity of this issue is above all apparent in the *summum bonum* ["supreme good"] of this "ethic": namely, the acquisition of money, and more and more money, takes place here simultaneously with the strictest avoidance of all spontaneous enjoyment of it. The pursuit of riches is fully stripped of all pleasurable (*eudämonistischen*), and surely all hedonistic, aspects. Accordingly, this striving becomes understood completely as an end in itself—to such an extent that it appears as fully outside the normal course of affairs and simply irrational, at least when viewed from the perspective of the "happiness" or "utility" of the single individual.[10] Here, people are oriented to acquisition as the purpose of life; acquisition is no longer viewed as a means to the end of satisfying the substantive needs of life. Those people in possession of spontaneous, fun-loving dispositions experience this situation as an absolutely meaningless reversal of a "natural" condition (as we would say today). Yet this reversal constitutes just as surely a guiding principle of [modern] capitalism as incomprehension of this new situation characterizes all who remain untouched by [modern] capitalism's tentacles.

This reversal implies an internal line of development that comes into close contact with certain religious ideas. One can ask why then "money ought to be made out of persons." In his autobiography, Franklin answers (although he is himself a bland Deist) with a maxim from the Bible that, as he says, his strict Calvinist father again and again drilled into him in his youth: "Seest thou a man vigorous in his **vocational calling** (*Beruf*)? He shall stand before kings" (Prov. 22:29). As long as it is carried out in a legal manner, the acquisition of money in the modern economic order is the result and manifestation of competence and proficiency in a *vocational calling. This competence and proficiency* is the actual alpha and omega of Franklin's morality, as now can be easily recognized. It presents itself to us both in the passages cited above and, without exception, in all his writings.[11]

In fact, this peculiar idea of a *duty to have a vocational calling*, so familiar to us today but actually not at all self-evident, is the idea that is characteristic of the "social ethic" of modern capitalist culture. In a certain sense, it is even of constitutive significance for it. It implies a notion of duty that individuals ought to experience, and do, vis-à-vis the content of their "vocational" activity. This notion appears regardless of the particular nature of the activity and regardless, especially, of whether this activity seems to involve (as it does for people with a spontaneous, fun-loving disposition) nothing more than a simple utilization of their capacity for labor or their treatment of it as only a material possession (as "capital").

Nevertheless, it is surely not the case that the idea of a duty in one's vocational calling could grow *only* on the soil of [modern] capitalism. Rather, our attempt later to trace its roots will take us to a period prior to [modern] capitalism. Naturally it will be argued here even less that, under *today's* capitalism, the subjective acquisition of these ethical maxims by capitalism's particular social carriers (such as businesspersons or workers in modern capitalist companies) constitutes a condition for capitalism's further existence. Rather, the capitalist economic order of today is a vast cosmos into which a person is born. It simply exists, to each person, as a factually unalterable casing (*unabänderliches Gehäuse*) in which he or she must live. To the extent that people are interwoven into the context of capitalism's market forces, the norms of its economic action are forced onto them. Every factory owner who operates in the long term against these norms will inevitably be eliminated from the economy. With the same degree of inevitability, every worker who cannot or will not adapt to the norms of the marketplace will become unemployed.

Thus, through a process of economic *selection*, the capitalism that today dominates economic life socializes and creates the economic functionaries that it needs, both owners of businesses and workers. Nevertheless, the limitations of the notion of "selection" as a means to explain historical phenomena can be grasped here vividly. In order for a particular type of organized life and a particular conception of a vocational calling adapted to the uniqueness of modern capitalism to be "selected" (that is, more than others), obviously they must first have originated among—and as a mode of thinking be **carried** by—*groups* of persons rather than simply by isolated individuals. Hence, it is the origin of this mode of thinking, and its carrier groups, that actually needs to be explained.

***

We can address the idea of naive historical materialism—that such "ideas" arise as a "reflection" or "superstructure" of economic situations—in more detail only later. It must suffice adequately for our purpose at this point to call attention to the fact that the capitalist spirit (according to our definition here) without a doubt existed *before* "capitalist development" in the colony (Massachusetts) where Benjamin Franklin was born. (In contrast to other regions in America, one complained in New England as early as 1632 about specific appearances of a particularly calculating type of profit seeking.) Moreover, for example, in the neighboring colonies that were later to become the southern states of the union, this capitalist spirit remained distinctly less developed despite the fact that the southern states were called into being by large-scale capitalists for *business* purposes. In contrast, the New England colonies were called into existence for *religious* reasons by ministers and seminary graduates, together with small-scale merchants, craftsmen, and farmers. Thus, in *this* case at any rate, the causal relationship between ideas and economic situations lies in the direction opposite from that which would be postulated by the "materialist" argument.

But the youth of these ideas—the capitalist spirit—is altogether more thorny than was assumed by the "superstructure" theorists, and its unfolding does not proceed in the manner of the blossoming of a flower. The capitalist spirit, according to the meaning of this concept thus far acquired, became prominent only after a difficult struggle against a world of hostile powers. The **frame of mind** (*Gesinnung*) apparent in the cited passages from Benjamin Franklin that met with the approval of an entire people would have been proscribed in the ancient world, as well as in the Middle Ages,[12] for it would have been viewed as an expression of filthy greed and completely undignified character. Indeed, antagonism to this frame of mind is found even today, particularly (and on a regular basis) in those social groups least integrated into or adapted to the modern capitalist economy. This was the case not because "the acquisitive instinct" in precapitalist epochs was perhaps less well-known or developed, as is so often said, or because the *auri sacra fames* [craving for gold] was then, or is even today, *smaller* outside modern, **middle-class** capitalism, as is depicted in the illusions of modern-day romantic thinkers. Such arguments will not isolate the distinction between the capitalist and precapitalist spirit: the *greed* of the mandarins in China, of the aristocrats in ancient Rome, and of the modern peasant is second to none. And as anyone can experience for himself, the *auri sacra fames* of the Naples cab driver, or *barcaiolo* [Venetian gondolier], representatives in Asia of similar trades, and craftsmen in southern Europe and Asia is even unusually *more intense*, and especially more unscrupulous, than that of, for example, an Englishman in the same situation.[13]

The universal sway of *absolute* unscrupulousness in establishing one's own self-interest as the legitimate operating assumption for the pursuit of money has been specifically characteristic of precisely those countries where the development of a middle-class capitalism—measured against the standards of modern Western capitalist development—has remained "backward." The absence of *coscienziosita* [conscientiousness] among [wage] workers[14] in such nations (such as Italy in comparison to Germany) has been, and to a certain extent still is, the major obstacle to the unfolding of modern capitalism, as every factory employer knows. Modern capitalism has as little use for *liberum arbitrium* [undisciplined] persons as laborers as it has for the businessman fully without scruples in the running of his company, as we already have learned from Franklin. Hence, because its strength has varied, an "instinct" to pursue money cannot be the decisive issue.

The *auri sacra fames* is as old as the history of humanity known to us. We shall see that those who without reservation surrendered themselves to it as an *instinct*—the Dutch captain, for example, who "would sail through hell for profit, even if he burned his sails"—were *in no way* representatives of that frame of mind from which the specifically modern capitalist spirit burst forth as *a mass phenomenon*. That is what matters here. Acquisition unrestrained by internally binding norms has existed in all periods of history; indeed, it has existed wherever its expression was not circumscribed. In relationships across tribes and among peoples fundamentally unknown to each other, as well as in warfare and piracy, trade unbounded by norms has been the rule. A double standard prevailed in such situations: practices considered taboo "among brothers" were permitted with "outsiders."

As an "adventure," capitalist acquisition has found a place in all those economies that have known valuable objects as quasi-money forms of exchange and offered the chance to utilize them for profit. These economies have been based on, for example, *commenda*,[15] tax farming,[16] state-guaranteed loans, and the financing of wars, state functionaries, and the courts of princes. Coexisting everywhere with these external modes of economic organization were persons with an adventurous frame of mind—who mocked all ethical restrictions on action. An absolute and willfully ruthless striving for profit often stood hard and fast alongside a strict adherence to age-old traditions. Then, as these traditions began to disintegrate, a more or less broad-ranging expansion of an unrestrained quest for gain took place. In some situations, it intruded even into the core of social groups. [1920]

Hence, adventure capitalism did not imply an ethical affirmation and shaping of this new situation. Rather, the intrusion of an unrestrained quest for gain was only *tolerated* as a new reality; it was treated with ethical indifference or as a disagreeable but unavoidable presence. This was the normal position taken by all ethical teachings. Moreover, and of more essential importance, this view characterized the practical behavior of the average person in the epoch prior to modern capitalism, namely, before a rational use of capital in a managed manner and a systematic capitalist organization *of work* became the dominant forces determining the orientation of economic activity. This toleration of the unrestrained quest for gain, however, constituted everywhere one of the strongest inner barriers against the adaptation of persons to the preconditions of an organized, middle-class capitalist economy. [1920]

In the sense of a certain norm-bound style of life that has crystallized in the guise of an "ethic," the spirit of capitalism has had to struggle primarily against a specific opponent: that type of experiencing, perceiving, and ordering of the world that we can denote ***economic* traditionalism**. Every attempt to offer a final "definition," however, must be postponed. Instead, and of course only in a provisional manner, we will attempt a clear rendering of this term by reference to a few special cases. The workers first capture our attention.

***

One of the technical means used by the modern employer to achieve the highest possible productivity from "his" workers, and to increase the intensity of work, is the *piece-rate* method of payment. People are paid according to the fruits of their labor. In agriculture, for example, the harvesting of the crops requires the highest possible intensity of labor field by field. This requirement is common not least because, owing to the unpredictability of the weather, extraordinarily large profits and losses depend upon the greatest conceivable acceleration of the harvesting. Accordingly, the piece-rate method is customarily employed. Wherever the size of the harvest and the intensity of the company's work rhythms increase, so does the employer's interest in accelerated harvesting. Thus, employers have repeatedly attempted to interest workers in increasing their productivity by increasing the piece rate. Indeed, in doing so employers believed they were offering workers an opportunity to earn, in very short periods of time, what appeared to them an extraordinary wage.

Just at this point, however, peculiar difficulties became apparent. Remarkably, increasing the piece rate often led to less productivity in the same period of time rather than more. This decline occurred because workers responded to the increase by decreasing their daily productivity. For example, a man has been accustomed to harvesting 2 ½ acres per day and to receiving one German mark for every acre of grain harvested. He thus earns 2 ½ marks every day. If the piece rate is raised to 1 ¼ marks per acre, he needs to harvest only 2 acres per day in order to earn the same amount as before, and this, according to the biblical passage, "allows enough for him." Yet the employer's hope of increasing productivity by increasing the piece rate has been disappointed (if the worker had harvested 3 acres, he would have earned 3 ¾ marks).

The opportunity of earning more appealed to him less than the idea of working less. He did not ask: "If I produce as much as possible, how much money will I earn each day?" Rather, he formulated the question differently: "How long must I work in order to earn the amount of money—2 ½ marks—I have earned until now and that has fulfilled my *traditional* economic needs?"

This example illustrates the type of behavior that should be called economic traditionalism. People do not wish "by nature" to earn more and more money. Instead, they wish simply to live, and to live as they have been accustomed and to earn as much as is required to do so. Wherever modern capitalism began its task of increasing the "productivity" of human work by increasing its intensity, it confronted, in the precapitalist economy, an infinitely obdurate barrier in the form of this definition of work. Even today modern capitalism everywhere encounters economic traditionalism the more "backward" (from the perspective of modern capitalism) are the very laborers it depends on.

But let us again return to our illustration. Owing to the incapacity of the higher piece rate to appeal to the "acquisitive sense," it would appear altogether plausible to attempt to do so by utilizing the opposite strategy: by *decreasing* piece rates, to force workers to produce *more* in order to maintain their accustomed earnings. Moreover, two simple observations seem to have held true in the past, as they do today: a lower wage and higher profit are directly related, and all that is paid out in higher wages must imply a corresponding reduction of profits. Capitalism has been guided by this axiom repeatedly, and even from its beginning, and it has been an article of faith for centuries that lower wages are "productive." In other words, lower wages were believed to enhance worker productivity. As Pieter de la Court [1618–85, Dutch textile manufacturer and strong proponent of fully unregulated trade and competition] contended (completely in accord in this respect with the old Calvinism, as we will see), people work only because, and only so long as, they are poor.

Nevertheless, the effectiveness of this presumably tried and proven strategy has limitations.[17] Capitalism surely required, for its development, the presence of population surpluses that kept the market costs of labor low. Indeed, under certain circumstances an overly large "reserve army" of workers facilitates capitalism's quantitative expansion. It slows down, however, its qualitative development, especially with respect to the transition to work in organizations that require intensive labor. A lower wage is in no way identical with cheaper labor. Even when scrutinized in reference to purely quantitative considerations, the productivity of work can be seen to sink, under all circumstances, when wages are too low to sustain good health. If retained in the long run, such a wage often leads plainly to a "selection of the least fit." The average farmer from Silesia harvests today, when he exerts himself fully, little more than two-thirds of the land in the same amount of time as the better paid and better nourished farmer from Pomerania or Mecklenburg. Compared to the Germans, the Poles' capacity for physical work declines more and more the farther to the east their homeland.

Even considered purely from the business point of view, lower wages fail, as a pillar of modern capitalist development, in all those situations where goods are produced that require any type of skilled labor, where expensive and easily damaged machines are used, and in general where a significant degree of focused concentration and initiative is demanded. In these circumstances the lower wage does not prove economically feasible, and its effects lead to the opposite of all that was originally intended. This holds in these situations for the simple reason that a developed sense of responsibility is absolutely indispensable. In addition, it is necessary to have a frame of mind that emancipates the worker, at least *during* the workday, from a constant question: With a maximum of ease and comfort and a minimum of productivity, how is the accustomed wage nonetheless to be maintained? This frame of mind, if it manages to uproot the worker from this concern, motivates labor as if labor were an absolute end in itself, or a "calling."

Yet such a frame of mind is not inherently given in the nature of the species. Nor can it be directly called forth by high or low wages. Rather, it is the product of a long and continuous process of education and socialization. Today, sitting triumphantly dominant, modern capitalism is able to recruit its workers in all industrial nations and in all the branches of industry in these nations relatively easily. Yet in the past, recruitment was everywhere an extremely difficult problem.[18] Even today, without the assistance of a powerful ally, modern capitalism does not always reach the goals that, as we will further note below, accompanied it in the period of its early development.

An illustration will again offer clarity. A portrait of the older traditional approach to work is very frequently provided [in the early twentieth century] by *female* workers, above all by those who are unmarried. An almost universal complaint among employers concerns the absolute incapacity and unwillingness of women workers to give up customary and once-mastered modes of work in favor of other, more practical work techniques, and their inability to adapt to new forms of labor, to learn, and to focus the mind's reasoning capacities, or even to use it. This view holds in particular for German young women. Efforts to organize work in a simpler and, especially, more productive manner come up against complete incomprehension. Increases in the piece rate [designed to raise production] strike against the wall of habit without the least effect.

The situation is often different only with young women from a specific religious background, namely for women from Pietist homes (not an unimportant point for our reflections). One hears often, and it is confirmed by occasional statistical studies,[19] that by far the most favorable prospects for socialization into the rhythms of the workplace exist among young women in this category. The capacity to focus one's thoughts in addition to an absolutely central element—the capacity to feel an "internal dedication to the work"—are found here unusually frequently. Indeed, these qualities combine with an organized approach to economic activity that, on the one hand, *calculates* earnings and their maximum potential and, on the other hand, is characterized by a **dispassionate** self-control and moderation, all of which increase productive capacities to an unusual degree. The foundation for perceiving work as an end in itself, or a "calling," as modern capitalism requires, is here developed in a most propitious manner. And the prospect for shattering the leisurely rhythm of economic traditionalism as a *consequence* of a religious education and socialization is at its highest.

This analysis derived from [early twentieth century] capitalism[20] has indicated to us yet again that it would be worthwhile simply to *ask* how these connections between people's capacity to adapt to [modern] capitalism, on the one hand, and their religious beliefs, on the other, could have been formulated during the youth of [modern] capitalism. That these connections existed in a similar manner earlier can be concluded from many fragmented observations. For example, the ostracism and persecution that Methodist workers in the eighteenth century encountered from their fellow workers, as implied in the frequent reports of the destruction of their tools, can in no way be understood exclusively or predominantly in terms of their religious eccentricities (of these England had seen quite enough, and of an even more striking character). Rather, their unambivalent "readiness to work hard," as one would say today, was the issue here.

Nonetheless, let us turn again to the present and specifically to employers. We must do so in order further to clarify the meaning of "economic traditionalism."

In his discussions of the genesis of capitalism,[21] [the German economic historian Werner] Sombart [1863–1941] distinguishes two great principles according to which economic history has unfolded: the "satisfaction of needs" and "acquisition." The development of economies tended toward one or the other depending, on the one hand, upon the extent to which personal *needs* were decisive or, on the other hand, the degree to which barriers were placed upon acquisition, an independent striving for *profit*, and the *possibility* of striving for profit. The type and direction of economic activity varied accordingly.

At first glance, Sombart's "satisfaction of needs" seems to correspond to what has here been called economic traditionalism. This is indeed the case *if* the concept of need is equated with *traditional need*. However, if it is not, then large numbers of businesses that must be considered "capitalist" (according to the form of their organization and even in the sense of Sombart's definition of "capital"[22]) fall out of the category of "acquisition" economy and move into the category of "satisfaction of needs" economy. For example, even businesses operated by private employers on the basis of the transformation of capital (that is, money or goods with a monetary value) into profit through the purchase of the means of production and the sale of products, or businesses undoubtedly capable of being organized as "capitalist," can retain the character of economic traditionalism. This situation, even in the course of the modern development of the economy, has not been simply the exception. Instead, it has been the rule, despite continuously reappearing interruptions and intrusions from a spirit of capitalism that has been repeatedly rejuvenated and become ever more powerful.

Rather than being in "lawful" dependency, the capitalist form of an economy and the spirit in which it is operated in fact exist generally in a less determinant relationship, namely, one of "adequacy" to each other. Nonetheless, if we provisionally employ the phrase *spirit of* (modern) *capitalism*[23] to refer to the particular frame of mind that, as in our example of Benjamin Franklin, strives systematically and rationally *in a calling* for legitimate profit, then we are doing so for historical reasons. We do so on the one hand because this frame of mind finds its most adequate form in the modern capitalist company and, on the other, because the capitalist company discovers in this frame of mind the motivating force—or spirit—most adequate to it.

Of course, it may happen that "spirit" and "form" do not come together at all. The "capitalist spirit" permeated Benjamin Franklin at a time when the organization of his publishing business did not vary from the older, traditional form typical in a handicraft shop. We shall also see that, on the threshold of the modern epoch, the capitalist entrepreneurs of the commercial aristocracy were by no means exclusively or predominantly the social carriers of that frame of mind here designated as the spirit of capitalism.[24] On the contrary, the upwardly mobile strata of the industrial middle classes were far more so. Similarly, in the nineteenth century, the classical representatives of this spirit were the Manchester or Rhineland-Westphalia upstart newcomers to wealth from modest circumstances, rather than the aristocratic gentlemen from Liverpool and Hamburg whose commercial fortunes were inherited from the distant past. Matters were not different even as early as the sixteenth century. The founders of the new *industries* of this period were predominantly upstart newcomers.[25]

For example, surely a bank, a wholesale export company, a large retail concern, or, finally, a large cottage industry that produces goods in homes can be operated only in the form of a capitalist business. Nevertheless, all of these businesses could be managed according to a spirit of strict economic traditionalism. In fact, it is *impossible* to carry out the operations of a large bank of issue[26] in a different manner, and the foreign trade of entire epochs has been based upon monopolies and regulations rooted strictly in economic traditionalism. The revolution that brought the ancient economic traditionalism to an end is still in full motion in retail trade (we are not referring to the type of small-scale businesses that are today calling out for state subsidies), and it is just this transformation that destroyed the old forms of the cottage-industry system (to which the modern forms of work in the home are related only in form). The course and significance of this revolution, even though these matters are well known, can be again illustrated by reference to a specific case.

Until the middle of the nineteenth century, the life of a cottage-industry worker in many branches of the textile industry in Europe[27] was altogether easygoing, at least compared to today. One can imagine the typical routine. Peasants arrived in the city home office with their woven fabric (often, as in the case of linens, mainly or entirely produced by hand out of basic materials). They then received for it, after a thorough (often certified) evaluation of the quality, the standard price. In those situations where markets were long distances away, the customers also traveled to the city. In search of traditional quality rather than specific patterns, they either purchased from the home-office warehouse or picked up orders placed long in advance. In turn, the employer placed further orders with the peasants for the particular cloth in demand.

According to this routine, the sending of letters sufficed and travel to visit customers occurred infrequently and at long intervals, if at all. Slowly and increasingly, the sending of samples became more common. Business hours were typically moderate (perhaps five to six hours a day and occasionally considerably less, but sometimes more if a busy season existed). Earnings, although small, were adequate to maintain a respectable standard of living and, in good times, to permit the saving of small sums. In general, a relatively high compatibility existed among competitors and a strong consensus regarding basic business practices. There was time for long daily visits to the taverns, early evening drinks, and long talks with a circle of friends. A comfortable tempo of life was the order of the day.

If one looked simply at the business character of the employer, at the indispensability of the movement of capital and its turnover within the business, and finally at the objective side of the economic process or the type of accounting, this was a "capitalist" form of organization in every respect. However, scrutiny of the *spirit* that inspired the employer also indicates that it was a "traditionalist" business; a traditional approach to life, rate of profit, amount of work, management of the business, and relationship to workers is apparent. The circle of customers remained constant as well. The manner of acquiring customers and markets was also traditional. All these factors dominated the operation of this business. Fundamental to this circle of employers, one can clearly state, was an "ethos."

At some point this ease and comfort were suddenly upset. Indeed, change occurred often even in the absence of an accompanying qualitative change of the organizational *form,* such as a changeover to a closed shop or the power loom. What happened frequently was simply that some young man from a family that ran a cottage industry moved out of the city and into the countryside, carefully selected weavers for his particular needs, and increasingly tightened their dependence and his supervision over them. In the process he transformed peasants into workers. At the same time he began to increase markets by directly catering to the final consumer: he took the retailing completely into his own hands, personally sought out customers, visited them regularly every year, and attempted above all to adapt the quality of his goods exclusively to the customers' needs and wishes. In these ways, he knew how to do justice to his customers, and simultaneously he began to institute a basic principle: "low prices, large sales."

Again and again, that which is always and universally the result of such a "rationalization" process occurred: whoever did not follow suit had to suffer loss and destruction as the consequences. The comfortable old ideal collapsed and crumbled in the face of a bitter competitive struggle. Considerable fortunes were won, yet they were not simply taken to the bank to earn interest. Rather, they were continuously reinvested in the business. And the old leisurely, easygoing approach to life yielded to a disciplined temperateness. Those who consumed little and *wanted* instead to acquire and earn rose to the top, and those who remained stuck in the old ways *had* to learn to do with less.[28]

Several cases are known to me in which small loans from one's relatives placed this entire revolutionary process into motion. As a rule, however, and important here, this transformation was *not* called forth by, for example, a massive influx of new *money*. Rather, a new *spirit* came into play: the spirit of modern capitalism. The question of the motivating forces behind the expansion of modern capitalism is not primarily one of the source of money reserves that can be used by capitalist firms but above all a question of the development of the spirit of capitalism. Wherever this spirit becomes active and is able to have an effect, it *acquires* the money reserves to be used as fuel for modern capitalism's activity—not the other way around.[29]

But the entrance of the spirit of capitalism did not foster peace. The earliest of its innovators regularly confronted a flood of mistrust, occasionally hatred, and above all moral indignation. Frequently outright legends were created about secret and dark skeletons in the early lives of proponents of this spirit (several cases of this sort are known to me). It is not very easy for anyone to be so naive as not to recognize that only an unusually firm character could protect such a "new style" employer from a loss of his calm self-control and from economic as well as moral catastrophe. In addition, clarity of vision and strength to act decisively were required. Furthermore and above all, under these new circumstances only very specific and highly developed "ethical" qualities would be capable of winning over the absolutely indispensable trust of customers and workers. Finally, only such qualities could make possible the lasting resilience necessary to overcome innumerable obstacles and, most important, to undertake the infinitely more intensive workplace tasks now required of the employer. Because these ethical qualities were of a specifically different *type* from those adequate to the economic traditionalism of the past, they could not be reconciled with the comfortable enjoyment of life.

As a rule, the bold and unscrupulous speculators or the adventurous persons in pursuit of riches, such as are encountered in all epochs of economic development, have not created this transformation. It has been scarcely visible to all who investigate external changes only (such as a massive influx of new money), alterations in the forms of organizations, or changes in the organization of the economy. Nevertheless, these ethical qualities have been decisive for the infusion of economic life with this new spirit of capitalism. Nor were the "great financiers" pivotal. Rather, a different group proved central: men raised in the school of hard knocks, simultaneously calculating and daring but above all *dispassionate*, *steady*, shrewd, devoted fully to their cause, and in possession of strict, middle-class views and "principles."

One might be inclined to believe that not the slightest connection exists between these *personal* moral qualities and any ethical maxims, let alone any religious ideas as such. One might be further inclined to see here an essentially negative relationship: one could contend that leading an organized life oriented to business assumes a capacity to *withdraw* oneself from long-standing religious tradition. Hence, according to this line of reasoning, liberal "Enlightenment" views would constitute the adequate foundation for the life organized on behalf of business activity. In fact this argument is in general correct *today*. As a rule, a religious undergirding of the life oriented to business is absent.

Furthermore, wherever a relationship between business activity and religious belief exists, it turns out to be a negative one, at least in Germany. People who are saturated by the capitalist spirit *today* tend to be indifferent, if not openly hostile, to religion. The thought of pious boredom in paradise has little appeal for their activity-oriented natures, and religion appears to this group as a mechanism that pulls people away from the very foundation of existence—their work. If one were to question these people regarding the "meaning" of their restless hunt, which never yields happiness with possessions already owned (and for this reason alone must appear meaningless from the point of view of an orientation of life fully devoid of a supernatural aspect), they would at times answer (if able to answer at all): "to care for the children and grandchildren." Nevertheless, because this motivation is apparently far from unique to them and influences in the same manner all those with the approach to business of "economic traditionalism," they would more frequently offer the simple and more correct answer: with its stable work, the business is "indispensable to life." This answer is indeed the single actual motivation, and it immediately renders obvious the *irrationality*, from the point of view of one's personal happiness, of this way of organizing life: people live for their business rather than the reverse.

Obviously the inclination to seek power and esteem, which is gratified by the simple fact of ownership, plays a role here. When an entire people becomes fascinated with all things quantitatively large, as in the United States, then this romantic obsession with great size has an impact, with irresistible charm, upon the "poets" among businesspersons. This remains so even though the actual leaders among them, and especially the perpetually successful, are by and large not seduced by this fascination. Moreover, the behavior typical now of upwardly mobile capitalist families in Germany—the harried attempts to acquire landed estates and the patent of nobility for sons who at the university and in the army officer corps had behaved in a manner designed to banish all memories of their social origins—must be seen for what it is: a product of the decadence of status-climbing latecomers.[30]

The **ideal type** of the capitalist employer,[31] as appeared in Germany in a number of distinguished examples, has had nothing to do with this kind of more crass or more fine snobbery and social climbing. Such employers shy away from ostentatious display and all unnecessary expenditures, as well as the conscious enjoyment of their power. Moreover, the reception of the many awards they receive, as evidence of the general societal respect for them, is discomfiting to them. In other words, their organized life often carries a certain ascetic aspect, just as was apparent in the "sermon" by Franklin quoted above (and an exploration of the historical significance of just this important point will soon be our task). It is actually in no way unusual, but highly common to find in Franklin a degree of detached modesty, indeed a modesty essentially more candid than that reserve he recommends in such a prudent manner to others. He "has nothing" from his wealth for himself personally, except that irrational sense of having "fulfilled his vocation" (*Berufserfüllung*).

Just this, however, is exactly that which appears to the precapitalist person so incomprehensible and puzzling, so vulgar and repulsive. That anyone could conceive of the idea of defining the exclusive goal of his life-long work as sinking into his grave weighed down with a heavy load of money and goods—this seems comprehensible to the precapitalist person only as the product of perverse drives: the *auri sacra fames*.

***

At the present time, in light of our political, legal, and economic institutions and the forms of business and the structures that are unique to our economy, Franklin's spirit of capitalism could be understood as a pure product of adaptation, as noted. The capitalist economic order, it could be argued, needs this devotion to a "calling" of moneymaking. This devotion could then be seen as a type of behavior, in respect to external consumer goods, closely tied to this economic structure and the conditions of the capitalist order's victory in the earlier economic struggle of existence, indeed to such an extent that any necessary connection between this "acquisitive" manner of organizing life and a unified "worldview" (*Weltanschauung*) of any sort must be entirely rejected *today*. It could be argued, in other words, that it is no longer necessary for this organization of life to be supported by the approval of any religious authority figures. Moreover, the influence of the norms of a church upon economic life, to the extent that they are still perceptible at all, could be viewed as an unjustifiable interference. The same could be said of all regulation of the economy by the state. Commercial-political and social-political interests then determine a person's "worldview." And those who do not adapt their organization of life to the conditions that make for success in capitalism's open market either fail or, at least, never move up.

This entire mode of argument, however, must itself be seen as a manifestation of our own time, a period in which modern capitalism has succeeded in emancipating itself from its old supporting framework. Capitalism, it will be remembered, managed to burst asunder in the late Middle Ages the old [feudal] forms of economic regulation only in alliance with the developing power of the modern state. We wish here to argue, in a preliminary fashion, that capitalism's relationship to the religious powers could have been exactly parallel, namely, a coalition between capitalism and religious belief tended to burst asunder the old economic traditionalism. It should be investigated here whether, and in what way, just this *was* the situation.

Surely it scarcely needs to be proven that the spirit of capitalism's comprehension of the acquisition of money as a "calling"—as an end in itself that persons were obligated to pursue—stood in opposition to the moral sensitivities of entire epochs in the past. The doctrine of *deo placere vix potest* [the merchant cannot be pleasing to God] was taken as genuine in medieval times (just as was the position of the Gospels against the taking of interest[32]), and was incorporated into canon law and applied to the activity of the businessman. This was also evident in the view of St. Thomas Aquinas [1224–74, the most significant philosopher and theologian of the Middle Ages], who characterized the striving for profit as moral turpitude (including even unavoidable and thus ethically permitted profit). Nonetheless, these positions held by the church stood in contrast to the radical opposition to the accumulation of wealth apparent in fairly broad circles. Indeed, these doctrinal positions already marked significant *accommodation* by Catholic doctrine to the interests of financial powers in the Italian cities, which were politically allied very closely with the church.[33] Yet even where Catholic doctrine accommodated still more, as for example happened with [the Dominican friar and bishop] Anthony of Florence [1389–1459], the perception never entirely disappeared that activity oriented to acquisition as an end in itself involved a fundamentally disgraceful situation, albeit one that existing realities made it necessary to tolerate.

A few ethical thinkers of the period, particularly adherents of the Nominalist school,[34] accepted as given the business practices of capitalism that had developed by that time. They then sought to demonstrate the legitimacy of those practices and above all to prove that commerce was necessary. Finally, they viewed the industriousness that arose out of trade as a legitimate source of profit and as ethically acceptable (though not without criticism). In general, however, the dominant teaching rejected the spirit of capitalist acquisition as moral turpitude, or at a minimum refused to value it as ethically positive. [1920]

"Moral" views, such as those of Benjamin Franklin, would have been simply inconceivable. Indeed, this was the position above all among capitalists themselves. Even when their life work followed religious traditions, they knew that their activities were at best ethically indifferent and only tolerated. Owing to the constant danger of a collision with the church's prohibition of usury, their activity remained suspect, indeed precisely with respect to the status of the believer's soul. As the sources indicate, on the occasion of the death of wealthy people quite considerable sums of money flowed from their pockets to religious institutions as "conscience money." In some cases this money even moved back to former debtors as compensation for sums unjustly taken as "usury."

The situation was different (aside from heretics and those viewed as possessing suspicious beliefs) only for those in patrician circles, for the nobility had already internally emancipated itself from religious traditions. Nevertheless, even skeptics and nonchurchgoers also believed it appropriate to make amends to the church through a lump sum donation to cover all eventualities. It seemed better to do so as insurance against the uncertainties of one's condition after death. At any rate (at least according to the more lax conception, which was very widespread), an external sign of submission to the commandments of the church was believed to be adequate to ensure salvation.[35] At precisely this point, either the *a*moral or even *im*moral nature of the activity of capitalists, skeptics, and nonchurchgoers, according to their *own* understanding of this activity, becomes evident.

***

How then does it come about that activity which, in the most favorable case, is barely morally tolerable, becomes a "calling" in the manner practiced by Benjamin Franklin? How is it to be explained historically that in Florence, the center of capitalist development in the fourteenth and fifteenth centuries and the marketplace for money and capital for all of the great political powers, striving for profit was viewed as either morally questionable or at best tolerated? Yet in the business relationships found in small companies in rural Pennsylvania, where scarcely a trace of large-scale commerce could be found, where only the beginning stages of a banking system were evident, and where the economy was continuously threatened with collapse into sheer barter (as a result of a simple lack of money), the same striving for profit became viewed as legitimate. Indeed, it became understood as the essence of a morally acceptable, even praiseworthy way of organizing and directing life.

To speak *here* of a "reflection" of "material" conditions in the "ideal superstructure" would be complete nonsense. Hence, our question: What set of ideas gave birth to the ordering of activity oriented purely to profit under the category of a "calling," to which the person felt an *obligation*? Just this set of ideas provided the ethical substructure and backbone for the "new style" employer's organized life.

Some have depicted **economic rationalism** as the basic characteristic of the modern economy in general (Sombart in particular, often in successful and effective discussions). Surely Sombart has done so correctly if "economic rationalism" refers to the increase in productivity that results from the organization of the production process according to *scientific* vantage points, hence the banishing of the situation in which gains were restricted owing to the naturally given "organic" limitations of people. This rationalization process in the arenas of technology and the economy undoubtedly also conditions an important part of the "ideals of life" in the modern, middle-class society in general. Work in the service of a rational production of material goods for the provision of humanity has without question always been hovering over the representatives of the capitalist spirit as a directing purpose of their life's labors. For example, one needs only to read about Franklin's efforts in Philadelphia in the service of community improvement to understand immediately this completely self-evident truth. Moreover, the joy and pride one feels in giving "work" to numerous people and in assisting the economic "flowering" (in the manner in which this term is associated, under capitalism, with population and trade figures) of one's hometown belongs obviously to the unique, and undoubtedly "idealistically" driven, satisfactions of the modern business establishment. And, likewise, the capitalist economy rationalizes on the basis of strictly *quantitative* calculations and is oriented to the sought-after economic success in a systematic and dispassionate manner. These operating principles are inherent in and fundamental to capitalism. They contrast directly with the situation of the peasant who lives from hand to mouth, to the guild craftsmen in the medieval epoch who maintained market advantages rooted in old customs, and to the "adventure capitalist" who was oriented to political opportunities and irrational speculation.

Thus it appears that the development of the capitalist spirit can be most easily understood as one component part in a larger and overarching development of rationalism as a whole. It appears further that this spirit should best be comprehended as derived from rationalism's basic position in respect to the ultimate problems of life. Hence, according to this interpretation, Protestantism would come into consideration historically only to the extent that it played a role as a "harbinger" of purely rationalistic views of life.

As soon, however, as one seriously attempts to formulate the problem of the development of the spirit of capitalism in this way, it becomes clear that such a simple approach to this theme is inadequate. The reason is that the history of rationalism *by no means* charts out a progressive unfolding, according to which all the separate realms of life follow a *parallel* developmental line. The rationalization of private law, for example, if understood as the conceptual simplification and organization of the subject matter of the law, attained its heretofore highest form in the Roman law of later antiquity. It remained least rationalized, however, in some nations with the most highly rationalized economies. England offers an example. During the period of the development of [modern] capitalism in this nation, the power of large guilds of lawyers prevented the rebirth of Roman law. In contrast, rationalized Roman law has consistently remained dominant in the Catholic areas of southern Europe [where modern capitalism, compared to England, remained underdeveloped].

[Two more examples for the nonparallel development of the separate realms of life must suffice.] First, the purely secularized philosophy of the eighteenth century [the Enlightenment] surely was not based alone, or even primarily, in the highly developed capitalist nations. This philosophy of Voltaire [1694–1778] is even today the broad common inheritance of the upper and (what is more important practically) middle strata, especially in the nations of Roman Catholicism. Second, if one understands by the phrase *practical rationalism* that way of organizing life according to which the world's activities are consciously referred back to the practical interests of the *particular person*, and are judged from his or her specific vantage point,[36] then this style of life was typically unique primarily to the *liberum arbitrium* [undisciplined] peoples. Even today practical rationalism permeates the flesh and blood of the Italians and the French. And we have already convinced ourselves this is not the soil that primarily nourishes persons who relate to their "calling" as a task (as [modern] capitalism needs).

A simple sentence should stand at the center of every study that delves into "rationalism." It must not be forgotten that one can in fact "rationalize" life from a vast variety of ultimate vantage points. Moreover, one can do so in very different directions. "Rationalism" is a historical concept that contains within itself a world of contradictions.

Our task now is to investigate from whose spiritual child this matter-of-fact form of "rational" thinking and living grew. The idea of a "calling," and of the giving over of one's self to *work* in a calling, originated here. As noted, the entire notion of a "calling" must appear fully irrational from the vantage point of the person's pure self-interest in happiness. Yet the dedication to work in the manner of a "calling" has in the past constituted one of the characteristic components of our capitalist economic culture. It remains so even today. What interests *us* here is precisely the ancestral lineage of that *irrational* element which lies in this, as in every, conception of a "calling."[37] ✦

Chapter III

LUTHER'S CONCEPTION OF THE CALLING

An audible echo from the religious realm unmistakably resonates even in the German *word Beruf*, and perhaps in an even more apparent manner in the equivalent English term **calling**: one's *task* is given by God. This echo becomes all the more perceptible the more vigorously we place the accent on this term in actual usage.

If we now trace this word historically and across the languages of the great civilizations, it quickly becomes apparent that an expression denoting a *calling* (in the sense of a position in one's life for a demarcated realm of work) is just as little known among the predominantly Catholic peoples as it was among the peoples of classical antiquity.[1] Such an expression, however, does exist among *all* predominantly Protestant peoples. It is further apparent that a diffuse, unique ethnic character of the languages in question (such as the expression *spirit of the German people* implies) is not the issue here. Rather the present-day meaning of the term *the calling* derives from *Bible translations*, and actually from the spirit of the translators rather than from the spirit of the original.[2]

In the translation into German by Luther, *Beruf* appears to be used earliest in our present-day meaning in a passage from the Old Testament in Jesus Sirach (11:20–21).[3] It then quickly acquired its present significance in the everyday language of all Protestant peoples. There had been *no* trace of this expression earlier, either in secularized literature or in sermons. As near as I can tell, it appears instead only in the writings of one German mystic, and his influence upon Luther is well-known.[4]

Moreover, just as the meaning of the word is new, so is (and this should be well-known) the *idea* new. The concept of the calling is a product of the Reformation. This is not to say that certain early signs of an appreciation of daily work, as found in the notion of a calling, were not already visible in the Middle Ages and even in (*late* Hellenistic) antiquity, as will be addressed later. At any rate, one aspect was unequivocally *new*: the fulfillment of duty in vocational callings became viewed as the highest expression that moral activity could assume. Precisely this new notion of the moral worth of devoting oneself to a calling was the unavoidable result of the idea of attaching religious significance to daily work. The earliest conception of a calling in this sense was produced in this manner.

Hence, the concept of *calling* expresses the central dogma of all Protestant denominations, a dogma that rejects Catholicism's division of the ethical commandments into *praecepta* [that which is commanded] and *consilia* [that which is advised]. The single means of living in a manner pleasing to God changes accordingly: an ascetic withdrawal from the world, as practiced by monks, and the clear surpassing of the world's routine morality of daily life that such asceticism implied, is now replaced by ***this-worldly work***. This work involves the fulfillment of duties, all of which derive from [the social and occupational] positions of each person. The "calling" for each person is defined through these positions.

Luther[5] developed these ideas in the course of the first decades of his reform activities. At the beginning, quite in keeping with the dominant medieval tradition (as exemplified, for example, by Thomas Aquinas)[6] Luther viewed this-worldly work as belonging to the realm of the flesh. Although work was said to be desired by God and the indispensable natural foundation of the devout life, work had no moral salience, any more than eating and drinking had.[7] However, with the more clear implementation of his notion of "salvation through the single believer's faith" (*sola fide*) in all its consistency, which resulted in an increasingly acute contrast to the Catholic evangelical councils of monks and friars (which Luther saw as "commanded by the devil"), the meaning of the calling became steadily more important to him.

To Luther, a monastic ***organization of life***, and the monk's perception of it as legitimate in the eyes of God, is now obviously of no value whatsoever. Moreover, Luther understands monasticism as a product of an egoistic lovelessness that withdraws from one's duties in the world. By contrast, this-worldly work in a vocation appears to him to be a visible expression of brotherly love, a notion he anchors in a highly naive manner indeed and in contrast (almost grotesquely) to the well-known passages of [the founder of modern economics], Adam Smith [1723–90].[8] Luther does so mainly by indicating that the division of labor forces every person to work for *others*. Owing, however, to the essentially scholastic[9] nature of this justification, this argument soon disappears. Luther emphasizes instead, and with increasing vigor, that the fulfillment of one's duties in the world constitutes, under all circumstances, the only way to please God. This fulfillment, and only this, is God's will. Therefore, every permissible calling is of absolutely equal validity before God.[10]

***

That this moral legitimation of vocational life was one of the Reformation's most influential achievements, and in particular the achievement of Luther, is truly beyond doubt. It may even rightly be understood as self-evident.[11] It stands worlds away from the deep hatred with which the contemplative voice of [the French mathematician and philosopher Blaise] Pascal [1623–62][12] repudiates all favorable evaluation of activity in the world. Such activity can be explained only by reference to vanity or slyness, according to Pascal's deepest conviction.[13] The broad-ranging **utilitarian *adaptation* to the world** practiced by Jesuit Probabilism[14] stands even further away from Reformation views. Yet how the practical significance of this achievement of Protestantism is to be presented in a detailed manner seems a conundrum. This achievement is more often dimly perceived than clearly recognized.

First of all, it is scarcely necessary to establish that Luther's writings, for example, cannot be spoken of as having an inner affinity with the capitalist spirit in the way in which we have until now defined this phrase (or by the way, in any manner whatsoever). Even those church circles that most eagerly praise every "achievement" of the Reformation are not today allied with capitalism in any of its forms. Even Luther himself would undoubtedly have harshly repudiated any relationship with the **frame of mind** that came to the fore with Franklin.

Of course, one should not take his complaints against the great adventure merchants, such as Fugger[15] and others like him, as evidence of his opposition to this frame of mind. Surely the struggle of Luther and others in the sixteenth and seventeenth centuries against the *privileged* position, either legal or factual, of certain large commercial companies can best be compared to the modern campaign against the privileges of trust companies, rather than be understood as a manifestation of the ***economic traditionalist*** frame of mind. The Huguenots and the Puritans, both supporters of the spirit of capitalism, were (alongside the Lutherans) also engaged in the bitter struggles against the large commercial companies against the House of Lombardy bankers and the *Trapeziten,*[16] and against the monopolists, bankers, and large-scale speculators favored by the Anglican Church and the kings and parliaments of England and France.[17] After the battle of Dunbar (September 1650), [Oliver] Cromwell [1599-1658][18] wrote to the Long Parliament: "Be pleased to reform the abuses of all professions, and if there be any one that makes many poor to make a few rich, that suits not a Commonwealth." Yet it is apparent from other passages that [unlike Luther] Cromwell is completely infused with a specifically "capitalist" mode of thinking.[19] In contrast, and even compared to the writings of late Scholasticism, Luther's numerous statements against usury and against interest in general reveal an altogether "backward" understanding of the essence of capitalist acquisition (viewed from the perspective of modern capitalism).[20] Of particular prominence was his support for the argument (already discredited by Anthony of Florence) that monetary measures remained incapable of enhancing productivity.

We need not, however, be more specific here regarding this point. The idea of a calling in the *religious* sense was capable of taking, when viewed from the vantage point of its consequences for the organization of life in the everyday world of work, a variety of forms. The achievement of the Reformation, in contrast to the Catholic position, was primarily to increase drastically the infusion of work (organized by a calling) with a moral accent and to place a **religious** value, or **reward**, on it. How the idea of a "calling," which gave expression to just this achievement, further unfolded depended on the particular formation of the notions of piety in the different Reformation churches.

***

The authority of the Bible, from which Luther believed he took the idea of the calling, actually generally favored economic traditionalism. In particular, the Old Testament never expresses an idea of surpassing the routine morality of daily life. This notion is not found in the Old Testament's classical prophecy and is otherwise visible only in scattered and incomplete passages. A religious idea extremely similar to that of the calling is formulated strictly only in one sense: Every believer must stay at his "livelihood" and leave the godless to strive for gain. This is the meaning of all those passages that directly address occupations. The Talmud makes the first break from this idea, but it is only a partial break and not a fundamental one. Jesus' position is characterized, in classical clarity, in the typical entreaty of the ancient Near East: "Give us this *day* our daily bread." Moreover, the presence of a radical element in Jesus' teachings that rejects the world as it is, as manifest in the μαμωνᾶς τῆς ἀδικίας [the sinfulness of ownership], excluded any *direct* linking of the modern idea of the calling with Jesus personally.[21]

In the era of the Christian apostles, as it is expressed in the New Testament and especially in St. Paul, the notion of a calling in one's worldly vocation was viewed either with indifference or, as in the Old Testament, essentially in the manner of economic traditionalism. The eschatological expectations that filled the first generations of Christians account for this indifference and traditionalism: because all changes awaited the coming of the Lord, the devout wished only to remain in the status and occupation in which God's "call" had found them—and to continue to labor as before. In this way, the faithful would not become impoverished and burdensome to fellow believers. And, in the end, the period of waiting would last only a short time.

Luther upheld economic traditionalism, and increasingly so, throughout the course of his development from approximately 1518 to approximately 1530. He read the Bible through the lens of his mood at the given time.[22] In the first years of his reform activity and as a consequence of his understanding of the calling essentially in terms of the basic survival of the person, Luther's thinking about the appropriate *type* of this-worldly activity was dominated by views having an inner affinity with the eschatological indifference of St. Paul (expressed in 1 Cor. 7:20–24).[23] Luther was convinced that people of every status can become saved; to lend importance to the *type* of calling in this short pilgrimage of life would be meaningless. Therefore, the striving for material gain that goes beyond one's own needs, Luther argues, must be a symptom of one's lack of grace. Indeed, because striving for gain appears to be possible only at the expense of others, this pursuit must be viewed as an unequivocal abomination.[24]

An increasing estimation of the significance of work in a calling develops for Luther, parallel to his own increasing engagement in the affairs of the world. As this occurs, he simultaneously comes to see each person's particular calling as, more and more, a special command of God to that person: the tasks incumbent upon a particular position must be fulfilled because Divine Providence has placed the believer in *this* position. After the peasant uprisings [1524–25] and the struggles against the *Schwarmgeister*,[25] Luther increasingly comes to see the objective historical order—into which God places the individual—as a direct manifestation of Divine Will.[26] The increasingly strong emphasis on the role of providential forces, even in life's disjointed happenings, now leads him more and more to emphasize the importance of Divine Will as "fate," an idea that proved compatible with economic traditionalism: the individual should basically *stay* in the calling and status in which God has first placed him. His striving in this life should remain within the boundaries of his existing life situation.

Hence, whereas Luther's economic traditionalism at the beginning was anchored in Pauline indifference to the world, his economic traditionalism later flowed out of an increasingly more intense belief in Divine Providence[27] that identified an unconditional obedience to God[28] with an unconditional submission to one's given lot. This way of thinking could not at all carry Luther to a fundamentally new way of linking work in a calling with *religious* principles, or in general to the formulation of a substantive foundation for such a linkage.[29] The purity of *doctrine*, as the single infallible criterion of Luther's church, had itself inhibited the development of new views in the realm of ethics. To Luther this doctrine stood as increasingly irrevocable after the [peasant] uprisings of the 1520s.

***

Thus, Luther's conception of the calling remained tied to economic traditionalism.[30] As a divine decree, the calling is something that must be *submitted to*: persons must "resign" themselves to it. This accent in Luther's writings outweighs the other idea also present in his thought: that work in a calling is one or actually *the* task given to people by God.[31] The development of orthodox Lutheranism stressed even further the idea of a resignation to one's calling.

With respect to ethical action, Lutheranism did not involve an ascetic notion of duty. Hence any possibility for a surpassing of the routine morality of daily life was eliminated. The negative consequences for ethical action become apparent once an acknowledgment of this aspect of Lutheranism is combined with its central features: the preaching of obedience to secular authority and believers' resignation to their life-situation as it is given to them. These admonitions for obedience and resignation constituted, in its earliest stage, Lutheranism's only ethical contribution.[32]

As will be explained when we turn to a discussion of medieval religious ethics, the idea of the calling in this formulation of Lutheranism had already been worked through for the most part by the German mystics. [Johannes] Tauler [1300–1361] established the principle of the equal value of clerical and this-worldly callings and the *lesser* value of the monastic forms of ascetic works and service.[33] These positions both resulted from the decisive significance he accorded to the ecstatic-contemplative incorporation of the divine spirit through the soul. Thus, compared to the mystics, Lutheranism implied, in a certain way, actually a step backwards. This occurred to the extent that (for Luther and more so for his church) the psychological underpinning for a rational vocational ethic became rather unstable, compared to the views of the mystics (which often remind one partly of the Pietist and partly of the Quaker psychologies of faith).[34] As has yet to be demonstrated, this instability developed precisely *because* Luther remained suspicious of mysticism's inclination toward ascetic self-discipline; he saw such self-discipline as a form of salvation through good works. For this reason, mysticism in Luther's church had to fade more and more into the background.

Hence, as can be ascertained so far, the idea of the calling for Luther had only an uncertain impact on that which *we* are here seeking to understand: [the emergence of the spirit of capitalism]. At this point we have not sought to determine more.[35] This conclusion, it must be noted, does not in the least imply that the Lutheran alterations of religious life may not have had a practical significance for the development of the spirit of capitalism. Indeed the contrary holds. Nonetheless, we can now see that Lutheranism's significance for the unfolding of this spirit is not to be *directly* derived from the position of *Luther* and his church in regard to a this-worldly vocational calling. Other Protestant denominations may more clearly establish a connection between the calling and the spirit of capitalism. It makes sense now for us to turn to those denominations that establish a connection between *practical* life and religious belief in a more direct manner than Lutheranism did.

***

The striking role of *Calvinism* and the Protestant ***sects*** in the history of capitalism's development has already been noted. Luther found in [the Swiss Reformation theologian Ulrich] Zwingli [1484–1531][36] a "spirit quite different" from his own, as did Luther's spiritual descendents, especially Calvinists. Catholicism considered, with a vengeance, Calvinism to be its real opponent, from its early stages and to the present.

These enmities can be viewed first by reference to purely political causes. As the Reformation was inconceivable without Luther's personal religious development and was spiritually determined in a lasting manner by his personality, an enduring practical impact of Luther's works would have been, without Calvinism, equally inconceivable. But the cause of the shared Catholic and Lutheran antipathy to Calvinism clearly lies in Calvinism's uniqueness. Even a superficial glance at Calvinism reveals a formulation of the relationship between the religious life and earthly *action* completely different from those found in both Catholicism and Lutheranism. This difference is evident even in literature that exclusively uses explicit religious motives. One need only compare, for example, the ending of *The Divine Comedy* [by Dante Alighieri, 1265–1321], where the poet in Paradise stands passive and speechless before the mystery of the Divine, to the conclusion of that poem we are accustomed to call the "Divine Comedy of Puritanism." After the description of the *expulsion* from Paradise, [the English poet John] Milton [1608–1674] concludes the last song of *Paradise Lost* as follows:

They, looking back, all the eastern side beheld
Of paradise, so late their happy seat,
Waved over by that flaming brand; the gate
With dreadful faces thronged and fiery arms.
Some natural tears they dropped, but wiped them soon:
The world was all before them, where to choose
Their place of rest, and Providence their guide.
They hand in hand with wandering steps and slow,
Through *Eden* took their solitary way.[37]

And a little earlier Michael had said to Adam:

. . . 'Only add
Deeds to thy knowledge answerable; add faith;
Add virtue, patience, temperance; add love,
By name to come called Charity, the soul
Of all the rest: then wilt thou not be loth

To leave this Paradise, but shall possess
A Paradise within thee, happier far.'[38]

Every person immediately feels that this powerful expression of the grave Puritan turning-to-the-world—that is, the valuing of life's matter-of-fact activities as a *task*—would never have been expressed by a medieval writer. Yet this turning-to-the-world is just as incompatible with Lutheranism, as is apparent, for example, in the hymns of Luther and [the poet and composer] Paul Gerhardt [1607–76].

We must be more specific at this point. This vague sense that significant differences exist here must now be replaced by a somewhat more precise conceptual *formulation* of these differences. Moreover, the inner causes of these differences [as rooted in the ethical uniqueness of Catholicism, Lutheranism, and Calvinism] must be investigated.

Task of the Investigation[39]

The appeal to "national character" (*Volkscharakter*) [as the source of these differences] is not only generally a confession of *ignorance* but, in this instance, entirely invalid as well. On the one hand, it would be historically incorrect to ascribe a unified "national character" to the English of the seventeenth century. "Cavaliers" and "Roundheads" [Puritans] perceived themselves not simply as two groups but as radically different human species, and whoever studies them attentively must agree with them on this point.[40] On the other hand, a contrast in national character between the English merchant adventurers and the old Hanseatic merchants in Hamburg is as little to be found as any significant distinction between the English and Germans at the end of the Middle Ages. Furthermore, those differences that did exist can be clearly explained by reference to varying political constellations.[41] The power of the religious movements, not alone but above all other factors, created the differences noted here, differences that are familiar to us even today.[42]

This investigation of the relationships between the old Protestant ethic and the development of the capitalist spirit begins with Calvin's innovations, with Calvinism, and with the other **Puritan** sects. Nevertheless, the selection of this point of departure should not be understood as implying an expectation to discover the capitalist spirit in one of the founders or representatives of these religious groups (the awakening of which would then be viewed, in some way, as the *goal* of his life work).

We surely will not be able to believe that any one of them considered the striving after the world's consumer goods as an end in itself; that is, as an ethical value.

Moreover, one point in particular should be kept in mind above all: Programs of ethical change were not the central issue for any of the religious reformers who must be examined for this investigation, such as Menno [Simons, 1492–1599, founder of the Mennonites], George Fox [1624–91, founder of the Quakers], and [John] Wesley [1703–91, co-founder of the Methodists]. These men were not the founders of societies for "ethical culture" or representatives of a humanitarian striving for social reform or cultural ideals. The salvation of the soul stood at the center of their lives and deeds—and that alone. Their ethical goals and the practical effects of their teachings were all anchored in the salvation theme and must be seen entirely as the *consequences* of purely religious motives. Furthermore, we must therefore be prepared to note that the cultural influences of the Reformation were to a great extent (and perhaps even predominantly from our particular vantage point) the unforeseen and even *unwanted* results of the [theological] labor of the Reformation figures. Indeed, the cultural influences stood often quite distant from, or precisely in opposition to, all that the religious reformers had in mind.

Hence, in its modest manner, the following study might perhaps constitute a contribution to the illumination of the way in which "ideas" become generally effective in history. In order, however, to prevent misunderstandings at the outset in regard to the manner in which we are here asserting that purely ideal motives may become effective forces, a few further small clarifications on this theme may be permitted. These clarifications can serve as concluding comments to the introductory discussion [presented immediately above and in chapters 1 and 2].

***

It should be directly stated that studies such as this one are in no way concerned with the attempt to *evaluate* the substantive ideas of the Reformation, by reference to either social-political or religious vantage points. Instead our goals concern aspects of the Reformation that must appear to persons with a religious consciousness as peripheral and related to superficial matters only. After all, it is our task to investigate and to clarify the impact that religious motives had on that web of development in the direction of our modern, specifically "this-worldly"-oriented life and culture generally—a development that grew out of innumerable, fragmented historical forces. Thus we are in the end asking a question: Which characteristic features of our modern life and culture should be *attributed* to the influence of the Reformation? In other words, to what extent did the Reformation serve as a historical cause of these characteristic features?

In asking this question, on the one hand we must of course emancipate ourselves from the point of view that the Reformation can be "deduced" from economic transformations as a "developmental-historical necessity." Constellations of innumerable historical forces had to interact if the newly created churches were to endure. By no means can reference to a "law of economic development" or, more generally, to economic points of view of whatever sort, do justice to the complexity of these developments. Rather, political processes, in particular, had to interact with economic forces.

On the other hand, we shall not defend here two foolish and doctrinaire theses[43] in any form: (1) that the capitalist spirit (in the still provisional use of this term utilized here) *could* have originated *only* as an expression of certain influences of the Reformation, and (2) that capitalism as an *economic system* was a creation of the Reformation. The latter position is rendered once and for all untenable by the simple fact that certain important *forms* of capitalist business companies are drastically older than the Reformation.[44] Instead, it should here be ascertained only whether, and to what extent, religious influences *co*-participated in the qualitative formation and quantitative expansion of this spirit across the globe. We wish further to assess which practical *aspects* of the *culture* upon which [modern] capitalism rests can be traced back to these religious influences.

In light of the immense confusion of the reciprocal influences among the material foundation, the forms of social and political organizations, and the various spiritual streams of the Reformation epoch, we can only proceed in the following manner. *First*, we will investigate whether (and in what ways) specific "elective affinities" (*Wahlverwandtschaften*) between certain forms of religious belief and a vocational ethic (*Berufsethik*) are discernible. Doing so will allow us, whenever possible, to illuminate the type of influence that the religious movement, as a consequence of these elective affinities, had upon the development of economic culture. In addition, the general *direction* of this influence upon economic culture, as a consequence of these elective affinities, can be clarified. Second, *only after* this influence has been satisfactorily established can an attempt be made to estimate to what degree the historical origin of the values and ideas of our modern life can be attributed to religious forces stemming from the Reformation, and to what degree to other forces. ✦

PART II

THE VOCATIONAL ETHIC

OF

ASCETIC PROTESTANTISM

Above all, . . . fundamental for our discussion is the investigation of the idea of a testifying to one's belief as the psychological point of origin for methodical ethics.

(p. 78)

Finally, and of central importance, the special life of the saint—fully separate from the "natural" life of wants and desires—could no longer play itself out in monastic communities set apart from the world. Rather, the devoutly religious must now live saintly lives in the world and amidst its mundane affairs. This rationalization of the organized and directed life—now in the world yet still oriented to the supernatural—was the effect of ascetic Protestantism's concept of the calling.

(p. 101)

A religion of predestination obliterates the goodness of God, for He becomes a hard, majestic king. Yet it shares with religions of fate the capacity for inducing nobility and rigor in its devotees

(Kalberg, *E & S*, p. 572)

CHAPTER IV

THE RELIGIOUS FOUNDATIONS OF THIS-WORLDLY ASCETICISM[1]

There have been four major historical **carriers** of **ascetic Protestantism** (in the manner in which "ascetic Protestanism" is used here): (1) Calvinism *in the form* it took in the major regions it dominated in Western Europe, especially during the seventeenth century; (2) Pietism; (3) Methodism; and (4) the **sects** that grew out of the baptizing movement (the Baptists, Mennonites, and Quakers).[1] None of these carriers of ascetic Protestantism were absolutely separate from any of the others, and the distinction vis-à-vis the nonascetic churches of the Reformation cannot be strictly maintained.

Methodism originated in the middle of the eighteenth century within the Church of England. Rather than aiming to create a new church, the founders of Methodism were more intent on awakening an ascetic spirit inside this state church. Indeed, Methodism became separate from the Anglican Church only later in the course of its development, and mainly after its transplantation to America.

Pietism grew out of the soil of English, and especially, Dutch Calvinism. Through barely perceivable linkages it remained tied to Calvinism until the end of the seventeenth century. Under the effective influence of [the German theologian Phillipp Jacob] Spener [1635–1705],[2] it then became, in a manner only partly grounded in dogma, incorporated into Lutheranism. It remained a movement inside the Lutheran church. Only the followers of [Count Nicolaus von] Zinzendorf [1700-1760],[3] who had been influenced in part by the Hussite and Calvinist echoes in the Moravian Brethren (*Herrnhuter*) sect,[4] were, like Methodists, pushed against their will to form a peculiar sort of sect outside the Lutheran Church.

Calvinism and the baptizing movement were sharply divided and hostile toward one another at the beginning of their development. The baptist sect of the later seventeenth century, however, became closely associated with Calvinism. At the beginning of this century the boundaries of these groups were permeable, as was even the case among the Independent sects in England and Holland. And as the history of Pietism demonstrates, the transition to Lutheranism was also gradual, as was that from Calvinism to the Anglican Church, despite the fact that Anglicanism was related to Catholicism through its external features as well as through the spiritual inclinations of its most devout adherents. Indeed, although the broad following of the ascetic movement (which will be referred to, in the most general sense of this amorphous term, as ***Puritanism***),[5] and especially its most ardent proponents, attacked the very foundation of Anglicanism, the differences between them became sharp only in the midst of conflicts and even then only gradually. Moreover, the relationship between these groups remains unchanged even if we completely leave aside the questions of governance and organizational structure that for the moment do not interest us.

Even the most important dogmatic differences, such as those concerning the doctrines of **predestination** and justification, merged into one another in a wide variety of combinations. Hence, the preservation of distinct church communities was quite often hindered, even at the beginning of the seventeenth century. Above all, and this is most important for us here, identical manifestations of the *moral* **organization of life** are found, regardless of whether we turn to the four carriers of ascetic Protestantism noted above or to any of the many denominations that arose out of them. We shall see that similar ethical maxims can be attached to various dogmatic foundations. Moreover, the highly influential literary devices employed in the organized care of the soul influenced one another in the course of time. This holds mainly with respect to the casuistic manuals[6] of the various faiths. Great similarities are found among them despite the notoriously different ways in which they organized practical life.

Thus, it might almost seem that we would do best to ignore the dogmatic foundations and ethical theories of these churches and sects. Instead we could focus our efforts purely on their moral practices (to the extent that they can be ascertained). To do so, however, would not be wise. Of course it is true that the dogmatic roots of ascetic morality, which varied across different denominations, died off after terrible struggles. Nonetheless, the original anchoring of ascetic morality to these dogmas not only left strong legacies in the "undogmatic" subsequent ethics; in addition, *only* knowledge of the content of the foundational ideas teaches us to understand how this ascetic morality was connected with the thought about the *next life*. Indeed, the next life absolutely dominated people's religious thinking at that time. The moral awakening, which considerably influenced the *practical* life of believers, would *not* have been set in motion without the overarching power held by the next life over the believer.

Obviously the issue for us does not involve what was theoretically and officially *taught* in the ethical manuals of the time. This is not to deny that such teachings certainly had a practical significance through their influence on church discipline, pastoral care, and preaching.[7] Our interest, however, is altogether otherwise: we shall investigate the mediation of those ***psychological motivations*** that gave direction to the organization of the believer's life and held the individual firmly to it. These motivations were created through religious belief and the practice of the religious life. However, they originated also and to a great degree (simply from) unique views of religious belief. People at that time brooded over seemingly abstract dogmas to a degree that becomes understandable to us today only if we comprehend the connection of these dogmas with practical-religious interests.

Now an exploration of a few dogmatic considerations[8] becomes indispensable. This remains so even though they must appear just as tedious to nontheologians as they will seem hurried and superficial to those well-versed in theology. We can only proceed by examining the religious ideas as **ideal types**, namely, as constructed concepts endowed with a degree of consistency seldom found in actual history. Precisely *because* of the impossibility of drawing sharp boundaries in historical reality, our only hope of identifying the particular effects of these religious ideas must come through an investigation of their most *consistent* [or "ideal"] forms.

A. Calvinism

Now the set of beliefs[9] around which the great political and cultural conflicts in the most highly developed capitalist nations in the sixteenth and seventeenth centuries—the Netherlands, England, and France—were fought was Calvinism.[10] Hence, we first turn to this denomination.[11]

The doctrine of *predestination* was seen at that time as Calvinism's most characteristic dogma, and this view remains generally true even today. To be sure, debates have been fought over the question of whether this doctrine constituted "the most essential" dogma of the **Reformed Church** or whether it was simply an "appendage."

Judgments about the extent to which a historical force is essential are of one of two types: they may be judgments rooted in values and faith (where the essential in regard to the historical force is understood as the single factor "of interest" or of lasting "value") or they may be judgments regarding the *causal* significance of the historical force in relation to other historical forces. Historical judgments regarding the attribution of causality are the same for the latter type.

Our question concerns the extent to which cultural-historical *effects* are to be attributed to the doctrine of predestination. These effects appear quite strong. The doctrine of predestination shattered [Johan von] Oldenbarneveldt's [1547–1619] struggle [against the Dutch state],[12] and the schism in the Anglican Church became irrevocable under [the anti-Puritan monarch] James I [1566–1625] owing to dogmatic differences over this doctrine between the Crown and Puritanism. Indeed, the *doctrine of predestination* came to be perceived as the primary danger posed by Calvinism to the state, and the state struggled against it.[13]

The great synods of the seventeenth century (**Dordrecht** and **Westminster** above all but also countless smaller ones) placed the elevation of this doctrine to canonical legitimacy at the center of their work. It served as the fixed point of reference for innumerable heroes of the *ecclesia militans* [militant factions]. In the eighteenth and nineteenth centuries this doctrine called forth divisions in the churches and became the battle cry of the Great Awakening movements. Hence, the doctrine of predestination cannot be overlooked. Yet it may no longer be familiar to every educated person today. For now, let us become acquainted with its major features through several passages from its authoritative source: the Westminster Confession of 1647. The Independents and baptizing sects took their positions on predestination from this document.

> Chapter 9 (of Free Will), No. 3. Man, by his fall into a state of sin, hath wholly lost all ability of will to any spiritual good accompanying salvation. So that a natural man, being altogether averse from that Good, and dead in sin, is not able, by his own strength, to convert himself, or to prepare himself thereunto.

> Chapter 3 (of God's Eternal Decree), No. 3. By the decree of God, for the manifestation of His glory, some men and angels are predestinated unto everlasting life, and others foreordained to everlasting death.

> No. 5. Those of mankind that are predestinated unto life, God before the foundation of the world was laid, according to His eternal and immutable

purpose, and the secret counsel and good pleasure of His will, hath chosen in Christ unto everlasting glory, out of His mere free grace and love, without any foresight of faith or good works, or perseverance in either of them, or any other thing in the creature as conditions, or causes moving Him thereunto, and all to the praise of His glorious grace.

No. 7. The rest of mankind God was pleased, according to the unsearchable counsel of His own will, whereby He extendeth, or withholdeth mercy, as He pleaseth, for the glory of His sovereign power over His creatures, to pass by, and to ordain them to dishonor and wrath for their sin, to the praise of His glorious justice.

Chapter 10 (of Effectual Calling), No. 1. All those whom God hath predestinated unto life, and those only, He is pleased in His appointed and accepted time effectually to call, by His word and spirit (out of that state of sin and death, in which they are by nature) . . . taking away their heart of stone, and giving unto them an heart of flesh; renewing their wills, and by His almighty power determining them to that which is good. . . .

Chapter 5 (of Providence), No. 6. As for those wicked and ungodly men, whom God as a righteous judge, for former sins doth blind and harden, from them He not only with-holdeth His grace, whereby they might have been enlightened in their understandings and wrought upon in their hearts, but sometimes also withdraweth the gifts which they had and exposeth them to such objects as their corruption makes occasion of sin: and withal, gives them over to their own lusts, the temptations of the world, and the power of Satan: whereby it comes to pass that they harden themselves, even under those means, which God useth for the softening of others.[14]

Milton's judgment on this doctrine was well-known: "Even if I land in Hell, this God will never command my respect."[15] Our concern, however, is not to evaluate this doctrine of predestination. Rather, we wish to assess its historical significance. We can only cast a glance at the question of this doctrine's origin and the contexts of ideas with which it merged in Calvinist theology.

Two possible paths led to the doctrine of predestination. The phenomenon of the religious feeling of salvation goes together with the feeling of certainty that the salvation destiny of every person must be exclusively attributed to the hand of an objective power—and one's own influence has not the slightest effect. The combination of these two pathways held especially for the most passionate and active believers, whom we see repeatedly in the history of Christianity since St. Augustine [354–430].[16] The powerful mood of happy certainty, which releases the tremendous tension caused by the feeling of sinfulness, seemingly breaks over the faithful with great suddenness. As it does so, any possibility of the idea that this unimaginable gift of salvation could be attributed, in any way, to the helpful effects of one's own actions is destroyed. The idea that one's state of grace may be connected to achievements or qualities of one's own belief and will is likewise banished.

At the peaks of his highest genius, when Luther was capable of writing his *On the Freedom of the Christian* [1521], this "secret decree" of God also constituted for him the most firm and absolutely singular (and unfounded) source of his religious state of grace.[17] Luther never formally abandoned the notion of predestination. Predestination, however, never acquired a central position in his theological thought; indeed it moved more and more into the background. The significance of the idea of predestination diminished to the same extent that Luther as a responsible political actor in the church was forced to become more of a "political realist." [Luther's ally Philipp] Melanchthon [1497–1560] quite intentionally avoided incorporating this "dangerous and gloomy" doctrine into the Augsburg Confession [1530].[18] Moreover, the church fathers of Lutheranism took a firm stand on this doctrine: salvation can be lost (*amissibilis*), but it can be won back through penitent humility and faithful trust in the word of God and the sacraments.

Precisely the opposite development occurred with Calvin: the significance of the doctrine of predestination noticeably increased in the course of his polemical debates over dogma with his opponents.[19] It was fully developed only in the third edition of Calvin's *Institutes* [1543], and it acquired its central position only after his death, in the great conflicts that the Dordrecht and Westminster synods attempted to bring to a close. For Calvin, unlike for Luther, this "horrible decree" (*decretum horribile*) is *not lived* but *thought*. Therefore, the significance of predestination increases with every further growth in the consistency of Calvin's thought in the direction of his religious interests: toward God alone and not individuals. God does not exist for people; rather, people exist to serve the Will of God.[20] Everything that takes place, including the fact that only a small part of humanity will be called to be saved (an idea Calvin never doubted), becomes meaningful only in light of their service to a single goal: the glorification of God's majesty. To apply the standards of earthly "justice" to His sovereign commands is nonsensical and an infringement upon His majesty.[21] *Free* and obedient to no law, God and God alone can make His decrees comprehensible and known to us. He does so only insofar as He finds it good to do so.

We can be certain regarding these fragments of the eternal truth, and only these fragments. All else, including the *meaning* of our individual destiny, is surrounded in dark mysteries that are impossible to fathom and to gauge. A complaint from the damned, for example, that their destinies were undeserved would be similar to animals grumbling about not having been born as human beings. Separated from God by an unbridgeable gulf, all creatures deserve from Him only eternal death (to the extent that He does not choose another way for the glorification of His majesty).

We know only that a part of humanity will be saved and the rest damned. To assume that service to God or faults of people could play a part in settling this destiny would be to understand God's absolutely free decisions, which have existed as absolutes from eternity, as capable of being changed by human influence. This idea is unthinkable. Out of the New Testament's image of the "father in heaven," who acts according to motives understandable by humans and who delights in the return of every sinner to the fold as a woman rejoices in finding lost coins, there develops here a transcendental Being totally inaccessible to human understanding. From eternity, and entirely according to God's inaccessible decisions, every person's destiny has been decided. Even the smallest detail in the universe is controlled.[22] Because His decrees are firm and unalterable, His grace cannot be lost once granted and cannot be attained once denied.

For the mood of a generation that devoted itself to the grandiose consistency of the doctrine of predestination, its melancholy inhumanity must have had one result above all: a feeling of unimaginable inner *loneliness of the solitary individual.*[23] The question of eternal salvation constituted people's primary life concern during the Reformation epoch, yet they were directed to pursue their life's journey in solitude. Moreover, the destiny they would encounter at journey's end had been unalterably set for them since eternity, and no one could help them.

Because only the "elect" can understand the divine word spiritually, no priests could assist believers. And performance of the sacraments would not be helpful: although commanded by God to increase His glory and therefore to be scrupulously observed, the sacraments did not constitute means to acquire divine grace. Rather, they existed only as subjective *externa subsidia* [external supplements] to one's faith. Indeed, no church existed to assist believers. Although the axiom *extra ecclesiam nulla salus* [there can be no salvation outside the Church] remained in place, in the sense that whoever stayed apart from the true church could not belong among the elect,[24] the damned also belonged to the (external) church. Moreover, the condemned *should* belong to the church and comply with its discipline. Membership was necessary for them not in order to acquire salvation (for this is impossible) but because they also, to serve God's glory, must be coerced to uphold His commandments. Finally, even God could not help the faithful. Christ died only for the predestined few,[25] and God had decided that his martyrdom would benefit them for all eternity.

This absolute disappearance of all aids to salvation through the church and the *sacraments* constituted an absolutely decisive contrast to Catholicism. And in Lutheranism this development had not been carried out in a fully consistent manner. That overarching process in the history of religion—the *elimination of magic* from the world's occurrences (*Entzauberung der Welt*)[26]—found here, with the doctrine of predestination its final stage. This development, which began with the prophecy of ancient Judaism in the Old Testament, rejected, in conjunction with Greek scientific thought, all *magical* means to the quest for salvation as superstition and sacrilege. Even at funerals the genuine Puritan scorned every trace of magical ceremony and buried his loved ones without song and ceremony. He did so in order to prevent the appearance of "superstition" in any form, that is, a trust in the efficacy for salvation of forces of a magical-sacramental type.[27] [1920]

There were not only no magical means that would turn God's grace toward believers He had decided to condemn, but no means of any kind. The resulting spiritual isolation of believers, when combined with the harsh teaching that the body was separated absolutely from God and worthless, provided the basis for Puritanism's absolutely negative position toward all aspects of culture and religion oriented to the sensuous and to **feelings**: they were useless for salvation and they promoted sentimental illusions and idolatrous superstition. Hence Puritanism fundamentally turned away from all culture that appeals to the senses.[28] Furthermore, the spiritual isolation of believers formed one of the roots for that individualism, which tends to be pessimistic and without illusions,[29] found in the "national character" and institutions of peoples with a Puritan past, the effects of which are influential even today. The contrast between this pessimistic individualism and the entirely different way in which the "Enlightenment" later viewed persons is striking.[30]

***

We find clear traces of the influence of the doctrine of predestination in basic manifestations of the organized life and view of life in the historical epoch of concern to us [the sixteenth and seventeenth centuries]. Even in later times this influence is still visible, namely, in those periods when this doctrine's validity as religious dogma was in the midst of disappearing. Predestination can actually be understood as only the *most extreme* form of the *exclusive* trust in *God*, the analysis of which constitutes our theme here. It is visible, for example, in the remarkably frequent repetition in the English Puritan literature of the warning against all trust in the helpfulness of others and in friendship.[31] Even the mild-mannered [English minister Richard] Baxter [1615–91] advised his flock to be deeply mistrustful, even of best friends. [The English theologian Lewis] Bayly [1565–1631] explicitly recommends that no one be trusted and that compromising information should not be communicated to anyone. God alone should be your confidant.[32]

In connection with this orientation of life in those regions of fully developed Calvinism, and in striking contrast to Lutheranism, the practice of the sacrament of private confession silently vanished, although the reservations of even Calvin himself related only to the possibility for sacramental misinterpretation. This change proved enormously significant, first of all for the nature of Calvin's influence upon the devout, and second, as a psychological stimulus for the development of the believer's ethical posture of sacramental confession. The mechanism of sacramental confession that had provided a regular "release" of an emotion-laden consciousness of guilt was now eliminated.[33]

The consequences of the abolition of confession for practical, everyday morality will be discussed later. The results for the general religious situation of believers are obvious. Despite the necessity of membership in the true church for one's salvation,[34] the interaction of the Calvinist with his God took place in a deep spiritual isolation. Whoever wishes to experience the unique effects[35] of this peculiar mood can turn to the book most widely read in all of Puritan literature, [John] Bunyan's [1628–1688] *Pilgrim's Progress* [1678].[36] The passages on [the hero] Christian's behavior are central. Once he recognizes that he has been living in the "city of the damned," Christian hastens to follow the call to commence his pilgrimage to the Heavenly City. Wife and children clinging to him, he staggers forth across the fields, sticking his fingers into his ears and crying "life, eternal life."

No refinement could better capture the mood of the devout Puritan, who is basically concerned only with himself and thinking only of his own salvation, than the naive disposition of this tinker, writing in his cell and receiving the applause of the entire world. In a manner somewhat reminiscent of [the Swiss novelist] Gottfried Keller's [1819–90] play, "Gerechte Kammacher" [The Righteous Comb-maker], this mood is expressed in the smug and ingratiating conversations Christian has along the way with others equally possessed. The thought that it would be pleasant to have his family by his side occurs to him only after he himself is safe.

Christian's tormenting fear of death and of the next life is the same as we experience so urgently and comprehensively with [the Catholic moral theologian] Alphonsus of Liguori [d. 1787], as [the church historian Johann von] Döllinger [1799–1890] describes him to us.[37] Just this [obsession with one's salvation] remains far distant from the spirit of prideful orientation to the existing world as expressed by Machiavelli in his depictions of the glory of the citizens of Florence. In their struggles against the pope and his prohibitions, these citizens place "the love of their native city above their fear for the salvation of their souls." Moreover, of course, the fears of Christian and Liguori remain even farther away from the sensibility that Richard Wagner [1813–83] bestows upon Siegmund before his fatal battle: "Then greet for me Wotan, greet for me Valhalla. . . . But truly [Brünnhilde], do not speak to me of Valhalla's cold delights."[38] Nevertheless, it must be noted that, in regard to the *effects* of their fears, Bunyan and Liguori characteristically diverge: the same fear that drives Bunyan's Christian to all forms of self-humiliation motivates Liguori to a hectic and systematic struggle with life. What is the origin of this distinction?

It appears at first to be puzzling. How can that tendency toward a spiritual loosening of the individual from the tightest ties that encircle him and hold him in the world be connected to Calvinism's undoubted superiority in respect to social organization?[39] As odd as it at first appears, precisely this superiority follows from the specific orientation that the Christian notion of "brotherly love" was now forced to acquire: Calvinist beliefs, which emphasized the spiritual isolation of each person, pushed this ideal away from its accustomed meaning.

This orientation derived first of all from dogma.[40] The world exists, and only exists, to serve the glorification of God. The predestined Christian exists, and only exists, in order to do his part to increase God's glory in the world through the implementation of His commandments. Indeed, God wants the Christian to engage in community activity *because* He wants the social organization of life to be arranged according to His commandments, and thus according to the goal of serving His greater glory. The social[41] work of the Calvinist is in the end work *in majorem gloriam dei* [for the greater glory of *God* (Weber's emphasis)]. It follows that work in a *calling* is also affected by this aim, and hence this-worldly work stands in service to the community as a whole.

Already with Luther we found that work in a calling, within an economy with a division of labor, was derived from the ideal of "brotherly love." But what remained for Luther an unstable, purely conceptual construction became, for the Calvinists, a central component of their ethical system. "Brotherly love," because it can only be in service to *God's* glory[42] and not to fulfill *physical desires*, [43] is expressed *primarily* in the fulfillment of the tasks of a **calling**, tasks that are given by *lex naturae* [natural law]. In the process, work in a calling becomes endowed with a peculiarly objective, *im*personal character, one in the service of the rational formation of the societal cosmos surrounding us. For just the marvelously purposeful construction and furnishing of this cosmos, which is apparently designed to serve the *usefulness* of the human species (according to the revelation of the Bible as well as natural insight), in fact allows work in the service of all impersonal, societal usefulness to promote the glory of God—and hence to be recognized as desired by Him.

In this manner, the complete elimination of the problem of theodicy,[44] as well as all those questions concerning the "meaning" of the world and of life which have caused so much anguish to other believers, was comprehended by the Puritans in a completely unproblematic manner. This was the case for the Jews as well, although for entirely different reasons. In a certain sense this elimination of the problem of theodicy held for the nonmystical strains of Christianity generally. In addition to this succinct rendering of the theodicy dilemma, a further force appeared with Calvinism, indeed one that cast its influence in the same direction: even though, in regard to religious matters, Calvinism placed the particular person fully on his own, a division between the "person" and the "ethic" (in Sören Kierkegaard's sense) did not exist for this version of ascetic Protestantism. [1920]

The significance of this argument for Calvinism's political and **economic rationalism** cannot be analyzed at this point. The source of the *utilitarian* orientation of the Calvinist ethic can be found here, as well as important peculiarities of the Calvinist conception of the calling.[45] We must now return once again to a consideration specifically of the doctrine of predestination.

***

The key problem for us, first, is clear: How was this doctrine *tolerated*[46] in an epoch in which the next life was not only more important than all of life's mundane and practical interests but also, in many respects, more certain?[47] A particular question must arise immediately for every single believer. It forces all such **this-worldly** interests into the background: Am *I* among the predestined who have been saved? How can *I* become certain of my status as one of the chosen?[48]

The question of salvation was not a problem for Calvin himself. He felt himself to be a "tool" of God's will and was certain of his state of grace. Accordingly, to the question—"How could persons become certain of their own election?"—Calvin basically offered only this answer: We should be content with the knowledge that God has chosen, and content with the steadfast trust in Christ that comes from true belief. Furthermore, he fundamentally rejected the assumption that people could discern from others' behavior whether they were chosen or condemned. According to Calvin, such a belief constituted a presumptuous attempt to intrude into God's secrets. The elect, he believed, in this life distinguish themselves in no external way from the condemned.[49] With the single exception of that *finaliter* [ultimate], steadfast, believing trust, all subjective experiences of the chosen few, as *ludibria spiritus sancti* [puppets of the Holy Spirit], are also possible among the damned. Thus the chosen are, and remain, God's *invisible* church.

As normally occurs, the situation for Calvin's epigone followers was different. The difference becomes apparent as early as [the French reformist theologian Theodor] Beza [1519–1605], and above all for the broad stratum of ordinary believers. The *certitudo salutis* [certainty of salvation] question must have become for them, in the sense of the *recognition* of one's state of grace, intensified to the point of absolutely overriding significance.[50] Wherever the doctrine of predestination was adhered to, the question of whether infallible signs (*Merkmale*) existed that allowed recognition of one's membership among the *electi* [chosen] could not be avoided. For the development of Pietism, which arose first from the soil of the Reformed Church, this question was of central significance. Indeed, in certain ways it remained, at times, even constitutive for Pietism. This was also true, however, outside Pietism. (When we consider below the very broad-ranging political and social significance of the Reformed doctrine and practice on communion, we will have to discuss the role played by the ascertainment of the individual's state of grace in regard to, for example, the question of admission to communion, that is, in regard to the religious ceremony that proved decisive for defining the social position of participants throughout the entire seventeenth century.)

It was impossible to retain Calvin's approach, at least to the extent that the question of one's *own* state of grace arose.[51] His answer to the question, which never formally abandoned orthodox [Lutheran] doctrine, in principle, referred to his own testimony: steadfast faith would produce salvation.[52] Above all, at the practical level of providing pastoral care for the devout, where the suffering caused by the doctrine of predestination was experienced at every turn, Calvin's response proved inadequate. These difficulties were addressed in various ways.[53] Insofar as the notion of "predestination" was not reinterpreted, rendered milder, or basically abandoned,[54] two interwoven types of advice for pastoral care emerged.

On the one hand, it became a matter of duty pure and simple for believers to *consider* themselves among the elect few and to repel every doubt about their state of grace as nothing more than the temptations of the devil.[55] This type of advice seemed plausible because a lack of self-confidence in one's status as chosen was believed to result from insufficient faith; and insufficient faith results only from the insufficient effects of God's grace. Thus, the admonition of the apostle—for the believer to "make firm" his or her own calling—is interpreted as a duty to acquire, in the course of one's daily struggle, the subjective certainty of predestination and justification. In place of humble sinners, to whom Luther promises grace if they trust themselves to God in penitent faith, Calvinism now bred self-confident "saints."[56] They were found often in those steel-hard (*stahlharten*) Puritan merchants of capitalism's heroic epoch. Indeed these "saints" are occasionally found even today.

On the other hand, a further type of advice was offered by those engaged in pastoral care to address the suffering caused by the uncertainty of one's salvation status. *Restless work in a vocational calling* was recommended as the best possible means to *acquire* the self-confidence that one belonged among the elect.[57] Work, and work alone, banishes religious doubt and gives certainty of one's status among the saved.

The reasons that this-worldly work in a calling could be understood as capable of *this* achievement (that it could be viewed, so to speak, as the suitable mechanism for the release of emotion-based religious anxiety) must be sought in deeply rooted peculiarities of the religious sensibility cultivated in the Reformed Churches. These unique aspects come to the fore most clearly when contrasted to Luther's doctrine: a justification of a certainty of salvation derives from faith alone. Schneckenburger's excellent lectures[58] analyze these differences in a subtle and objective manner and without value judgments. For the most part, the following brief observations simply tie into his discussion.

***

As Lutheran theology developed in the course of the seventeenth century, the ultimate religious experience for Lutheran piety was the *unio mystica* [sacred, mystical union] with the Divine.[59] As indicated by this expression, which is unknown in Reformist doctrines in this form, of importance is a substantial feeling of God (*Gottesgefühl*), namely, the sensation of an actual penetration of the Divine into the soul of the devout. This penetration must be understood as having the same qualitative effects that contemplation had upon the German mystics. It is characterized by its *passive* character, which is oriented to fulfillment of a desire for *rest* in God, and by its purely devotional looking inward (*Innerlichkeit*).

As is well-known from the history of philosophy, a religious devotion oriented to mysticism can become closely allied with a decidedly down-to-earth sense of reality in respect to the empirically given. Indeed, as a consequence of mysticism's rejection of dialectical doctrines, this kind of religious devotion may often directly underpin this practical sense of reality. Moreover, in a similar manner mysticism can also indirectly support the rational organization of life. Nevertheless, mysticism's relationship to the world's everyday tasks and occupations naturally displays an incapacity to bestow a positive evaluation upon external activity. Lutheranism, however, added a further element [the effect of which was to move this religion even more in this direction]. The *unio mystica* in Lutheranism combined, because of original sin [which stains all humans], with a deep feeling of personal unworthiness. This feeling should carefully maintain the *poenitentia quotidiana* [daily penitence] of the Lutheran believer; its goal was to preserve humility and candor, both of which were indispensable for the forgiveness of sins.

In contrast, from the beginning Reformist religious devotion stood in opposition to Pascal's quietistic flight from the world and to Lutheranism's purely inwardly-oriented, devotional mood of piety. The Reformed Church precluded, as a consequence of God's absolute transcendence vis-à-vis the human species and hence His incomprehensibility, the real penetration of the Divine into the human soul. According to Calvin, *finitum non est capax infiniti* [the finite is not capable of understanding the infinite]. Instead, the coming together of God with His chosen elect could only occur and enter the consciousness of believers in a different manner: God *operated* (*operatur*) in the devout and they were conscious of His powers. Hence, believers were aware that their *action* arose out of the belief that was caused by God's grace. This belief in turn, the faithful also knew, legitimized itself through the quality of this action, which was caused by God.

***

Highly significant differences in regard to the crucial conditions for the believer's salvation status[60] are now becoming articulated, as are distinctions pivotal for the classification of all practical religious devotion in general. Namely, it is now apparent that the religious virtuoso can convince himself of his own state of grace insofar as he feels himself to be *either* a vessel *or* a tool of divine power. In the case of the former, his religious life tends toward a mystical culture of feelings; in the latter, it tends toward ascetic *action*. While Luther stood closer to the former case, Calvinism belonged to the latter. The Reformed devout wanted, as did Lutherans, to be saved *sola fide:* on the basis of faith alone. However, because to Calvin all sheer feelings and moods remained suspect, even though they might appear lofty,[61] a **testifying** to belief, as given by its objective *effects* upon action, had to be offered. Only then could belief provide a secure foundation for the *certitude salutis*. The call to salvation must be *fides efficax*,[62] or an "effectual calling" (as stated in the **Savoy Declaration** [1658]).

One may now pose the next question: By *what* signs were the Reformed devout able, beyond a doubt, to recognize the right belief? By leading an organized Christian life that served to increase *God's glory*. Exactly what fulfills this goal is to be derived from His will. And this will is revealed directly in the Bible or indirectly out of the purposeful orders of the world (*lex naturae*)[63] created by Him. One's own state of grace can be determined largely through a comparison of the state of one's own soul to the soul of the elect (the patriarchs of the Old Testament come to mind).[64] Only the chosen actually *have* the *fides efficax:*[65] only they are capable, on the basis of a *regeneratio* [regeneration] and the sense of holiness (*sanctificatio*) that thereby follows, of dedicating their entire life to increasing God's glory through actual (and not simply apparent) good works. To the extent that believers are aware of their transformation, at least in terms of its fundamental character and enduring purpose to be obedient [*propositum oboedientiae*], as resting upon a power living in them[66] that seeks to increase His glory (hence a power not only willed by God but above all *caused*[67] by God), they acquire the highest reward Calvinism strives for: the certainty of grace.[68]

That this certainty is to be attained is confirmed by 2 Cor. 13:5.[69] Yet good works are absolutely unsuitable to serve as means for the acquisition of this certainty: because even the saved are still mere humans determined by human wants and desires, all that even they do falls infinitely short of God's demands. Nevertheless, good works are indispensable as *signs* of election.[70] They are technical means, but not ones that can be used to purchase salvation. Rather, good works serve to banish the anxiety surrounding the question of one's salvation.[71] In this sense they are occasionally openly described as "indispensable for salvation" or directly linked to the *possessio salutis* [possession of salvation].[72]

At a practical level, this doctrine basically means that God helps those who help themselves.[73] Thus, as it is also noted on occasion, the Calvinist *himself creates*[74] his salvation. More correctly: the Calvinist creates for himself the *certainty* of his salvation. *Unlike* in Catholicism, however, the creation of this certainty *cannot* be built from a gradual accumulation of single, service-oriented good works. It is comprised instead of the *systematic self-control* necessary, in *every moment*, when the believer stands before the alternatives: Am I among the saved or among the damned? With this point we arrive at a very important stage in our discussion.

***

It is frequently noted that this development of ideas in the Reformed churches and sects, which has been worked out with increasing clarity,[75] has been subject to criticism from the Lutheran side. "Salvation through good works" (*Werkheiligkeit*),[76] it is argued, is actually the issue here. Now although Calvinism has correctly defended itself by rejecting any identification of its *dogmatic* position with the Catholic doctrine of good works, this criticism from Lutheranism holds as soon as the point of reference becomes the *practical* consequences for daily life of the average Reformed believer.[77] For there has never been perhaps a more intense form of religious valuation of moral *action* than that which Calvinism produced in its followers. Key, however, for the practical significance of this type of "salvation through good works" is first of all the recognition of the *qualities* that characterize the corresponding organization of one's life, and the qualities that distinguish it from the everyday life of the average medieval Catholic.

One can attempt to formulate the distinction [between the Catholic and Calvinist orientations to daily action] roughly in this way. The normal lay Catholic[78] in the medieval period, in regard to ethical matters, lived in a sort of "hand to mouth" fashion. First of all he conscientiously fulfilled his traditional duties. Above and beyond these duties, however, his "good works" normally were not necessarily connected. At any rate, the Catholic's good works and duties were surely not of necessity **rationalized** into a life-*system*. Rather, they remained a series of *isolated* actions that the faithful could carry out as the situation required: whether to atone for specific sins, to follow more closely the advice of one's priest, or at the end of the believer's life, to acquire insurance credits, so to speak. Of course it is true that this Catholic ethic was an "ethic of conviction" (*Gesinnungsethik*), yet the concrete *intentio* of the *isolated* actions decided their value. Moreover, the *isolated* actions—good or bad—were credited to the believer and influenced his life on earth as well as his eternal destiny. Entirely realistically, the Catholic Church concluded that the human species was *not* an absolutely and clearly determined unity to be valued as such. Rather, people's moral lives were viewed as (normally) influenced by conflicting motives and often by contradictory modes of behavior. Of course, the church demanded also of believers a *principled* transformation of life to conform to God's commandments, as an ideal. Even this demand, however, was in turn weakened (for the average believer) by one of the church's most important mechanisms of power and socialization: confession. Its function was deeply interwoven with the internal uniqueness of Catholic religious devotion.

The "elimination of magic" from the world—namely, the exclusion of the use of magic as a means to salvation[79]—was not followed through with the same degree of consistency in Catholicism as in Puritanism (and before it only in Judaism). To the Catholic,[80] the *salvation through the sacraments* was available as a mechanism that compensated for his own shortcomings, and the priest was a magician who carried out the miracle of transubstantiation in the mass. The pivotal power had been bestowed upon the priest. The faithful could turn to him for assistance in contrition and penitence. Because the priest provided the means of atonement and bestowed hope for salvation and certainty of forgiveness, he granted the believer a *relief* from tremendous *tension*. By contrast, the Calvinist's destiny involved the necessity of living inseparable from this tension. [1920]

Calvinists must live amidst this tension, and no mechanism existed for lessening it. A friendly and humane comforting did not exist for believers. Moreover, they could not hope that hours of weakness and frivolity could be compensated for with intensified good will during other hours, as could Catholics and Lutherans. The Calvinist God did not demand isolated "good works" from His faithful; rather, if salvation were to occur, He required an intensification of good works into a *system*.[81] There was here no mention of that genuinely humane cycle, followed by the Catholic, of sin, repentance, penitence, relief, and then further sin. Nor was there any discussion in Calvinism of devices or mechanisms (such as a defined period of punishment) that would balance one's entire life account and then provide, through the means of grace offered by the church, atonement for sins. [1920]

In Calvinism, the practical-ethical action of the average believer lost its planless and unsystematic character and was molded into a consistent, *methodical* organization of his life as a whole. It is surely no accident that the name *Methodists* remained attached to the carriers of the last great reawakening of Puritan ideas in the eighteenth century, just as the term *Precisians* (which is substantively fully synonymous with Methodism) was used to refer to their seventeenth-century spiritual ancestors.[82] For only through a fundamental transformation of the meaning of one's entire life—in every hour and every action[83]—could the effect of grace, namely a raising of believers out of the *status naturae* [natural state] and into the *status gratiae* [state of grace], be testified to through action.

The life of this "saint" was exclusively oriented to a transcendent goal: salvation. Precisely *for this reason*, however, its this-worldly, practical course was thoroughly *rationalized* and exclusively dominated by a single point of view: to increase God's glory on earth. Nowhere has this vantage point—*omnia in majorem dei gloriam* [all for the greater glory of God]—been taken with such complete seriousness.[84] Yet only a life guided by constant reflection could constitute a life empowered to overcome the *status naturae*. Indeed, with this alteration of meaning in the direction of an ethical organization of life, Descartes' *cogito ergo sum* was taken over by the early Puritans.[85] This rationalization now provided Reform piety with its uniquely *ascetic* character. Moreover, in this manner it established its inner affinity[86] with, as well as its unique contrast to, Catholicism. Similar developments, of course, were not foreign to Catholicism.

***

Christian asceticism undoubtedly contains within itself highly diverging features in regard to external appearance as well as meaning. In its highest forms in the West, however, asceticism bore a thoroughly *rational* character as early as the Middle Ages. Some forms of asceticism were rational even in antiquity. The world-historical significance of the way that monks in the West led their lives in an organized manner rests precisely upon Western monasticism's asceticism, as does the contrast of Western monasticism to the monasticism of the Orient (in terms of its general classification rather than in its entirety). The organization of life in Western monasticism was emancipated from all random flight from this-world and all heroic self-torture. This liberation held, in principle, even as early as St. Benedict [480–547], more so for the [French Benedictine] monks of Cluny [910], yet more so for the [French] Cistercians [1098], and, finally, most decisively for the Jesuits [1534].[87] This organized life, which was systematized, thoroughly shaped, and methodical-rational, had the goal of overcoming the *status naturae.* Thus, it enabled believers to escape the power of irrational drives and all dependence upon the world and nature as given, to subordinate life to the supremacy of the organized will,[88] and to subject their actions to a permanent self-*control* and a *reflection* upon their ethical implications. Hence this methodical-rational organization of life sought to train the monk objectively (to become a worker in service to God's kingdom) and, in this manner, subjectively (to guarantee the salvation of his soul).

Just as it constituted the goal of the *exercitia* [religious exercises] of St. Ignatius [of Loyola, 1491–1556] and the highest forms of rational monastic virtues in general,[89] this *active* self-control constituted also Puritanism's defining practical ideal of life.[90] Even in the reports on the trials of its martyrs one can see that the reserved calm of the Puritan faithful stood opposed to the confused rambunctiousness of noble prelates and state officials, whom the devout held in the deepest contempt.[91] Indeed, just this high esteem for a reserved self-control comes to the fore even now in the best representatives of the English and American "gentleman."[92] As can be said for every "rational" asceticism, Puritan asceticism (in the everyday language of today[93]) worked to render the devout capable of calling forth and then acting upon their "constant motives," especially those motives that the believer, through the practice of asceticism itself, "trained" against the "emotions."

In this manner, and in *this* formal-psychological meaning of the term, Puritan asceticism socialized the believer to become a personality. In contrast to a number of popular ideas, the Puritan goal was to be able to lead an alert, conscious, and self-aware life. Hence the destruction of the spontaneity of the instinct-driven enjoyment of life (*triebhaften Lebensgenusses*) constituted the most urgent task. The aim was to bring *order* into the believer's way of leading his or her life and asceticism was the most important *mechanism* for doing so.

On the one hand, all these decisive themes are found as fully developed[94] in the rules of Catholic monasticism as in the basic tenets of the Calvinist organized life.[95] The tremendous power of these religious groups to overcome the *status naturae* rests upon this methodical taking hold of the entire person. As evident, in particular if compared to Lutheranism, precisely this feature of Calvinism undergirded its capacity as an *ecclesia militans* to insure the success of the cause of Protestantism. On the other hand, the basis for the *contrast* between Calvinist and Catholic asceticism is obvious: the privilege of advice from the *consilia evangelica* [Catholic Church hierarchy] disappeared in Calvinism. The restructuring of Christian asceticism followed from this development; it now became purely *this*-worldly.

This is not to say that the "methodical" life in medieval Catholicism remained confined to the cells of the monastery; that was by no means the case either in theory or in practice. Rather, as has already been pointed out, despite the greater moral moderation of Catholicism, an ethically unsystematic life did *not* fulfill, even for the this-worldly life, its highest ideals.[96] For example, a powerful attempt to achieve the full penetration of everyday life by asceticism was undertaken in the Third Order of St. Francis. It was not the only such attempt, as is well-known. Indeed, works such as *Nachfolge Christi* [The Disciples of Christ][97] clearly demonstrate—directly *through* the manner of their strong effect—that the mode of organized life they preached was perceived as morally *higher* than that morality viewed as simply fulfilling the minimum basic requirement, namely, the morality of everyday life. This remained the case even though daily life morality was actually *not* evaluated according to standards, as Puritanism had already begun to do. Furthermore, the *practice* of certain Catholic religious institutions, above all the granting of indulgences, repeatedly had to cross paths with the rudiments of a systematic, this-worldly asceticism (and for this reason the granting of indulgences during the period of the Reformation was perceived as the church's fundamental weakness rather than as a peripheral abuse).

The decisive difference involved another issue, however. In medieval Catholicism, the person who lived methodically in the religious sense par excellence was *actually only the monk*. And he remained the only figure to do so. Hence, the more intensively asceticism took hold of the individual the *more* it drove him *out of* everyday life and into the monastery, precisely because the uniquely holy life was to be found only in a *surpassing* of everyday morality.[98] Luther first abolished this mode of leading the religious life, and Calvinism here simply followed Luther.[99] It must be emphasized that Luther abolished the monasteries not as an actor fulfilling some "developmental historical trend" (*Entwicklungstendenz*), but entirely because of his personal experiences (which were, by the way, at the beginning quite unclear in regard to the direction in which they would lead; later, however, they were driven further by the *political* situation).

The essence of the type of religious devotion that now came to the fore was captured by [the German mystic and popular author] Sebastian Franck [1499–1542].[100] The significance of the Reformation could be found, Frank argued, in this new situation: now *every* Christian must be a monk for an entire lifetime. A dam was now erected that prevented asceticism from flowing out of everyday life, and those persons of passionate and serious spiritual nature (the best representatives of which had heretofore been delivered into monasticism) were now instructed to pursue their ascetic ideals *inside* a this-worldly, vocational calling.

Calvinism, however, in the course of its development, added a positive element: the idea of the necessity of *testifying to one's belief* in a this-worldly vocational calling.[101] In adding this element, Calvinism bestowed a *positive motivation* toward asceticism upon broader strata of persons endowed with religiously oriented natures. In place of the spiritual aristocracy of the monk outside of and above the world, there now appeared, once its ethic was anchored in the doctrine of predestination, a spiritual aristocracy of saints predestined from eternity, *in* the world.[102] With its *character indelebilis* [unchangeable character], this aristocracy was eternally separate from the other part of humanity: the damned. In principle unbridgeable and, because of its invisibility, more mysterious[103] than the division that visibly separated the medieval monk from the world, this gulf between the saved and the damned invaded *all* social perceptions with a hard and piercing acuity. In light of his sinfulness, an attitude of compassionate helpfulness towards one's neighbor (coming from an awareness of one's own weakness) was not the appropriate response of the elect chosen by the grace of God (who thus were saints). More suitable instead was a hatred and contempt for the sinner as an enemy of God, one who carried with him the marks of the eternally condemned.[104]

This mode of perceiving the social world was capable of such an intensification that, under certain conditions, it could flow into the formation of *sects*. As happened with the "Independents" of the seventeenth century,[105] such a flow occurred when genuine Calvinist belief (divine glory requires that the damned, through the church, be brought to submit to His commandments) was outweighed by the conviction that God would be disgraced if the condemned were found among His devout flock, if the damned participated in the sacraments, or if they (as pastors) administered them.[106] In a word, a movement toward the formation of sects was set into motion wherever the Donatist view of the church appeared as a consequence of the idea that a testifying to one's belief is necessary, as happened in the case of the Calvinist Baptists.[107] In those situations where the demand for a "pure" church as a community of the elect was not followed fully to its logical end, and thus did not lead to the formation of a new sect, various new arrangements for church governance arose out of the attempt to separate the chosen from the damned. A special position, it was believed, must be retained for the elect. Church administrators and the minister, for example, must be among the saved.[108]

***

Of course, the ascetic organization of life received its firm norms from the Bible. The action of the faithful could be continuously oriented to these norms and believers clearly needed them as guidelines. For us, the most important aspect of the Calvinists' often-noted "mastery of the Bible" is their view that the *Old* Testament, because its moral rules were just as inspiring as those of the New Testament, must be accorded dignity at a level of complete *equality* with the New Testament (at least to the extent that they perceived these moral rules as not exclusively addressing the historical situation of Judaism and as not explicitly abrogated by Christ). The law of God was given as an ideal for *believers* in particular and it stood as a valid norm even if it was never fully to be reached.[109] For Luther, in contrast, the exact opposite held, at least at the beginning: he extolled the *freedom* from subordination to the Old Testament laws as a divine privilege bestowed upon the faithful.[110] Yet in the entire orientation of life of the Puritans one feels the effect of Hebrew wisdom, as found in the passages they read most (Proverbs and certain Psalms). The sense of a closeness to God but also of a fully **dispassionate** dimension is clear. The *rational* character of this Hebrew wisdom is particularly apparent: the suppression of the mystical and, in general, of the *feeling* aspect of religion. Sanford[111] correctly traced this aspect to the influence of the Old Testament.

Nevertheless, Old Testament rationalism was essentially of a petty-bourgeois and traditional character. The powerful pathos of the great prophets and many of the psalms was a component of it, as were elements that later provided points of linkage to the development of a religious devotion specifically based on feelings.[112] This connection took place as early as the Middle Ages. Thus, it was Calvinism's *own* components, namely, its foundational ascetic character, that in the end again led it to select out and assimilate the congenial elements of Old Testament piety.

Now the systematization of a life organized around ethical principles, as common to both Calvinist Protestant asceticism and the rational forms of life within the Catholic monastic orders, becomes manifest purely externally in the way in which the "precise" Puritan Christian perpetually *monitored* his state of grace.[113] Indeed, even the devout believers' diaries (in which sins, temptations, and acts that indicated progress toward grace were perpetually recorded, even in tables) were shared alike by modern Catholic piety, which was mainly a Jesuit creation (namely in France), and the most zealously church-oriented Calvinist circles.[114] However, whereas the keeping of a diary in Catholicism served to insure the completeness of the believer's confession or to offer to the *directeur de l'ame* [director of the soul] the documents necessary for authoritarian guidance of the (mostly female) faithful, the Reformed Christian *himself*, with the help of these diaries, "felt his own" pulse. Significant moral theologians all note the importance of these diaries, and Benjamin Franklin's daily accounting offers a classical example; his tabular-statistical entries marked his progress in cultivating particular virtues.[115] In contrast, the old medieval conception of God's accounting (found even in the ancient world), as depicted by Bunyan, reaches such a point of characteristic tastelessness that the relationship of the sinner to God is compared to the relationship between a customer and a shopkeeper: whoever once falls into debt may at best pay off the cumulative interest, using the yield of all his acts of service, but never the debt itself.[116]

As he monitored his own behavior, the later Puritan monitored also the behavior of God and discovered His finger in every single detail of life. Moreover, and in opposition to the teachings of Calvin himself, the

Puritan knew why God had decided in this or that way. Hence the striving to make life holy and sanctified could almost assume the character of a business.[117] A penetrating Christianization of the entire being was the consequence of this *methodicalness* now required for the leading of a life organized around ethical principles. In contrast to Lutheranism, Calvinism forced this methodical organization of life upon the believer.

If one wishes to acquire a correct understanding of the particular effect Calvinism had on believers, one must keep continuously in mind that this *methodicalness* was decisive. It follows, on the one hand, that just *this* Calvinist version of Christianity could first have had this influence upon believers. It also follows, on the other hand, that other Protestant denominations must have had an effect in the same direction if their ethical motivations were the same in regard to the decisive point: the idea of testifying to belief through one's action. [1920]

***

Until now we have been concerned with Calvinist religious devotion. Accordingly, we have assumed that the doctrine of predestination forms the dogmatic framework for Puritan morality in the sense of a methodical-rational and ethical organization of life. We have done so because this doctrine in fact extended far beyond the circle of the religious grouping that in every way remained strict adherents of Calvin, the "Presbyterians." It was contained not only in the Savoy Declaration of the Independents of 1658, but also in the Baptist-influenced confessions of Hanserd Knollys [1599–1691] of 1689.[118] Although the greatest community-organizing and administrative genius of Methodism, John Wesley, believed in the universality of grace, the great agitator of the first Methodist generation and its most consistent thinker [and co-founder], George Whitefield [1714–70], adhered to the doctrine of predestination. So also did the occasionally highly influential circle around Lady [Selina Countess of] Huntingdon [1707–91, Whitefield's disciple, who organized his followers into a cohesive body of Calvinist-Methodists in Wales].

In the fateful epoch of the seventeenth century, according to the magnificent consistency of this doctrine, believers were considered to be the tools of God and the executors of His providential decrees. Precisely this idea was cultivated and maintained in England by the warring representatives of the "holy life."[119] The doctrine of predestination, in conveying this notion of believers as God's tools, forestalled a premature collapse of religion-oriented action into a purely utilitarian ethos of good works. The concerns of this world would have been the focus of such an ethos and this utilitarian posture would never have been capable of bringing the faithful to make unheard of sacrifices on behalf of irrational and ideal goals. Moreover, in an ingenious manner, the doctrine of predestination linked absolute determinism, the complete transcendence of the supernatural realm, and the belief in unconditionally valid norms.[120] Simultaneously, this linkage was in principle much more *modern* than the milder doctrines that addressed more the feelings of the devout and subjected even God to moral laws. Above all, as will be repeatedly apparent in the sections below, fundamental for our discussion is the investigation of the idea of a *testifying* to one's belief as the psychological point of origin for methodical ethics.

***

We proceeded above by examining the doctrine of predestination and its significance for everyday life. In addition, because the idea of testifying through action to belief recurs on a regular basis among the denominations still to be considered, it proved feasible to study this idea first, with Calvinism, in its "pure form." In other words, we constructed a model of the way in which belief and ethics are connected; this model can now be "applied" to the further denominations. In this exercise, because the consequences of the doctrine of predestination were the most broad-ranging, it was necessary to begin with this doctrine.[121]

Within Protestantism, the *doctrine of predestination* had great consequences among its earliest followers, in particular with respect to the ascetic formation of an organized life. Lutheranism, however, most thoroughly blocked its impact. Indeed, Lutheranism formed the *most principled* antithesis to Calvinism. A (relative) lack of moral awareness (*sittlichen Ohnmacht*) arose from Lutheranism rather than an ascetic organization of life. Apparently, the Lutheran *gratia amissibilis* [loss of grace], which could always be won back again through penitent contrition, contained *as such* no motivational push toward a systematic, rational formation of the believer's ethical life (which is important for us as a product of ascetic Protestantism).[122] Rather, Lutheran piety left largely unaltered the spontaneous vitality of instinctive action and the untempered life based on feelings. It lacked this motivational push toward an uninterrupted self-control and hence toward a *planned* regulation of one's own life in any sense. Here Lutheranism stood in contrast to the motivational impulse contained in the bleak teachings of Calvinism.

A religious genius, such as Luther, could live spontaneously in this atmosphere of uninhibited openness to the world and without danger of sinking back into the *status naturae*, as long as the strength of his enthusiasm lasted! Also the simple, delicate, and peculiarly devotional form of piety that adorns some of the most distinguished representatives of Lutheranism is rarely found on the soil of genuine Puritanism. Lutheranism's morality unbounded by firm rules is likewise also not discovered in this Puritanism. Rather, parallels to Lutheranism are far more likely to be found, for example, in the mild Anglican religious devotion of [the theologians Richard] Hooker [*ca.* 1554–1600] and [William] Chillingsworth [1602–44], among others. For average Lutheran believers (and even for the more sincere), nothing was more certain than that they would be pulled out of the *status naturae* only temporarily, that is, so long as the influence upon them of a particular confession or sermon lasted.

The striking difference between the ethical standards of the courts of Reformist and Lutheran princes was well-known in the Reformation period. The Lutheran courts had sunk into drunkenness and raw behavior.[123] In comparison to the asceticism of the baptizing movement, the helplessness of the Lutheran clergy, with its sermons based upon pure faith alone, was similarly common knowledge. What one perceives today in the Germans as the behavior of easy-going congeniality (*Gemütlichkeit*) and a "lack of affected mannerisms"[124] contrasts to the behavior of the Anglo-Saxons. A more thorough destruction of the spontaneity of the *status naturae,* as apparent even in physiognomy, occurred in England and the United States. Upon meeting Americans and English, Germans are normally inclined to perceive precisely this destruction of spontaneity as strange, namely, as a certain internal constraint, a narrowness of manifest emotional range, and a general inhibitedness. These are all contrasts in the organization and direction of life that fundamentally result from the *lesser* penetration of asceticism into the life of the Lutheran believer as compared to that of the Calvinist. The aversion of every spontaneous "child of the world" to asceticism is evident in this child's every sensation. As a result of its doctrinal teachings on the acquisition of salvation, Lutheranism lacks the psychological motivation capable of endowing the organization of life with a systematic element. If present, this element would have compelled a methodical rationalization of the Lutheran's life.

***

This motivation toward a methodical rationalization of life, which conditions the ascetic character of piety, *could* undoubtedly be produced through a variety of religious ideas, as we will soon see. Calvinism's doctrine of predestination offered only *one* among diverse possibilities. Nevertheless, we have become convinced that this doctrine not only possessed an entirely unique consistency; in addition, it stood out because of a great psychological effectiveness.[125] If considered exclusively from the vantage point of the religious motivation provided by their asceticism, the *non*-Calvinist ascetic movements must be seen as involving a *weakening* of Calvinism's internal consistency.

Although not always the case in the empirical-historical course of development, the Reformist form of asceticism was, for the most part, either imitated by the other ascetic movements or taken as a comparative and complementary point of reference. The latter view arose when its basic principles were diverged from or expanded upon. At times, an asceticism appeared which was no different from Calvinism in terms of its consistency, despite its anchoring in different beliefs. This development, wherever it occurred, generally resulted from church *government*. This theme, however, must be discussed in a different context.[126]

B. Pietism

Viewed *historically*, the idea of predestination is also the point of departure for the ascetic movement normally referred to as *Pietism*. As long as it remained inside the Reformist Church, a drawing of firm boundaries between Pietist Calvinists and non-Pietist Calvinists is nearly impossible.[127] Almost all of the major representatives of Puritanism have at times been considered to be Pietists. Moreover, it is fully legitimate to view all of the interconnections between the doctrine of predestination and the idea that the devout must testify to their belief as Pietist expansions upon Calvin's original doctrine. As noted, all of these interconnections are grounded in the interest in acquiring a state of subjective certainty regarding one's salvation (*certitudo salutis*).

The origin of asceticism's revival within Reformed communities has been, especially in Holland, very often associated with a rejuvenation of the doctrine of predestination, which had from time to time been forgotten or had become less viable. For this reason, in the case of England, one tends normally not to use the term "Pietism" at all.[128] But even Reformed Pietism on the Continent (in Holland and along the lower Rhine River [in southwestern Germany]) was, at first, primarily simply an intensification of Reformed asceticism, just as was the religious devoutness of Bayly, for example. The defining emphasis was so thoroughly shifted to the *praxis pietatis* [practice of piety in daily life] that dogmatic orthodoxy fell into the background and occasionally seemed merely a matter of indifference. Along with other sins, dogmatic errors at times might also occur among the predestined. And experience indicated that, for numerous Christians, the effects of their faith became manifest over time, despite their unfamiliarity with the basic theological issues. On the other hand, it became evident that mere theological knowledge would not at all introduce the sense of certainty regarding salvation that followed from a testifying to belief through conduct.[129]

Hence, membership among the elect could not be testified to through theological knowledge.[130] For this reason, amidst a mistrust of theology[131] and despite Pietism's continued official affiliation with the scholars and theologians (which belongs among its characteristic features), it began to gather the followers of the *praxis pietatis* into **conventicles** set apart from the world's mundane activities.[132] In doing so, Pietism wished to bring the invisible church of saints back to earth and to render it visible. The Pietists hoped to accomplish this, however, without following through in a fully consistent manner, that is, by supporting the formation of sects. Instead, protected in the conventicle community and separate from the world's influences, the Pietists attempted to lead lives oriented in all details to the will of God. In doing so, also in the visible aspects of their daily lives, they sought to remain certain of their own elect status. Through an intensified asceticism, the *ecclesiola* [assembly] of true converts wished already in this life to enjoy (as did all Pietist groups) the blissfulness of community with God.

This latter effort contained an element internally related to the Lutheran *unio mystica*. It very often led to a stronger cultivation of the element of *feeling* in religion than would be acceptable to the average Reformed Christian. To the extent that *our* vantage points come into consideration, *this* was the decisive feature to be addressed regarding the "Pietism" that developed in the soil of the Reformed Church. For those specific forms of medieval religious devotion possessing an inner affinity to feelings (which were fully foreign to Calvinist piety) channeled practical religious devotion in the direction of a this-worldly enjoyment of salvation, instead of in the direction of an ascetic struggle to acquire a certainty of salvation in the next life. Moreover, along the way, feelings *could* become subject to such an intensification that religious devotion acquired a clearly hysterical character.

As is familiar to us from innumerable examples, through a neuropathically grounded alternation between half-conscious conditions of religious ecstasy and periods of nervous exhaustion (which are perceived as "distant from God"), Pietists in *effect* aimed for the direct opposite of the dispassionate and strict discipline that took hold of all people adhering to the Puritan's systematized holy life. That is, Pietists aimed for a weakening of those "inhibitions" that bolstered the Calvinist's rational personality against the "affects."[133] Similarly, in the process the Calvinist idea of the depravity of all physical desires, if understood by Pietists in terms of *feelings* (for example, in the form of regret, shame, and guilt), *could* lead to a deadening of vitality in one's vocational calling.[134] Even the idea of predestination *could*, in contrast to the genuine tendency of rational Calvinist religious devotion, lead to fatalism if it became the object of a conversion based on mood and *feelings*.[135] Finally, the need to separate the chosen from the world *could*, if a powerful intensification of *feeling* occurred, lead to a kind of quasi-communistic, cloister-like community. This occurred repeatedly in Pietism and even in the Reformed church.[136]

As long, however, as Reformed Pietism did not strive for this extreme effect (which was produced by a cultivation of *feelings*) and sought instead to acquire certainty of salvation through a this-worldly *vocational* calling, Pietist principles had in the end two practical effects. They led to a *still* stricter ascetic control of the organized life in one's calling, and they anchored in religion the ethical significance of the calling even more firmly than did normal Reformed Christians (who were viewed by the "fine" Pietists as second-class believers practicing merely a worldly "respectability"). In Pietism, the religious aristocracy of the elect, who strove all the more to the forefront to the same extent that the development of Reformist asceticism was taken seriously, were henceforth organized voluntarily in the form of conventicles inside the church, as occurred in Holland. By contrast, in English Puritanism the religious aristocracy pushed in part for a formal distinction between active and passive believers in the *governing* of the church and (corresponding to the above analysis) in part for the formation of separate sects.

***

German Pietism, which is associated with the names of Spener, [the German theologian August Hermann] Francke [1663–1727], and Zinzendorf,[137] was founded on the soil of Lutheranism. It leads away from the doctrine of predestination. Nevertheless, this development does not necessarily take us away from the train of thought from which this doctrine had logically arisen. This proximity is visible in particular in the influence exercised by English-Dutch Pietism upon Spener, as he himself noted. It is apparent as well, for example, in the readings undertaken by Bayly in his first conventicles.[138]

At any rate, from *our* particular vantage point, in the end Pietism implies the penetration, into those geographical regions untouched by Calvinism, of the methodically cultivated and monitored life, that is, an *ascetic organization of life*.[139] Lutheranism, however, must have experienced this rational asceticism as a foreign element, and the lack of consistency in German Pietist doctrine was a result of the problems that grew out of the difficulties Lutheranism experienced with asceticism. In order to ground dogmatically the systematic-religious organization of life, Spener combines Lutheran trains of thought with distinctly Reformist elements: the notion that good works as such are undertaken with a view to the *honor* of God[140] and the Lutheran belief (which also resonated with the Reformed Church) in the possibility for the elect to arrive at a relative degree of Christian perfection.[141]

Yet precisely the element of logical consistency is lacking in Spener's theorizing. Although the organized Christian life was also essential for the Pietism of Spener (who was strongly influenced by mysticism[142]), he weakened its systematic character. In a somewhat unclear, but essentially Lutheran, way of describing more than grounding, Spener never attempted to derive the *certitudo salutis* [certainty of salvation] from a striving by the believer toward elect status. Instead of the idea of a testifying through conduct to one's belief, he selected the less strict Lutheran notion of faith (as discussed earlier) as the mechanism through which the believer could feel certain of his salvation.[143]

As long, however, as the rational-ascetic component in Pietism retained the upper hand over the element of feeling, the ideas decisive for our vantage point again and again came forcefully to the fore. First, the methodical development of the believer's own holiness in the direction of ever higher degrees of consolidation and perfection, as monitored by conformity to *God's laws,* constitutes in Pietism a *sign* of one's state of grace.[144] Second, it is God's providence *at work* in just this improvement by the faithful; after patient waiting and *methodical reflection,* He is giving a favoring sign to believers.[145] Work in a calling was also for Francke the ascetic means *par excellence.*[146] He was firmly convinced (as were the Puritans, as we shall see) that God himself, through the success of the believer's work, was blessing His chosen.

Moreover, as a surrogate (*surrogat*) for the "double decree" [according to which a few were saved and most were condemned], Pietism created ideas that were essentially the same, although less vibrant, than those following from the idea of predestination (for example, the idea that God's special grace had established an aristocracy of the elect).[147] The same psychological consequences of this idea followed for both Pietists and Calvinists (as described above). Included among them, for example, was so-called *Terminism,*[148] which had been generally imputed to Pietism by its opponents (doubtless incorrectly). Although it was universal, this teaching assumed that salvation would be offered either only once in a lifetime (and then at a specific moment) or at some moment for the last time.[149] Those who miss this particular moment can no longer be helped by the axiom of universal grace. Thus, Terminists found themselves in the same situation as those under Calvinism who had been neglected by God.

In effect, this Terminist theory came quite close, for example, to Francke's position. Abstracted from his personal experiences and widely dispersed throughout Pietism (and perhaps even dominant within it), his theory assumed that grace could be acquired only under unique circumstances. It would appear once and in a particular manner, namely, after "penitence" had led to a "breakthrough."[150] Yet not everyone, according to the Pietists' own views, was predisposed to have such an experience. On the one hand, those unable to induce it, in spite of instructions by the Pietists in the use of ascetic methods to this end, were viewed by the chosen as belonging to a type of passive

Christian. On the other hand, through the creation of a *method* for bringing about "penitence," the attainment of God's grace also became, in effect, for the Pietists the goal of a *rational* human program. And the many reservations regarding private confession (which were shared broadly among Pietists, although not by Francke, for example), as indicated by the repeated questions addressed to Spener, especially by Pietist *pastors*, arose out of this idea of grace as reserved for a few only. These reservations, as also occurred in Lutheranism, contributed to a weakening of the foundations of the confessional. It was now more and more believed that the *effect* of grace, as acquired through repentance and as visible in holy *conduct*, must be decisive for admission to Confession. Mere "contrition" would never suffice.[151]

Zinzendorf's idea of a religious *self*-judgment repeatedly merged into the idea of the believer as a "tool" in God's hands. This merging occurred even though, as a result of orthodox attacks, this idea vacillated. Admittedly, the conceptual framework of Zinzendorf—this remarkable "religious dilettante," as [the distinguished German Protestant theologian Albrecht] Ritschl [1822–89] called him—can scarcely be clearly comprehended in respect to the themes important for us.[152] Zinzendorf described himself repeatedly as a representative of "Pauline-Lutheran Christianity" and as *against* the "Pietistic-Jansenists,"[153] who were fixated upon the *commandments*. Zinzendorf, however (despite his own Lutheranism,[154] which he continuously emphasized), permitted the practices of the Brethren Congregation.[155] As is evident in their notarized protocol of August 12, 1729, he even supported them in spite of positions that clearly corresponded in many respects to the Calvinist idea of an aristocracy of the elect.[156] The much discussed attribution of the Old Testament to Jesus Christ, in the protocols of November 12, 1741, expressed a somewhat similar notion (also externally). Moreover, of the three "branches" within the Brethren Congregation, the more Calvinist branch and the more Moravian branch were from the beginning essentially oriented to the vocational ethic of the Reformed Church. Finally, fully in accordance with the Puritan position, Zinzendorf expressed the view (in his talks with John Wesley) that, even though the chosen may not always be aware of their elect status, *others* could *recognize*, from the manner of their conduct, their status as among the saved.[157]

***

By contrast, however, the element of feeling became very prominent in the particular piety of the Herrnhuter branch of the Brethren movement.[158] These believers repeatedly sought out Zinzendorf, in particular, in order to thwart directly the tendency in his community toward the striving, in the Puritan sense, to elect status through asceticism.[159] Instead, they wished to bend the notion of good works in a Lutheran direction.[160] Moreover, there developed in Zinzendorf's Pietism, influenced by those who rejected the conventicles and wished to maintain Confession, an essentially Lutheran-influenced tendency to bind the mediation of salvation to the sacraments. Finally, certain aspects of Zinzendorf's own positions had the effect of strongly counteracting the rationalism of the organized and directed life; for example, his view that the *childlike nature* of the religious experience is best understood as a sign of its genuineness (a basic principle particular to him), and that the drawing of *lots* constitutes a device to reveal God's will.

Indeed, such views standing against the rational organization of the believer's life became so prominent that, as far as Zinzendorf's impact is concerned,[161] on the whole anti-rational, *feeling*-based elements played the greater role (as apparent in the piety of the Herrnhuter much more than in other branches of Pietism).[162] The connection between moral conduct and the forgiveness of sins in [the Pietist Bishop August Gottlieb] Spangenberg's [1704–92][163] volume, *Idea Fidei Fratrum* [Idea of Brotherly Trust], is likewise weak,[164] as in Lutheranism in general. Zinzendorf's rejection of the Methodist striving for perfection corresponds, here as well as elsewhere, to his basically eudaemonistical ideal. He wished, namely, to allow believers, even in the *present*,[165] to experience salvation (or "blessedness") through *feelings*. Moreover, Zinzendorf opposed advising the faithful to follow the Calvinist route; that is, he opposed the effort to acquire certainty of salvation for the *next life* through rational work and an organization of their present lives.[166]

Nonetheless, [other elements in Zinzendorf's teachings had the effect of introducing the organized and directed life among believers]. An idea unique to the Brethren Congregation remained viable in Zinzendorf's theology: the idea that the decisive value in the activity of the Christian life lies in missionary work and (as thereby brought into association with it) in work in a calling.[167] In addition, the practical rationalization of life from the standpoint of *utility* was an essential component of Zinzendorf's view of life.[168] Similar to other representatives of Pietism, this rationalization followed for him, on the one hand, from his firm dislike of philosophical speculation (which, he believed, endangered religious belief) and his corresponding favoring of isolated empirical information,[169] and on the other hand from the professional missionary's shrewd knowledge of the world. As the fulcrum of missionary activity, the Brethren Congregation was also a business organization, one that directed its members into paths of inner-worldly asceticism. Exactly in the manner of a business, Pietist asceticism first sought "tasks" to undertake and then, in a dispassionate and planned manner, to organize life in reference to them.

However, the ideal of the Christian apostles' missionary life, from which arose the glorification of the charisma of apostolic *propertylessness* among the "disciples" (chosen by God through "predestination"),[170] opposed Pietism's further development in this direction. Indeed, this apostolic ideal constituted an obstacle that effectively meant a partial rejuvenation of the privilege of receiving advice from the *consilia evangelica* [Catholic Church hierarchy]. This development certainly inhibited in Pietism the creation of a rational ethic, in the manner of Calvinism, for the believer's vocational calling, even though it was not precluded (as the example of the baptizing movement's transformation will shortly demonstrate). An idea of work as occurring *solely* "for the sake of a calling" [as in Calvinism] strongly prepared the pathway—far more effectively and on the basis of an internal relationship—toward such a vocational ethic.

***

In summary, if we consider German Pietism from the vantage point that *for us* is here central, we must confirm, all in all, a vacillation and instability in regard to the religious anchoring of its asceticism. The anchoring of Pietism in asceticism is considerably weaker than the iron-clad consistency of Calvinism's grounding in asceticism. In part Lutheran influences and in part the *feeling* character of Pietist religious devotion account for the weakening of asceticism in Pietism.

To depict this feeling component as, compared to *Lutheranism*, something unique to Pietism is surely a great simplification.[171] In any event, however, in comparison to *Calvinism*, the intensity of the rationalization of life in Pietism must necessarily be less. The reason is that the inner motive deriving from the thought of having to testify, over and over again from the beginning, to a state of grace that gives security for an eternal *future* has in Pietism, owing to its orientation to the believer's feelings, been re-directed onto the *present*. In place of the certainty that the predestined ever strove to attain anew through restless and successful work in a calling, there came humility, timidity, exhaustion, and insecurity.[172] In part, these qualities were a consequence of an awakening of feelings in Pietism oriented exclusively to spiritual experiences, and in part they resulted from the Lutheran form of confession. Although indeed viewed in many ways with deep skepticism, Pietism still tolerated this form of confession for the most part.[173]

Precisely that uniquely Lutheran way of seeking salvation is manifest in all this. The "forgiveness of sins" rather than a practical "striving toward holiness" is crucial here. In place of the systematic and rational searching to acquire and maintain certain *knowledge* of one's future (next-worldly) salvation stands the need to *feel* a (this-worldly) reconciliation and community with God now. As in economic life, where the inclination to enjoy the present conflicts with the rational organization of the "economy" (which is rooted of course in a provision for the future), so it is, in a certain sense, in the arena of religious life.

Hence, on the one hand the orientation of religious need toward a spiritual *feeling*-emotion (*Gefühlsaffektion*) in the present evidently implies, in contrast to the need of the Reformed elect to testify to their belief (which is oriented exclusively to the next world), a *hindrance* upon any formation of motivations toward the rationalization of this-worldly *action*. On the other hand, the Pietist's orientation to the present and feelings was nonetheless clearly capable of developing a more *methodical* penetration by religion into the entire organization of life than the orientation to faith of the orthodox Lutheran, which remained bound to scripture and the sacraments. From Francke and Spener to Zinzendorf, Pietism as a whole developed an *increasing* emphasis on the feeling aspect of belief. This emphasis, however, was not the result of some "developmental tendency" inherent to Pietism that expressed itself in this manner. Rather, these differences vis-à-vis Lutheranism and Calvinism followed from contrasts in the religious (and social) contexts out of which their leading representatives arose. This point cannot be explored now, nor can a further theme: how the uniqueness of German Pietism became manifest in its social and geographical *distribution* in Germany.[174]

At this point, we should once again remind ourselves that Pietism's emphasis on the believer's feelings, in contrast to the Puritan elect's religious organization of life, is of course a distinction that shades off into a series of gradual transitions. Nevertheless, if a reference to one practical consequence of this difference may be permitted here (at least in a provisional way), one could note that the virtues cultivated in Pietism tended more often to be those developed on the one hand by the civil servant, middle-management employee, worker, and craftsman "dedicated and devoted to their occupations,"[175] and on the other hand by the employer who adopts a predominantly patriarchal and *condescending* stance toward his workers that is pleasing to God (in the manner of Zinzendorf). In comparison, the virtues cultivated by Calvinism appear to stand in a relationship of greater **elective affinity** to the restrained, strict, and active posture of capitalist employers of the middle class.[176] Finally, as Ritschl[177] has already emphasized, the *purely* feeling-based variety of Pietism is a religious toy for the "leisure classes."

This discussion has in no way offered an exhaustive characterization of Pietism. Nevertheless, the conclusions arrived at here correspond to certain differences in the unique economic orientations of peoples under the influence of the Pietist or the Calvinist forms of asceticism. These differences are visible even today.

C. Methodism

The linking of a feeling-based, yet also ascetic, religious devotion with an increasing indifference to, or rejection of, the dogmatic foundations of Calvinist asceticism also characterizes *Methodism*, the English-American counterpart to continental Pietism.[178] The name already indicates what struck contemporaries as unique to its followers: the "methodical" and systematic organization of life with the aim of attaining the *certitudo salutis*. *This* was the concern of the faithful from the beginning in this church also, and the question of certainty regarding salvation remained at the center of all religious seeking.

Despite all the differences between them, the undoubted affinity of Methodism with certain branches of German Pietism[179] is visible above all in the carrying over of this methodicalness, in particular, into the inducement of the *feeling-based* act of "conversion." Moreover, owing to Methodism's orientation from the beginning to missionary work among the common people, the feeling component (awakened in

John Wesley through Herrnhuter-Lutheran influences) took on a very strongly *emotional* character, especially on American soil. Belief in God's undeserved grace (and with it, simultaneously, the direct awareness of exculpation and forgiveness) resulted under certain circumstances from an intensification of the penitence struggle to the point of the most alarming states of ecstasy. Indeed, Methodists in America preferred to seek this ecstasy on the "anxious bench."[180]

This emotional religious devotion entered into a peculiar coalition, despite significant inner difficulties, with an ascetic ethic that had been stamped, once and for all, with an element of Puritan *rationality*. In contrast to Calvinism, which held all orientation to feelings to be a delusion and therefore suspect, Methodism, in principle, at first viewed the purely *felt* absolute certainty of forgiveness as the single, undoubted foundation for the *certitudo salutis*. Believers were convinced that this state of feeling flowed from the unmediated presence of the Holy Spirit, the appearance of which could be normally specified by day and hour. According to Wesley's teachings, which present a consistent intensification of Calvinist doctrine on the striving of the devout toward salvation (though they were also a decisive departure from this orthodoxy), one who is saved in this manner can acquire "salvation" even in this life. By virtue of the effect of divine grace within the believer, such "salvation" occurs through a second (normally separate and likewise often sudden) spiritual process: a striving toward salvation that leads to the acquisition of a consciousness of *perfection*, in the sense of being without sin.

However difficult it may be to reach this goal (which is acquired for most only near the end of life), a striving to reach it is absolutely necessary. It guarantees definitely the *certitudo salutis* and substitutes a happy certainty for the "moody" brooding of the Calvinists.[181] Moreover, striving to attain this consciousness of perfection marks the true convert, to himself and to others, as a person over whom sin, at least, "no longer has any power." Therefore, despite the decisive significance to Methodists of *feelings*, which offer evidence to believers themselves of their salvation, an orientation to *God's laws*, because it indicates holy conduct, must also be maintained.

***

[Wesley further clarified the nature of this conduct.] Wherever he struggled against those who, in his time, advocated the performance of good works as the means toward salvation, his efforts ultimately had the effect of rejuvenating again an old Puritan idea: good works are not the actual cause of salvation, but only the means to recognize whether one is among the saved. Moreover, this recognition can occur only if the good works are carried out exclusively for God's glory. To Wesley, the correct conduct did not *alone* suffice, as he had learned from his own experience; rather, the *feeling* of being among the saved must also be present. (Wesley himself occasionally described good works as a "condition" for salvation, and he emphasized, in the Declaration of August 9, 1771,[182] that those who fail to perform good works are not among the truly devout.) In this manner, the Methodists have continuously stressed that they are distinguished from the Anglican Church, namely, by the type of their piety rather than by their doctrine. For Methodists, the significance of the "fruit" of belief was normally grounded in 1 John 3:9 ["No one born of God commits sin; for God's nature abides in him, and he cannot sin because he is born of God"], and conduct was understood as a clear *sign* of membership among the saved.

Nevertheless, difficulties remained for Methodists.[183] For those devout who held to the doctrine of predestination, a displacement of the *certitudo salutis* away from a consciousness of being among the saved, which had followed from the ascetic organization of life itself and the continuous testifying through conduct to one's belief, and toward the unmediated *feeling* of grace and perfection[184] (because the certainty of the believer's *perseverantia* [resoluteness] now became connected to the penitence struggle, which occurred only *once*) signified one of two outcomes. Either, as in the case of weak natures, a bleak interpretation of "Christian freedom" as unreachable, and hence a collapse of the methodical organization of life followed; or, whenever this conclusion was rejected, a certainty among the saved[185] that climaxed in dizzying heights—namely, a *feeling-based* intensification of the Puritan model.

In light of attacks by opponents, Methodists sought to address these two outcomes. On the one hand, they did so through an increased emphasis on the normative validity of the Bible and the indispensability of a testifying to belief through conduct.[186] On the other hand, and as a consequence of this increased emphasis, they did so by strengthening anti-Calvinist doctrines within Methodism, namely, Wesley's teaching that grace can be lost. Wesley's vulnerability[187] to strong Lutheran influences, as mediated by the Brethren Congregation, strengthened this development and increased the *indeterminateness* of the religious orientation of Methodist morality.[188] In the end, essentially only the concept of "regeneration" was consistently maintained: the belief that a directly manifest certainty of salvation based on feeling resulted from the believer's *faith*. Regeneration served as the indispensable foundation for the believer's state of grace and it implied striving toward salvation. To the extent this process of making the believer holy followed, this implied a freedom (at least fictitious) from the power of sin, and as well a corresponding devaluation of the significance of the external means of grace, especially the sacraments. In any event, an intensification of the doctrine of predestined grace and Election characterized the "Great Awakening" that everywhere followed Methodism (for example, in New England).[189]

***

Thus for *our* investigation, in terms of its ethic, Methodism appears to be a social formation as precariously grounded as Pietism. The striving for the "higher life," however, also served Methodism, as it did Pietism, as a "second blessing," namely, as a type of surrogate doctrine of predestination. Moreover, growing from the soil of England, Methodism oriented its ethical practice fully toward England's Reformed Christianity, wishing to be its "revival." Accordingly, the emotional act of conversion was *methodically* induced. Once attained, a pious enjoyment of a sense of community with God did not exist in Methodism, unlike in Zinzendorf's Pietism based on feeling. Rather, awakened feeling in Methodism was immediately guided into the pathway of a rational striving for perfection.

Hence, the emotional character of Methodist religious devotion never led to a spiritual Christianity based on feeling in the manner of German Pietism. That this distinction was connected to a theology in Methodism that placed less emphasis on development of the feeling of *sinfulness* (in part precisely owing to the emotional pathway followed in the conversion process) has already been demonstrated by Schneckenburger, and his argument has remained unchallenged in subsequent scholarship. Rather, the *Reformist* foundation of Methodism's religious sensibility remained central. The arousal of feelings took the form of an occasional, *korybantenartig* [boisterous] but then restrained, enthusiasm. As such, it failed to detract from the rational character of the Methodist organization of life.[190]

In this way, Methodism's "regeneration" produced in the end only a *complementary* component to the pure idea of salvation through good works: a religious anchoring of the ascetic organization of life after the idea of predestination had been abandoned. The sign offered by conduct, which was indispensable as an indication of the believer's true conversion (its "precondition," as Wesley occasionally noted), was substantively the same as in Calvinism. In the following discussion of the idea of the calling,[191] we will see that Methodism, as a later theology,[192] contributed nothing new to its development.[193] Hence it can be essentially left aside.

D. The Baptizing Sects and Churches[194]

The Pietism of the European Continent and the Methodism of the Anglo-Saxon peoples are secondary developments both in respect to their ideas and their historical unfolding.[195] On the other hand, the second (next to Calvinism) *independent* carrier of Protestant asceticism was the *baptizing* movement and the sects[196] that arose from it in the course of the sixteenth and seventeenth centuries, either directly or through the assimilation of its forms of religious thinking: namely, the *Baptists*, *Mennonites*, and, above all, the *Quakers*.[197] With these sects, we arrive at religious communities that possess ethics resting in principle upon a foundation opposed to Reformist doctrines. The following brief overview, which of course calls attention only to that which is important to *us* here, will not do justice to the diversity of this movement. Once again, the primary emphasis will be placed on developments in the older capitalist countries.

We have already become acquainted with the rudiments of the idea that is historically, and in principle, most important in all of these communities (although its scope for cultural development can become fully clear to us only in a different context): the "believers' church."[198] According to this notion, the religious community (the "visible church" in the terminology of the churches of the Reformation[199]) was no longer viewed as a sort of repository of trust established to serve supernatural aims, that is, as an *institution* (*Anstalt*) that necessarily included both the saved and the unsaved, whether in order to increase the glory of God (Calvinism) or to mediate salvation to persons (Catholicism and Lutheranism). Rather, the religious community now became viewed as a community of *sincere believers and the elect*—and only these persons.

In other words, it existed as a "sect"[200] rather than as a "church." The manifest principle of the sect—exclusively those adults who have innerly acquired and then overtly declared sincere belief are to be baptized—should symbolize this understanding of the religious community.[201]

For the baptizing sects, "justification" of a person's devoutness *through* this belief, which was confirmed repeatedly and insistently in all discussions among the faithful, was radically different from the idea of a "public" *imputation* of devoutness to a person, as prevailed in the orthodox dogma of the old Protestantism [Lutheranism].[202] Rather, this justification in the sects involved more of a *spiritual conversion to belief* in Christ's sacrifice and gift of salvation. This conversion occurred through an individual *revelation*, that is, through the effect of the Holy Spirit inside the believer—and *only* in this manner. This revelation was offered to everyone. The devout must simply wait for the Holy Spirit and avoid resisting His arrival through their sinful attachment to the mundane world.

As a consequence, the significance of faith—in the sense of the knowledge of church doctrine, though also in the sense of a penitent focusing on God's grace—moved now into the background. Instead, a renaissance of the spiritual-religious ideas of early Christianity (though naturally with strong modifications) occurred.[203] The sects, for example those for which Menno Simons created in his *Book of Fundamentals* of 1539 an acceptably closed doctrine, wanted to be *the* true, blameless Church of Christ, as did the other baptizing sects. Like the original community of apostles, they wished to be constituted exclusively from believers *personally* awakened and called by God. The elect, and only the elect, are brothers in Christ, for they, like Christ, have been created spiritually directly from God.[204] To the first baptizing communities, the consequence of these ideas was apparent: faith did not suffice. Instead, members should practice a strict *avoidance* of "the world." Only absolutely necessary interactions with nonmembers were permitted. Moreover, following the exemplary life of the first generations of Christians, sect members must engage in the strictest study of the Bible. Indeed, as long as the old spirit of these sects remained alive, this principle of avoidance of the world never fully disappeared.[205]

These motives dominated the baptizing sects' early period. They retained from this period a principle that we have already become acquainted with from Calvinism (even though somewhat differently grounded): the absolute *condemnation of all deification of human wants and desires*, for their cultivation rendered worthless the reverence owed exclusively to God.[206] The fundamental importance of this principle will repeatedly come to the fore. The organization of life according to the Bible was viewed by the first generation in the baptizing communities from Switzerland and southwest Germany in a radical manner similar to that found originally in St. Francis: a sharp rejection of all worldly pleasures and a strict conformity with the lives of the apostles should prevail. In fact the lives of many of the first adherents of these sects remind one of the life of St. Giles [the eighth century monk and "helper in need" in France and Switzerland].

This exceptionally strict adherence to the authority[207] of the Bible, however, stood somewhat weakly against the spiritual character of religious devoutness. What God had revealed to the prophets and the apostles was not all that He could, or wanted, to reveal. On the contrary, according to the testimony of the early Christian community (as the German mystic [Kaspar von] Schwenckfeld [1489–1581][208] taught against Luther, and [the Quaker] Fox later taught against the Presbyterians), the long-term endurance of scripture constituted the single identifying mark of the true church. This mark was manifest in the daily lives of the faithful (rather than simply as a written document) and as the effective power of the Holy Spirit, who speaks directly to those individuals who want to hear Him. A well-known doctrine arose from this idea of continuing revelation, which was later developed by the Quakers in a consistent fashion. According to it, the inner manifestation of the Holy Spirit as reason and *conscience* is of ultimate importance. With this teaching, the exclusive authority of the Bible was pushed aside, though not its validity.

Simultaneously, a further development was introduced that ultimately resulted in the radical removal of all remnants of the Catholic Church's doctrine of salvation. Together with all churches that upheld predestination (and above all the strict Calvinists), all denominations with adult baptism practiced the most radical devaluation of all sacraments as means to salvation. In the case of the Quakers, this removal included the abandonment of even the sacraments of christening and communion.[209] Hence, a process that "eliminated magic" from the world was placed into motion by these denominations and carried through to its final conclusion. Only that "inner light" of continuing revelation now enabled believers to acquire true understanding, even of the biblical revelations of God.[210]

On the other hand, at least according to Quaker teachings, which here drew matters out to their full conclusion, the effect of this inner light could be extended to persons who had never known the biblical form of revelation. The dictum *extra ecclesiam nulla salus* [no salvation outside of the Church] was valid only for this *in*visible church of those penetrated by the Holy Spirit. *Without* the inner light, human beings, and even persons guided by natural reason, remained pure creatures of desires and wants.[211] All baptizing congregations, including the Quakers, felt the Godlessness of such persons to be reprehensible, indeed almost as much as did the Calvinists. Nevertheless, the rebirth that the Holy Spirit brings, if we *wait for Him* and inwardly give ourselves over to Him, *can* lead to a condition—because caused by God—in which the power of sin is completely overcome.[212] This condition can be so intense that relapses, or even the loss of the state of grace, actually become impossible. Yet, as a rule (as later in Methodism), the attainment of this intense condition does not occur. Rather, a developmental process much more determines the degree of perfection achieved by an individual.

All baptizing communities, however, wanted *pure* congregations, in the sense of members of blameless conduct. The inner disengagement from the world and its mundane interests and the unconditional submission to the domination of God, who speaks to believers through their conscience, were also themselves unerring signs of one's saved status. Corresponding conduct was thus a necessity for salvation. As a gift from God, salvation could not be earned. Nevertheless, those who lived according to their conscience—and only these devout believers—were permitted to view themselves as among the saved. In this sense "good works" were *causa sine qua non* [indispensable] if believers were to see themselves as among the saved.

***

It is apparent that this series of ideas, which we have summarized from the writings of [the Quaker Robert] Barclay [1648–1686], is the same as the Reformed doctrine for all practical purposes. Surely it was developed under the influence of Calvinist asceticism, which existed before the rise of the baptizing sects in England and Holland. During the entire first period of his missionary activity, George Fox preached on behalf of a serious and spiritual conversion to this asceticism. Because the baptizing sects rejected the notion of predestination, however, the specifically *methodical* character of their morality rested psychologically primarily on the idea of *waiting* for the effect of the Holy Spirit. Even today this idea provides the defining characteristic of the "Quaker Meeting." It has been aptly analyzed by Barclay.

The overcoming of the instinctive and the irrational, as well as the passions and the prejudices—that is, of the "natural" human being—is the aim of this silent waiting. People must be silent in order to create the deep stillness in the soul that alone allows God to speak to them. Of course, the effect of this "waiting" *could* be to lead to conditions of anxiety or to prophecies regarding the future. Moreover, under certain conditions, and as long as eschatological hopes continued to exist, waiting might flow into an outburst of chiliastic[213] enthusiasm, as is possible in all similarly grounded types of piety (and as actually occurred in the sects that imploded in Münster).[214] "Waiting" was somewhat altered, however, as members of the baptizing congregations began to stream into this-worldly vocational callings. The original idea—God speaks only when creaturely drives are silent—was changed. The devout were now apparently taught to *deliberate* calmly before acting and to orient their action only after a careful investigation of the individual *conscience*.[215] This calm, dispassionate, and supremely *conscience*-bound disposition of character then became manifest in the practical life of the later baptizing communities (as occurred also, and to an unusual degree, among the Quakers).[216]

In the first generation, of course, things had been different. The leaders of the baptizing movement's oldest congregations were irredeemably radical in turning away from the mundane world. *Not all* believers, however, even in this period viewed the strict organization of life, in accord with the ideals of poverty of the apostles, as unconditionally required for proof of one's saved status. Even wealthy persons were found in this generation. Indeed, even before Menno, who stood squarely on the soil of the this-worldly vocational virtues and in support of private property, the serious and strict morality of the baptizing groups had in practice turned in this direction. The facilitating groundwork for this turn had already been laid by Reformist ethics,[217] and the pathway in the direction of an *other*-worldly, monastic form of asceticism had been, since Luther, precluded. He had condemned monasticism as not in conformity with the Bible's teachings and as involving an ethos of good works. The baptizing congregations, as had others, followed Luther on these points.

Despite these developments toward the notion of a this-worldly vocational calling, the baptizing sects did not yet move unequivocally in this direction. Even leaving aside the quasi-communistic communities of the early period (which cannot be discussed here), residuals remained of the radical turning away from the mundane world evident in the movement's oldest congregations. One baptizing sect, the so-called Dunckers (*Dompelaers*) [in Germany, founded in 1708],[218] has continued to condemn higher forms of education up to our own time, as well as every possession that went beyond life's basic necessities. Moreover, for Barclay, for example, the notion of "being true to one's vocational calling" is not conceptualized in the manner of the Calvinists or even the Lutherans. Instead, following St. Thomas of Aquinas, Barclay comprehended it as *naturali ratione* [naturally rational], namely, as an unavoidable *result* of the entanglement of the faithful in the world's activities.[219]

Nevertheless, and even though we can see in these views a weakening of the Calvinist notion of the calling similar to that found in many of Spener's statements and in German Pietism, the intensity of interest in a this-worldly vocational calling among the baptizing sects essentially *increased*. There were various reasons. First, the increase resulted from a rejection of employment in all state offices, a rejection that was originally understood as stemming from a religious duty to withdraw from the world. This view endured, at least in practice, for the Mennonites and Quakers (even after it had been abandoned in principle) as a consequence of their strict refusal to use weapons and to swear oaths (refusals that disqualified a person to hold civil service positions). Second, together with this disqualification there developed an insurmountable opposition in all of the baptizing denominations to every sign of an aristocratic style of life (*Lebensstil*). This opposition arose in part as a consequence of the prohibition against all deification of human wants and desires (as it did for the Calvinists) and in part as a result of the apolitical (or even anti-political) principles just mentioned.

In these ways the entire dispassionate and conscientious, methodical organization of life among the baptizing communities was pushed down the pathway of the *a*political vocational life. In the process, the immense significance awarded by their salvation doctrine to the monitoring of action by the conscience (the very capacity to do so was viewed as an individualized revelation from God) now gave a particular orientation to conduct in vocational life. In turn, this conduct had great significance for the development of important aspects of the capitalist spirit.

This theme of this-worldly asceticism will become more familiar to us in the following chapter. However, it can be addressed only to the extent that it appears possible to do so without entering into a consideration of the entire political and social ethics of Protestant asceticism. We will then note (if a single point may here be alluded to) that the specific form taken by this-worldly asceticism among the baptizing congregations, especially the Quakers,[220] was expressed, according to the judgment of the seventeenth century, in the practical testifying of believers to that important principle of the capitalist "ethic" previously cited in the treatise by Benjamin Franklin: "honesty is the best policy."[221] In contrast, we will surmise that the effects of Calvinism are more to be seen in the direction of unchaining the private economy's energy to expand. For Goethe's maxim, despite the formal legality of the business activity of the Calvinist "saints," remained in the end often valid also for these devout believers: "Those who act are always without a conscience; only those who observe have a conscience."[222]

The full significance of a third important reason that contributed to the intensity of the baptizing denominations' this-worldly asceticism can be addressed only in another context. Nevertheless, a few observations on this subject may be made now, if only to justify the procedure chosen here for our presentation.

***

We have intentionally decided here *not* to commence our discussion with a consideration of the objective social institutions of the old Protestant churches and their ethical influence. We have especially decided not to begin with a discussion of *church discipline*, even though it is very important. Instead, we will first examine the effects on *each believer's* organization of life that are possible when *individuals* convert to a religious devoutness anchored in asceticism. We will proceed in this manner for two reasons: this side of our theme has until now received far less attention, and the effect of church discipline cannot be viewed as always leading in the same direction.

In those regions where a Calvinist state church held sway, the authoritarian supervision (*kirchenpolizeiliche Kontrolle*) of the believer's life was practiced to a degree that rivaled an inquisition. This supervision *could* work even *against* that emancipation of individual energies originating out of the believer's ascetic striving to methodically acquire a sense of certainty as belonging among the saved. It did so under certain circumstances. Just as mercantilist regimentation by the state could indeed give birth to industries but not (at least not alone) to the capitalist "spirit" (which this regimentation crippled in various ways, wherever it assumed a despotic-authoritarian character), the church's regimentation of asceticism could have the same effect. Wherever the church developed too far in a harshly authoritarian direction, it coerced believers into adhering to specific forms of external behavior. In doing so, however, under certain circumstances the church then crippled the individual's motivation to organize life in a methodical manner.

Every explanation of this point[223] must note the great difference between the effects of the despotic-authoritarianism of state *churches* and the effects of the despotism of *sects*. The latter rests upon voluntary subjection. The creation by the baptizing movement, in all its denominations, of "sects" rather than "churches" contributed to the intensity of its asceticism. Such intensity occurred as well, to varying degrees, in the Calvinist, Pietist, and Methodist communities. In *practice*, all were pushed in the direction of forming voluntary communities.[224]

***

It is now our task to follow out the effect of the Puritan idea of a vocational calling on how people *acquire goods and* ***earn a living***. We are now prepared to do so, having attempted to offer in this chapter a sketch of the way in which the religious anchoring of the calling idea developed. Although differences in details and variations in emphasis exist in the diverse communities of religious asceticism, the vantage points decisive for us have been present and manifest, in effective ways, in all of these groups.[225]

To recapitulate, decisive again and again for our investigation was the conception of the religious "state of grace." Reappearing in all the denominations as a particular status, this state of grace separated people from the depravity of physical desires and from "this-world."[226] Although attained in a variety of ways depending upon the dogma of the particular denomination, possession of the state of grace could *not* be guaranteed through magical-sacramental means of any kind, through the relief found in confession, or through particular good works. Rather, it could be acquired only through a *testifying to belief.* Sincere belief became apparent in specifically formed conduct unmistakably different from the style of life of the "natural" human being. For the person testifying to belief there followed a *motivation* to *methodically supervise* his or her state of grace. An organizing and directing of life ensued and, in the process, its penetration by *asceticism*.

As we noted, this ascetic style of life implied a *rational* formation of the entire being (*Dasein*) and the complete orientation of this being toward God's Will. Moreover, this asceticism was *no longer opus supererogationis*, [an achievement within the capability of only a few], but one expected of all who wished to become certain of their salvation. Finally, and of central importance, the special life of the saint—fully separate from the "natural" life of the wants and desires—could no longer play itself out in monastic communities set apart from the world. Rather, the devoutly religious must now live saintly lives *in* the world and amidst its mundane affairs. This *rationalization* of the organized and directed life—now in the world yet still oriented to the supernatural—was the effect of ascetic Protestantism's *concept of the calling*.

At its beginning, Christian asceticism had fled from the world into the realm of solitude in the cloister. In renouncing the world, however, monastic asceticism had in fact come to dominate the world through the church. Yet, in retreating to the cloister, asceticism left the course of daily life in the world by and large in its natural and untamed state. But now Christian asceticism slammed the gates of the cloister, entered into the hustle and bustle of life, and undertook a new task: to saturate mundane, *everyday* life with its methodicalness. In the process, it sought to reorganize practical life into a rational life *in* the world rather than, as earlier, in the monastery. Yet this rational life in the world was *not of* this world or *for* this world. In our further exposition we will attempt to convey the results of this dramatic turn. ✦

CHAPTER V

ASCETICISM AND THE SPIRIT OF CAPITALISM

In order to comprehend the connections between the basic religious ideas of ***ascetic Protestantism*** and the maxims of everyday economic life, it is necessary above all to draw upon those theological texts that can be recognized as having crystallized out of the practice of pastoral care. In this [sixteenth- and seventeenth-century] epoch, everything depended upon one's relationship to the next life, and one's social position depended upon admission to the sacrament of communion.[1] Moreover, through pastoral care, church discipline, and preaching, the clergy's influence grew to such an extent (as any glance in the collected *consilia, casus conscientiae*, and other church documents will indicate[2]) that we today are *simply no longer* capable of comprehending its broad scope. Religious forces, as they became transmitted to populations through *these regular practices* of the clergy and became legitimate and accepted, were decisive for the formation of "national character."[3]

In contrast to later discussions in this chapter, we can *here* treat *ascetic Protestantism* as *a* unity. Because, however, English ***Puritanism,*** which grew out of Calvinism, provides the most consistent foundation for the *idea of a vocational* ***calling***, we are placing one of its representatives at the center of our analysis (in accord with our previous procedures). *Richard Baxter* [1615–1691] is distinguished from many other literary representatives of the Puritan ethic on the one hand by his eminently practical and peace-loving position and on the other by the universal acknowledgment accorded his works, which have been repeatedly reprinted and translated.

Baxter was a Presbyterian and apologist for the Westminster Synod, although in terms of dogma he moved gradually away from an orthodox Calvinism (like so many of the best clergymen of his time). Because he was hostile to every revolution, all sectarianism, and even the fanatical zeal of the "saints," he opposed Cromwell's usurpation. Yet Baxter remained unusually tolerant of all extreme positions and impartial toward his opponents. His own projects were essentially oriented toward a practical advancement of the religious-moral life. On behalf of these endeavors he offered his services, as one of the most successful practitioners of pastoral care known to history, equally to Parliament, to

Cromwell, and to the Restoration.[4] He continued to do so until he departed from his pulpit, which took place before St. Bartholomew's Day.[5]

Baxter's *Christian Directory* [1673] is the most comprehensive compendium of Puritan moral theology. Moreover, it is oriented throughout to the practical issues he dealt with in his pastoral care. In order to offer appropriate comparisons, Spener's *Theological Considerations* [1712], as representative of German Pietism, Barclay's *Apology* [1701], as representative of the Quakers, and occasionally other representatives of the ascetic ethic[6] will be referred to (generally in the endnotes, however, owing to space restrictions).[7]

***

If we examine Baxter's *Saints' Everlasting Rest* [1651] or his *Christian Directory* or even related works by others,[8] we are struck at first glance, in his judgments regarding wealth[9] and its acquisition, by his emphasis on the New Testament ebionitic[10] proclamations [which scorned wealth and idealized the poor].[11] Wealth as such is a serious danger and its temptations are constant. Moreover, in light of the overriding significance of God's kingdom, the pursuit[12] of wealth is seen as both senseless and morally suspect. Indeed, to Baxter, New Testament asceticism appeared oriented *against* every **striving** to acquire the products of this world in a far more pointed manner than Calvin, who never saw wealth among the clergy as a barrier to clerical effectiveness. On the contrary, according to Calvin wealth led to a thoroughly desirable increase of clerical prestige, and he allowed the clergy to acquire profit from their fortunes wherever it could be invested without causing difficulties. Yet in Puritan writings examples that condemn the pursuit of money and material goods can be accumulated without end. They can be contrasted with the ethical literature of the late medieval period, which was far less strict on this point. Moreover, the Puritan literature's suspicion of wealth was thoroughly serious. Its decisively ethical meaning and context, however, can be articulated only after somewhat closer scrutiny.

What is actually morally reprehensible is, namely, the *resting* upon one's possessions[13] and the *enjoyment* of wealth. To do so results in idleness and indulging desires of the flesh and above all in the distraction of believers from their pursuit of the "saintly" life. Furthermore, the possession of goods is suspect *only because* it carries with it the danger of this resting. The "saint's everlasting rest" comes in the next world. On earth, in this life, in order to become certain of one's state of grace, a person must "work the works of Him who sent him, while it is day" [John 9:4]. According to the will of God, which has been clearly revealed, *only activity*, not idleness and enjoyment, serves to increase His glory.[14]

Hence, of all the sins, *the wasting of time* constitutes the first and, in principle, the most serious. A single life offers an infinitely short and precious space of time to "make firm" one's own election. The loss of time through sociability, "idle talk,"[15] sumptuousness,[16] and even through more sleep than is necessary for good health[17] (six to eight hours at most) is absolutely morally reprehensible.[18] Franklin's maxim — "time is money"—is not yet expressed by Baxter, yet this axiom holds in a certain spiritual sense. Because every hour not spent at work is an hour lost in service to God's greater glory, according to Baxter, time is infinitely valuable.[19] Thus, inactive contemplation is without value and in the end explicitly condemned, at least if it occurs at the expense of work in a calling,[20] for it pleases God *less* than the active implementation of His will in a calling.[21] At any rate, Sundays exist for contemplation. For Baxter, it is always those who are idle in their vocational callings who have no time for God, even on the day of rest.[22]

Accordingly, a sermon on the virtues of hard and continuous physical or mental *work* is continuously repeated, occasionally almost with passion, throughout Baxter's major treatise.[23] Two motives come together here.[24]

First, work is the tried and proven *mechanism* for the practice of *asceticism*. For this reason, work has been held in high esteem in the Catholic Church from the beginning,[25] in sharp contrast not only to the Middle East but also to almost all the regulations followed by non-Christian monks throughout the world.[26] Indeed, work constitutes a particular defense mechanism against all those temptations summarized by the Puritan notion of the "unclean life." The part played by these temptations is by no means a small one. Sexual asceticism in Puritanism is different only in degree, and not in principle, from that in monastic practice. As a result of the Puritan conception of marriage, sexual asceticism is more comprehensive simply because, even in marriage, sexual intercourse is permitted *only* as a means, desired by God, to increase His glory through the fulfillment of His commandment: "be fruitful and multiply."[27] Just as it is a bulwark against all religious doubt and unrestrained torment, the admonition "work hard in your calling" constitutes a prescription against all sexual temptations (as do a temperate diet, vegetarianism, and cold baths).[28]

Second, in addition and above all, as ordained by God, the purpose of life *itself* involves work.[29] [The Apostle] Paul's maxim applies to everyone without qualification: "if anyone will not work, let him not eat."[30] An unwillingness to work is a sign that one is not among the saved.[31]

The divergence of Puritanism from medieval Catholicism becomes clearly evident here. Thomas Aquinas also interpreted Paul's maxim. Work is simply a *naturali ratione* [naturally rational] necessity, according to him,[32] in order to maintain the life of the individual and that of the community. Paul's maxim, however, ceases to hold wherever this aim is not relevant, for it offers simply a general prescription for all and fails to address each person's situation. That is, it does not pertain to those people who can, without working, live from their possessions. Similarly, contemplation as a spiritual form of activity in God's kingdom naturally takes priority over this maxim in its literal sense. In addition, according to popular theology, the highest form of monastic "productivity" was to be found in the increase of the *thesaurus ecclesiae* [the church's spiritual treasures] through prayer and choir service.

These violations of the ethical duty to work were, of course, abandoned by Baxter. In addition, and with great emphasis, he hardened his basic principle that even wealth does not free people from Paul's unconditional maxim.[33] For Baxter even those with many possessions shall not eat without working. As God's commandment, this maxim remains in effect even if it is not necessary for people to work in order to fulfill their needs. The wealthy, just like the poor, must be obedient to this principle.[34] Besides, God's providence reserves a calling for everyone without distinction. It is to be recognized by each person, and each person should work within his calling, according to Baxter. Moreover, this calling is not, as in Lutheranism,[35] a fate to which believers must submit and reconcile themselves. Rather, it is God's command to each person to act on behalf of His honor.

This seemingly inconsequential nuance had broad-ranging psychological consequences. It went together with the Puritan understanding of the **providential** interpretation of the economic cosmos familiar to us from the Scholastics.[36] Yet the Puritan outlook (*Anschauung*) constituted a further development of Scholasticism's ideas. Here we can once again, and most conveniently, make a connection to the thinking of Aquinas.

***

The notion of a societal division of labor and occupational stratification has been conceptualized, by Aquinas as well as others, as a direct manifestation of God's divine plan. The placement of people into this cosmos, however, follows *ex causis naturalibus* [from natural causes] and is random (or, in the terminology of the Scholastics, "contingent"). Luther, as we noted, viewed the placement of people in given status groups and occupations (which followed out of the objective historical order) as a direct manifestation of God's will. Thus, a person's abiding *persistence* in the position and circumscribed situation assigned to him by God constituted a religious duty.[37] It was all the more so because the ways in which Lutheran piety connected the devout to the mundane "world" as given were, in general, from the beginning uncertain, and remained so. Ethical principles, in reference to which the world could be transformed, were not to be extracted from Luther's constellation of ideas (which never became fully severed from Paul's notions of indifference to the world). Hence, Lutherans had to take the world simply as it was. *This acceptance*, and only this acceptance, could become, in Lutheranism, endowed with a notion of religious duty.

The Puritan view nuanced the providential character of the interplay of societal forces with private economic interests in a different way. Here the providential purpose of occupational stratification can be recognized from its *fruits*. This view is consistent with the Puritan proclivity toward a pragmatic interpretation, and Baxter offers statements on this theme that remind one (on more than one occasion) immediately of Adam Smith's familiar deification of the division of labor.[38]

Because the specialization of occupations makes it possible for workers to develop skills, it leads, Baxter argues, to a quantitative and qualitative increase in worker productivity and thus serves the "common best" [common good] (which is identical with the prosperity of the greatest possible number). So far, the motivation remains purely utilitarian and closely related to points of view already common in the secular literature of the period.[39] But just at this point the characteristic Puritan element comes to the fore. Baxter places a discussion of the motivation involved at the center of his analysis:

> Outside of a firm calling, the workplace achievements of a person are only irregular and temporary. This person spends more time being lazy than actually working.

Moreover, Baxter's manner of concluding this discussion also reveals the Puritan dimension:

> And he (the worker with a vocational calling) will perform his work *in an orderly fashion* while others are stuck in situations of constant confusion; their businesses fail to operate according to time or place[40]. . . Therefore a 'certain calling' (or 'stated calling' at other passages) is best for everyone.

Intermittent work, into which the common day laborer is forced, is often unavoidable, but it is always an unwanted, transitional condition. The systematic-methodical character required by this-worldly asceticism is simply lacking in the life "without a calling" (*Beruflosen*).

Also, according to the ethic of the Quakers, a person's vocational calling should involve a consistent, ascetic exercise of virtues. One's state of grace is ***testified to*** through the *conscientiousness* with which the believer, with care[41] and methodicalness, pursues his calling. Rational work in a calling is demanded by God rather than work as such.

The Puritan idea of a calling continually emphasizes this methodical character of vocational asceticism rather than, as with Luther, the resignation to one's lot as irredeemably assigned by God.[42] Hence, for Puritanism the question of whether one may combine multiple callings is unequivocally answered affirmatively—if doing so proves beneficial to the common prosperity or to the individual[43] and is not injurious to anyone, and if it does not lead to a situation in which one becomes "unfaithful" to one of the combined callings. Indeed, even the *change* of vocational callings is not at all viewed as reprehensible, if carried out in a responsible manner. On the contrary, when made for the purpose of securing a vocation more pleasing to God[44] (that is, corresponding to the general rule here, to a more useful calling), then the initiative should be taken.

Most important, the usefulness of a vocational calling is assessed mainly in moral terms, as is its corresponding capacity to please God. A further criterion is closely bound to this moral dimension, namely, according to the degree of importance of the goods produced in the calling for the "community." A third criterion, one clearly the most important at the practical level, is also central in assessing a calling's usefulness: its economic *profitability* for the individual.[45] For if his God, whom the Puritan sees as acting in all arenas of life, reveals a chance for turning a profit to one of His faithful, He must do so with clear intentions in mind. Accordingly, the believer must follow this opportunity and exploit it:[46]

> If God show you a way in which you *may*, in accordance with His laws, *acquire more profit* than in another way, without wrong to your soul or to any other and if you refuse this, choosing the less profitable course, *you then cross one of the purposes of your calling. You are refusing to be God's steward*, and to accept His gifts, in order to be able to use them for Him when He requireth it. *You may labour, for God, to become rich,* though not for the flesh and sin.[47]

Hence, wealth is only suspect when it tempts the devout in the direction of lazy restfulness and a sinful enjoyment of life. The striving for riches becomes suspect only if carried out with the end in mind of leading a carefree and merry life once wealth is acquired. If, however, riches are attained within the dutiful performance of one's vocational calling, striving for them is not only morally permitted but expected.[48] This idea is explicitly expressed in the parable of the servant who was sentenced to hell because he failed to make the most of the opportunities entrusted to him.[49] *Wishing* to be poor, it was frequently argued, signifies the same as wishing to be sick.[50] Indeed, it would be abominable and detrimental to God's glory if poverty came to be viewed as sanctified. Furthermore, begging by those capable of working is not only sinful (as indolence) but also, according to the apostles, opposed to brotherly love.[51]

Just as the endowment of the stable vocational calling with ascetic significance sheds an ethical glorification around the modern *specialized expert*, the providential interpretation of one's chances for profit glorified the *business*person.[52] Asceticism on the one hand despises equally the refined nonchalance of the feudal noble and the parvenu-like ostentation of boasters. On the other hand, it shines a full beam of ethical approval upon the **dispassionate**, "self-made man" of the **middle class**.[53] A common remark—"God blesseth his trade"—refers to these saints[54] who have followed God's every decree with success. Moreover, the entire force of the *Old Testament God*,[55] which required His disciples to become pious in *this* life,[56] must have influenced the Puritans in the same direction. According to Baxter's advice, the devout must monitor and supervise their own state of grace through comparisons to the spiritual condition of biblical heroes.[57] In doing so, they must "interpret" the words of the Bible as if they were reading "paragraphs of a law book."

Of course Old Testament scripture was not entirely clear. We noted that Luther first employed the concept of calling, in its ***this-worldly*** sense, in a translation of a passage from the Book of Jesus Sirach. According to its entire mood of devotion, however, and despite its Hellenic influences, this book belongs to those sections of the (expanded) Old Testament [the Apocrypha][58] that convey more traditional influences. Characteristically, Jesus Sirach appears to possess, even today, a special attraction for Lutheran German peasants[59] and those broad streams of German Pietism more bound to Lutheranism.[60]

In light of their harsh either-or distinction between the Divine and depraved human beings, the Puritans criticized the Apocrypha as uninspired.[61] Among the canonical books, the Book of Job then became all the more central. On the one hand, it manifested a glorification of God's absolutely sovereign majesty, separate from all human standards, an idea highly congenial to Calvinist views. On the other, as breaks forth again in Job's concluding passages and combined with this idea of a majestic God, it presents a God who will, with certainty, bless His faithful—and will do so in this life, also in a material sense (as exclusively stated in this book).[62] Though of secondary importance to Calvin, this promise proved important for Puritanism. At the same time, the Puritan interpretation abandoned all Near Eastern quietism, which came to the fore in some of the most devotional verses of Psalms and Proverbs. Similarly, in his discussion of a passage in the First Letter to the Corinthians, Baxter interpreted away its traditional overtones. Doing so proved essential for his concept of the calling. In light of these developments, the Puritans all the more placed an emphasis upon those Old Testament passages that praised *formal correctness in terms of religious law* in one's conduct as constituting a sign of God's approval.

[Further interpretations also moved in this direction.] The Puritans opposed the theory that the law of Moses had lost its legitimacy with the founding of Christianity. They argued instead that only those passages relating to Jewish ceremonial or historically conditioned statutes were invalid, and that otherwise this law, as an expression of *lex naturae* [natural law], had possessed its validity from eternity and therefore must be retained.[63] This interpretation allowed on the one hand the elimination of statutes not easily adaptable to modern life, and on the other a powerful strengthening of a spirit of self-righteous and dispassionate legality suitable to Puritanism's this-worldly asceticism. Once in place, this development enabled numerous related features of Old Testament morality to flow freely into ascetic Protestantism.[64]

***

Therefore, correctly understood, the repeated depiction of the basic ethical orientation of English Puritanism in particular, even by its contemporaries (as well as more recent writers), as "English Hebraism"[65] is fully appropriate. Nevertheless, one should not think of this English Hebraism as the Palestinian Judaism from the period of the Old Testament's origin. Rather, one should recall the later Judaism that developed gradually under the influence of formal-legal and Talmudic learning over many centuries. Even then one must be extremely cautious regarding historical parallels. The mood of ancient Judaism, which was by and large oriented toward an appreciation of life's spontaneity as such, was far removed from the specific uniqueness of Puritanism.

Yet it should not be overlooked that Puritanism remained far distant as well from the economic ethic of medieval and modern Judaism in respect to features decisive for the development of the capitalist *ethos*. Judaism stood on the side of an "adventure" capitalism in which political or speculative motives were central. In a word, the economic ethic of Judaism was one of *pariah* capitalism.[66] By contrast, Puritanism carried the ethos of a rational, middle-class *company* and the rational organization of *work*. It took from Judaism's ethic only that which proved adaptable to this framework. [1920]

To chart out the characterological consequences of the penetration of life by Old Testament norms would be impossible in the context of this sketch (however stimulating a task, although until now it has not been adequately undertaken even for Judaism itself).[67] An analysis of the inner habitus of the Puritans in its entirety (*inneren Gesamthabitus*), in addition to the relationships already discussed, would also have to consider how it accompanied a grandiose rebirth of their belief in being the chosen people of God.[68] Just as even the mild-mannered Baxter thanks God for allowing him to be born in England and in the true church, and not elsewhere, this thankfulness for one's own blamelessness (which was caused by God's grace), penetrated the mood of life[69] of the Puritan middle class. It conditioned the formalistic, exacting, hard character of these representatives of the heroic epoch of capitalism.

***

We can now seek to clarify those aspects of the Puritan conception of the calling and promotion of an ascetic ***organization of life*** that must have *directly* influenced the development of the capitalist style of life.

As we have seen, asceticism turned with all its force mainly against the *spontaneous enjoyment* of existence and all the pleasures life had to offer. This aspect of asceticism was expressed most characteristically in the struggle over the *Book of Sports* [1637][70] which James I and Charles I raised to the level of law in order explicitly to confront Puritanism. Charles ordered the reading of this law from all pulpits. The fanatic opposition of the Puritans to the king's decree that, on Sundays, certain popular amusements would be legally allowed after church services, arose *not* only on account of the resulting disturbance of the Sabbath day of rest. Rather, the more important source of this opposition was the fully premeditated disruption the decree implied of the ordered and organized life practiced by the Puritan saints. Moreover, the king's threat to punish severely every attack on the legality of these sporting activities had a single clear purpose: to banish this Puritan movement that, owing to its *anti-authoritarian ascetic* features, posed a danger to the state. Monarchical-feudal society protected the "pleasure seekers" against the crystallizing middle-class morality and the ascetic ***conventicles*** hostile to authority, just as today capitalist society seeks to protect "those willing to work" against the class-specific morality of workers and the trade unions hostile to authority.

In opposition to the feudal-monarchical society, the Puritans held firm to their most central feature in this struggle over the *Book of Sports*, namely, the principle of leading an organized life anchored in asceticism. Actually, Puritanism's aversion to sports was not a fundamental one, even for the Quakers. However, sports must serve a rational end; they must promote the relaxation indispensable for further physical achievement. Hence, sports became suspect whenever they constituted a means for the purely spontaneous expression of unrestrained impulses. They were obviously absolutely reprehensible to the extent that they became means toward pure enjoyment or awakened competitive ambition, raw instincts, or the irrational desire to gamble. Quite simply, the enjoyment of life as if it were only *physical drives*, which pulls one equally away from work in a calling and from piety, was the enemy of rational asceticism as such. This enmity remained, regardless of whether the enjoyment of life presented itself in the form of monarchical-feudal society's sports or in the common man's visits to the dance floor or the tavern.[71]

Correspondingly, Puritanism's position toward those aspects of culture devoid of any direct relevance to religious matters was also one of suspicion and strong hostility. That is not to say that a sombre, narrow-minded scorn for culture was contained in Puritan ideals. Precisely the opposite holds, at least for the sciences (*Wissenschaften*) (with the exception of Scholasticism, which was despised).[72] Moreover, the great representatives of Puritanism were deeply submerged in the humanism of the Renaissance, the sermons in the Presbyterian wing drip with references to classical antiquity,[73] and even the radicals (although they took offense at it) did not reject this humanist learning in theological polemics. Perhaps no country was ever so overpopulated with "graduates" as New England in the first generation of its existence. Even the satires of opponents, such as *Hudibras* [1663–78] by [Samuel] Butler [1612-80], turn quickly to the armchair scholarship and sophomoric dialectics of the Puritans. Their learning *in part* goes together with the high religious esteem for knowledge that followed from the Puritans' rejection of the Catholic *fides implicita* ["confusing faith," as the Puritans perceived it].

Matters are distinctly different as soon as one moves into the arena of nonscientific literature[74] and to the realm of art which appeals to the senses. Asceticism now blankets like a frost the life of merry olde England. Its influence was apparent not only on secular festivals. The angry hatred of the Puritans persecuted all that smacked of "superstition" and all residuals of the dispensation of grace through magic or sacraments, including Christmas festivities, the may pole celebration,[75] and all unrestricted use of art by the church.[76] The survival in Holland of a public space within which the development of a masterful, often coarse and earthy, realistic art[77] could occur demonstrates in the end that the authoritarian regimentation of morality by the Puritans was not able to exercise a complete domination. The influence of court society and the landlord stratum, as well as members of the lower middle class who had become wealthy and sought joy in life, all contested in Holland the impact of Puritanism. This resistance took place after the short domination of the Calvinist theocracy had dissolved into a staid state church. As a consequence of this development, Calvinism suffered a distinct loss in ascetic energy and thus its capacity to attract believers perceptibly declined.

The theater was reprehensible to the Puritans.[78] As in literature and art, radical views could not survive once eroticism and nudity had been strictly banned from the realm of the possible. The notions of "idle talk," "superfluities,"[79] and "vain ostentation," all of which designated to the Puritans irrational, aimless, and thus not ascetic, behavior (and surely not conduct serving God's glory but only human goals), surfaced quickly. Hence, dispassionate instrumentalism was given a decisive upper hand over and against every application of artistic tendencies. This purposiveness was especially important wherever the direct decoration of the person was involved, as for example in respect to dress.[80] The foundation in ideas for that powerful tendency to render styles of life uniform, which today supports the capitalist interest in the "standardization" of production,[81] derived from the Puritans' rejection of all "glorification of human wants and desires."[82]

***

Certainly, in the midst of these considerations, we should not forget that Puritanism contained within itself a world of contradictions. It must be recognized that the instinctive awareness among Puritan leaders of the eternal greatness of art certainly transcended the level of art appreciation found in the milieu of the [feudalism-oriented] "cavaliers."[83] Furthermore, and even though his "conduct" would scarcely have found grace in the eyes of the Puritan God, a unique genius such as Rembrandt was, in the direction of his creativity, fundamentally influenced by his sectarian milieu.[84] These acknowledgments, however, fail to alter the larger picture: the powerful turn of the personality in an inward-looking direction (which the further development of the Puritan milieu could cultivate and, in fact, co-determined) influenced literature for the most part. Even in this realm, however, the impact of ascetic Protestantism would be felt only in later generations.

We cannot here investigate further the influences of Puritanism in all these ways. Nevertheless, we should note that *one* characteristic barrier always opposed ascribing legitimacy to the joy experienced from aspects of culture serving pure aesthetic pleasures or to the pure enjoyment of sports: *this pleasure should not cost anything*. Persons are only administrators of the cultural performances that the grace of God has offered. Hence, every dime expended for them must be justified, just as in the example of the servant in the Bible.[85] It remains doubtful at least whether any part of this money should be spent for a purpose that serves one's own pleasure rather than the glory of God.[86]

Who among us, whose eyes are open, has not seen manifestations of this outlook even at the present time?[87] The idea of a person's *duty* to maintain possessions entrusted to him, to which he subordinates himself as a dutiful steward or even as a "machine for producing wealth," lies upon his life with chilling seriousness. And as one's possessions become more valuable, the more burdensome becomes the feeling of responsibility to maintain them intact for God's glory and to increase their value through restless work—*if* the ascetic temper meets the challenge. The roots of this style of life also extend back to the Middle Ages (at least particular roots), as is true of so many components of the modern capitalist spirit.[88] This spirit, however, first found its consistent ethical foundation in the ethic of ascetic Protestantism. Its significance for the development of [modern] capitalism is obvious.[89]

***

Let us summarize the above. On the one hand, this-worldly Protestant asceticism fought with fury against the spontaneous *enjoyment* of possessions and constricted *consumption*, especially of luxury goods. On the other hand, it had the psychological effect of *freeing* the *acquisition of goods* from the constraints of the traditional economic ethic. In the process, ascetic Protestantism shattered the bonds restricting all striving for gain—not only by legalizing profit but also by perceiving it as desired by God (in the manner portrayed here). The struggle against the desires of the flesh and the attachment to external goods was *not*, as the Puritans explicitly attest (and also the great Quaker apologist, Barclay), a struggle against rational *acquisition*; rather, it challenged the irrational use of possessions. That which remained so familiar to feudal sensibilities—a high regard for the *external* display of luxury consumption—was condemned by the Puritans as a deification of human wants and desires.[90] According to them, God wanted a rational and utilitarian use of wealth on behalf of the basic needs of the person and the community.

Hence, this-worldly asceticism did *not* wish to impose *self-castigation* upon the wealthy.[91] Instead, it wanted that wealth to be used for necessary, *practical*, and *useful* endeavors. The notion of "comfort," typically for the Puritans, encompasses the realm of the ethically permissible use of goods. Thus, it is naturally not by chance that one observes the development of the style of life attached to this notion, earliest and most clearly, precisely in those most consistent representatives of the Puritan life outlook: the Quakers. In opposition to the glitter and pretense of feudalism's pomp and display, which rests upon an unstable economic foundation and prefers a tattered elegance to low-key simplicity, the Puritans placed the ideal of the clean and solid comfort of the middle-class "home."[92]

***

In terms of capitalism's *production* of wealth, asceticism struggled against greed. It did so in order to confront both the danger it presented to social order and its *impulsive* character. The Puritans condemned all "covetousness" and "mammonism," for both implied the striving for wealth—becoming rich—as an end in itself, and wealth as such constituted a temptation.

The nature of asceticism again becomes clear at this point. Its methodical-rational organization of life was the power "that perpetually wanted good and perpetually created evil,"[93] namely, evil in the manner conceived by asceticism: wealth and its temptations. For asceticism (together with the Old Testament and completely parallel to the ethical valuation of "good works") defined the pursuit of riches, if viewed as an *end* in itself, as the peak of reprehensibility. At the same time, it also viewed the acquisition of wealth, when it was the *fruit* of work in a vocational calling, as God's blessing. Even more important for this investigation, the religious value set on restless, continuous, and systematic work in a vocational calling was defined as absolutely the highest of all ascetic means for believers to testify to their elect status, as well as simultaneously the most certain and most visible means of doing so. Indeed, the Puritan's sincerity of belief must have been the most powerful lever conceivable working to expand the life outlook that we are here designating as the spirit of capitalism.[94]

Moreover, if we now combine the strictures against consumption with this unchaining of the striving for wealth, a certain external result [that is, one with an impact outside the realm of religion] now becomes visible: *the formation of capital* through *asceticism's compulsive saving*.[95] The restrictions that opposed the consumption of wealth indeed had their productive use, for profit and gain became used as *investment* capital.

Of course, the strength of this effect cannot be determined exactly in quantitative terms. The connection became so apparent in New England, however, that it did not escape early on the eye of a historian as distinguished as John Doyle.[96] But it was also apparent in Holland, where a strict Calvinism ruled for only seven years. The greater simplicity of life that dominated the Dutch regions of ascetic Protestantism led, among the enormously wealthy, to an excessive desire to accumulate capital.[97] Furthermore, it is evident that the tendency for middle-class fortunes to be used for the acquisition of noble status (which has existed in all epochs and countries, and even today quite significantly in Germany) must have been inhibited to a measurable extent by the hostility of Puritanism to all feudal forms of life. English writers on the mercantilism of the seventeenth century traced the superiority of Dutch over English capitalism back to the English practice (as in Germany) of regularly investing newly acquired fortunes in land. On this basis (for the purchase of land is not the only issue), newly wealthy persons sought to make the transition to feudal habits of life and to noble status. The result was clear: such land could not be used for capitalist investment.[98]

An esteem for *agriculture* was even present among the Puritans. Indeed, it constituted a particularly important arena for making a living (for example, in the case of Baxter) and was highly conducive to piety. Yet the Puritan engagement in agriculture diverged from feudalism: it involved productive farming rather than merely owning land as a landlord. In the eighteenth century, it was oriented more toward "rational" commercial farming than toward the acquisition of a country manor and entry into the nobility.[99] Since the seventeenth century, the division between the "squirearchy," which were the **social carriers** of "merry olde England," and the Puritan circles, whose societal power varied across a broad spectrum, cut through English society.[100] Both streams—on the one hand a spontaneous and naive taking pleasure in life and on the other a strictly regulated, reserved self-control and ethical restraint—stand even today alongside each other in any portrait of the English "national character."[101] A similarly sharp polarity runs through the earliest history of North American colonization between the "adventurers," who wanted to build plantations with the labor of indentured servants and to live like feudal lords, and the middle-class frame of mind of the Puritans.[102]

As far as its power extended, the Puritan life outlook promoted under all circumstances the tendency toward a middle-class, economically *rational* organization of life. This outlook was, of course, far more important than the mere facilitating of the formation of capital. Indeed, it was the most substantial and, above all, only consistent social carrier of this middle-class mode of organizing life. Just this rational organization of life stands at the source of modern "economic man" (*Wirtschaftsmenschen*).[103]

***

Of course, these Puritan ideals of life failed to meet the challenge whenever the test—the "temptations" of wealth (which were well known even to the Puritans themselves)—became too great. We find the most sincere followers of the Puritan spirit very frequently among those in the middle class who operated small businesses, among farmers and the *beati possidentes* [those in possession of salvation]—all of whom must be understood as having been at the beginning of an *upwardly mobile* journey.[104] Yet we find that many in these groups were prepared quite frequently to betray the old ideals.[105] Such betrayal even occurred among the Quakers. The predecessor of this-worldly asceticism, the monastic asceticism of the Middle Ages, repeatedly fell victim to this same fate. Whenever the rational organization of the economy had fully developed its productive powers in the cloister milieu, which was characterized by a strict regulation of life as a whole and limited consumption, then the accumulated wealth was either used to acquire land and noble status (as occurred in the era before the Reformation) or it threatened the dissolution of monastic discipline. One of the numerous "reform movements" in monasticism had to intervene if this occurred. In a certain sense, the entire history of the religious orders reveals a constantly renewed struggle with the problem of the secularizing effects of wealth.

On a larger scale, the same is true for Puritanism's this-worldly asceticism. The powerful "revival" of Methodism, which preceded the flowering of English industrialism near the end of the eighteenth century, can be appropriately compared with the "reform movements" in the monastic orders. A passage[106] from John Wesley himself can be noted now, for it is well suited to stand as a motto for all that has been stated here. It indicates how the main figures in the ascetic movements were themselves completely aware of the apparently so paradoxical relationships presented here and understood these connections fully.[107]

> I fear, wherever riches have increased, the essence of religion has decreased in the same proportion. Therefore I do not see how it is possible, in the nature of things, for any revival of true religion to continue long. For religion must necessarily produce both industry and frugality, and these cannot but produce riches. But as riches increase, so will pride, anger, and love of the world in all its branches. How then is it possible that Methodism, that is, a religion of the heart, though it flourishes now as a green bay tree, should continue in this state? For the Methodists in every place grow diligent and frugal; consequently they increase their possession of material goods. Hence they proportionately increase in pride, in anger, in the desire of the flesh, the desire of the eyes, and the pride of life. So, although the form of religion remains, the spirit is swiftly vanishing away. Is there no way to prevent this continual decay of pure religion? We ought not to prevent people from being diligent and frugal; *we must exhort all Christians to gain all they can, and to save all they can; that is, in effect, to grow rich.* [Weber's emphasis] [1920]

(There follows the admonition that those who have "acquired all they can and saved all they can" should also "give all they can"—in order to grow in grace and to assemble a fortune in heaven.) In this passage from Wesley one sees the connection, in all its details, illuminated in the analysis above.[108] [1920]

Exactly as Wesley noted here, the significance for economic development of the powerful early religious movements was to be found mainly in the ascetic effects of their *socialization*. To him, their full *economic* impact developed, as a rule, only after the peak of their *pure* religious enthusiasm. As the paroxysms of the search for God's kingdom gradually dissolved into the dispassionate virtues of the vocational calling and the religious roots of the movement slowly withered, a utilitarian orientation to the world took hold. In the popular imagination, if we follow [the Irish scholar of English and French literature Edward] Dowden [1843–1913], "Robinson Crusoe"—the *isolated economic man* (who is engaged in missionary activities in his spare time)—now took the place of Bunyan's "pilgrims" scurrying through the "amusement park of vanity" on their solitary spiritual quest for God's kingdom.[109] If then, further, the basic principle "to make the best of *both* worlds" came to prevail, then, finally (as Dowden similarly already observed) the good conscience had also to be included among the series of factors comprising the comfortable, middle-class life (as is so beautifully expressed in the German adage about the "soft pillow"[110]). That which the religiously lively epoch of the seventeenth century bequeathed to its utilitarian heirs was above all a startlingly good conscience (we can say without hesitation, *pharisaically* good) as concerns the acquisition of money. Elsewhere, such gain and acquisition occurred alone on the basis of legal forms.[111] Now, with Puritanism, every residual of the medieval proverb *deo placere vix potest* has disappeared.[112]

***

A specifically *middle-class vocational ethos* (*Berufsethos*) arose. Now the middle-class employer became conscious of himself as standing in the full grace of God and as visibly blessed by Him. If he stayed within the bounds of formal correctness, if his moral conduct remained blameless, and if the use he made of his wealth was not offensive, this person was now allowed to follow his interest in economic gain, and indeed *should* do so. Moreover, the power of religious asceticism made available to the businessperson dispassionate and conscientious workers. Unusually capable of working, these employees attached themselves to their work, for they understood it as bestowing a purpose on life that was desired by God.[113]

In addition, religious asceticism gave to the employer the soothing assurance that the unequal distribution of the world's material goods resulted from the special design of God's providence. In making such distinctions as well as in deciding who should be among the chosen few, God pursued mysterious aims unknown to terrestrial mortals.[114] Calvin had argued early on (in a passage frequently cited) that the "people," the overwhelming majority of skilled and unskilled workers, would continue to obey God only if kept poor.[115] The Dutch (Peter de la Court and others) "secularized" this statement; to them, most persons *worked* only if driven to do so by necessity. In turn, this formulation of a key idea regarding the functioning of the capitalist economy then merged into the plethora of theories on the "productivity" of low wages. Here again, and in full conformity with the developmental pattern we have repeatedly observed, as the religious roots of an idea died out a utilitarian tone then surreptiously shoved itself under the idea and carried it further.[116]

Now let us turn away from the Puritan employer and briefly toward the other side, namely, the perspective of the worker. Zinzendorf's branch of Pietism, for example, glorified workers who were loyal to their callings, lived in accord with the ideals of the apostles, and never strove for gain—hence, workers endowed with the charisma of Christ's disciples.[117] Similar views were widespread, in an even more radical form, among the baptizing congregations in their early stages. Of course, the entire corpus of literature on asceticism, which is drawn from almost *all* religions [East and West], is permeated with the point of view that loyal work is highly pleasing to God, even if performed for low wages by people at a great disadvantage in life and without other opportunities. *Here* Protestant asceticism added nothing new as such. It dramatically deepened, however, this point of view. In addition, it created the norm on which its impact *exclusively depended*: the psychological *motivation* that arose out of the conception of work as a *calling* and as the means best suited (and in the end often as the *sole* means) for the devout to become certain of their state of salvation.[118] Furthermore, on the other hard, in interpreting the employer's acquisition of money also as a "calling," Protestant asceticism legalized the exploitation of this particular willingness to work.[119]

***

It is obvious how powerfully the *exclusive* striving for the kingdom of God—through fulfillment of the duty to work in a vocational calling and through strict asceticism, which church discipline naturally imposed in particular upon the propertyless classes—must have promoted the "productivity" of work in the capitalist sense of the word.[120] For the modern worker, the view of work as a "vocational calling" became just as characteristic as the view of gain as a "vocational calling" became for the modern employer. New at the time, this situation was reflected in the keen observations on Dutch economic power of the seventeenth century by the insightful Englishman Sir William Petty [see p. 10]. He traced its growth back to the especially numerous "Dissenters" (Calvinists and Baptists) in Holland, who viewed *"work and the industrious pursuit of a trade as their duty to God."*[121]

The "organic" societal organization, in the form of the fiscal monopoly it assumed in the Anglicanism under the Stuarts [1603–1714] and especially in [Archbishop William] Laud's [1573–1645][122] conceptions, involved specific features. First, a coalition of state and church with the "business monopolists" arose. Second, this alliance became anchored in Christian social ethics. Puritanism stood against this coalition. They passionately opposed *this* type of economy, one in which the state offered privileges to merchants, cottage industries, and colonial capitalism. Instead, Puritans upheld a type of capitalism in which a person's competence and initiative-taking capacity provided the individualistic *motivation* for rational-legal acquisition. In England, where the industrial monopolies privileged by the state as a whole soon disappeared, Puritanism decisively participated in the creation of newly emerging industries. It did so in spite of and against the state's authoritarian powers.[123] [1920]

The Puritans [William] Prynne [1600–1669] and [Matthew] Parker [1504–74][124] rejected every common undertaking with "courtiers and operators" in the mold of large-scale capitalists, for they perceived such people as members of an ethically suspect class. Moreover, the Puritans did so on the basis of pride in their own superior middle-class business ethics (*Geschäftsmoral*). In turn, precisely this ethos constituted the true reason for the persecution of Puritans by large-scale capitalists. Even as late as [the eighteenth-century the novelist Daniel] Defoe [1660–1731] suggested a struggle against Puritans. He sought to win this conflict by arguing in favor of boycotts against all businesses that changed banks and the cancellation of bank and stock accounts. [1920]

The contrast between the two types of capitalist conduct paralleled to a very great extent the religious contrasts. Even in the eighteenth century the opponents of the Puritans repeatedly satirized them as carriers of a "spirit of shopkeepers" and persecuted them as the ruin of old English ideals. The contrast between Puritan and Jewish economic ethics is also anchored *here* and even contemporaries (Prynne) knew that the former, and not the latter, was the middle-class economic ethic.[125] [1920]

***

One of the constitutive components of the modern capitalist spirit and, moreover, generally of modern civilization, was the rational organization of life on the basis of the *idea of the calling*. It was born out of the spirit of *Christian asceticism*. Our analysis should have demonstrated this point. If we now read again the passages from Benjamin Franklin cited at the beginning of this essay, we will see that the essential elements of the frame of mind he described as the "spirit of capitalism" are just those that we have conveyed above as the content of Puritan vocational asceticism.[126] In Franklin, however, this "spirit" exists without the religious foundation, which had already died out.

The idea that modern work in a vocational calling supposedly carries with it an *ascetic* imprint is, of course, also not new. The limitation of persons to specialized work, which necessitates their renunciation of the Faustian multi-dimensionality of the human species, is in our world today the precondition for doing anything of value at all. This is a lesson that already *Goethe*, at the peak of his wisdom in his *Wilhelm Meister's Years of Travel* [1829] and in his depiction of the final stage of life through his [most famous character] Faust [1808], wished to teach us.[127] He instructs us that this basic component of asceticism in the middle-class style of life—if it wishes to be a style at all—involves today an inescapable interaction in which the conduct of "specialized activity," on the one hand, and "renunciation," on the other, mutually condition each other. For Goethe this acknowledgment implied a farewell to an era of full and beautiful humanity—and a renunciation of it. For such an era will repeat itself, in the course of our civilizational development, with as little likelihood as a reappearance of the epoch in which Athens bloomed.

The Puritan *wanted* to be a person with a vocational calling; today we *are forced* to be. For to the extent that asceticism moved out of the monastic cell, was transferred to the life of work in a vocational calling, and then commenced to rule over this-worldly morality, it helped to construct the powerful cosmos of the modern economic order. Tied to the technical and economic conditions at the foundation of mechanical and machine production, this cosmos today determines the style of life of all individuals born into it, *not* only those directly engaged in earning a living. This pulsating mechanism does so with overwhelming force. Perhaps it will continue to do so until the last ton of fossil fuel has burnt to ashes. According to Baxter, the concern for material goods should lie upon the shoulders of his saints like "a lightweight coat that could be thrown off at any time."[128] Yet fate allowed a steel-hard casing (*stahlhartes Gehäuse*)[129] to be forged from this coat. To the extent that asceticism attempted to transform and influence the world, the world's material goods acquired an increasing and, in the end, inescapable power over people—as never before in history.

Today the spirit of asceticism has fled from this casing, whether with finality, who knows? Victorious capitalism, in any case, ever since it came to rest on a mechanical foundation, no longer needs asceticism as a supporting pillar. Even the rosy temperament of asceticism's joyful heir, the Enlightenment, appears finally to be fading. And the idea of an "obligation to search for and then accept a vocational calling" now wanders around in our lives as the ghost of beliefs no longer anchored in the substance of religion. Wherever the "conduct of a vocation" cannot be explicitly connected to the highest cultural values of a spiritual nature, or wherever, conversely, individuals are not forced to experience it simply as economic coercion—in both situations persons today usually abandon any attempt to make sense of the notion of a vocational calling altogether. The pursuit of gain, in the region where it has become most completely unchained and stripped of its religious-ethical meaning, the United States, tends to be associated with purely competitive passions. Not infrequently, these passions directly imprint this pursuit with the character of a sporting contest.[130]

No one any longer knows who will live in this steel-hard casing and whether entirely new prophets or a mighty rebirth of ancient ideas and ideals will stand at the end of this prodigious development. Or, however, if neither, whether a mechanized ossification, embellished with a sort of rigidly compelled sense of self-importance, will arise. Then, indeed, if ossification appears, the saying might be true for the "last humans"[131] in this long civilizational development:

> narrow specialists without mind, pleasure-seekers without heart; in its conceit, this nothingness imagines it has climbed to a level of humanity never before attained.[132]

***

Here, however, we have fallen into the realm of value-judgments and judgments rooted in faith, with which this purely historical analysis should not be burdened. The further *task* is a different one: to chart the significance of ascetic rationalism.[133] The above sketch has only hinted at its importance.

Its significance for the content of ethical *social policy* must now be charted, that is, for the type of organization and the functions of social communities, ranging from the conventicle to the state. Having done that, we must analyze the relationship of ascetic rationalism to the ideals and cultural influences of humanistic rationalism.[134] Further, we must investigate the relationship of ascetic rationalism to the development of philosophical and scientific empiricism, to the unfolding of technology, and to the development of nonmaterial culture (*geistige Kulturgüter*), in general.[135] Then, finally, we need to pursue the historical course of ascetic rationalism, beginning with the first signs of this-worldly asceticism in the Middle Ages and moving all the way to its dissolution in pure utilitarianism. We should then need to trace this development in its *particular historical* manifestations and through the particular regions of the expansion of ascetic religious devotion. Only after the completion of such investigations can the *extent* of ascetic Protestantism's civilizational significance be demarcated in comparison to that of other elements of modern civilization that can be changed and shaped in response to the actions of persons.

This study has attempted, of course, merely to trace ascetic Protestantism's influence, and the particular *nature* of this influence, back to ascetic Protestantism's motives in regard to one, however important, point.[136] The way in which Protestant asceticism was in turn influenced, in its development and characteristic uniqueness, by the entirety of societal-cultural conditions, and especially *economic* conditions, must also have its day.[137] For certain, even with the best will, the modern person seems generally unable to imagine *how* large a significance those components of our consciousness rooted in religious beliefs have actually had upon culture, national character, and the organization of life. Nevertheless, it is not, of course, the intention here to set a one-sided spiritualistic analysis of the causes of culture and history in place of an equally one-sided "materialistic" analysis. *Both* are *equally possible*.[138] Historical truth, however, is served equally little if either of these analyses claims to be the conclusion of an investigation rather than its preparatory stage.[139] ✦

The Protestant Sects and the Spirit of Capitalism[1]

Translated by Hans H. Gerth and C. Wright Mills

For some time in the United States a principled "separation of state and church" has existed. This separation is carried through so strictly that there is not even an official census of denominations, for it would be considered against the law for the state even to ask the citizen for his denomination. We shall not here discuss the practical importance of this principle of the relation between religious organizations and the state.* We are interested, rather, in the fact that scarcely two and a half decades ago the number of "persons without church affiliation" in the U.S.A. was estimated to be only about 6 percent;[2] and this despite the absence of all those highly effective premiums which most of the European states then placed upon affiliation with certain privileged churches and despite the immense immigration to the U.S.A.

It should be realized, in addition, that church affiliation in the U.S.A. brings with it incomparably higher financial burdens, especially for the poor, than anywhere in Germany. Published family budgets prove this, and I have personally known of many burdened cases in a congregation in a city on Lake Erie, which was almost entirely composed of German immigrant lumberjacks. Their regular contributions for religious purposes amounted to almost $80 annually, being paid out of an average annual income of about $1,000. Everyone knows that even a small fraction of this financial burden in Germany would lead to a mass exodus from the church. But quite apart from that, nobody who visited the United States fifteen or twenty years ago, that is, before the recent Europeanization of the country began, could overlook the very intense church-mindedness which then prevailed in all regions not yet flooded by European immigrants.** Every old travel book reveals that formerly church-mindedness in America went unquestioned, as compared with recent decades, and was even far stronger. Here we are especially interested in one aspect of this situation.

---

* The principle is often only theoretical; note the importance of the Catholic vote, as well as subsidies to confessional schools.

** The opening by prayer of not only every session of the U. S. Supreme Court but also of every Party Convention has been an annoying ceremonial for quite some time.

Hardly a generation ago when businessmen were establishing themselves and making new social contacts, they encountered the question: "To what church do you belong?" This was asked unobtrusively and in a manner that seemed to be apropos, but evidently it was never asked accidentally. Even in Brooklyn, New York's twin city, this older tradition was retained to a strong degree, and the more so in communities less exposed to the influence of immigration. This question reminds one of the typical Scotch *table d'hôte*, where a quarter of a century ago the continental European on Sundays almost always had to face the situation of a lady's asking, "What service did you attend today?" Or, if the Continental, as the oldest guest, should happen to be seated at the head of the table, the waiter when serving the soup would ask him: "Sir, the prayer, please." In Portree (Skye) on one beautiful Sunday I faced this typical question and did not know any better way out than to remark: "I am a member of the *Badische Landeskirche* and could not find a chapel of my church in Portree." The ladies were pleased and satisfied with the answer. "Oh, he doesn't attend any service except that of his own denomination!"

If one looked more closely at the matter in the United States, one could easily see that the question of religious affiliation was almost always posed in social life and in business life which depended on permanent and credit relations. However, as mentioned above, the American authorities never posed the question. Why?

First, a few personal observations [from 1904] may serve as illustrations. On a long railroad journey through what was then Indian territory, the author, sitting next to a traveling salesman of "undertaker's hardware" (iron letters for tombstones), casually mentioned the still impressively strong church-mindedness. Thereupon the salesman remarked, "Sir, for my part everybody may believe or not believe as he pleases; but if I saw a farmer or a businessman not belonging to any church at all, I wouldn't trust him with fifty cents. Why pay me, if he doesn't believe in anything?" Now that was a somewhat vague motivation.

The matter became somewhat clearer from the story of a German-born nose-and-throat specialist, who had established himself in a large city on the Ohio River and who told me of the visit of his first patient. Upon the doctor's request, he lay down upon the couch to be examined with the [aid of a] nose reflector. The patient sat up once and remarked with dignity and emphasis, "Sir, I am a member of the _____ Baptist Church in ____ Street." Puzzled about what meaning this circumstance might have for the disease of the nose and its treatment, the doctor discreetly inquired about the matter from an American colleague. The colleague smilingly informed him that the patient's statement of his church membership was merely to say: "Don't worry about the fees." But why should it mean precisely that? Perhaps this will become still clearer from a third happening.

On a beautiful clear Sunday afternoon early in October I attended a baptism ceremony of a Baptist congregation. I was in the company of some relatives who were farmers in the backwoods some miles out of M. [a county seat] in North Carolina. The baptism was to take place in a pool fed by a brook which descended from the Blue Ridge Mountains, visible in the distance. It was cold and it had been freezing during the night. Masses of farmers' families were standing all around the slopes of the hills; they had come, some from great distances, some from the neighborhood, in their light two-wheeled buggies.

The preacher in a black suit stood waist deep in the pond. After preparations of various sorts, about ten persons of both sexes in their Sunday-best stepped into the pond, one after another. They avowed their faith and then were immersed completely—the women in the preacher's arms. They came up, shaking and shivering in their wet clothes, stepped out of the pond, and everybody "congratulated" them. They were quickly wrapped in thick blankets and then they drove home. One of my relatives commented that "faith" provides unfailing protection against sneezes. Another relative stood beside me, and being unchurchly in accordance with German traditions, he looked on, spitting disdainfully over his shoulder. He spoke to one of those baptized, "Hello, Bill, wasn't the water pretty cool?" and received the very earnest reply, "Jeff, I thought of some pretty hot place (Hell!), and so I didn't mind the cool water." During the immersion of one of the young men, my relative was startled.

"Look at him," he said. "I told you so!"

When I asked him after the ceremony, "Why did you anticipate the baptism of that man?" he answered, "Because he wants to open a bank in M."

"Are there so many Baptists around that he can make a living?"

"Not at all, but once being baptized he will get the patronage of the whole region and he will outcompete everybody."

Further questions of "why" and "by what means" led to the following conclusion: Admission to the local Baptist congregation follows only upon the most careful "probation" and after closest inquiries into conduct going back to early childhood (Disorderly conduct? Frequenting taverns? Dance? Theatre? Card Playing? Untimely meeting of liability? Other Frivolities?) The congregation still adhered strictly to the religious tradition.

Admission to the congregation is recognized as an absolute guarantee of the moral qualities of a gentleman, especially of those qualities required in business matters. Baptism secures to the individual the deposits of the whole region and unlimited credit without any competition. He is a "made man." Further observation confirmed that these, or at least very similar phenomena, recur in the most varied regions. In general, *only* those men had success in business who belonged to Methodist or Baptist or other ***sects*** or sectlike conventicles. When a sect member moved to a different place, or if he was a traveling salesman, he carried the certificate of his congregation with him; and thereby he found not only easy contact with sect members but, above all, he found credit everywhere. If he got into economic straits through no fault of his own, the sect arranged his affairs, gave guarantees to the creditors, and helped him in every way, often according to the Biblical principle, *mutuum date nihil inde sperantes* [Lend, expecting nothing in return] (Luke 6:35).

The expectation of the creditors that his sect, for the sake of their prestige, would not allow creditors to suffer losses on behalf of a sect member was not, however, decisive for his opportunities. What was decisive was the fact that a fairly reputable sect would only accept for membership one whose "conduct" made him appear to be morally qualified beyond doubt.

It is crucial that sect membership meant a certificate of moral qualification and especially of business morals for the individual. This stands in contrast to membership in a "church" into which one is "born" and which lets grace shine over the righteous and the unrighteous alike. Indeed, a church is a corporation which organizes grace and administers religious gifts of grace, like an endowed foundation. Affiliation with the church is, in principle, obligatory and hence proves nothing with regard to the member's qualities. A sect, however, is a voluntary association of only those who, according to the principle, are religiously and morally qualified. If one finds voluntary reception of his membership, by virtue of religious *probation*, he joins the sect voluntarily. It is, of course, an established fact that this selection has often been very strongly counteracted, precisely in America, through the proselyting of souls by competing sects, which, in part, was strongly determined by the material interests of the preachers. Hence, cartels for the restriction of proselyting have frequently existed among the competing denominations. Such cartels were formed, for instance, in order to exclude the easy wedding of a person who had been divorced for reasons which, from a religious point of view, were considered insufficient. Religious organizations that facilitated remarriage had great attraction. Some Baptist communities are said at times to have been lax in this respect, whereas the Catholic as well as the Lutheran churches were praised for their strict correctness. This correctness, however, allegedly reduced the membership of both churches.

Expulsion from one's sect for moral offenses has meant, economically, loss of credit and, socially, being declassed.

Numerous observations during the following months confirmed not only that church-mindedness *per se*, although still (1904) rather important, was rapidly dying out; but the particularly important trait, mentioned above, was definitely confirmed. In metropolitan areas I was spontaneously told, in several cases, that a speculator in undeveloped real estate would regularly erect a church building, often an extremely modest one; then he would hire a candidate from one of the various theological seminaries, pay him $500 to $600, and hold out to him a splendid position as a preacher for life if he would gather a congregation and thus preach the building terrain "full." Deteriorated churchlike structures which marked failures were shown to me. For the most part, however, the preachers were said to be successful. Neighborly contact, Sunday School, and so on, were said to be indispensable to the newcomer, but above all association with "morally" reliable neighbors.

Competition among sects is strong, among other things, through the kind of material and spiritual offerings at evening teas of the congregations. Among genteel churches also, musical presentations contribute to this competition. (A tenor in Trinity Church, Boston, who allegedly had to sing on Sundays *only*, at that time received $8,000.) Despite this sharp competition, the sects often maintained fairly good mutual relations. For instance, in the service of the Methodist church which I attended, the Baptist ceremony of the baptism, which I mentioned above, was recommended as a spectacle to edify everybody. In the main, the congregations refused entirely to listen to the preaching of "dogma" and to confessional distinctions. "Ethics" alone could be offered. In those instances where I listened to sermons for the middle classes, the typical bourgeois morality, respectable and solid, to be sure, and of the most homely and sober kind, was preached. But the sermons were delivered with obvious inner conviction; the preacher was often moved.

Today the kind of denomination [to which one belongs] is rather irrelevant. It does not matter whether one be Freemason,* Christian Scientist, Adventist, Quaker, or what not. What is decisive is that one be admitted to membership by "ballot," after an *examination* and an ethical *probation* in the sense of the virtues which are at a premium for the inner-worldly asceticism of Protestantism and hence, for the ancient puritan tradition. Then, the same effect could be observed.

Closer scrutiny revealed the steady progress of the characteristic process of "secularization," to which in modern times all phenomena that originated in religious conceptions succumb. Not only religious associations, hence sects, have this effect on American life. Sects exercised this influence, rather, in a steadily decreasing proportion. If one paid some attention it was striking to observe (even fifteen years ago) that surprisingly many men among the American **middle classes** (always outside of the quite modern metropolitan areas and the immigration centers) were wearing a little badge (of varying color) in the buttonhole, which reminded one very closely of the rosette of the French Legion of Honor.

When asked what it meant, people regularly mentioned an association with a sometimes adventurous and fantastic name. And it became obvious that its significance and purpose consisted in the following: Almost always the association functioned as a burial insurance, besides offering greatly varied services. But often, and especially in those areas least touched by modern disintegration, the association offered the member the (ethical) claim for brotherly help on the part of every brother who had the means. If he faced an economic emergency for which he himself was not to be blamed, he could make this claim. And in several instances that came to my notice at the time, this claim again followed the very principle, *mutuum date nihil inde sperantes*, or at least a very low rate of interest prevailed. Apparently, such claims were willingly recog-

* An assistant of Semitic languages in an eastern university told me that he regretted not having become "master of the chair," for then he would go back into business. When asked what good that would do the answer was: As a traveling salesman or seller he could present himself in a role famous for respectability. He could beat any competition and would be worth his weight in gold.

nized by the members of the brotherhood. Furthermore—and this is the main point in this instance—membership was again acquired through balloting after investigation and a determination of moral worth. And hence the badge in the buttonhole meant, "I am a gentleman patented after investigation and probation and guaranteed by my membership." Again, this meant in business life above all, tested *credit worthiness*. One could observe that business opportunities were often decisively influenced by such legitimation.

All these phenomena, which seemed to be rather rapidly disintegrating—at least the religious organizations—were essentially confined to the middle classes. Some cultured Americans often dismissed these facts briefly and with a certain angry disdain as "humbug" or backwardness, or they even denied them; many of them actually did not know anything about them, as was affirmed to me by William James. Yet these survivals were still alive in many different fields, and sometimes in forms which appeared to be grotesque.

These associations were especially the typical vehicles of social ascent into the circle of the entrepreneurial middle class. They served to diffuse and to maintain the bourgeois capitalist business ethos among the broad strata of the middle classes (the farmers included).

As is well known, not a few (one may well say the majority of the older generation) of the American "promoters," "captains of industry," of the multi-millionaires and trust magnates belonged formally to sects, especially to the Baptists. However, in the nature of the case, these persons were often affiliated for merely conventional reasons, as in Germany, and only in order to legitimate themselves in personal and social life—not in order to legitimate themselves as businessmen; during the age of the Puritans, such "economic supermen" did not require such a crutch, and their "religiosity" was, of course, often of a more than dubious sincerity. The middle classes, above all the strata ascending with and out of the middle classes, were the bearers of that specific religious orientation which one must, indeed, beware viewing among them as only opportunistically determined.*

* "Hypocrisy" and conventional opportunism in these matters were hardly stronger developed in America than in Germany where, after all, an officer or civil servant "without religious affiliation or preference" was also an impossibility. And a Berlin ("Aryan!") Lord Mayor was not confirmed officially because he failed to have one of his children baptized. Only the direction in which conventional "hypocrisy" moved differed: official careers in Germany, business opportunities in the United States.

Yet one must never overlook that without the universal diffusion of these qualities and principles of a methodical way of life, qualities which were maintained through these religious communities, capitalism today, even in America, would not be what it is. In the history of any economic area on earth there is no epoch, [except] those quite rigid in feudalism or patrimonialism, in which capitalist figures of the kind of Pierpont Morgan, Rockefeller, Jay Gould, et al. were absent. Only the technical *means* which they used for the acquisition of wealth have changed (of course!). *They* stood and they stand "beyond good and evil." But, however high one may otherwise evaluate their importance for economic transformation, they have never been decisive in determining what economic mentality was to dominate a given epoch and a given area. Above all, they were not the creators and they were not to become the bearers of the specifically Occidental middle class mentality.

This is not the place to discuss in detail the political and social importance of the religious sects and the numerous similarly exclusive associations and clubs in America which are based upon recruitment by ballot. The entire life of a typical Yankee of the last generation led through a series of such exclusive associations, beginning with the Boys' Club in school, proceeding to the Athletic Club or the Greek Letter Society or to another student club of some nature, then onward to one of the numerous notable clubs of businessmen and the middle class or finally to the clubs of the metropolitan plutocracy. To gain admission was identical to a ticket of ascent, especially with a certificate before the forum of one's self-feeling; to gain admission meant to have "proved" oneself. A student in college who was not admitted to any club (or quasi-society) whatsoever was usually a sort of pariah. (Suicides because of failure to be admitted have come to my notice.) A businessman, clerk, technician, or doctor who had the same fate usually was of questionable ability to serve. Today, numerous clubs of this sort are bearers of those tendencies leading toward aristocratic status groups which characterize contemporary American development. These status groups develop alongside of and, what has to be well noted, partly in contrast to the naked plutocracy.

In America mere "money" in itself also purchases power, but not social honor. Of course, it is a means of acquiring social prestige. It is the same in Germany and everywhere else; except in Germany the appropriate avenue to social honor led from the purchase of a feudal estate to the foundation of an entailed estate, and acquisition of titular nobility, which in turn facilitated the reception of the grandchildren in aristocratic "society." In America, the old tradition respected the self-made man more than the heir, and the avenue to social honor consisted in affiliation with a genteel fraternity in a distinguished college, formerly with a distinguished sect (for instance, Presbyterian, in whose churches in New York one could find soft cushions and fans in the pews). At the present time, affiliation with a distinguished club is essential above all else. In addition, the kind of home is important (in "the street" which in middle-sized cities is almost never lacking) and the kind of dress and sport. Only recently descent from the Pilgrim fathers, from Pocahontas and other Indian ladies, et cetera has become important. This is not the place for a more detailed treatment. There are masses of translating bureaus and agencies of all sorts concerned with reconstructing the pedigrees of the plutocracy. All these phenomena, often highly grotesque, belong in the broad field of the Europeanization of American "society."

In the past and up to the very present, it has been a characteristic precisely of the specifically American democracy that it did *not* constitute a formless sand heap of individuals, but rather a buzzing complex of strictly exclusive, yet voluntary associations. Not so long ago these associations still did not recognize the prestige of birth and *inherited* wealth, of the office and educational diploma; at least they recognized these things to such a low degree as has only very rarely been the case in the rest of the world. Yet, even so, these associations were far from accepting anybody with open arms as an equal. To be sure, fifteen years ago an American farmer would not have led his guest past a plowing farmhand (American born!) in the field without making his guest "shake hands" with the worker after formally introducing them.

Formerly, in a typical American club nobody would remember that the two members, for instance, who play billiards once stood in the relation of boss and clerk. Here equality of gentlemen prevailed absolutely. This was not always the case in the German-American clubs. When asking young German merchants in New York (with the best Hanseatic names) why they all strove to be admitted to an American club instead of the very nicely furnished German one, they answered that their (German-American) bosses would play billiards with them occasionally, however not without making them realize that they (the bosses) thought themselves to be "very nice" in doing so. To be sure, the American worker's wife accompanying the trade unionist to lunch had completely accommodated herself in dress and behavior, in a somewhat plainer and more awkward fashion, to the middle class lady's model.

He who wished to be fully recognized in this democracy, in whatever position, had not only to conform to the conventions of middle class society, the very strict men's fashions included, but as a rule he had to be able to show that he had succeeded in gaining admission by ballot to one of the sects, clubs, or fraternal societies, no matter what kind, were it only recognized as sufficiently legitimate. And he had to maintain himself in the society by proving himself to be a gentleman. The parallel in Germany consists in the importance of the *Couleur*[*] and the commission of an officer of the reserve for *commercium* and *connubium*, and the great status significance of qualifying to give satisfaction by duel. The thing is the same, but the direction and material consequence characteristically differ.

He who did not succeed in joining was no gentleman; he who despised doing so, as was usual among Germans,[**] had to take the hard road, and especially so in business life.

However, as mentioned above, we shall not here analyze the social significance of these conditions, which are undergoing a profound transformation. First, we are interested in the fact that the modern position of the secular clubs and societies with recruitment by ballot is largely the product of a process of *secularization*. Their position is derived from the far more exclusive importance of the prototype of these voluntary associations, to wit, the sects. They stem, indeed, from the sects in the homeland of genuine Yankeedom, the North Atlantic states. Let us recall, first, that the universal and equal franchise within American democracy (of the Whites! for Negroes and all mixtures have, even today, no de facto franchise) and likewise the "separation of state and church" are only achievements of the recent past, beginning essentially with the nineteenth century. Let us remember that during the colonial period in the central areas of New England, especially in Massachusetts, full citizenship status in the church congregation was the precondition for full citizenship in the state (besides some other prerequisites). The religious congregation

* Student fraternity, comparable to a "Greek letter society."

** But note above. Entry into an American club (in school or later) is always the decisive moment for the loss of German nationality.

indeed determined admission or non-admission to political citizenship status.[3]

The decision was made according to whether or not the person had *testified* his religious qualification through conduct, in the broadest meaning of the word, as was the case among all Puritan sects. The Quakers in Pennsylvania were not in any lesser way masters of that state until some time before the War of Independence. This was actually the case, though *formally* they were not the only full political citizens. They were political masters only by virtue of extensive gerrymandering.

The tremendous social significance of admission to full enjoyment of the rights of the sectarian congregation, especially the privilege of being admitted to the *Lord's Supper*, worked among the sects in the direction of breeding that ascetist professional ethic which was adequate to modern capitalism during the period of its origin. It can be demonstrated that everywhere, including Europe, the religiosity of the ascetist sects has for several centuries worked in the same way as has been illustrated by the personal experiences mentioned above for [the case of] America.

When focusing on the religious background[4] of these Protestant sects, we find in their literary documents, especially among those of the Quakers and Baptists up to and throughout the seventeenth century, again and again jubilation over the fact that the sinful "children of the world" distrust one another in business but that they have confidence in the religiously determined righteousness of the pious.[5]

Hence, they give credit and deposit their money only with the pious, and they make purchases in their stores because there, and there alone, they are given honest and *fixed prices*. As is known, the Baptists have always claimed to have first raised this price policy to a principle. In addition to the Baptists, the Quakers raise the claim, as the following quotation shows, to which Mr. Eduard Bernstein drew my attention at the time:

> But it was not only in matters which related to the law of the land where the primitive members held their words and engagements sacred. This trait was remarked to be true of them in their concerns of trade. On their first appearance as a society, they suffered as tradesmen because others, displeased with the peculiarity of their manners, withdrew their custom from their shops. But in a little time the great outcry against them was that they got the trade of the country into their hands. This outcry arose in part from a strict exemption of all commercial agreements between them and others and *because they never asked two prices for the commodities they sold.*[6]

The view that the gods bless with riches the man who pleases them, through sacrifice or through his kind of conduct, was indeed diffused all over the world. However, the Protestant sects consciously brought this idea into connection with this kind of religious conduct, according to the principle of early capitalism: "Honesty is the best policy." This connection is found, although not quite exclusively, among these Protestant sects, but with characteristic continuity and consistency it is found *only* among them.

The whole typically bourgeois ethic was from the beginning common to all asceticist sects and conventicles and it is identical with the ethic practiced by the sects in America up to the very present. The Methodists, for example, held to be forbidden:

(1) To make words when buying and selling (haggling').

(2) To trade with commodities before the custom tariff has been paid on them.

(3) To charge rates of interest higher than the law of the country permits.

(4) 'To gather treasures on earth' (meaning the transformation of investment capital into 'funded wealth').

(5) To borrow without being sure of one's ability to pay back the debt.

(6) Luxuries of all sorts.

But it is not only this ethic, already discussed in detail,* which goes back to the early beginnings of asceticist sects. Above all, the social premiums, the means of discipline, and, in general, the whole organizational basis of Protestant sectarianism with all its ramifications reach back to those beginnings. The survivals in contemporary America are the derivatives of a religious regulation of life which once worked with penetrating efficiency. Let us, in a brief survey, clarify the nature of these sects and the mode and direction of their operation.

Within Protestantism the principle of the "believer's church" first emerged distinctly among the Baptists in Zürich in 1523–24.[7] This principle restricted the congregation to "true" Christians; hence, it meant a voluntary association of really sanctified people segregated from the world. Thomas Münzer had rejected infant baptism; but he did not take the next step, which demanded repeated baptism of adults baptized as

* In *The Protestant Ethic and the Spirit of Capitalism.*

children (anabaptism). Following Thomas Münzer, the Zürich Baptists in 1525 introduced adult baptism (possibly including anabaptism). Migrant journeymen-artisans were the main bearers of the Baptist movement. After each suppression they carried it to new areas. Here we shall not discuss in detail the individual forms of this voluntarist inner-worldly asceticism of the Old Baptists, the Mennonites, the Baptists, the Quakers, nor shall we again describe how every asceticist denomination, Calvinism[8] and Methodism included, were again and again constrained into the same path.

This resulted either in the **conventicle** of the exemplary Christians *within* the church (Pietism), or else the community of religious "full citizens," legitimated as faultless, became masters *over* the church. The rest of the members merely belonged as a passive status group, as minor Christians subject to discipline (Independents).

In Protestantism the external and internal conflict of the two structural principles—of the "church" as a compulsory association for the administration of grace, and of the "sect" as a voluntary association of religiously qualified persons—runs through the centuries from Zwingli to Kuyper and Stöcker. Here we merely wish to consider those consequences of the voluntarist principle which are practically important in their influence upon conduct. In addition, we recall merely that the decisive idea of keeping the Lord's Supper pure, and therefore excluding unsanctified persons, led also to a way of treating church discipline among those denominations which failed to form sects. It was especially the predestinarian Puritans who, in effect, approached the discipline of the sects.[9]

The central social significance of the Lord's Supper for the Christian communities is evidenced in this. For the sects themselves, the idea of the purity of the sacramental communion was decisive at the very time of their origin.[10] Immediately the first consistent voluntarist, Browne, in his "Treatise of Reformation without tarying for anie" (presumably 1582), emphasized the compulsion to hold communion at the Lord's Supper with "wicked men" as the main reason for rejecting Episcopalianism and Presbyterianism.[11] The Presbyterian church struggled in vain to settle the problem. Already under Elizabeth (Wandworth Conference) this was the decisive point.*

* The English Presbyterians under Elizabeth wished to recognize the 39 articles of the Church of England (with reservations concerning articles 34 to 36, which are here of no interest).

The question of *who* might exclude a person from the Lord's Supper played an ever-recurrent role in the Parliament of the English Revolution. At first (1645) ministers and elders, that is, laymen, were to decide these matters freely. Parliament attempted to determine those cases in which exclusion should be permissible. All other cases were to be made dependent on the consent of Parliament. This meant "Erastianism," against which the Westminster Assembly protested sharply.

The Independent party excelled in that it admitted only persons with tickets to communion, besides the local residents recognized to be in good standing. Members from outside congregations received tickets only upon recommendation by qualified members. The certificates of qualification (letters of recommendation), which were issued in case of removal to another place or in case of travel, also occur in the seventeenth century.[12] *Within* the official church, Baxter's conventicles (associations), which in 1657 were introduced in sixteen counties, were to be established as a kind of voluntary censorship bureau. These would assist the minister in determining the qualification and exclusion of scandalous persons from the Lord's Supper.[13] The "five dissenting brethren" of the Westminster Assembly—upper-class refugees who had lived in Holland—had already aimed at similar ends when they proposed to permit voluntaristic congregations to exist *beside* the parish and also to grant them the right to vote for delegates to the synod. The entire church history of New England is filled with struggles over such questions: who was to be admitted to the sacraments (or, for instance, as a godfather), whether the children of non-admitted persons could be baptized,* under what clauses the latter could be admitted, and similar questions. The difficulty was that not only was the worthy person allowed to receive the Lord's Supper, but he *had* to receive it.[14] Hence, if the believer doubted his own worth and decided to stay away from the Lord's Supper, the decision did not remove his sin.[15] The congregation, on the other hand, was jointly responsible to the Lord for keeping unworthy and especially reprobated persons[16] away from communion, for purity's sake. Thus the congregation was jointly and especially responsible for the administration of the sacrament by a worthy minister in a state of grace. Therewith, the primordial problems of church constitution were resurrected. In vain Baxter's compromise proposal attempted to mediate by suggesting that

* Even the Brownist petition to King James of 1603 protested against this.

at least in case of an emergency the sacrament should be received from an unworthy minister, thus from one whose conduct was questionable.[17]

The ancient Donatist principle of personal charisma stood in hard and unmitigated opposition to the principle of the church as an institution administering grace,[18] as in the time of early Christianity. The principle of instituted grace was radically established in the Catholic Church through the priest's *character indelebilis* [indestructible integrity], but it also dominated the official churches of the Reformation. The uncompromising radicalism of the Independentist world of ideas rested upon the religious responsibility of the congregation as a whole. This held for the worthiness of the ministers as well as for the brethren admitted to communion. And that is how things still stand in principle.

As is known, the Kuyper schism in Holland during recent decades had far-reaching political ramifications. It originated in the following manner: Against the claims of the Synodal church government of the Herformde Kerk der Nederlanden, the elders of a church in Amsterdam, hence *laymen*, with the later prime minister Kuyper (who was also a plain lay elder) at the helm, refused to acknowledge the confirmation certificates of preachers of outside congregations as sufficient for admission to communion if from their standpoint such outside preachers were unworthy or unbelieving.[19] In substance, this was precisely the antagonism between Presbyterians and Independents during the sixteenth century; for consequences of the greatest importance emerged from the joint responsibility of the congregation. Next to the voluntarist principle, that is, free admission of the qualified, and of the qualified alone, as members of the congregation, we find the principle of the sovereignty of the local sacramental community. Only the local religious community, by virtue of personal acquaintance and investigation, could judge whether a member was qualified. But a church government of an inter-local association could not do so, however freely elected such church government might be. The local congregation could discriminate only if the number of members was restricted. Hence, in principle, only relatively small congregations were appropriate.[20]

Where the communities were too large for this, either conventicles were formed, as in Pietism, or the members were organized in groups, which, in turn, were the bearers of church discipline, as in Methodism.[21] The extraordinarily strict moral discipline[22] of the self-governing congregation constituted the third principle. This was unavoidable because of the interest in the purity of the sacramental community (or, as among the Quakers, the interest in the purity of the community of prayer). The discipline of the asceticist sect was, in fact, far more rigorous than the discipline of any church. In this respect, the sect resembles the monastic order. The sect discipline is also analogous to monastic discipline in that it established the principle of the novitiate.* In contrast to the principles of the official Protestant churches, persons expelled because of moral offenses were often denied all intercourse with the members of the congregation. The sect thus invoked an absolute boycott against them, which included business life. Occasionally the sect avoided any relation with non-brethren except in cases of absolute necessity.[23] And the sect placed disciplinary power predominantly into the hands of laymen. No spiritual authority could assume the community's joint responsibility before God. The weight of the lay elders was very great even among the Presbyterians. However, the Independents, and even more, the Baptists signified a struggle against the domination or the conurecration by theologians.[24] In exact correspondence this struggle led naturally to the clericalization of the lay members, who now took over the functions of moral control through self-government, admonition, and possible excommunication.[25] The domination of laymen in the church found its expression, in part, in the quest for freedom of the layman to preach (liberty of prophesying).[26] In legitimizing this demand, reference was made to the conditions of the early Christian community. This demand was not only very shocking to the Lutheran idea of the pastoral office but also to the Presbyterian idea of God's order. The domination of laymen, in part, found its expression in an opposition to any professional theologian and preacher. Only charisma, neither training nor office, should be recognized.**

The Quakers have adhered to the principle that in the religious assembly anyone could speak, but he alone should speak who was moved by the spirit. Hence no professional minister exists at all. To be sure, today this is, in all probability, nowhere radically effected. The official "legend" is that members who, in the experience of the congregation, are especially accessible to the spirit during service are

---

* In all probability among all sects there existed a period of probation. Among the Methodists, for example, it lasted for six months.

** Already Smyth in Amsterdam demanded that when preaching the regenerate must not even have the Bible in front of him.

seated upon a special bench opposite the congregation. In profound silence the people wait for the spirit to take possession of one of them (or of some other member of the congregation). But during service in a Pennsylvania college, unfortunately and against my hopes, the spirit did not take hold of the plainly and beautifully costumed old lady who was seated on the bench and whose charisma was so highly praised. Instead, undoubtedly by agreement, the spirit took hold of a brave college librarian who gave a very learned lecture on the concept of the "saint."

To be sure, other sects have not drawn such radical conclusions, or at least not for good. However, either the minister is not active principally as a "hireling,"[27] holding only honorific position, or else he serves for voluntary honorific donations.* Again his ministerial service may be a secondary occupation and only for the refunding of his expenses;** or he can be dismissed at any time; or a sort of missionary organization prevails with itinerant preachers[28] working only once in a while in the same "circuit," as is the case with Methodism.[29] Where the office (in the traditional sense) and hence the theological qualification were maintained,[30] such skill was considered as a mere technical and specialist prerequisite. However, the really decisive quality was the charisma of the state of grace, and the authorities were geared to discern it.

Authorities, like Cromwell's triers (local bodies for the handling of certificates of religious qualification) and the ejectors (ministerial disciplinary office),*** had to examine the fitness of the ministers to serve. The charismatic character of authority is seen to have been preserved in the same way in which the charismatic character of the membership in the community itself was preserved, just as Cromwell's army of Saints allowed only religiously qualified persons to pass the Lord's Supper to them, so Cromwell's soldiers refused to go into battle under an officer who did not belong to his sacramental community of the religiously qualified.[31]

---

* The latter was demanded for all preachers in the Agreement of the People of 1 May 1649.

** Thus the local preachers of the Methodists.

*** Thus, in accordance with the proposal of 1652 and essentially also in accordance with the church constitution of 1654.

Internally, among the sect members, the spirit of early Christian brotherliness prevailed, at least among the early Baptists and derived denominations; or at least brotherliness was demanded.[32] Among some sects it was considered taboo to call on the law courts.* In case of need, mutual aid was obligatory.[33] Naturally, *business* dealings with nonmembers were not interdicted (except occasionally among wholly radical communities).

Yet it was self-understood that one preferred the brethren.** From the very beginning, one finds the system of certificates (concerning membership and conduct),[34] which were given to members who moved to another place. The charities of the Quakers were so highly developed that in consequence of the burdens incurred their inclination to propagandize was finally crippled. The cohesiveness of the congregations was so great that, with good reason, it is said to be one of the factors determining New England settlements. In contrast to the South, New England settlements were generally compact and, from the beginning, strongly urban in character.***

It is obvious that in all these points the modern functions of American sects and sectlike associations, as described in the beginning of this essay, are revealed as straight derivatives, rudiments, and survivals of those conditions which once prevailed in all asceticist sects and conventicles. Today they are decaying. Testimony for the sectarian's immensely exclusive "pride in caste" has existed from the very beginning.****

Now, what part of this whole development was and is actually decisive for our problem? Excommunication in the Middle Ages also had political and civic consequences. Formally this was even harsher than where sect freedom existed. Moreover, in the Middle Ages only Christians could be full citizens. During the Middle Ages it was also possible to proceed through the disciplinary powers of the church against a

* The Methodists have often attempted to sanction the appeal to the secular judge by expulsion. On the other hand, in several cases, they have established authorities upon which one could call if debtors did not pay promptly.

** With the Methodists this is expressly prescribed.

*** Doyle in his work which we have repeatedly cited ascribes the industrial character of New England, in contrast to the agrarian colonies, to this factor.

**** Cf., for example, Doyle's comments about the status conditions in New England, where the families bearing old religious literary tradition, not the "propertied classes," formed the aristocracy.

bishop who would not pay his debts, and, as Aloys Schulte has beautifully shown, this possibility gave the bishop a credit rating over and above a secular prince. Likewise, the fact that a Prussian Lieutenant was subject to discharge if he was incapable of paying off debts provided a higher credit rating for him. And the same held for the German fraternity student. Oral confession and the disciplinary power of the church during the Middle Ages also provided the means to enforce church discipline effectively. Finally, to secure a legal claim, the opportunity provided by the oath was exploited to secure excommunication of the debtor.

In all these cases, however, the forms of behavior that were favored or tabooed through such conditions and means differed totally from those which Protestant asceticism bred or suppressed. With the lieutenant, for instance, or the fraternity student, and probably with the bishop as well, the enhanced credit rating certainly did not rest upon the breeding of personal qualities suitable for business; and following up this remark directly: even though the effects in all three cases were intended to have the same direction, they were worked out in quite different ways. The medieval, like the Lutheran church discipline, first, was vested in the hands of the ministerial officeholder; secondly, this discipline worked—as far as it was effective at all—through authoritarian means; and, thirdly, it punished and placed premiums upon concrete individual acts.

The church discipline of the Puritans and of the sects was vested, first, at least in part and often wholly, in the hands of laymen. Secondly, it worked through the necessity of one's having to hold one's own; and, thirdly, it bred or, if one wishes, selected qualities. The last point is the most important one.

The member of the sect (or conventicle) had to have qualities of a certain kind in order to enter the community circle. Being endowed with these qualities was important for the development of rational modern capitalism, as has been shown in the first essay.* In order to hold his own in this circle the member had to *testify* repeatedly that he was endowed with these qualities. They were constantly and continuously bred in him. For, like his bliss in the beyond, his whole social existence in the here and now depended upon his "testifying" to his belief. The Catholic confession of sins was, to repeat, by comparison a means of *relieving* the person from the tremendous internal pressure under which the sect mem-

* *The Protestant Ethic and the Spirit of Capitalism.*

ber in his conduct was constantly held. How certain orthodox and heterodox religious communities of the Middle Ages have been forerunners of the ascetic denominations of Protestantism shall not here and now be discussed.

According to all experience there is no stronger means of breeding traits than through the necessity of holding one's own in the circle of one's associates. The continuous and unobtrusive ethical discipline of the sects was, therefore, related to authoritarian church discipline as rational breeding and selection are related to ordering and forbidding.

In this as in almost every other respect, the Puritan sects are the most specific bearers of the inner-worldly form of asceticism. Moreover, they are the most consistent and, in a certain sense, the only consistent antithesis to the universalist Catholic Church—a compulsory organization for the administration of grace. The Puritan sects put the most powerful individual interest of social self-esteem in the service of this breeding of traits. Hence *individual* motives and personal self-interests were also placed in the service of maintaining and propagating the "middle class" Puritan ethic, with all its ramifications. This is absolutely decisive for its penetrating and for its powerful effect.

To repeat, it is not the ethical *doctrine* of a religion, but that form of ethical conduct upon which *premiums* are placed that matters.[35] Such premiums operate through the form and the condition of the respective goods of salvation. And such conduct constitutes "one's" specific "ethos" in the sociological sense of the word. For Puritanism, that conduct was a certain methodical, rational way of life which—given certain conditions—paved the way for the "spirit" of modern capitalism. The premiums were placed upon "testifying" oneself before God in the sense of attaining salvation—which is found in *all* Puritan denominations—and "testifying" oneself before men in the sense of socially holding one's own within the Puritan sects. Both aspects were mutually supplementary and operated in the same direction: they helped to deliver the "spirit" of modern capitalism, its specific *ethos*: the ethos of the modern *bourgeois middle classes*.

The ascetic conventicles and sects formed one of the most important historical foundations of modern "individualism." Their radical break away from patriarchal and authoritarian bondage,[36] as well as their way of interpreting the statement that one owes more obedience to God than to man, were especially important.

Finally, in order to understand the nature of these ethical effects, a comparative remark is required. In the *guilds* of the Middle Ages there was frequently a control of the general ethical standard of the members similar to that exercised by the discipline of the ascetic Protestant sects.[37] But the unavoidable difference in the effects of guild and of sect upon the economic conduct of the individual is obvious.

The guild united members of the same occupation; hence it united *competitors*. It did so in order to limit competition as well as the rational striving for profit which operated through competition. The guild trained for "civic" virtues and, in a certain sense, was the bearer of middle class "rationalism" (a point which will not be discussed here in detail). The guild accomplished this through a "subsistence policy" and through traditionalism. In so far as guild regulation of the economy gained effectiveness, its practical results are well known.

The sects, on the other hand, united men through the selection and the breeding of ethically qualified *fellow believers*. Their membership was not based upon apprenticeship or upon the family relations of technically qualified members of an occupation. The sect controlled and regulated the members' conduct *exclusively* in the sense of formal *righteousness* and methodical asceticism. It was devoid of the purpose of a material subsistence policy which handicapped an expansion of the rational striving for profit. The capitalist success of a guild member undermined the spirit of the guild—as happened in England and France—and hence capitalist success was shunned. But the capitalist success of a sect brother, if legally attained, testified of his worth and of his state of grace, and it raised the prestige and the propaganda chances of the sect. Such success was therefore welcome, as the several statements quoted above show. The organization of free labor in guilds, in their Occidental medieval form, has certainly—very much against their intention—not only been a handicap but also a precondition for the capitalist organization of labor, which was, perhaps, indispensable.[38] But the guild, of course, could not give birth to the modern middle class capitalist *ethos*. Only the methodical way of life of the ascetic sects could legitimate and put a halo around the economic "individualist" impulses of the modern capitalist ethos. ✦

Max Weber's 'Prefatory Remarks' to Collected Essays in the Sociology of Religion (1920)

Translated by Stephen Kalberg

Any child of modern European culture will, unavoidably and justifiably, address universal-historical[1] themes with a particular question in mind: What combination of circumstances called forth the broad range of ideas and cultural forces that on the one hand arose in the West, and only in the West, and on the other hand stood—at least as we like to imagine—in a line of historical development endowed in *all* civilizations with significance and validity?

Science, developed to the stage that we today recognize as "valid," exists only in the West. Empirical knowledge, reflection on the world and the problems of life, philosophical and theological wisdom of the deepest kind, extraordinarily refined knowledge and observation—all this has existed outside the West, above all in India, China, Babylon, and Egypt. Yet a fully developed systematic theology appeared only in Hellenic-influenced Christianity (even though some beginnings were apparent in Islam and a few sects in India). And despite empirical knowledge, Babylonian, and every other type of astronomy, lacked a mathematical foundation (rendering the development, in particular, of Babylonian astronomy all the more astonishing), which would be provided only later by the Greeks. A further product of the Hellenic mind, the idea of rational "proof," was absent from geometry in India. This mind also first created mechanics and physics. Moreover, although natural sciences in India were quite well developed as concerns observation, they lacked the rational experiment, which was essentially a product of the Renaissance (although beginnings can be found in the ancient world). The modern laboratory was also missing in the natural sciences developed in India. For this reason, medicine in India, which was highly developed in terms of empirical technique, never acquired a biological, and especially, a biochemical foundation. A rational chemistry was absent from all regions outside the West.

The scholarly writing of history in China, which was very advanced, lacked the rigor of Thucydides [*ca.* 460–400 BCE].[2] Precursors of

Machiavelli [1489–1527] existed in India, yet all Asian theorizing on the state omitted a systematic approach comparable to Aristotle's [384–322 BCE], as well as rational[3] concepts in general. A rational jurisprudence based on rigorous juridical models and modes of thinking of the type found in Roman law and the Western law indebted to it was absent outside the West, despite all beginnings in India (School of Mimamsa)[4] and the comprehensive codification of law in the Near East especially—and in spite of all the books on law written in India and elsewhere. A form of law similar to canon law cannot be found outside the West.

Similar conclusions must be drawn for art. The musical ear, apparently, was developed to a more refined degree among peoples outside the West than in the West to this day; or, at any rate, not less so. The most diverse sorts of polyphonic music have expanded across the globe, as did also the simultaneous playing of a number of instruments and singing in the higher pitches. All of the West's rational tone intervals were also widely calculated and known elsewhere. However, unique to the West were many musical innovations. Among them were rational, harmonic music (both counterpoint and harmony); formation of tone on the basis of three triads and the major third;[5] and the understanding of chromatics and enharmonics since the Renaissance harmonically and in rational form (rather than by reference to distance). Others were the orchestra with the string quartet as its core and the organization of ensembles of wind instruments; the bass accompaniment; and the system of musical notation (which made possible the composition and rehearsal of modern works of music and their very survival over time). Still other innovations were sonatas, symphonies, and operas (although organized music, onomatopoeia, chromatics, and alteration of tones have existed in the most diverse music as modes of expression). Finally, the West's basic instruments were the means for all this: the organ, piano, and violin.

[The situation is similar in architecture.] As a means of decoration, pointed arches existed outside the West, both in the ancient world and in Asia. Presumably, the juxtaposition of pointed arches and cross-arched vaults was not unknown in the Middle East. However, the rational utilization of the Gothic vault as a means to distribute thrust and to arch over variously formed spaces and, above all, as a principle of construction for large monumental buildings and as the foundation for a *style* that incorporated sculpture and painting, as was created in the Middle Ages—all this was missing outside the West. A solution to the weight problem introduced by domes was also lacking outside the West, even though the technical basis for its solution was taken from the Middle East. Every type of "classical" rationalization[6] of the entire art world—as occurred in painting through the rational use of both linear and spatial perspective—was also lacking outside the West, where it began with the Renaissance.

Printing existed in China. Yet a printed literature intended *only* to be printed and made possible exclusively through printing—"daily newspapers" and "periodicals," mainly—originated only in the West.

Universities of all possible types existed also outside the West (China and the Islamic world), even universities that look externally similar to those in the West, especially to Western academies. A rational and systematic organization into scientific disciplines, however, with trained and specialized professionals (*Fachmenschentum*), existed only in the West. This becomes especially evident if these disciplines are viewed from the vantage point of whether they attained the culturally dominant significance they have achieved in the West today.

Above all, the cornerstone of the modern state and modern economy—specialized *civil servants*—arose only in the West. Only precursors of this stratum appeared outside the West. It never became, in any sense, as constitutive for the social order as occurred in the West. The "civil servant," of course, even the civil servant who performs specialized tasks, appeared in various societies, even in ancient times. However, only in the modern West is our entire existence—the foundational political, technical, and economic conditions of our being—absolutely and inescapably bound up in the casing (*Gehäuse*) of an *organization* of specially trained civil servants. No nation and no epoch has come to know state civil servants in the way that they are known in the modern West, namely, as persons trained in technical, commercial, and above all, legal areas of knowledge who are the social carriers of the most important everyday functions of social life.

[And what about the state?] The organization of political and social groups on the basis of *status* has existed historically on a broad scale. Yet the *Ständestaat* in the Western sense—*rex et regnum*—has appeared only in the West.[7] Moreover, parliaments of periodically elected "representatives," with demagogues and party leaders held responsible as "ministers" to parliamentary procedures, have come into existence only in the West. This remains the case even though "political parties," of course, in the sense of organizations oriented to the acquisition of political power and the exercise of influence on political policy, can be found throughout the world. The "state," in fact, as a political institution (*Anstalt*) operated according to a rationally enacted "constitution" and rationally enacted laws, and administered by civil servants possessing *specialized* arenas of competence and oriented to rules and "laws," has existed with these distinguishing features only in the West, even though rudimentary developments in these directions have crystallized elsewhere.

The same may be said of that most fateful power of our modern life: *capitalism*.

A "drive to acquire goods" has actually nothing whatsoever to do with capitalism, as little as has the "pursuit of profit," money, and the greatest possible gain. Such striving has been found, and is to this day, among waiters, physicians, chauffeurs, artists, prostitutes, corrupt civil servants, soldiers, thieves, crusaders, gambling casino customers, and beggars. One can say that this pursuit of profit exists among "all sorts and conditions of men" [Sir Walter Besant],[8] in all epochs and in all countries of the globe. It can be seen both in the past and in the present wherever the objective possibility for it somehow exists.

This naive manner of conceptualizing capitalism by reference to a "pursuit of gain" must be relegated to the kindergarten of cultural history methodology and abandoned once and for all. A fully unconstrained compulsion to acquire goods cannot be understood as synonymous with capitalism, and even less as its "spirit." On the contrary, capitalism *can* be identical with the *taming* of this irrational motivation, or at least with its rational tempering. Nonetheless, capitalism is distinguished by the striving for *profit*, indeed, profit is pursued in a rational, continuous manner in companies and firms, and then pursued *again and again*, as is *profitability*. There are no choices. If the entire economy is organized according to the rules of the open market, any company that fails to orient its activities toward the chance of attaining profit is condemned to bankruptcy.

***

Let us begin by *defining terms* in a manner more precise than often occurs. For us, a "capitalist" economic act involves first of all an expectation of profit based on the utilization of opportunities for *exchange*; that is, of (formally) *peaceful* opportunities for acquisition. Formal and actual acquisition through violence follows its own special laws and hence should best be placed, as much as one may recommend doing so, in a different category.[9] Wherever capitalist acquisition is rationally pursued, action is oriented to *calculation* in terms of capital. What does this mean?

Such action is here oriented to a systematic utilization of skills or personal capacities on behalf of earnings in such a manner that, at the close of business transactions, the company's money *balances*, or "capital" (its earnings through transactions), exceed the estimated value of all production costs (and, in the case of a longer lasting company, *again and again* exceed costs). It is all the same whether goods entrusted to a traveling salesman are involved and he receives payment through barter, so that the closing calculation takes place in goods, or whether the assets of a large manufacturing corporation (such as buildings, machines, cash, basic materials, and partly or entirely manufactured goods) are weighed against its production costs. Decisive in both situations is that a *calculation* of earnings in money terms takes place, regardless of whether it is made on the basis of modern accounting methods or primitive, superficial procedures. Both at the beginning of the project and at the end there are specific calculations of balances. A starting balance is established and calculations are carried out before each separate transaction takes place; at every stage an instrumental assessment of the utility of potential transactions is calculated; and, finally, a concluding balance is calculated and the origin of "the profit" ascertained.

For example, the beginning balance of the *commenda* transaction [see ch. 2, note 15] involves, for example, a designation of the amount of money agreed upon by both parties regarding what the relevant goods *should* be worth (assuming they have not already been given a monetary value). A final balance forms the estimate on the basis of which a distribution of profit and loss takes place. Calculation lies (as long as each case is rational) at the foundation of every single activity of the *commenda* partners. However, an actual exact accounting and appraisal may not exist, for on some occasions the transaction proceeds purely by reference to estimates or even on the basis of traditions and conventions. Indeed, such estimation appears in every form of capitalist enterprise even today wherever circumstances do not require more exact calculation. These points, however, relate only to the *degree* of rationality of capitalist acquisition.

Important for the formation of the *concept* of capitalism is only that economic action is decisively influenced by the *actual* orientation to a comparison of estimated monetary expenses with estimated monetary income, however primitive in form the comparison may be. Now in this sense we can see that, insofar as our documents on economies have reached into the distant past, "capitalism" and "capitalist" enterprises, at times with only a moderate degree of rationalization of capital accounting, have existed in *all* the world's civilizations. In other words, "capitalism" and "capitalist" enterprises have been found in China, India, Babylon, Egypt, the ancient Mediterranean, and medieval Europe, as well as in the modern West. Not only entirely isolated enterprises existed in these civilizations; rather, also businesses are found completely oriented to the continuous appearance of new companies and to a continuity of "operations." This remained the situation even though trade, over long periods, did not become perpetual, as it did in the West; instead, it assumed the character of a series of separate enterprises. A business context—the development of different "branches" for business—congealed only gradually and only slowly influenced the behavior of the *large-scale* commercial traders. At any rate, the capitalist enterprise has been an enduring, highly universal, and ancient organization. Also capitalist businessmen, not only as occasional entrepreneurs but as persons oriented permanently to business, have been ancient, enduring, and highly universal figures.

***

The West, however, has given birth to types and forms of capitalism (as well as to directions for its unfolding) that have provided the foundation for the development of capitalism to an extent and significance unknown outside the West. Merchants have engaged in wholesale and retail trade, on a local as well as international scale, throughout the world. Businesses offering loans of every sort have existed widely, as have banks with the most diverse functions (although for the most part functions essentially similar to those of Western banks of the sixteenth century). Sea loans,[10] *commenda*, and *kommandit*[11] types of businesses and formal associations have been widespread. Wherever the financing of public institutions through *currency* has occurred,[12] financiers have appeared—in Babylon, ancient Greece, India, China, and ancient Rome. They have financed above all wars, piracy, and all types of shipping and construction projects; as entrepreneurs in colonies they have served the international policy goals of nations. In addition, these *adventure* capitalists have acquired plantations and operated them using slaves or (directly or indirectly) forced labor; they have leased land and the rights to use honorific titles; they have financed both the leaders of political parties standing for re-election and mercenaries for civil wars; and, finally, as "speculators" they have been involved in all sorts of money-raising opportunities.

This type of entrepreneur—the adventure capitalist—has existed throughout the world. With the exception of trade, credit, and banking businesses, his money-making endeavors have been mainly either of a purely irrational and speculative nature or of a violent character, such as the capture of booty. This has taken place either through warfare or the continuous fiscal exploitation of subjugated populations.

Promoter, adventure, colonial, and, as it exists in the West, modern finance capitalism can be characterized often, even today, in terms of these features. This becomes especially apparent whenever capitalism is oriented to warfare, although it holds even in periods of peace. Single (and only single) components of large-scale international commerce today, as in the past, approximate adventure capitalism.

However, in the *modern* era the West came to know an entirely different type of capitalism. Absent from all other regions of the globe, or existing only in preliminary developmental stages, this capitalism appeared side-by-side with adventure capitalism and took as its foundation the rational-capitalist[13] organization of (legally) *free labor.* With *coerced* labor, a certain degree of rational organization had been attained only on the plantations of antiquity, and to a very limited extent, on the ancient world's *ergasteria*.[14] An even lesser degree of rationality was reached in agricultural forced-labor enterprises generally, the workshops of medieval manors, and in manor-based cottage industries utilizing the labor of serfs at the dawning of the modern era. Outside the West, free labor has been found only occasionally. Even the existence of actual "cottage industries" has been documented with certainty only rarely outside the West. And the use of day laborers, which naturally can be found everywhere, did not lead to manufacturing and not at all to a rational, apprenticeship-style organization of skilled labor of the type practiced in the West's Middle Ages. This must be said despite a very few, very unusual exceptions, and even these diverged significantly from the modern Western organization of industrial work in companies (especially from those companies that, through support from the state, held market monopolies).

However, the rational organization of industrial companies and their orientation to *market* opportunities, rather than to political violence or to irrational speculation, does not constitute the only distinguishing mark of Western capitalism. The modern, rational organization of the capitalist industrial firm would not have been possible without two prior important developments: (1) the *separation of the household from the industrial company*, which absolutely dominates economic life today, and, connected closely to this development, (2) the appearance of rational *accounting*.

The spatial separation of the place of labor or sales from the place of residence can be also found elsewhere (in the Oriental bazaar and in the *ergasteria* of other cultures). Capitalist associations with accounting procedures separate from personal accounts existed in East Asia as well as in the Middle East and the ancient world. Nonetheless, compared to the modern situation in which company operations are fully independent, these examples show only very limited beginnings. This remained the case above all because the *internal* preconditions for independent business operation—rational *accounting* methods and a *legal* separation of company wealth from personal wealth—were either entirely absent or developed only to preliminary stages.[15] Instead, outside the West, industry-oriented endeavors tended to become simply one component of the feudal manor's *household* activities (the *oikos*). [Karl Johann] Rodbertus [1805–65] has already noted that all developments toward the *oikos* deviated distinctly from the route taken by capitalist activity in the West. Indeed, as he argues, and despite a number of apparent similarities, the *oikos* stood starkly in opposition to the Western pathway.[16]

***

All these particular aspects of Western capitalism, however, in the end acquired their present-day significance as a result of their connection to the capitalist organization of *work*. Even what one is inclined to call "commercialization"—the development of stocks and bonds and the systematization, through stock markets, of speculation—must be seen as taking place in the context of a capitalist organization of labor. All this, even the development toward "commercialization," if it had been possible at all, would never have unfolded to anywhere near the same proportion and dimension if a capitalist-rational organization of work had been lacking. Hence, all of these new factors would never have significantly influenced the social structure and all those problems associated with it specific to the modern West. Exact calculation, the foundation for everything else, is possible only on the basis of *free* labor.[17]

And as the world outside the modern West has not known the rational organization of work, it has also not known, and for this reason, rational *socialism*. Now, of course, just as history has experienced a full spectrum of types of economies, ranging from those, on the one hand, oriented to city development and city-organized food supply policies, mercantilism, the social welfare policies instituted by princes, the rationing of goods, a thorough regulation of the economy, and protectionism, and on the other hand to *laissez-faire* theories (also in China), the world has also known socialist and communist economies of the most diverse sorts. State socialist (in [ancient] Egypt) and cartel-monopolistic versions of socialism can be found, as can types of communism more rooted in (a) heterogeneous consumer organizations, (b) private sphere values of intimacy and the family, (c) religious values, and (d) military values. However (despite the existence everywhere at one time or another of guilds and brotherhood corporations, various legal distinctions between cities and provinces in the most diverse form, and cities that granted specific market advantages to particular groups), just as the concept of "citizen" is entirely missing except in the West and the concept of "bourgeoisie" is completely absent outside the modern West, so also the notion of a "proletariat" as a *class* is absent. Indeed, it could not appear outside the West precisely because a rational organization *of free labor* in *industrial enterprises* was lacking. "Class struggles" between strata of creditors and debtors, between those who owned land and those who did not (whether serfs or tenant sharecroppers), between persons with economic interests in commerce and consumers or owners of land—all these conflicts have existed for centuries in various constellations. Yet even the struggles typical in the West's medieval period between domestic industry entrepreneurs and their wage workers [the putting-out system] are found elsewhere only in a rudimentary form. The modern opposition between large-scale industrialists, as employers, and free workers paid a wage is completely lacking outside the West. And thus a situation of the type known to modern socialism also could not exist.

***

Hence, for us, as we investigate the universal history of civilizations, and even if we proceed by reference exclusively to issues directly related to the economy, the central problem in the end *cannot* be the unfolding of capitalist activity everywhere and the various forms it took. That is, our concern cannot be whether it appeared more as adventure capitalism, commercial capitalism, or a capitalism oriented to the opportunities for profit offered by war, politics, and state administration. Rather, the central problem must ultimately involve the origin of ***middle-class*** *industrial* capitalism with its rational organization of *free labor.* Or, rendered in the terms of cultural history: The central problem must ultimately concern the origin of the Western middle class and its particular features. Of course, this theme is closely interwoven with the question of the origin of the capitalist organization of labor. Yet it is naturally not exactly the same—for the simple reason that a "middle class," in the sense of a stratum of people, existed before the development of this specifically Western capitalism anchored in the capitalist organization of labor. However, obviously this was the case *only* in the West.

Now evidently the capitalism specific to the modern West has been strongly influenced above all by advances in the realm of *technology.* The nature of the rationality of modern Western capitalism is today determined by the calculability of factors that are technically decisive. Indeed, these factors are the foundation for all more exact calculation. In turn this calculability is rooted fundamentally in the characteristic uniqueness of Western science, and especially in the natural sciences grounded in the exactness of mathematics and the controlled experiment.

The development of these sciences, and the technology that is based upon them, acquired—and continues to acquire—pivotal invigorating impulses from opportunities offered by capitalism. Market opportunities, that is, as rewards, are connected to the economic applications of these technologies. However, it must also be emphasized that the origin of Western science cannot be explained by the availability of such economic opportunities. Calculation, even with decimals, existed also in the algebra of India, where the decimal system was discovered. Yet in India it never led to modern calculation and accounting methods; this mode of calculation was first placed into *operation* only in the West's developing capitalism. Similarly, the origin of mathematics and physics was not determined by economic interests, yet the *technical* application of scientific knowledge was. Important for the quality of life of the broad population, this application was conditioned by economic rewards—and these crystallized precisely in the West. These rewards, however, flowed out of the particular character of the West's *social* order. It must then be asked: From *which* components of this unique social order did these rewards derive? Surely not all of its features have been of equal importance.

The rational structure of *law* and administration has undoubtedly been among the most central elements of this social order. This is the case for the simple reason that modern-rational industrial capitalism, just as it requires calculable technical means in order to organize work, also needs a calculable law and administration that function according to formal rules. Of course adventure capitalism and a trade-based capitalism oriented to speculation, as well as all types of capitalism determined by political considerations, can well exist without calculable law and administration. However, a rational industrial firm—with fixed capital and reliable *calculation*, and operating in a private economy—is not possible without this type of law and administration.

Yet this type of law and administration, in *this* degree of legal-technical and formal perfection, was placed at the disposal of the economy and its development *only* in the West. Hence, one must ask: What was the source of this type of law in the West? Undoubtedly, in addition to other circumstances, *also* economic interests paved the way for the rule of a stratum of jurists who were professionally trained in rational law and who, in a disciplined and regular manner, practiced and administered law. This is evident from every investigation. Yet these economic interests were not the exclusive, or even the primary, causal forces in the rise of this stratum to importance. Moreover, economic interests did not of themselves *create* this type of law. Rather, entirely different powers were active in respect to this development. And why then did capitalist interests not call forth this stratum of jurists and this type of law in China or India? How did it happen that scientific, artistic, and economic development, as well as state-building, were not directed in China and India into those tracks of *rationalization* specific to the West?[18]

***

The issue in all of the cases mentioned above evidently involves a characteristic aspect of a specifically formed "rationalism" of Western civilization. Now this word can be understood as implying a vast spectrum of matters.[19] There is, for example, "rationalization" of mystical contemplation, that is, of a type of behavior that is specifically "irrational" if viewed from the perspective of other realms of life.[20] Similarly, there may be rationalization of the economy, technology, scientific work, education, warfare, administration, and the practice of law. One may further "rationalize" each one of these arenas from vantage points and goals of the most diverse sort and ultimate orientations. What may appear "rational" viewed from one angle may appear "irrational" when viewed from another.

Hence, we must note that rationalizations have occurred in the various arenas of life in highly varying ways and in all circles of cultural life.[21] It is necessary, in order to identify the ways in which the multiple rationalization paths have characteristically varied according to cultural and historical factors to assess *which* arenas have been rationalized and in what directions. Again, important here above all are the special *characteristic features* of Western rationalism and, within this particular type of rationalism,[22] the characteristic features of modern Western rationalism. Our concern is to identify this uniqueness and to explain its origin.

Every attempt at explanation, recognizing the fundamental significance of economic factors, must above all take account of these factors. Nevertheless, the opposite line of causation should not be neglected if only because the origin of economic rationalism depends not only on an advanced development of technology and law but also on the capacity and disposition of persons to **organize their lives** in a practical-rational manner. Wherever magical and religious forces have inhibited the unfolding of this organized life, the development of an organized life oriented systematically toward *economic* activity has confronted broad-ranging internal resistance. Magical and religious powers, and the ethical notions of duty based on them, have been in the past among the most important formative influences upon the way life has been organized.

***

Two older essays have been placed at the beginning of this collection on the sociology of religion [see pp. lviii–lxiv]: [*The Protestant Ethic and the Spirit of Capitalism* and "The Protestant Sects and the Spirit of Capitalism"].[23] By reference to *one* important point, both attempt to shed light on that aspect of the problem normally most difficult to understand: the influence of certain religious ideas on the origin of an "economic **frame of mind**," that is, on the "ethos" of an **economic form**. This theme will be addressed by offering an example of the connections between the modern economic ethos and the rational economic ethic of ascetic Protestantism. Thus, these two essays investigate only *one* side of the causal relationship.[24]

The later essays, which constitute the Economic Ethics of the World Religions (EEWR) series, attempt to explore *both* causal relationships[25] to the extent necessary for the discovery of points of *comparison* with the West's development, which will later be analyzed further.[26] They do so by offering an overview of the relationships between, on the one hand, the most important religions and the economy, and on the other hand, between the most important religions and the social stratification in their milieu. Only in this way will it be at all possible to pursue a relatively clear line of causal *attribution* that enables a determination of which components of the religion-defined Western economic ethic (that are characteristic for it and do not appear in non-Western economic ethics) became causal forces.

Thus, no claim is made that the EEWR essays seek to serve as something close to a comprehensive analysis of civilizations, albeit in an ever so compressed form. Rather, in respect to every theme, they intentionally and insistently emphasize that which stood—and stands today—in *contrast* to the line of development of Western civilization. They are, in other words, on the occasion of a depiction of the Western pathway of development, [as in *The Protestant Ethic and the Spirit of Capitalism*], entirely oriented to what seems to be important from the vantage point of *such contrasts*. No other mode of procedure appeared possible in light of [the] particular goal [here to determine the causal effect of the characteristic components of the economic ethic of Western religions]. Nonetheless, in order to avoid misunderstanding, the limitations of these studies must be explicitly noted at the outset.

In yet another manner the uninitiated, if not also others, must be warned against overestimating the significance of these analyses. To area specialists on China, India, or Egypt, as well as to experts on Semitic culture, these studies will offer no new research findings. It can only be hoped that these specialists discover nothing *essential* to the subject here that must be judged as objectively *incorrect*. The author cannot know to what extent he has succeeded in coming as close to this ideal, at least, as a non-specialist might be at all capable. It is certainly completely obvious that a person dependent on translations, and, moreover, forced to orient himself in a specialist literature (that is frequently highly debated and on which he cannot arrive at independent judgments) in order to use and evaluate a massive amount of documentary and literary material, has every reason to think of the value of his achievement in very modest terms. This is all the more the case because the number of available translations of the actual "source" material (that is, inscriptions and documents) in part to this day (especially for China) remains very small in proportion to that which exists in the original and is important. The completely *provisional* character of these essays follows from all these factors, especially for those sections that concern Asia.[27]

Only the specialist is entitled to render a final judgment on these investigations. Moreover, these studies were written only because, understandably, analyses by specialists oriented to the particular goal enunciated above and undertaken from the special angle pivotal here did not hitherto exist. Indeed, they are destined, far more so and in a different sense from specialized studies, soon to become "out-of-date"—although this, in the end, can be said of every scientific study.[28] Nonetheless, however hazardous, an encroachment into other social science disciplines cannot be avoided when one pursues such comparative themes. Yet one must acknowledge the consequence of doing so: a sense of deep resignation regarding the degree of one's success.

Fashion and the yearning of intellectuals today easily leads to the conclusion that the specialist can be pushed aside or, in order to please a public in search of a "show," humiliated by being reduced to the level of a subordinate worker. Almost all of the sciences are indebted to dilettantes for achievements of some sort, and often for the contribution of quite valuable vantage points. However, science would come to an end if dilettantism became its operating principle. Whoever wishes a "show" should best visit the cinema; it will offer, even in literary form, a massive schedule of events touching on just this thematic complex.[29] Nothing stands more distant from the dilettantes' frame of mind than the completely dispassionate analyses offered in these (according to my intention) strictly empirical investigations.

And, I would like to add, those who wish to hear a "sermon" should visit a **conventicle**. Not a single word will be expended on behalf of the relative *value* of the civilizations compared here.[30] It is true that the path of human destiny deeply scars the breast of each person who glances at even a short historical epoch. But all will be better off keeping their insignificant personal commentaries to themselves, just as one does when standing before an ocean vista and towering mountain peaks—unless one knows oneself to be called and endowed with the gift of artistic expression or prophetic powers. In most other cases the loquacious discussion of "intuition" only veils a lack of distance to the beauty of nature—which must be judged no differently from a lack of distance on persons.[31]

***

It needs to be justified how it came about that, on behalf of the goals pursued here, the author did not use *ethnographic* research to anywhere near the extent (in light of its present-day development) naturally indispensable for a fully convincing analysis, especially of religious devoutness in Asia. This omission occurred not only because there are limitations to the human capacity for work. Rather, it appeared permissible mainly because our concern here must necessarily be what holds together the religion-determined ethic of those strata that constituted the "carriers of culture" in their respective geographical regions. The influences exerted by *their* particular mode of organizing life concern us. Now it is completely correct that these influences, in their particularity, can actually be comprehended accurately only if the ethnographic-anthropological record is utilized. Hence, it is explicitly conceded and emphasized that a deficiency exists on this score and that ethnographers may legitimately raise objections to these studies. I will hope to be able to rectify this omission in part when I turn to a systematic treatment of the sociology of religion.[32] However, given the limited purposes of the Economic Ethics of the World Religions series, such an undertaking would have moved beyond the framework of its analysis. These investigations had to be content with attempting to unveil, as far as possible, the points of *comparison* to our *major* Western religions.

Finally, the *anthropological* side of the problem should also be considered. If we again and again discover in the West, and *only* in the West, specific *types* of rationalizations (and also in arenas of life [such as religion, the economy, and law] that seemingly developed independently from one another), then naturally a certain assumption appears plausible: heredity is playing a decisive role. The author confesses that he is inclined, personally and subjectively, to estimate highly the importance of biological heredity. However, despite the significant achievements of anthropological research at this time, I do not see any manner of exactly comprehending, or even hinting at in terms of probabilities, the share of heredity—namely, according to its extent, and above all, type and points of impact—in the development investigated *here*.

As one of its major tasks, sociological and historical research will have to reveal as many as possible of those influences and causal chains that are satisfactorily explainable as reactions to the effect of [biological] fate on the one hand and that of social milieu on the other. Only then, and only when, in addition, the comparative study of racial neurology and psychology moves beyond its rudimentary beginnings of today (which are promising in many ways, if one examines the discrete studies), can one *perhaps* hope for satisfactory results even for the problem studied here.[33] Yet any development in this direction appears to me for the time being not to exist and any referral to "heredity" would be, it seems to me, tantamount to both a premature abandonment of the extent of knowledge perhaps possible *today* and a displacement of the problem onto (at this time still) unknown factors. ✦

Notes for *The Protestant Ethic*

Chapter I

1. From the voluminous literature on this study I am citing only the most comprehensive criticisms. (a) Felix Rachfahl, "Kalvinismus und Kapitalismus," *Internationale Wochenschrift für Wissenschaft, Kunst und Technik* (1909), nos. 39–43. In reply, see my article, "Antikritisches zum Geist des Kapitalismus," *Archiv für Sozialwissenschaft und Sozialpolitik* 30 (1910): 176–202. Rachfahl then replied in his "Nochmals Kalvinismus und Kapitalismus," 1910, nos. 22–25, of the *Internationale Wochenschrift.* Finally, my "Antikritisches Schlusswort" (Final Word), *Archiv* 31 (1910): 554–99. [These essays, and further "critical" comments and "anti-critical" responses by Weber (1907–10), have been collected into one volume. See *Max Weber: Die protestantische Ethik II,* edited by Johannes Winckelmann (Gütersloh: Gütersloher Verlag, 1978). Weber's responses to his critics are now available in English. See *The Protestant Ethic Debate: Max Weber's Replies to His Critics, 1907–1910,* edited by David Chalcraft and Austin Harrington (translated by Harrington and Mary Shields, Liverpool: Liverpool University Press, 2001). Weber occasionally refers in the notes below to "the critics" and to his "anti-critical" replies. These terms refer to this early debate.] (Brentano, in the criticism presently to be referred to, evidently did not know of this last phase of the discussion, as he does not refer to it.) I have not incorporated anything in this edition from the rather unproductive (unavoidably) polemics against Rachfahl. He is an author whom I otherwise admire, but who has in this instance ventured into a field he has not thoroughly mastered. I have only added a few supplementary references from my anti-critical replies, and have attempted, in new passages and footnotes, to make impossible any future misunderstanding. (b) Werner Sombart, *Der Bourgeois* (Munich and Leipzig: Duncker & Humblot, 1913) [*The Quintessence of Capitalism* (New York: Howard Fertig, 1967)]. I shall return in the notes below to this volume. Finally, (c) Lujo Brentano in part 2 of the appendix to his Munich address (in the Academy of Sciences, 1913) on *Die Anfänge* [Beginnings] *des modernen Kapitalismus* [see note 15 below], which was published in 1916. [See ch. 3, excursus 2 on "Puritanism and Capitalism," pp. 117–57]. I shall also refer to this criticism in the notes in the proper places.

I invite anyone who may be interested to convince himself by comparison that in revision I have *not* left out, changed the meaning of, weakened, or added materially *different* statements to *a single essential sentence* of my essay. There was no occasion to do so, and the development of my argument will convince anyone who still doubts. Sombart and Brentano engaged in a more bitter quarrel with each other than with me. I consider Brentano's criticism of Sombart's book [published in 1911; translated in 1913 as *The Jews and Modern Capitalism* (New York: Burt Franklin)] in many points well founded, but often very unjust, even apart from the fact that Brentano does not himself seem to understand the real essence of the problem of the Jews (which is entirely omitted from this essay, but will be dealt with later). [See *Economy and Society* (*E&S*) (Berkeley: University of California Press, 1976), pp. 611–23; *Ancient Judaism* (New York: Free Press, 1952)].

From theologians I have received numerous valuable suggestions in connection with this study. Its reception on their part has been in general friendly and objective, even when wide differences of opinion on particular points were apparent. This is all the more valuable to me since I would not have been surprised by a certain hostility toward the way in which these matters were necessarily treated here. What to a theologian is *valuable* in his religion naturally cannot play a very large part in this study. We are concerned with what, if *evaluated* from a religious point of view, are often quite external and unrefined aspects of religious life. These aspects, however, precisely because they were external and unrefined, have often had the strongest influence.

Another book that, besides containing many other themes, is a very welcome confirmation of and supplement to this essay, insofar as it addresses our problem, is the important work of [Ernst] Troeltsch, *The Social Teaching of the Christian Churches,* 2 vols. (New York: Harper & Row, 1960 [1912]). It treats the entire history of the ethics of Western Christianity from a very comprehensive, and unique, point of view. I here refer the reader to Troeltsch for general comparison, as I cannot refer to his work repeatedly in respect to particular points. Troeltsch is principally concerned with the *doctrines* of religion, while I am interested rather in the practical effect of religion. [entire note from 1920]

2. The deviant cases are explained (not always but frequently) if we note that the religion of an industry's labor force is naturally, in the *first* instance, determined by the religion of the locality in which the industry is situated (that is, from which its labor is drawn). This circumstance often alters the impression given at first glance by statistics on religious affiliation, for instance in [the highly Catholic] state of North-Rhine Westphalia. Furthermore, figures can naturally be relied upon only if the particular occupations have become thoroughly specialized. Otherwise, in some situations, very large employers may be thrown together, under the category "proprietors of companies," with "master craftsmen," who work alone. Above all, the fully developed capitalism of *today,* especially so far as its broad, unskilled labor force is concerned, has become independent of any influence that religion *may* have had in the past. More on this point later.

3. Compare, for example, Hermann Schell, *Der Katholizismus als Prinzip des Fortschrittes* (Würzburg: Andreas Gobel, 1899), p. 31, and Georg Freiherr von Hertling, *Das Prinzip des Katholizismus und die Wissenschaft* (Freiburg: Herder, 1899), p. 58.

4. One of my students has thoroughly studied the most complete statistical material we possess on this subject: the denominational affiliation statistics of [the state of] Baden. See Martin Offenbacher, "Konfession und soziale Schichtung," *Eine Studie über die wirtschaftliche Lage der Katholiken und Protestanten in Baden* (Tübingen and Leipzig: Mohr, 1901), vol. 4, pt. 5, of the *Volkswirtschaftliche Abhandlungen der badischen Hochschulen.* The facts and figures used for illustrative purposes below all originate from this study.

5. Germans (Protestants) and Poles (Catholics) lived side by side until World War II in what is today western Poland (Silesia) [sk].

6. For example, in 1895 in [the state of] Baden, for every 1,000 Protestants a tax of 954,060 marks was collected for property that produced taxable income; 589,000 marks was collected for every 1,000 Catholics. It is true that the Jews, with more than four million marks for every 1,000 Jews, were far ahead of the rest. (For details see Offenbacher, *op. cit.*, p. 21.)

7. On this point compare the whole discussion in Offenbacher's study.

8. Offenbacher provides for Baden more detailed evidence also on this point in his first two chapters.

9. As innumerable commentators have noted, *Herrschaft* is a particularly difficult term to translate. It implies both legitimate authority and a coercive, dominating component. I will employ (following the translation in Weber's major analytic work, *E&S*) "domination" throughout. This appears appropriate as Weber occasionally uses the term *Autorität* (authority) in *The Protestant Ethic* volume [sk].

10. The population of Baden was composed in 1895 as follows: Protestants, 37.0 percent; Catholics, 61.3 percent; Jews, 1.5 percent. The percentage of students who attended the *noncompulsory* schools [beyond the primary level] were, however, divided as follows (Offenbacher, p. 16):

	Protestant	Catholic	Jews
	Percent	Percent	Percent
Gymnasien	44	46	9
Realgymnasien	60	30	10
Oberrealschulen	52	40	8
Realschulen	50	39	11
Höhere Bürgerschulen ..	49	40	11
Average	48	42	10

[Moving from top to bottom of this table, the curricula in the schools move away from an emphasis on the classical liberal arts, including ancient languages, and toward modern languages, science, and mathematics. This school system was replaced with a three-track system in the 1950s. On the basis of re-computation, Offenbacher's statistics were revised slightly by the German editor (Winckelmann). I have rounded his percentages.]

The same proportions may be observed in Prussia, Bavaria, Württemberg, the German-speaking territories, and Hungary (see figures in Offenbacher, pp. 18 ff.).

11. The figures in the preceding note indicate that Catholic attendance at secondary schools, which is regularly one-third less than the Catholic share of the total population, is exceeded, by a small percentage, *only* in the case of the *Gymnasien* (mainly as a result of preparation for theological studies). With reference to the subsequent discussion it may further be noted as characteristic that, in Hungary, those affiliated with the *Reformed* [Calvinist] church exceed even the average Protestant [Lutheran] record of attendance at secondary schools. (See Offenbacher, p. 19, note.)

12. For the figures see Offenbacher (p. 54) and the tables at the end of his study.

13. This is especially well illustrated by passages in the studies of Sir William Petty [*Political Arithmetick* (London: Henry Mortlock, 1687)] (which will be referred to repeatedly later).

14. Petty's occasional reference [to the contrary in] the case of *Ireland* is very simply explained by the fact that the Protestant stratum lived in Ireland only as absentee landlords. If his illustrations had meant to maintain more he would have been wrong (as is well-known), as is demonstrated by the position of the "Scotch-Irish." The typical relationship between Protestantism and capitalism existed in Ireland just as elsewhere. (On the Scotch-Irish see C. A. Hanna, *The Scotch-Irish,* 2 vols., [New York: Putnam, 1902].) [1920]

15. This is not, of course, to deny that the historical-political, external situations had exceedingly important consequences. I shall show later that many Protestant sects were small and hence homogeneous minorities, as were actually all the *strict* Calvinists outside of Geneva and New England (even where they were in possession of political power). This [external situation] was of fundamental significance for the development of believers' entire orientation of life in the sects, and this orientation then reacted back upon the participation of the faithful in economic life.

That *migrants* from all the religions of the earth—from India, Arabia, China, Syria, Phoenicia, Greece, Lombardy—have universally been the social carriers, to other countries, of the *commercial education* in highly developed areas has nothing to do with our problem. (Brentano, in the essay I shall often cite, *Die Anfänge des modernen Kapitalismus* (Munich: *Akademie der Wissenschaften*, 1916) refers to his own family. But *bankers* of foreign extraction have existed at *all* times, and in all countries, as the social carriers of commercial experience and connections. These bankers are not unique to *modern* capitalism, and were looked upon with ethical mistrust by the Protestants [see below]. The case of the Protestant families from Locarno [Italy], such as the Muralts, Pestalozzi, and others, who migrated to Zurich, was different. They very soon became the social carriers of a specifically modern capitalist [industrial] development.) [1920]

16. Offenbacher, *op. cit.,* p. 68.

17. Weber is here referring to the French Huguenots [sk].

18. Weber refers here to those churches that take the early Christianity of the apostles as their ideal [sk].

19. Unusually acute observations on the characteristic uniqueness of the different religions in Germany and France, and the interweaving of their differences with other cultural elements in the conflict of nationalities in Alsace, are to be found in the excellent study by Werner Wittich, "Deutsche und französische Kultur im Elsass" [German and French Culture in Alsace-Lorraine], *Illustrierte Elsässische Rundschau* (1900; also published separately).

20. St. Francis lived in voluntary poverty and preached a doctrine of brotherly love and optimism [sk].

21. Naturally only *then*, we wish to make clear, if the *possibility* of capitalist development in the relevant area was *at all* present.

22. Weber is here thinking of monks as entrepreneurial, as they often were in the High Middle Ages [sk].

23. On this point see, for instance, Dupin de St. André, "L'ancienne église réformée de Tours. Les membres de l'église," *Bulletin de la société de l'histoire du Protestantisme,* vol. 4 [1856], p. 10. Here again one could (and this idea will be appealing especially to those persons who evaluate this theme from the perspective of Catholicism) view the desire for *emancipation* from monastic

control (or even control by the church) as the driving motive. But this view is opposed not only by the judgment of contemporaries (including Rabelais), but also, for example, by the qualms of conscience raised in the first national synods of the Huguenots (for example, 1st Synod, C. partic. qu. 10 in J. Aymon, *Synodes nationaux de l'Eglise réformée de France* [1710], p. 10), as to whether a *banker* might become an elder of the church. Furthermore, and in spite of Calvin's unambiguous stand, repeated discussions took place in the same synods regarding the permissibility of taking interest. These discussions were occasioned by the questions of extremely conscientious members of the congregations. In part these discussions arose because a high percentage of church members were also participants in business and banking circles—and hence had a direct interest in these questions. These discussions arose, however, *at the same time* also because it was hoped by these circles that the wish to practice *usuraria pravitas* [depraved usury]—and to do so without supervision through the confession—could be considered as *not* central. (The same—see below—is true of Holland. Let it be said explicitly that the prohibition of the charging of interest by Canon Law will play absolutely no part in *this* investigation).

24. W. Eberhard Gothein, *Wirtschaftsgeschichte des Schwarzwaldes* [Economic History of the Black Forest], vol. 1 [Strasbourg: Trubner, 1892; reprinted in German in 1970 (New York: Burt Franklin)], p. 67.

25. The brief observations by Sombart relate to this point. See Sombart, *Der moderne Kapitalismus* (Leipzig: Duncker & Humblot [1902]), p. 380. Later, in by far the weakest (in my opinion) in respect [to the importance of Calvinism] of his larger studies, *The Quintessence of Capitalism* [*op. cit.*], Sombart defended, unfortunately, a completely incorrect "thesis." I will return to it occasionally below [see notes 12 and 32 of ch. 2]. Sombart's study was influenced by the weak investigation by Franz Keller, *Unternehmen und Mehrwert* (Paderborn: Schriften der Görresgesellschaft, no. 12, 1912). Keller's volume contains many good observations (although they are not, in *this* respect, new). Nonetheless, his study remains *below* the standard set by other works of modern Catholic apologetics. [See note 31, ch. 2.] [1920]

26. It has been thoroughly established that the simple fact of a change of residence is among the most effective means of intensifying labor (see note 15 above). The same Polish girl who at home was not to be shaken loose from her traditional laziness by any chance of earning money, however tempting, seems to change her entire nature and become capable of unlimited expenditures of energy when she becomes a migratory worker in a foreign milieu, such as [German] Saxony. The exact same transformation is manifest in the case of Italian laborers. The socializing influence that occurs with movement into a higher "cultural milieu" is not here in the least the decisive factor (although it does, of course, play a part). This conclusion is evident if only because the same [intensification of work] occurs also wherever the *type* of work (such as agricultural labor) is the same in the foreign milieu as at home. Indeed, this intensification occurs despite the temporary decline in workers' standard of living (as a result of the accommodation, in the foreign milieu, in migrant labor camps) that would never be tolerated at home. The simple fact of working in completely unaccustomed and different surroundings breaks through the worker's traditional ways—and this new milieu is the "socializing" force. It is hardly necessary to note how much of American economic development is based upon such effects. The similar significance of the Babylonian Exile for the Jews in ancient times is apparent (one would like to say, obvious in the inscriptions). The same is true for the Parsenes [today in Iran and Iraq, and reformed Zoroastrians known as followers of Mazdaism]. However, for the Protestants, as apparent even in the unmistakable differences among believers in the orientation to the economy in the Puritan New England colonies in contrast to Catholic Maryland, the Episcopal South, and denominationally mixed Rhode Island, the influence of unique religious factors is apparent. Indeed, this influence clearly indicates that religion plays an *independent* role. The same must be said of the Jain sect in India.

27. It is well known to be, in most of its forms, a more or less *moderated* Calvinism or Zwinglianism. [1920]

28. In Hamburg, which is almost entirely Lutheran, the *only* fortune going back to the seventeenth century is that of a well-known *Reformed* family. (This example was kindly called to my attention by Professor A. Wahl). [1920]

29. Hence, the assertion that such a connection [between Calvinism and the capitalist spirit] exists is not "new." E. de Laveleye [*Protestantism and Catholicism in Their Bearing upon the Liberty and Prosperity of Nations* (London: John Murray, 1875)] and Matthew Arnold [*St. Paul and Protestantism* (London: Smith, Elder, 1906)], among others, have addressed this connection. On the contrary, "new" is only its questioning, which is entirely unfounded. The task here is *to explain* this connection. [1920]

30. Naturally, this does not mean that official Pietism, like other religious denominations, did not at a later date, as a result of [enduring] patriarchal proclivities, oppose certain "progressive" features of the capitalist economy (for example, the transition from cottage industry to the factory system). As we will often note, precisely that which a religion *strives for* as an ideal must be distinguished clearly from the actual *result* of the religion's influence upon the organization of its believers' lives.

(In a [recent] article I have offered my own examples, from a study of a factory in Westphalia, of the particular adaptability of Pietist workers. See "Zur Psychophysik der gewerblichen Arbeit" [On the Psychological-Physics of Industrial Work], reprinted in *Max Weber Gesamtausgabe* (Tübingen: Mohr 1995/1924), I/11, ed. by Wolfgang Schluchter, pp. 42–178. [1920]

31. Knox was a leading Calvinist reformer in Scotland. Voët, a professor for Near Eastern languages in Holland, influenced significantly Pietist doctrine. Calvin and Luther are discussed in depth in chapters 3 and 4 [sk].

Chapter II

1. Weber generally places the term *spirit* in quotation marks, although I have omitted them for ease of reading. By doing so he wishes (a) to express his awareness that controversy surrounded this term and (b) to emphasize that he is using it in this study in a specific and unique manner (and thus to distance his usage, above all, from that of the major figure of German Idealism, G. W. F. Hegel [1770–1831]) [sk].

2. Weber here alludes to a few central aspects of his sociological methodology: (a) historical concepts must refer to "historical individuals" (unique cases); (b) classificatory schemes (*genus proximum, differentia specifica*) are too abstract to capture uniqueness and hence are useful *only* as preliminary conceptual tools; (c) concepts do not "replicate reality," for "reality" varies depending on the investigator's particular research question (or "vantage point" upon reality); and (d), following from the above, concepts can be formulated only after an assessment by researchers of the "cultural significance" of potential constituent elements and a selection accordingly. All the above points are central to Weber's sociological methodology based on "subjective meaning," "interpretive understanding," and "ideal types." See " 'Objectivity' in Social Science and Social Policy," in *The Methodology of the Social Sciences,* translated and edited by Edward A. Shils and Henry A. Finch (New York: Free Press, 1949). See also the "Basic Concepts" chapter in *E&S* (pp. 3–22). See Fritz Ringer, *Max Weber's Methodology* (Cambridge, MA: Harvard University Press, 1997); John Drysdale, "How Are Social-Scientific Concepts Formed? A Reconstruction of Max Weber's Theory of Concept Formation," *Sociological Theory* 14 (March 1996): 71–88 [sk].

3. The final [five short] passages are from *Necessary Hints to Those That Would Be Rich*, in *Works* (1736) (Sparks edition [Chicago, 1882], vol. 2, p. 80). The earlier are passages from *Advice to a Young Tradesman* (1748) (Sparks edition, vol. 2, pp. 87 ff.). [The italics in the text are Franklin's.]

4. This book (Frankfurt, 1855; Vienna and Leipzig, 1927) is well known to be a fictional paraphrase of Lenau's impressions of America. As a work of art, the book would today be somewhat difficult to enjoy. However, it is unsurpassed as a document of the differences (now long since blurred over) between German and American sensibilities; indeed, one could say, of the spiritual life of the Germans (which has remained *common* to all Germans since the German mysticism of the Middle Ages, despite all the differences between German Catholics and German Protestants) in contrast to Puritan-capitalist "can-do" energy. [See ch. 3.]

5. Sombart has used this quotation as a motto for his section on "the genesis of capitalism" (*Der moderne Kapitalismus, op. cit.*, vol. 1 [see pp. 193–634], p. 193. See also p. 390).

6. Which obviously does not mean either that Jakob Fugger was a morally indifferent or an irreligious man, or that Benjamin Franklin's ethic is *completely* covered by the above quotations. It scarcely required Brentano's quotations (*Die Anfänge des modernen Kapitalismus, op. cit.*, pp. 151 f.) to protect this well-known philanthropist from the misunderstanding that Brentano seems to attribute to me. The problem is actually just the reverse: how could such a philanthropist come to write precisely *these sentences* (the especially characteristic form of which Brentano neglected to reproduce) in the manner of a moralist? [1920]

7. This way of formulating the problem constitutes the basis for our differences with Sombart. The very considerable practical significance of this difference will become clear later. It should, however, be noted here that Sombart has by no means neglected this ethical aspect of the capitalist employer. However, in his train of thought, capitalism calls forth this ethical aspect. We must, on the contrary, for our purposes, take into consideration the opposite hypothesis. A final position on this difference can only be taken up at the end of this investigation. For Sombart's view see *op. cit.*, vol. 1, pp. 357, 380, etc. His reasoning here connects with the brilliant conceptualizations offered in [Georg] Simmel's *Philosophie des Geldes* [Leipzig: Duncker & Humblot, 1900] [*The Philosophy of Money* (London: Routledge, 1978)] (final chapter). I will speak later [see notes 12 and 31] of the polemics which Sombart has brought forward against me in his *The Quintessence of Capitalism*. At this point any thorough discussion must be postponed.

8. "I grew convinced that *truth, sincerity,* and *integrity* in dealings between man and man were of the utmost importance *to the felicity of life*; and I formed written resolutions, which still remain *in my journal book* to practise them ever while I lived. Revelation had indeed no weight with me as such; but I entertained an opinion that, though certain actions might not be bad because they were forbidden by it, or good because it commanded them, yet probably these actions might be forbidden *because* they were bad for us, or commanded *because* they were beneficial to us in their own nature, all the circumstances of things considered" [*Autobiography*, ed. by F. W. Pine (New York: Henry Holt, 1916), p. 112].

9. "I therefore put myself as much as I could out of sight and started it—that is, the project of a library which he had initiated—as a scheme of a *number of friends,* who had requested me to go about and propose it to such as they thought lovers of reading. In this way my affair went on smoothly, and I ever after practised it on such occasions; and from my frequent successes, can heartily recommend it. The present little sacrifice of your vanity will afterwards be amply repaid. If it remains *awhile* uncertain to whom the merit belongs, someone more vain than yourself will be encouraged to claim it, and then even envy will be disposed to do you justice by plucking those assumed feathers and restoring them to their right owner" [*Autobiography*, *ibid.*, p. 140].

10. Brentano *(op. cit.,* pp. 125; 127, note 1) takes this remark as an occasion to criticize the later discussion of "that rationalization and intensification of discipline" to which this-worldly asceticism has subjected men. That, he says, is a "rationalization" toward an "irrational" organization of life. This is in fact quite correct. Something is never "irrational" in itself but only from a particular "rational" vantage point. For the nonreligious person every religious way of organizing life is irrational; for the hedonist every ascetic organization of life is "irrational" even if it may be, measured against *its* ultimate values, a "rationalization." If this essay wishes to make any contribution at all, may it be to unveil the many-sidedness of a concept—the "rational"—that only appears to be straightforward and linear. [1920] [See "The Social Psychology of the World Religions," in *From Max Weber*, edited by H. H. Gerth and C. W. Mills (New York: Oxford, 1946), p. 293; "Prefatory Remarks" below, pp. 159–60. See also S. Kalberg, "Max Weber's Types of Rationality," *American Journal of Sociology* 85, no. 5 (1980): 1145–79].

11. In reply to Brentano's (*Die Anfänge des modernen Kapitalismus, op. cit.,* pp. 150 ff.) very detailed but somewhat imprecise apologia for Franklin, whose ethical qualities I have allegedly misunderstood, I refer only to this statement. It should have been sufficient, in my opinion, to render this apologia superfluous. [1920]

12. I will take this opportunity to interweave a few "anti-critical" remarks prior to embarking upon the main argument. Sombart (*The Quintessence of Capitalism, op. cit.,* note 1, ch. 1) occasion-

ally argues on behalf of the indefensible assertion that this "ethic" of Franklin is a "word-for-word" repetition of some writings of that great and universal genius of the Renaissance, Leon Battista Alberti [1404–1472]. In addition to writing theoretical treatises on mathematics, sculpture, painting, architecture, and love (he was personally a woman-hater), he authored a four-volume treatise on the household (*Libri della famiglia* [*Book on the Family*]). (Unfortunately, I have not at this writing been able to acquire the new edition by G. Mancini [Firenze: Carnesecchi e Figli, 1908] and thus must use the older edition by Bonucci [Florence, 1843–49, 5 vols.].)

The passage from Franklin is printed above word for word [see pp. 14–15]. Where, then, are corresponding passages found in Alberti's work, especially the maxim that stands at the beginning—"time is money"—and the admonitions that follow it? As far as I know, the only passage that bears the slightest resemblance is found toward the end of the first book of *Della Famiglia* (ed. Bonucci, vol. 2, p. 353). Alberti speaks here in very general terms of money as the *nervus rerum* [major driving force] of the household, which, consequently, must be especially well-managed. These same terms are earlier found [in ancient Rome] in Cato when he writes *de re rustica* [*on the rural areas*].

Moreover, to treat Alberti, who always emphasized his descent from one of the most distinguished feudal families of Florence ("*nobilissimi cavalieri*"; *Della Famiglia*, in *ibid.*, pp. 213, 228, 247, etc. [Bonucci ed.]), as a man of "mongrel blood" (and filled with envy for the noble families owing to his illegitimate birth, which was to him not in the least socially disqualifying) is quite incorrect. Likewise, it is incorrect to argue that, as a businessman, he was excluded from association with the nobility.

Characteristic for Alberti is surely his recommendation to become engaged in *large* businesses, for these businesses alone are worthy of *nobile e onesta famiglia* [persons from noble and honest families] and *libero e nobile animo* [free and noble souls] (*ibid.*, p. 209). Moreover, large businesses require less labor (see *Del governo della Famiglia,* bk. 4, pp. 55, 116, in the edition published for the Pandolfini); *therefore,* a putting-out business for wool and silk is the best business. Furthermore, ordered and strict budgetary practices are recommended, in other words, an assessment of expenditures by reference to income. Hence, involved here is mainly a principle that concerns proper *budgeting* rather than a principle related to *acquisition* (as Sombart especially [as a specialist on this subject] should have recognized). Similarly, in his discussion of the nature of money (*ibid.*), Alberti's concern is with the investment of *wealth* (money or *possessioni*) and not with the utilization of capital. All this is *santa masserizia* [prudent management], as represented in Alberti's book by the statements of "Gianozzo." As protection against the uncertainties of fate, he recommends the early habituation to continuous activity, which, by the way, alone maintains healthfulness in the long run (see *Della famiglia,* pp. 73–74) *in cose magnifiche è ample* [in magnificent and grand affairs] (p. 192), and an avoidance of laziness, which always presents a threat to continued employment. Hence, as a precaution against the possibility of unexpected changes, [Alberti advises] the careful learning of skills appropriate to one's social status (however, every *opera mercenaria* [work motivated by a desire for material gain] is unsuitable to one's social status) (bk. 1, p. 209).

[An entire array of activities praised by Alberti would be] viewed by every Puritan as sinful "deification of human wants and desires": Alberti's idea of *tranquillita dell' animo* [peace of mind], his strong tendency toward the Epicurean λάΘε βιώσας (*vivere a sè stesso,* [leading a self-sufficient life]; *ibid.*, p. 262), his special dislike of any office (as a source of unrest, as a place where enemies are created, and as a source of entanglement in corrupt business practices) (*ibid.*, p. 258), his idealizing of life in a country villa, his nurturing of self-confidence from thinking about his ancestors, and his consideration of the honor of his family (which, because of the importance of honor, should keep its fortune together, as is the Florentine custom, and not divide it up) as the decisive standard and purpose [for his business activity]. Indeed, in the eyes of Benjamin Franklin, all of these proclivities would have expressed (for he remained unacquainted with them) the pomposity of the aristocracy.

One should further note the high prestige of all endeavors that require a broad, liberal arts education (*industria* [industriousness] is primarily oriented to literary and [broadly understood] scientific labor). This labor is viewed as the single endeavor actually worthy of the dignity of human beings. Basically, only the illiterate Gianozzo understands *masserizia*—in the sense of "rational budgeting" as the means to live independently from others and to avoid the fall into poverty—as equal in dignity to the tasks of the educated. Because of this perception, Gianozzo explains the origin of "rational budgeting" by reference to [the wisdom of] an old priest rather than by noting [its actual origins in] the ethic of medieval monks (see below).

One could place all of the above comments next to Benjamin Franklin's ethic and organized life (and, above all, that of his Puritan ancestors). In order to measure the depth of the differences one would note the orientation [on the one hand] of Renaissance literati [writers and scholars] toward a humanistic aristocracy, and [on the other] the orientation of the treatises and sermons of the Puritans toward the masses of a business-oriented middle class (more precisely, the *Kommis* [merchants].) Alberti's economic rationalism, which is comprehensively supported by references to ancient authors, is in its essence most similar to the treatment of economic matters in the works of Xenophon (who remained unknown to him), Cato, Varro, and Columella (all of whom he quotes). However, especially in Cato and Varro, *acquisition* as such stands in the foreground in an entirely different way than is the case for Alberti. Furthermore, Alberti's (admittedly infrequent) discussions on the use of the *fattori*—the division of labor and discipline—to influence the unreliability of the peasants, etc., indeed sounds very much like a transposition of Cato's teachings on common sense, practical wisdom, and prudent behavior, acquired from the realm of the ancient slave-using household, onto the cottage industry and the manufacturing milieu, both of which are based upon free labor rather than slave labor.

When Sombart (whose referral to the ethic of the Stoics is quite incorrect) discovers economic rationalism as "developed to its greatest external consistency" as early as Cato, one must say that (if this description is correctly understood) he is not entirely incorrect. One can indeed bring together the *diligens pater familias* [conscientious family patriarch] of the Romans with the ideal of the *massajo* [prudent management] of Alberti under the same category. Characteristic for Cato, above all, is that a landed estate is valued and judged as an object for the *investment* of wealth. Nonetheless, the concept of *industria* [in Alberti] is differently shaded as a result of the influence of Christianity.

And here the difference becomes clear. In the concept of *industria,* which originates out of monastic asceticism and which was developed by monastic writers, lies the seed of an *ethos*. This ethos was fully developed later in the exclusively *this*-worldly asceticism (see below!) of Protestantism (*thus,* as will be often emphasized, a relationship [existed between the other-worldly asceticism of the monastery and ascetic Protestantism's this-worldly asceticism], although asceticism, by the way, was *less* closely related to the official church dogma of St. Thomas Aquinas than to the Florentine and Siennese mendicant-ethicists). This *ethos* of asceticism is lacking in Cato and also in Alberti's own writings. Instead, for both, the issue is one of common sense, practical wisdom, and prudent behavior rather than ethics. Franklin's writings also involve utilitarian considerations. However, the ethical element in the sermon to young merchants is entirely unmistakable. Moreover, it constitutes—and this is what matters to us here—that which is characteristic. A lack of carefulness in handling money signifies to him that one has, so to speak, "murdered" embryos which could have been used for the creation of capital. For this reason, such carelessness is also an *ethical* defect.

An inner affinity between the two (Alberti and Franklin) exists in fact only insofar as Alberti (who, although called pious by Sombart, actually—despite taking the sacraments and holding a Roman benefice [as mediated through the church], and with the exception of two colorless passages in his writings—*did not himself in any way,* like so many humanists, employ religious motives as points of orientation for the organization of life he recommended) had *not yet* related his recommendation for "economic efficiency" to religious conceptions, while Franklin *no longer* did so. Utilitarianism, as apparent in Alberti's preference for the wool and silk cottage industries as well as in his mercantilist social utilitarianism ("that many people should be given employment"; see Alberti, *ibid.*, p. 292), justifies, at least formally, economic activity in both of these arenas. Indeed, Alberti's writings on this subject offer a very appropriate example for that type of, so to speak, immanent economic "rationalism" that in fact exists as a "reflection" of economic conditions. Yet this interest of authors purely "in the thing itself" has been found everywhere and in all eras, and not less in the Chinese classical period [700–400 BCE] and in ancient Greece and Rome than during the Renaissance and Enlightenment epochs. There can be no doubt that, just as in antiquity in the writings of Cato, Varro, and Columella, and is the case also here with Alberti and his contemporaries, economic *ratio* [rationalism] was to a great extent developed out of the teaching of *industria*. However, how can one believe that such a *teaching* by the literati [educated stratum] could develop the power to radically transform life in the same manner as occurs when a religious belief places *salvation premiums* upon a specific (in this case, methodical-rational) way of organizing life?

[The utilitarian organization of life that follows from such teachings by the literati] looks quite different from a *religion*-oriented "rationalization" of the organization of life (and hence, in the process, eventually also of the conduct of economic activity). The contrast is visible in a number of (highly diverging) religious groupings, in addition to the Puritans of all denominations: the Jains [in northern India], the Jews, certain ascetic sects of the Middle Ages, [the followers of the pre-Reformation English theologian John] Wyclif [*ca.* 1320–84], the Moravian Brotherhood (an offshoot of the Hussite movement [which was influenced by Wyclif]), the Skoptsi and Stundists in Russia, and numerous religious orders.

The decisive point in regard to the distinction [between the religious groupings and the groupings oriented to utility] is that (if one may note this important point before commencing the argument) a religion-anchored ethic, and the behavior called forth by it, places completely specific, and as long as the religious belief remains viable, highly effective *psychological premiums* (not oriented to economic interests) upon this behavior; namely, premiums not available to Alberti's teachings on common sense, practical wisdom, and prudent behavior. Only to the extent that these premiums constitute an effective influence upon the believer's action (and they are often primarily influential—and this is the central point—in a significantly different *direction* from the influence of the theological *teachings,* for they also are only "teachings") do they acquire an independent (*eigengesetzlichen*) directional impact upon the organization of life, and, in this way, upon the economy. To state it clearly: this is actually the point of this entire essay. And I had not expected that this message would be so completely overlooked.

I will address on another occasion the relative welcoming of capitalism by theological ethicists of the High Middle Ages (in particular Anthony of Florence and Bernard of Siena, both of whom Sombart has likewise seriously misinterpreted). In any event, Alberti did not belong to this circle. And he took only the concept of *industria* from monastic lines of thought; this remains clear regardless of which mediating links came into play. Alberti, Pandolfini, and their kind are representatives of the frame of mind (although outwardly obedient) already emancipated spiritually from the church. Indeed, despite all ties to the existing Christian ethic, they remained for the most part oriented to a "pagan" frame of mind with roots in antiquity. Brentano believes that I have "ignored" the significance of precisely this frame of mind with respect to its significance for the development of modern teachings on the economy (and also on modern economic policy).

It is in fact correct that I did not address *this* line of causality [and for a simple reason]: it did not belong in a study on the *Protestant ethic* and the spirit of capitalism. Far from attempting to deny its significance (which will be demonstrated at another time), I am rather (and for good reasons) of the opinion that the spheres of influence and directional influence of the "pagan" frame of mind were completely *different* from those of the Protestant ethic. (And the practical, and by no means insignificant, predecessors of this ethic were the [ascetic Protestant] sects and the Wyclif-Hussite ethic.) It was *not* the *organization of life* (of the rising middle class) that influenced the formation of the Protestant ethic but the politics of statesmen and princes. These two indeed partly, but by no means always, converging causal lines [—on the one hand the psychological, salvation premiums that religious belief places on the organization of life, thereby bestowing upon it an independent directional impact and, on the other hand, the politics of statesmen and princes—] should at the outset be kept cleanly separate.

As concerns Benjamin Franklin, it must be noted that his tracts on the private economy (which were used in his time as basic readings in the schools) with respect to *this* point in fact belong to a category of works that have influenced *practical* life. In contrast, Alberti's massive works are hardly known outside of learned circles. However, I have explicitly cited Franklin as a man who stood completely beyond the Puritan regimentation of life; by his time, it had become considerably weaker. He remained as well uninfluenced by the English "Enlightenment" as a whole (which is often presented as having close ties to Puritanism). [entire note from 1920]

13. Unfortunately Brentano (*op. cit.* [ch. 1, note 15]) has thrown every kind of striving for gain (regardless of whether peaceful or in warfare) into one pot. He has then defined the exclusive pursuit of *money* (instead of land) as that which is unique to "the capitalist" pursuit of gain (in contrast, for example, to the feudal striving for gain). He also opposes every further distinction, even though doing so could have led to clear concepts. In addition, he rejects the concept formulated here for the purpose of this investigation, the "spirit" of (modern!) capitalism (p. 131). He does so on the basis of an assertion incomprehensible to me: he contends that he has already included in his presuppositions that which should be proven. [1920]

14. The observations of Sombart are relevant in every respect. See *Die deutsche Volkswirtschaft im neunzehnten Jahrhundert* [The German Economy in the Nineteenth Century (Berlin: Georg Bondi Publishers, 1903)], p. 123. I do not at all, in particular, need to emphasize—although this study goes back, with respect to its pivotal vantage points, to many of my earlier projects—how much the formulation of these vantage points are indebted to the simple existence of Sombart's manifold investigations and their acute formulations. This indebtedness remains also when Sombart's studies move along a pathway different from the one chosen here—in fact *precisely* when this occurs. Furthermore, those who feel stimulated time and again by Sombart's opinions to oppose strongly his views, and directly to reject some of his theses, are obligated to clarify explicitly their reasons for doing so.

15. *Commenda* involved a contract in which one partner provided capital (money, or, for example, ships, merchandise, or equipment) and the other sought to render a profit for both parties from the capital. See Weber, *General Economic History*, pp. 206–07 [sk].

16. Common in the ancient world, particularly in Rome and Egypt, tax farming involved the large landholder's farming out of the collection of public taxes to an entrepreneur. The latter paid a fixed fee to the lord and retained all sums collected above this fee. See *E&S*, pp. 965–66, 1045–46 [sk].

17. Of course, we cannot here address the question of *where* these limitations lie, nor can we evaluate the well-known theory on the connection between high wages and the high productivity of labor. This theory was first suggested by [Thomas] Brassey [*Work and Wages* (New York: D. Appleton & Co., 1872)]. It was then formulated and upheld theoretically by Brentano [*Über das Verhältnis von Arbeitslohn und Arbeitszeit zur Arbeitsleistung* (Leipzig, 1875, 1893)] and simultaneously, historically and analytically, by [Gerhart] Schulze-Gaevernitz [*Der Großbetrieb* (Leipzig: Duncker & Humblot, 1892)]. The discussion was again opened by [Wilhelm] Hasbach's penetrating studies (see "Zur Charakteristik der englischen Industrie," in *Schmollers Jahrbuch* [1903, pp. 385–91, 417 ff.]), and is not yet finally settled. It is here sufficient for us to note (as is not, and cannot be, doubted by anyone) that low wages and high profits, as well as low wages and favorable opportunities for profit, do not simply go together with industrial development. That is, simply mechanical operations involving money do not at all call forth a "socialization" into a capitalist [economic] culture, and thereby the possibility of [the development of] a capitalist economy. All examples selected here are purely illustrative.

18. Therefore, the importation, *even of capitalist* industries, has often not been possible without large emigration movements out of older culture areas. Sombart is correct in noting the contrast between the "skills" of persons and the trade secrets of craftsmen, both of which take persons as their point of orientation, on the one hand, and scientific, objectified modern technology on the other. This distinction hardly existed in the period of capitalism's origin. Indeed, the (so-to-speak) ethical qualities of the worker under capitalism (and, to a certain extent, also the ethical qualities of the employer) were often regarded, as a result alone of their scarcity, as more valuable than the craftsman's skills, which had become ossified in centuries-old traditionalism. And even industry today, when it selects a location to build, is not at all able to make this decision simply independently of the qualities a population has acquired as a result of longstanding traditions and socialization practices that have prepared it for intensive work. Corresponding to the ideas widespread in scientific circles today, this dependence upon the qualities of the local population, once first observed, is

gladly attributed to hereditary racial qualities instead of to tradition and socialization. But to do so, in my view, is of very doubtful validity.

19. See my "Zur Psychophysik der gewerblichen Arbeit." [See note 29, ch. 1.] [1920]

20. The foregoing observations could be misunderstood. A well-known type of businessperson demonstrates a proclivity to lend support, for his own purposes, to the sentence "religion must be maintained among the people." This proclivity combines with the (earlier not infrequent) proclivity of broad circles (especially the Lutheran clergy, owing to its general sympathy for the authoritarian powers-that-be) to make themselves available to these powers as "secret police." Indeed, wherever able to do so, these circles labeled the [labor] strike as sinful and the unions as promoters of "greed," etc. These are occurrences that have nothing to do with the illustrations of concern to us here. The examples discussed in the text do not involve isolated instances. Instead, these illustrations point to very frequent occurrences that, as we will see, reappear in a recognizable and typical pattern.

21. *Der moderne Kapitalismus, op. cit.,* vol. I, p. 62.

22. *Ibid.,* p. 195.

23. We are referring here, of course, to that *modern* rational *business* that is unique to the West, rather than to the capitalism of usurers, purveyors of warfare, traders in offices, tax farmers, large merchants, and financial magnates. This latter capitalism has, for 3,000 years, spread across the globe from China, India, Babylon, Greece, Rome, Florence, and into the present. See the "Prefatory Remarks" [essay in this volume]. [1920]

24. The assumption (and this should be emphasized here) is by no means justified *a priori* that, on the one hand, the technique of the capitalist enterprise and, on the other, the spirit of "work as a vocational calling," which endows capitalism with its expansive energy, must have had their *original* sustaining roots in the same social groupings. Religious beliefs relate to social relationships in the same [imprecise] manner.

Historically, Calvinism was one of the social carriers of the socialization practices that gave rise to the "capitalist spirit." Yet, in the Netherlands, for example, those who possessed great fortunes were not predominately followers of the strictest Calvinism; rather, they were Arminians (for reasons that will be discussed later). In the Netherlands as well as elsewhere, the "typical" social carriers of the capitalist ethic and the Calvinist Church were persons from the upwardly mobile *middle* and *lower-middle* strata. The owners of businesses came out of these strata.

However, exactly this situation conforms very well with the thesis presented here. Persons who possessed great fortunes and large-scale merchants have existed in all epochs, yet a rational-capitalist organization of *industrial* work in a middle class first became known in the development that occurred between the Middle Ages and the modern period. [1920]

25. On this point see the good Zurich dissertation by J. Maliniak (1913). [*Die Entstehung der Exportindustrie und des Unternehmerstandes in Zürich im 16. und 17. Jahrhundert* (Zürich: *Züricher volkswirtshaftliche Studien*, vol. 2, 1913).]

26. These banks (*Notenbank*) issued their own currency. They are called "federal reserve banks" in the United States [sk].

27. The following picture has been compiled "ideal typically" from different branches of the textile industry at a variety of locations. Of course, for the illustrative purpose served by this picture, it is irrelevant that the course of this revolution did not occur, in any of the examples we have in mind, in precisely the manner portrayed in this ideal-typical construct. On the formation of the ideal type, Weber's central methodological tool, see *E&S*, pp. 19–22, and the "Objectivity" essay *(op. cit..* pp. 90–107).]

28. Also for this reason it is no accident that this period—the beginning era of economic rationalism when German industry first began to flap its wings—is accompanied by, for example, a complete decline in the aesthetic design of the products commonly used in daily life. [1920]

29. This is not to imply that movement in the supply of precious metals can be depicted as being without economic consequences. [1920]

30. Weber here wishes to convey that a pattern of behavior in Germany different from the "American fascination"—the search for status in Germany through the acquisition of "landed estates and the patent of nobility"—does not constitute a viable alternative to the American situation.

Rather, the German behavior "must be seen for what it is," namely, a legacy from the feudal past [sk].

31. This refers to that type of employer *we* have made the object of our discussion here. We are not referring to any sort of empirical average. (On the "ideal type" concept see my ["Objectivity" essay; *ibid.*].) [1920]

32. This is perhaps the appropriate place briefly to address observations in the already cited book by Franz Keller (see note 24, ch. 1) and the observations by Sombart that relate to it (in *The Quintessence of Capitalism*), at least to the extent that they belong here. It is actually quite amazing that an author [Keller] criticizes a study in which the canonical prohibition of charging interest is *not at all mentioned* (except in *one* passing remark that had *no* relationship to the entire line of argument). Keller does so on the assumption that precisely this prohibition of interest (parallels to which are to be found in almost all religious ethics around the world) constitutes the distinguishing feature of the Catholic ethic as opposed to the ethics of the Reformation churches and sects. One should really criticize only those studies that one has really read, or in those cases when their arguments, if read, have not already been forgotten. The struggle against *usuraria pravitas* [depraved usury] runs through Huguenot and Dutch church history of the sixteenth century. The Lombards (that is, the bankers) were often excluded from communion solely because they were bankers (see ch. 1, note 22). The more tolerant view held by Calvin (which, by the way, did not prevent the plan to include a usury litmus test in the first draft of the ordination regulations) was not victorious until [Claudius] Salmasius [1588–1653]. Hence, the opposition between the Catholic ethic and the ethics of Reformation churches and sects did not concern *this* issue [as Keller argues]; quite the contrary.

Still worse, however, are [Keller's] arguments that do rightfully belong here. Compared to the works of [F. X.] Funck ["Über die ökonomischen Anschauungen der mittelalterlichen Theologen," in: *Zeitschrift für die gesammelte Staatwissenschaft* 25 (1869)] and other Catholic scholars (and Keller has not, by the way, in my opinion fully acknowledged the contribution of Funck or these scholars), and in opposition to the investigations of Wilhelm Endemann, which are today out of date in regard to details yet still remain fundamental [see *Studien in der Roman.-Kanon. Wirtschafts- und Rechtslehre, 1874–83* (Berlin: J. Guttentag; 2 vols., reprinted 1962)], they make a painful impression of superficiality.

To be sure, Keller has abstained from the excesses apparent in some remarks by Sombart (*The Quintessence of Capitalism*). Sombart notes that the "pious gentlemen" (referring basically to Bernhard of Siena and Anthony of Florence) "wished to excite the spirit of business in any way possible." [They wished to do so, Sombart argues,] by interpreting the prohibition against usury in a way that excluded the (in my terminology) "productive" investment of capital [from this prohibition]. Yet this manner of treating the prohibition against the taking of interest is hardly different from what has occurred across the entire world. Keller has kept his distance from such excesses. (Furthermore, Sombart places the Romans among the "heroic peoples," yet presumably—and this constitutes an irreconcilable contradiction, in view of his other books—sees economic rationalism as having developed "to its final consistency" as early as Cato [234–149 BCE]. This inconsistency is noted here only in passing. Nonetheless, it serves to indicate the quality of *The Quintessence of Capitalism*, a book "with a thesis" in the worst sense of this expression.)

Sombart has also completely distorted the significance of the prohibition against the taking of interest. This cannot be set forth here in detail. Its significance was earlier [in our scholarly research] often exaggerated, and later strongly underestimated; now (in an era of Catholic, as well as Protestant, millionaires) it has been turned upside down—for apologetic purposes. As is well known, and in spite of the grounding in the Bible (!) of a prohibition against the taking of interest, interest was not abolished until the last century. This took place by order of the *Congregatio Sancti Officii* [the highest judiciary body in the Catholic Church], yet only *temporum ratione habita* [for a limited period, and as a consequence of specific, this-worldly circumstances] and *indirectly*. That is, priests were prevented (because they wished to preserve their claims for obedience in the event of a re-institution of the right to take interest) from asking questions in the confessional about *usuraria pravitas*, for fear of unsettling the faithful.

Anyone who has even begun to undertake a thorough study of the extremely tangled history of the church's doctrine on usury cannot claim (in view of the endless controversies over, for example, the permissibility of purchasing bonds, the discounting of notes and various other contracts, and above all in light of the order of the *Congregatio Sancti Officii* mentioned above concerning a *municipal* loan) that the prohibition of taking interest concerned only emergency loans, that it had the purpose of "preserving capital," and, indeed, that it served "to aid capitalist businesses" [as Sombart does]. The truth is that the church began to reconsider the prohibition of interest only at a rather late time. The common forms of purely business investment, when this occurred, were *not* loans at fixed interest rates but the *fœ nus nauticum, commenda, societas maris*, and the *dare ad proficuum de mari* types of loans (loans made according to categories of risk, and shares of gain and loss were adjusted within fixed upper and lower limits within each category of risk). (In view of the nature of the employer's borrowing, loans *had* to be of these types.) Yet these loans were not defined as falling under the ban (although a few rigorous canonists disagreed).

However, when investment at a fixed rate of interest became possible and common, and discounting practices became widespread, these types of loans encountered clearly perceptible difficulties stemming from the prohibition against the taking of interest. Frequent punitive measures were taken against the merchant guilds (black lists were formed!). Nevertheless, even in these cases, the church proceeded [against the violators] in a *purely* legalistic-formal manner. In any event, the church did not, as Keller argues, exhibit any tendency to "protect capital."

Finally, the church's attitude toward capitalism, *to the extent* that it can be ascertained at all, on the one hand was determined by a traditional (and mostly more diffusely experienced) hostility against the encompassing power of capital; because *impersonal*, the ethical regulation of its flow was scarcely possible [see *E&S*, pp. 346, 584–85, 600, 635–40, 1186–87] (as still reflected in Luther's comments on the Fuggers [a family of financial magnates] and on moneymaking as such). On the other hand, the church's attitude toward capitalism was determined by the necessity for accommodation.

Nevertheless, this theme does not belong here. As noted, the prohibition against taking interest and its destiny [in relationship to the Catholic Church] has, for us, at most only a symptomatic significance (and even in this regard only to a limited extent). [For a classic work on this theme written in the Weberian tradition, see Benjamin Nelson, *The Idea of Usury: From Tribal Brotherhood to Universal Otherhood* (Chicago: University of Chicago Press, 1969).]

The economic ethic of the Scots, and especially of certain fourteenth century mendicant theologians, primarily Bernhard of Siena and Anthony of Florence (hence, friar writers of a specifically rational *ascetic* orientation), undoubtedly deserves a separate treatment. In light of the major focus here, an examination of this economic ethic could take place only in a secondary fashion, which would not do justice to it. Moreover, if the attempt were nonetheless made, I would be forced here, in these "anti-critical" statements, to examine that which I wish to note later in discussing the *positive* relationship of the Catholic economic ethic to capitalism. Bernhard of Siena and Anthony of Florence go to great pains (and here they can be seen as precursors of many Jesuits) to legitimize the profit of the *merchant*; because (they argue) it constitutes a reward for the merchant's "industria" [industriousness], profit is ethically *permitted*. (Of course, obviously, even Keller cannot claim more.)

The concept and the high evaluation of *industria* obviously derives *ultimately* from monastic and mendicant asceticism. However, it also originates clearly from the concept of *masserizia* [see note 12], which Alberti borrowed from clerical sources (as he conveys to us through the words of Gianozzo). We will later address the way in which the monastic and mendicant ethic constitutes a precursor of the this-worldly ascetic denominations of Protestantism. (The beginnings of similar conceptions can be found in the ancient world with the Cynics, as is apparent from the tombstones in late Hellenic cemeteries [300–100 BCE], and—although as a consequence of entirely different social configurations—in Egypt.) That element that is decisive for us is *entirely lacking* in the ancient world (and with Alberti as well), namely, exactly what is characteristic for ascetic Protestantism, as we will note later: the conception of offering *testimony* to oneself of one's own salvation—that is, of offering the *certitudo salutis* [sense of being certain of one's salvation]—through the exercise of a vocational calling.

The psychological *reward* that ascetic Protestantism placed upon *industria* arose from this source (and is of necessity missing in Catholicism, for the simple reason that the means toward salvation in this religion were simply different). Ethical *teachings*, and their effects upon behavior, constituted the concern for these authors [whether Alberti, the Cynics, or the ancient Egyptians], whereas for the ascetic Protestant theologians, the issue involved practical motivations, as conditioned by the salvation interests of the faithful. Moreover, while the concern for Alberti, the Cynics, and the ancient Egyptians was one of *accommodation* [to the world as it exists], as is very easy to see, the issue for this-worldly asceticism involved [in respect to practical behavior] lines of argumentation deducted from direction-giving, internally consistent religious postulates. (Anthony of Florence and Bernard of Siena have, by the way, received from authors long ago better treatment than they received from F. Keller.) Furthermore, even these accommodations [to the world as it exists] by Alberti and the ancient authors, have remained, to the present day, controversial.

The significance of the ethical conceptions of early monasticism, as *symptomatic* [of the ascetic Protestant notion of offering testimony to one's salvation through a calling], should by no means be viewed as completely nonexistent. Nevertheless, the actual "beginnings" of the religious ethic that flowed into the *modern* concept of a *vocational calling* can be found in the [ascetic] sects and the unorthodox religious groupings. These early traces are primarily to be found in Wyclif, even though his significance is certainly highly overestimated by von Brodnitz (*Englische Wirtschaftsgeschichte* [vol. 1, 1918]). To him, Wyclif's influence had such a strong impact that Puritanism found nothing more to do. But all this cannot (and should not) be delved into here. We cannot conduct a parallel debate regarding the question of how, and to what extent, the Christian ethics of the Middle Ages *actually* participated in creating the preconditions for the capitalist spirit. [entire note from 1920]

33. The words μηδὲν ἀπελπίζοντες [without hoping for anything from it] (Luke 6:35), and the translation of the Vulgate, *nihil inde sperantes* [hoping for nothing from it], are presumably (according to Adelbert Merx) a misrepresentation of μηδένᾳ ἀπελπίζοντες (or *meminem desperantes*) [do not despair regarding anyone (do not give up on anyone)]. These words decree the granting of loans to *all* brothers, including those who are indigent, and do so without speaking at all about interest. The passage *Deo placere vix potest* [the merchant cannot be pleasing to God] is now thought to be of Arian origin (which is, for our argument, a matter of indifference). [1920]

34. This school, which grew out of medieval Scholasticism, stood (as "realists" and empiricists opposed to all speculative metaphysics) against Catholic orthodoxy [sk].

35. We are instructed how, in this situation, a compromise with the prohibition of usury occurred, for example, in book I, section 65, of the statutes of the *Arte di Calimala* (at present I have only the Italian edition put out by Emiliani-Guidici, *Storella dei Com.* [Florence, 1866], vol. 3, p. 246). "Procurino i consoli con *quelli frate, che parrà loro*, che perdono si faccia e come fare si possa il meglio per l'amore di ciascuno, del dono, merito o guiderdono, ovvero interesse per l'anno presente e secondo che altra volta fatto fue." In other words, the issue here concerns the attempt by guilds to find a way for their members, owing to their official position within the organization, to be exempt from the prohibition against usury. This must be done, however, it is noted, without undermining the church's authority. The instructions that follow, as well as those for example immediately preceding (sect. 63), to record all interest and profits as "gifts," are very characteristic of the view of investment profit as amoral. The formation today by stock exchange traders of black lists against those who criticize orthodox procedures often corresponds to the scorn for those who pleaded, against the church court, for an exemption to the prohibition of usury.

36. On "practical rationalism" (and Weber's other types of rationalism), see S. Kalberg, "Max Weber's Types of Rationality," *op. cit.* (see note 10).

37. We will discover that the "birth of the calling" did not follow *logically* from ascetic Protestantism's doctrine of predestination. On the contrary, despair and bleakness followed logically from this doctrine. The revisions formulated by Richard Baxter, which concerned the pastoral care of believers, introduced the "calling" of significance to Weber or, more precisely, the notion of testifying to one's belief through conduct. These revisions could not be deduced rationally from the doctrine of predestination. See chapter 4 (especially note 76) [sk].

Chapter III

1. Of the ancient languages, only *Hebrew* has any similar concept—most of all in the word מְלָאכָה. It is used for priestly functions (Exod. 35:21; Neh. 21:22; 1 Chron. 9:13, 23:4, 26:30), for business in the service of the king (especially 1 Sam. 8:16; 1 Chron. 4:23, 29:6), for the service of a *royal* official (Esther 3:9, 9:3), of a *superintendent* of labor (2 Kings 12:12), of a slave (Gen. 39:2), of labor in the fields (1 Chron. 27:26), of *craftsmen* (Exod. 31:5, 35:21; 1 Kings 7:14), for traders (Ps. 107:23), and for worldly activity of any kind in the passage, Sirach 11:20, to be discussed later [on the Book of Jesus Sirach, see note 58 of ch. 5 below]. The word is derived from the root לאך, to send, thus meaning originally a "task." That it originated in the ideas current in Solomon's bureaucratic kingdom of serfs, built up as it was according to the Egyptian model, seems evident from the above references. In meaning, however, as I learn from A. Merx, this root concept had become lost even in antiquity. The word came to be used for any sort of "labor," and in fact became fully as colorless as the German *Beruf*, with which it shared the fate of being used primarily for mental functions. The expression (חק), "assignment," "task," "lesson," which also occurs in Sirach 11:20, and is translated in the [pre-Christian Greek version of the Old Testament, the] Septuagint with διθήκη, is also derived from the terminology of the bureaucratic regime of the time that enforced servitude, as is דְּבַר־יוֹם (Exod. 5:13, cf. Exod. 5:14), where the Septuagint also uses διαθήκη for "task." In Sirach 43:10 it is rendered in the Septuagint with κρίμα. In Sirach 11:20 it is evidently used to signify the fulfillment of *God's* commandments, being thus related to our "calling." On this passage in Jesus Sirach, reference may here be made to Smend's well-known book on Jesus Sirach [*Die Weisheit des Jesus Sirach* (Berlin, 1906)] on these verses and to his *Index zur Weisheit des Jesus Sirach* (Berlin, 1907) for the words διαθήκη, ἔργον, πόνος. (As is well known, the Hebrew text of the Book of Sirach was lost, but was rediscovered by Schechter, and in part supplemented by quotations from the Talmud. [See Solomon Schecter, *The Wisdom of Ben Sira* (New York: Macmillan, 1899)]. Luther did not possess it, and these two Hebrew concepts could not have had *any* influence on *his* use of language. See below on Prov. 22:29.)

In Greek there is no term corresponding in ethical connotation to the German or English words at all. Where Luther, quite in the spirit of modern usage (see below), translates Jesus Sirach 11:20 and 11:21, *bleibe in deinem Beruf* [stay in your calling], the Septuagint has at one point ἔργον, at the other, which however seems to be an entirely corrupt passage, πόνος (the Hebrew original speaks of the spark of divine help!). Otherwise in antiquity τά προσήκοντο is used in the general sense of "duties." In the works of the Stoics, κάματος occasionally carries similar connotations, though its linguistic source is diffuse and insignificant (called to my attention by Albrecht Dieterich). All other expressions (such as τάξις, etc.) have no ethical connotations.

In Latin what we translate as "calling" (a person's specialized and sustained activity that is normally his source of income and thus, in the long run, the economic basis of his existence) is expressed, aside from the commonplace *opus*, with an ethical content somewhat related to that of the German word. This occurred either by *officium* (from *opificium,* which was originally devoid of an ethical dimension but later, especially in Seneca *De benef,* bk. 4, p. 18, came to mean *Beruf*), by *munus* (derived from the compulsory obligations to the old civic community) or, finally, by *professio.* This last word was also characteristically used in this sense for public obligations, and was probably derived from the old tax declarations of the citizens. It later came to be applied in the special modern sense of the liberal professions (as in *professio bene dicendit*). In *this* narrower meaning it had a significance in every way similar to the German *Beruf* (even in the more spiritual sense of the word, as is apparent when Cicero says of someone *non intelligit quid profiteatur*, in the sense of "he does not recognize his own profession"), except that it is, of course, definitely this-worldly and without any *religious* connotation. This is even more true of *ars,* which in Imperial times was used for handicraft. The Vulgate translates the above passages from Jesus Sirach at one point with *opus*, at another (verse 21) with *locus,* which implies in this case something like social station. The addition of *mandaturam tuorum* derives from the ascetic Jerome. Brentano quite rightly notes this origin; however, he never calls attention, here or elsewhere, *precisely* to the fact that *mandaturum tuorum* was characteristic of the ascetic origin of the term (before the Reformation other-worldly, afterwards this-worldly). It is, by the way, uncertain from what text Jerome's translation was made. An influence of the old liturgical meaning of מְלָאכָה does not appear to be impossible.

In the Romance languages only the Spanish *vocación*, in the sense of an inner "call" to something, is found. This was carried over from the clerical office and its connotation partly corresponds to that of the German word. However, it was never used to mean "calling" in the external sense. In the Romance Bible translations, the Spanish *vocación* and the Italian *vocazione* and *chiamamento,* which otherwise have a meaning partly corresponding to the Lutheran and Calvinist usage to be discussed presently, are used only to translate the κλῆσις of the New Testament, which refers to the call of the gospel to eternal salvation (which in the Vulgate is *vocatio).* Oddly, Brentano, *op. cit.* [ch. 1, note 15], maintains that this fact, which I have myself adduced to defend my view, is evidence *for* the existence of the concept of the vocational calling in the sense that it had later. But it is nothing of the kind. κλῆϊσις should have been translated as *vocatio.* But where and when in the Middle Ages would it have been used in our sense? The fact of this translation, and the *lack* of any application of the word to a this-worldly connotation, *in spite of this translation*, makes the case.

Chiamamento is used in this manner along with *vocazione* in the Italian Bible translation of the fifteenth century, which is printed in the *Collezione di opere inedite e rare* (Bologna, 1887). On the other hand, the modern Italian translations use *vocazione*. The words used in the Romance languages for "calling," in the *external*, this-worldly sense of regular acquisitive activity, in contrast carry (as appears in all the dictionaries and from a report of my honorable friend, Professor Baist of Freiburg) no religious connotation whatever. This remains the case regardless of whether they are derived from *ministerium* or *officium* (both of which originally had a certain ethical dimension), or from *ars, professio* and *implicare* (*impeigo*) (which entirely omitted an ethical dimension from the beginning). The passages in Jesus Sirach mentioned at the beginning, where Luther used *Beruf*, are translated as follows: in French (verse 20, *office;* verse 21) as *labeur* (a Calvinist translation); Spanish translations (verse 20, *obra;* verse 21) are as *lugar* (following the Vulgate) recently *posto* (a Protestant translation). The Protestants of the Latin countries, since they were minorities, did not exercise (possibly did not even make the attempt) such a creative influence over their respective languages, as Luther did over the less highly rationalized (in an academic sense) German used in state offices.

2. However, the concept is developed only partially in the Augsburg Confession and only implicitly. Article XVI (ed. by Theodor Kolde [Gütersloh.: Bertelsmann, 1906], p. 43) teaches,

> For it is the case that the Gospel . . . does not stand against secular rulership, the police, and marriage; rather, the Gospel wishes that believers maintain the given rulership, police powers, and marriage as elements in God's order. Each in their own station in life, believers must practice Christian love and appropriate good works, each doing so *according to his calling*.

(The Latin: *et in talibus ordinationibus exercere caritatem.* p. 42.) Thus, the consequence to be drawn is apparent: that people must obey the given authority. At least *primarily*, it is clear that the "calling" is understood as an *objective* order in the sense of the passage at 1 Cor. 7:20. And Article XXVII of the Augsburg Confession (Kolde, p. 83) discusses a "calling" (in Latin: *in vocatione sua*) only in connection with those statuses and positions ordained by God, such as the clergy, secular rulers, princes, and lords. Nonetheless, this is the case in German only in the concordance volume; in the main text the relevant sentence is omitted.

Only in Article XXVI (Kolde, p. 81) is the term "calling" used in a manner that encompasses the way the term is used today:

> . . . self-castigation should serve the purpose of maintaining the strength and health of the body (rather than earning of grace), for the body must not hinder persons from that which they have been, according to their calling, commanded to do. (The Latin: *juxta vocationem suam.*)

3. According to the lexicons, kindly confirmed by my colleagues Professors Braune and Hoops, the word *Beruf* (Dutch *beroep*, English *calling*, Danish *kald,* Swedish *kallelse*) does *not* occur in any

of the languages that now contain it, in its present this-worldly sense, before Luther's translation of the Bible.

The Middle High German, Middle Low German, and Middle Dutch words, which *sound* like it, all *mean* the same as *Ruf* in modern German. They also include, and *especially* so, the idea of a "calling" (*Vokation*) of a candidate to an *ecclesiastical office* by those with the power of appointment. This is a special case, which is also often mentioned in the dictionaries of the Scandinavian languages. The word is also occasionally used by Luther in this sense. However, even though this special use of the word [as referring to the formal appointment to a position] may have promoted its change of meaning, the modern conception of *Beruf* undoubtedly goes back linguistically to the Bible translations, especially by Protestants. Other beginnings are to be found, as we shall see later, only in [the mystic Johannes] Tauler [1300–61]. *All* the languages predominantly influenced by the *Protestant* Bible translations have the word. *All* languages for which this was not the case (such as the Romance languages) do not have the word, or at least not in its modern meaning.

Luther translates two quite different concepts with [the single] term *Beruf.* First the Pauline κλῆῖσις, in the sense of the call from God, to eternal salvation. See 1 Cor. 1:26; Eph. 1:18; 4:1, 4; 2 Thess. 1:11; Heb. 3:1; 2 Pet. 1:10. All these cases concern the *purely* religious idea of the call, as announced in the gospel, by the apostles; the word κλῆῖσις has nothing to do with this-worldly callings in the modern sense. The German Bibles before Luther's translation use *ruffunge* (that is, all early printed works in [my] Heidelberg [University] Library), and sometimes instead of *by God called* state *by God summoned.* Second, however, as we have already seen, Luther translates the words in Jesus Sirach discussed in the previous note (in the Septuagint ᾆν τῷ ᾆργῳ σου παλαιώθητι and καὶ ᾆμμενε τῷ πόνῳ σου), with "beharre in deinem *Beruf*" [stay in your *calling*] and "bliebe in deinem *Beruf*" [stay in your *calling*] instead of "bliebe bei deiner *Arbeit*" [stay in your *work*]. The later (authorized) Catholic translations (for example that of Fleischütz; Fulda, 1781) have (as in the New Testament passages) simply followed him. Luther's translation of the passage in the Book of Sirach is, so far as I can see, the *first* case in which the German word *Beruf* appears in its present, *purely* this-worldly sense. (The preceding exhortation, verse 20, στῖθι εν διαθήκῃ σου, he translates *bleibe in Gottes Wort* [stay in God's word] although Sirach 14:1 and 43.10 show that, corresponding to the Hebrew חק, which—according to the citations to the Talmud—Sirach used, διαθήκη really did mean something similar to our calling, namely one's "fate" or "assigned task." [1920])

In its later and present sense the word *Beruf* did *not* exist in the German language. As far as I can see, it also did not exist in the works of the older Bible translators or preachers. The German Bibles before Luther rendered the passage from Sirach as *work.* [The Franciscan] Berthold of Regensburg [1210–1272], at the points in his sermons where today we would say *Beruf* [calling] uses the word *Arbeit* [work]. Thus, the usage was the same as in antiquity. The first passage I know in which *Beruf* is not used but nonetheless *Ruf* (as a translation of κλῆσις) is used, in the sense of purely worldly labor, is found in the fine sermon of the German mystic Tauler [see p. 44] on Ephesians 4 (*Works*, Basel edition, f. 117.5). It concerns peasants who cause trouble. To Luther, they would be better off "if only they would follow their own call (*Ruf*) rather than the [Catholic] clergy, who do not represent their own call." The word in this sense did not find its way into everyday speech. And although Luther's usage at first vacillates between *Ruf* and *Beruf* (see *Werke,* Erlangen edition, vol. 51, p. 51), a direct influence from Tauler is by no means certain (although Luther's [*The Freedom of a Christian* (Philadelphia: Muehlenberg Press, 1957 [1521])] is in many respects similar to this sermon of Tauler). But in the purely *worldly* sense of Tauler, Luther did *not* at the beginning use the word *Ruf.* (This position opposes [the distinguished Luther scholar, Heinrich Seuse] Denifle [1844–1905], *Luther and Luthertum* [1903], p. 163.)

Now evidently in the Septuagint the advice of Sirach contains (apart from the general exhortation to trust in God) no relationship to a specifically religious *valuation* of this-worldly work in a calling. The term πόνος, or toil, in the untenable second passage would be rather the opposite, were it not corrupted. What Jesus Sirach says corresponds simply to the exhortation of the Psalmist ("Dwell in the land, and nourish yourself in a respectable manner"—Psa. 37:3); this idea also comes out clearly in connection with the warning (verse 21) not to let oneself become enamored with the works of the godless, since it is easy for God to make a poor man rich. Only the opening exhortation to remain in the קח (verse 20) has a certain relatedness to the κλῆῖσις of the gospel. Nevertheless, Luther did not here use the word *Beruf* for the Greek διαθήκη. The bridge between Luther's two, seemingly quite unrelated, uses of the word *Beruf* is found in the first letter to the Corinthians and its translation.

In the usual modern editions, the whole context in which the passage stands is as follows, 1 Cor. 7:17–24 (English, King James version [American revision, 1901]):

> (17) Only as the Lord hath distributed to each man, as God hath called each, so let him walk. And so ordain I in all churches. (18) Was any man called being circumcised? Let him not become uncircumcised. Hath any man been called in uncircumcision? Let him not be circumcised. (19) Circumcision is nothing and uncircumcision is nothing; above all keep the commandments of God. (20) Let each man abide in that calling wherein he was called [ἐν τῇ κλήσει η ἐκλήθη; this expression is undoubtedly from the Hebrew, as Professor Merx tells me]. (21) Wast thou called being a bondservant? Care not for it; nay, even if thou canst become free use it rather. (22) For he that was called in the Lord being a bondservant is the Lord's freedman; likewise he that was called being free is Christ's bondservant. (23) Ye were bought with a price; become not bondservants of men. (24) Brethren, let each man, wherein he was called, therein abide with God.

The remark follows verse 29 that time is "short." Well-known commandments motivated by eschatological expectations follow: (31) to possess women as though one did not have them; to buy as though one did not have what one had bought, etc. Luther, in verse 20, following the older German translations, even in his 1523 exegesis of this chapter, renders κλῆῖσις with *call,* and interprets it as [related to] one's social status (Erlangen edition, vol. 51, p. 51.)

In fact it is obvious that the word κλῆσις in this passage, and *only* here, corresponds evidently to the Latin *status* and the German *Stand* (status of marriage, status of a servant, etc.). However, this usage of "status" is of course not, as Brentano assumes (*op. cit.* [ch. 1, note 15], p. 137), the same as *Beruf* in the modern sense. Brentano can hardly have read this passage, or what I have said about it, very carefully. A word that at least reminds us of *Beruf* (and it is etymologically related to ἐκκλησία, or an assembly which has been called) occurs in Greek literature (so far as the lexicons inform us) only once. It can be found in a passage from Dionysius of Halicarnassus. This word, which corresponds to the Latin *classis* (a word borrowed from the Greek) refers to those citizens who have been called to perform military service. Theophylaktos (eleventh-twelfth century) interprets 1 Cor. 7:20: ἐν ο ἴῳ βιῳ καὶ ἐν οἴῳ τάγματι καὶ πολιτεύματι ὢν ἐπ῾στεν,εν [one should stay in the position one has been called into—in life, in classes, and in one's activities as a citizen]. (My colleague Professor Deissmann called my attention to this passage.) Nonetheless, the modern *Beruf,* even in our passage, does *not* correspond to κλῖσις. Luther, however, having translated κλῖσις as *Beruf* in the eschatologically motivated exhortation—everyone should remain in his present status—naturally would, on account of the *objective similarity* of the exhortations alone when he later came to translate the Apocrypha [see ch. 5, note 58], also use *Beruf* for πᾴνῳς to refer to the traditionalistic and anti-chrematistic advice given by Jesus Sirach, namely, that each should remain in his own occupation. This is what is decisive and characteristic. As has been pointed out, the passage in 1 Cor. 7:17 does not use κλῆῖσις at all in the sense of *Beruf,* which implies a demarcated realm of achievements.

In the meantime (or at about the same time), in the Augsburg Confession of 1530 the Protestant dogma regarding the uselessness of the Catholic attempt to surpass this-worldly morality was formulated. The expression "every person according to his calling (*Beruf*)" then became used (see previous note). This expression came to the forefront in Luther's translation. In addition, his translation also stressed his significantly increased estimation (which occurred at the beginning of the 1530s) of the *sacredness* of the order in which the individual is placed. This emphasis resulted, on the one hand, from Luther's increasingly clearly defined belief in the completely unusual character of divine rulership, even over the details of life; on the other hand, it resulted from his increasing proclivity to accept this-worldly orders as ones that God wishes to remain unchanged. *Vocatio,* in the traditional Latin, was used to designate the divine call to a *life* of holiness, especially in a monastery or as a priest. And now, under the influence of Luther's dogma, this term came to denote, for Luther, work in a this-worldly calling. For, while he now translated πόνος and ἔργον in Jesus Sirach as *Beruf* (for which earlier *only* the Latin analogies, which derived from the translations by *monks*, had been available), some years earlier, in translating Proverbs (see verses 22, 29), he had still translated the Hebrew מְלָאכָה, which anchored the ἔργον in the Greek text of Ecclesiastes. This Hebrew מְלָאכָה, in the same manner as the German *Beruf* and the Scandinavian *kald*, and *kallelse*, derived in particular from a *spiritual* notion of *Beruf*. Similarly, in other passages (Gen. 39:2), it was translated as *Geschäft* (Septuagint ἔργον, Vulgate *opus;* in the English Bibles as *business,* and correspondingly in the Scandinavian and all the other translations before me).

Hence, the creation of the term *Beruf* by Luther in the sense in which we understand it today remained, for a time, entirely *Lutheran*. Because the Apocrypha [from which Luther had partly derived his concept] remained to the Calvinists entirely illegitimate, they accepted the Lutheran *concept* of a calling only later. They did so when the consequences of the development that placed the notion of an interest in "testifying to" one's belief came to the forefront. The Calvinists then sharply accentuated Luther's "calling." However, the Calvinists never had a corresponding *term* available to them from the first translations from the Romance languages [Spanish, French, and Italian]. Moreover, they never possessed the power to create such a word as an idiom in their own language, which was already too rigid and inflexible to allow for this possibility.

The concept of *Beruf* became integrated in its present sense into the secular literature as early as the sixteenth century. The Bible translators *before* Luther had used the word *Berufung* [appointment to a position] for the Greek κλῆϊσις (as, for example, in the Heidelberg translations of 1462–66 and 1485; the Eck translation of 1537 states *in dem Ruf, worin er beruft ist* [in the call, to which one is called]). Most of the later Catholic translations directly follow Luther. The first translation of the Bible in England, by Wyclif (1382), used *cleping* (the Old English word that was later replaced by *calling,* a borrowed term). This practice—of using a word that already corresponded to the later usage of the Reformation—is certainly characteristic of this type of Lollard ethics, [as practiced by followers of Wyclif]. On the other hand, Tyndale's translation of 1534 utilizes the idea in terms of *status:* "in the same *state* wherein he was called." This is the case also with the Geneva Bible of 1557. The official translation by Cranmer (1539) substituted *calling* for *state*, while the (Catholic) Bible of Rheims (1582), exactly like the Anglican court Bibles of the Elizabethan era, with their indebtedness to the Vulgate, characteristically return to "vocation."

Murray [unidentified] has already appropriately noted that Cranmer's Bible translation in England is the source of the Puritan conception of "calling" in the sense of *Beruf* (used in reference to trade). *Calling* is used in this sense as early as the middle of the sixteenth century. By 1588, "unlawful callings" are referred to, and "greater callings," in the sense of "higher" occupations, etc., are noted in 1603 (see Murray). Brentano's idea *(op. cit.,* p. 139) is highly remarkable. To him, because only a *free* man could engage in a *Beruf* in the Middle Ages, and freemen were *missing* at that time in the business-oriented vocations, *vocatio* was not translated as *Beruf.* For this reason, to him, this concept remained unknown. However, because the entire societal organization of mediaeval industry, in contrast to antiquity, rested upon free labor (and merchants, above all, were almost always free), I do not really understand this assertion.

4. Weber is here most likely referring to Johannes Tauler. See p. 44 [sk].

5. Compare the following paragraphs with the instructive discussion by K. Eger, *Die Anschauung Luthers vom Beruf* [*Luther's View of the Calling*] (Giessen, 1900). Perhaps the only serious omission in this work, which almost all other theological writers also omit, concerns the analysis of the *lex naturae* concept. This discussion lacks adequate clarity. On this theme see the review by Ernst Troeltsch of Seeberg's *Dogmengeschichte*. Above all, see also the relevant sections in Troeltsch's *Social Teachings of the Christian Churches* [New York: Harper & Row, 1960 (1911)].

6. [St. Thomas Aquinas interpreted Aristotle and synthesized numerous streams of ancient and medieval theology.] The stratification of people into social statuses and occupational groups is the work of divine *providence*, according to him. This stratification implies to him the existence of an objective societal *cosmos*. A *particular person's* decision to take up a particular "calling" (as we would say today, whereas Thomas speaks of *ministerium* or *officium*) results from *causæ naturales* [natural causes]. To him:

> Hæc autem diversificatio hominum in diversis officiis contingit primo ex divina providentia, quæ ita hominum status distribuit, . . . secundo etiam ex causis naturalibus, ex quibus contingit, quod in diversis hominibus sunt diversæ inclinationes ad diversa officia. . . . [This stratification of people into various occupations derives, firstly, from God's providence, according to which the positions people hold are allotted. This apportioning derives, secondly, from natural causes, for different proclivities toward the various occupations exist in different persons.] (See his Quæst. quodlibetal, bk. 7, Art. 17*c*.)

Pascal's evaluation of the "calling" is quite similar when he notes that *chance* decides the choice of a calling. See on Pascal, Adolf Köster, *Die Ethik Pascals* [Tübingen: H. Laupp, 1908]. Only the most closed of the "organic" religious ethics [in the sense of stable elements interrelated with one another in a firm manner]—those from India—are different in this respect. The contrast between the Thomistic and Protestant concepts of the calling are so obvious that we can, for now, refer simply to the quotation above [in the previous note]. (And, furthermore, the contrast of Catholicism to Lutheranism is clear, despite the close relationship in later Lutheranism, especially in regard to an emphasis upon the providential.) We will, at any rate, return later to Catholicism's notion of the calling. On Thomas, see Maurenbrecher, *Thomas von Aquino's Stellung zum Wirtschaftsleben seiner Zeit* [Leipzig: J.J. Weber, 1898]. Otherwise, Luther's agreement with Thomas, which appears to be the case in respect to a series of details, results in fact more from the influence upon Luther of the general teachings of the Scholastics, than from the teachings of Thomas in particular. According to the arguments of Denifle, Luther in fact appears to have been insufficiently acquainted with the works of Thomas. See Denifle, *op. cit.* [p. 180] (p. 501) and Walter Koehler, *Ein Wort zu Denifles Luther* [Tübingen: Mohr, 1904] (p. 25).

7. In Luther's *The Freedom of a Christian*, *op. cit.*, (a) this-worldly duties are understood as involving a *lex naturæ* (interpreted by Luther to mean the natural order of the world), and adherence to them is necessary owing to the "double" [good and evil] natures of the human being. Hence, it follows (Erlangen edition 27, p. 188) that people are *in fact* bound to their bodies and to the social community. (b) In light of this situation, human beings (p. 196) will (and this point connects to the first as a *second* legitimation [for fulfillment of this-worldly duties]), *if* they are believing Christians, come to the conclusion that God's decision to grant salvation, which resulted from genuine love [of His children], must be remunerated by loving one's neighbor. This connection between "faith" and "love" is a very loose one. (c) However, it combines with the old ascetic legitimation of work (p. 190), namely as a mechanism that provides the "spiritual" person with mastery over the physical body. Therefore, work (d) (and here the connection [with work as a mastery mechanism] is taken a step farther, and again the idea of *lex naturae*—now as natural morality—becomes valid, although in a different usage), a particular *drive*, one planted within the species by God (even with *Adam* [before the Fall] and one which Adam held to "solely to please God." Finally (e) (pp. 161 and 199), in connection with Matthew 7:18 f., the idea appears that proficient work in a calling is a consequence of the new life that has been acquired, through faith, by the believer. Moreover, proficient work must have had this cause. Nevertheless, the decisive Calvinist idea—"the capacity to work itself constitutes an internal and external testifying to the person's devoutness"—has not yet developed [from this idea that proficient work derives from faith]. The utilization of such heterogeneous elements [five in all, as above] is explained by the powerful temperament that drives Luther's *The Freedom of a Christian*.

8. "It is not from the benevolence of the butcher, the brewer, or the baker, that we expect our dinner, but from their regard to their own interest. We address ourselves, not to their humanity, but to their self-love; and never talk to them of our own necessities, but of their advantages" (*Wealth of Nations* [1776], bk. 1, ch. 2).

9. This term refers to the major theological and philosophical teachings of the period 1000–1500. They were rooted in the authority of Christianity's founders on the one hand and Aristotle and his interpreters on the other [sk].

10. "Omnia enim per te operabitur (Deus), mulgebit per te vaccam et servilissima quæque opera faciet, ac maxima pariter et minima ipsi grata erunt" [Through you, God will sacrifice all. He will, through you, milk a cow, as he will also, through all, perform the most servile work. In addition, the

smallest and largest tasks will each become welcome tasks.] (Luther, "Exegesis of Genesis," *Exegetica opera Latina*, edited by Christian S. Elsperger, vol. 7, p. 213 [Erlangen: Heyer, 1831]). The idea is found before Luther in [the major figure of early German mysticism] Tauler, who placed the spiritual and the worldly "callings," in terms of their value, in principle at an equal level. Luther and German mysticism share this position, one that contrasts to [Catholic] Thomism. This contrast to Catholicism becomes manifest in that Thomas [Aquinas], in order firmly to retain the moral value of contemplation, though also because he was writing from the standpoint of a mendicant who must beg for a living, found it necessary to interpret Paul's maxim—"whoever does not work shall not eat"—in a certain way. Namely, Thomas viewed this maxim as imposed upon the human species as a whole (and actually, as *lege naturae* [through the law], completely indispensable), rather than upon each person. This hierarchical variation in the prestige of work articulated by Thomas, from the *opera servilia* [servile tasks] of the peasants on up, is connected to the specific character of the Catholic mendicants; for material reasons, it was necessary for them to live in the towns. Such gradation was equally foreign to the German mystics and to Luther, the peasant's son. While attributing equal prestige to all occupations, both the mystics and Luther viewed the general stratification of the social order as willed by God. For the decisive passages in regard to Thomas Aquinas, see Maurenbrecher, *op. cit.* [note 6], pp. 65 f.

11. All the more astonishing is the belief by some scholars that such an innovation could have passed over the *action* of persons without the least effect. I confess, I don't understand this. [1920]

12. Pascal believed that God's grace cannot be coerced or acquired; rather, it must be awaited [sk].

13. "Vanity is so deeply embedded in the human heart that a camp-follower, a kitchen-helper, or a porter all boast and seek admirers . . . (Faugeres, 1st ed., p. 208. cf. Koester, *op. cit.,* pp. 17, 136 ff.). On the principled position on the calling taken at Port Royal and by the Jansenists (which will be also briefly noted later), see now the excellent study by Dr. Paul Honigsheim, *Die Staats- und Soziallehren der französischen Jansenisten im 17ten Jahrhundert* [Darmstadt: Wissenschaftliche Buchhandlung, 1969 (1914)]. See especially pp. 138ff. Although printed separately, this volume belongs to Honigsheim's comprehensive study of the *Vorgeschichte der französischen Aufklärung* [Early History of the French Enlightenment]. [1920]

14. Because our knowledge can never give to us absolute certainty, "probabilities" must be assessed with respect to actions. If good reasons can be offered, action can be viewed as legitimate [sk].

15. In regard to the Fuggers, Luther states: "It cannot be right and godly that, in the course of a single human life, such a large and regal fortune is accumulated." His view essentially expresses the [typical] peasant's mistrust of wealth. Similarly, Luther considers the purchase of stocks ethically suspect because they are "a newly discovered clever thing." In other words, because stocks are, to him, *incomprehensible*. This position is similar to the position of the modern clergy on investment in commodities. (See *Grosser Sermon vom Wucher* [Major Sermon on Usury], Erlangen edition, 20, p. 109).

16. Bankers were called *trapeziten* in ancient Greece. See Weber, *General Economic History,* p. 224 [sk].

17. Hermann Levy develops the contrast appropriately. See *Die Grundlagen des ökonomischen Liberalismus in der Geschichte der englischen Volkswirtschaft* (Jena, 1912) [English Economic Liberalism (London: Macmillan, 1913)]. Note also, for example, the petition of 1653 by the Levellers in Cromwell's army against monopolies and companies. See Samuel R. Gardiner, *History of the Commonwealth and Protectorate* [London: Longmans, Green & Co., 1894–1903], vol. 2, p. 179. On the other hand, [Archbishop William] Laud's regime [1629–1640] sought a "Christian-social" organization of the economy led by the monarchy and the church. The monarch expected political and fiscal-monopolistic advantages from this economy. The Puritans oriented their struggle against just such plans. [1920]

18. An aristocrat, member of parliament, and strict Puritan, Cromwell led the opposition forces against the English monarchy in the English Civil War (1641–49) [sk].

19. This statement can be best understood by reference to the example of the manifesto addressed to the Irish. With this document, in January, 1650, Cromwell opened his war of extermina-

tion against the Irish and answered the manifestos of the Irish (Catholic) clergy from Clonmacnoise of December 4 and 13, 1649. The pivotal sentences:

> Englishmen had good inheritances [manorial estates] (in Ireland, namely) which many of them *purchased with their money* . . . they had good leases from Irishmen for long time to come, *great stocks thereupon*, houses and plantations erected *at their cost and charge*. . . . You broke the union . . . at a time when Ireland was in perfect peace and when, through the *example of English industry, through commerce and traffic*, that which was in the nation's hands was better to them than if all Ireland had been in their possession . . . *Is God, will God be with you*? I am confident He will not.

This manifesto, which reminds one of editorials in the English press at the time of the Boer War [between England and South Africa, 1899–1902], is not unique for the reason that the "capitalist" interests of the English were defined as the legitimating reason for the war. This line of argument could very well have been likewise used in negotiations, for example, between Venice and Genoa over the extent of their respective spheres of influence in the Orient. (Strangely, and although I have emphasized this argument here, Brentano holds it against me; see *Die Anfänge des modernen Kapitalismus*, *op. cit.*, p. 142). Rather, unique to this manifesto is that Cromwell legitimizes (with the deepest personal conviction, as everyone who knows his character will attest, and directly to the Irish themselves) the oppression of the Irish by calling upon God to note the circumstances; namely, that English capital had socialized the Irish to *work*. The manifesto is printed in Thomas Carlyle, *Oliver Cromwell's Letters and Speeches* [London,: Chapman-Hall, 2nd ed., 1846]. It is reprinted in Samuel R. Gardiner, *op. cit.* pp. 163 f.

20. A further exploration of this theme cannot be pursued here. See the writers cited in note 22 below.

21. See the remarks in Adolf Jülicher's fine book, *Die Gleichnisreden Jesu,* (Tübingen: Mohr, 1886–99), vol. 2, pp. 108, 636 f.

22. On the following see, above all, again the discussion in Karl Eger, *op. cit.* Also note Schneckenburger's fine work, which is even today not yet out of date: *Vergleichende Darstellung der lutherischen und reformierten Lehrbegriffe* (Stuttgart: J.B. Metzler, 1855). Christoph E. Luthardt's *Die Ethik Luthers in ihren Grundzgen* (Leipzig: Dorfling und Franke, 1866; only this edition is available to me) does not offer an analysis of the *development* (see p. 84). See further Reinhold Seeberg, *Lehrbuch der Dogmengeschichte,* (Erlangen: A. Deichart, 1895–1898), vol. 2, pp. 262 ff. The article on *Beruf* in the *Realenzyklopädie für protestantische Theologie und Kirche* is without value. It contains all sorts of rather shallow observations on everything imaginable, such as the women question, etc., instead of a scientific analysis of the concept and its origin. From the national economics school's literature on Luther, I will refer here only to Schmoller's studies ("Zur Geschichte der Nationalökonomischen Ansichten in Deutschland während der Reformationszeit," *Zeitschrift für die gesamte Staatswiss.,* vol. 16 [1860]), Wiskemann's prize essay (1861), and the study by Frank G. Ward ("Darstellung und Würdigung von Luthers Ansichten vom Staat und seinen wirtschaftlichen Aufgaben," *Conrads Abhandlungen,* vol. 21 [Jena, 1898]. As far as I can see, the literature on Luther on the occasion of the 400th anniversary of the Reformation (some of which is excellent) has not offered a significantly new contribution to *this* particular problem. Naturally, on Luther's social ethics (and the Lutheran social ethic) see the relevant sections of Troeltsch's *Social Teachings of the Christian Churches (op. cit.)*.

23. *Auslegung des 7. Kap. des 1. Korintherbriefes* (1523, Erlangen edition, vol. 51, pp. 1f). Here Luther still interprets the idea of the freedom "of every calling" before God, as alluded to in this Corinthians passage, to mean that (a) rules pertaining to the regulation of human beings should be repudiated (such as monastic vows, the prohibition of mixed marriages). He also interprets this passage (b) to imply that the fulfillment of customary, this-worldly duties to one's neighbor (which is in itself *indifferent* to God) should be intensified into a commandment *to love one's neighbor*. Actually, his central discussions concern, in view of the *lex naturae* dualism [see note 6 above], the question of the believer's just action before God (for example, at pp. 55, 56).

24. Sombart correctly takes a passage from Luther as his motto for his presentation of the "craftsman spirit" (namely, a spirit of traditionalism):

> You must be prepared to seek, from such a business, nothing other than your basic sustenance. You can do so by calculating the amount of expected business, and then by being attentive to the cost of your room and board, the effort you must invest, and the potential dangers of your activity. Finally, you must attend to the pricing of your goods (whether higher or lower) in such a manner that you receive a wage for your work and troubles. (Martin Luther, *Von Kaufhandlung und Wucher* [*On Business and Usury*], 1524)

Luther's basic approach here remains thoroughly in conformity with the writings of Thomas Aquinas.

25. A social revolutionary sect during Luther's time that wished to erect God's kingdom on earth. Its adherents supported a subjective piety based on feelings, adult baptism, and a strict church discipline [sk].

26. As early as Luther's letter to H. von Sternberg (where Luther states in 1530 that he is dedicating his exegesis of the 117th Psalm to Sternberg), the (lower) nobility "stratum" is viewed as founded by God, in spite of its moral degradation (Erlangen edition, vol. 40, p. 282). The decisive significance that the disturbances in Münster [see ch. 4, note 214] had upon the development of this view are apparent from this letter (p. 282). See also Eger, *op. cit.,* p. 150.

27. Luther's polemics against a transcending of the given order of things in the world through a withdrawal from the world into monasteries constituted the point of departure for his analysis in 1530 of the 111th Psalm, verses 5 and 6 (Erlangen edition, vol. 40, pp. 215–16). However, the *lex naturae* (in contrast to positive law, which is manufactured by the emperor and jurists) is now clearly *identical* with *divine justice*: it is God's creation. Moreover, divine justice includes, in particular, the stratification of the people into *status groups* (p. 215). Luther emphasizes strongly here that the equality of status groups exists only before *God.*

28. As Luther taught especially in his *Von Konzilien und Kirchen* (1539) and *Kurzer Bekenntnis vom heiligen Sakrament* (1545).

29. The idea of the Christian's *testifying to his faith* in work in a vocational calling and in the organization of life remains, with Luther, in the background. This idea, so important for us, dominated Calvinism. A passage from Luther's *Von Konzilien und Kirchen* (1539, Erlangen edition, vol. 25, p. 3) indicates how far it remains in the background: "In addition to the seven major axioms" (by reference to which one recognizes the true church) "are now *several external signs* that allow one to recognize the holy Christian church . . . if we are not drunkards, and if we are not lascivious, proud, haughty, and ostentatious, but chaste, modest, and sober." According to Luther, these signs are not as certain as "the others" (doctrinal purity, prayer, etc.) "because heathens behaved in these ways, indeed to the extent that they occasionally have appeared more holy than Christians."

Calvin's own position, as will be discussed (unlike Puritanism's), was only slightly different. At any rate, Christians, according to Luther, serve God only *in vocatione* [*in* a vocation], not *per vocatione* [*for* a vocation] (Eger, *op. cit.*, pp. 117 ff.). The idea of *a testifying to belief*, on the other hand (more, nonetheless, in its Pietist than in its Calvinist manifestation), at least in incipient, fragmented forms, can be found in the German mystics, even though applied for them in a purely psychological manner. See, for example, the passage by Denifle cited by Reinhold Seeberg, *Lehrbuch der Dogmengeschichte, op. cit.* [note 22], vol. 1, p. 195. See also the already noted statements by Tauler; see note 3 above.

30. His final position is well expressed in some parts of his exegesis of Genesis [see note 10] (vol. iv, p. 109): "Neque hæc fuit levis tentatio, intentum esse suæ vocationi et de aliis non esse curiosum. . . . Paucissimi sunt, qui sua sorte vivant contenti. . . . (p. 111). Nostrum autem est, ut vocanti Deo pareamus . . . (p. 112). Regula igitur hæc servanda est, ut unusquisque maneat in sua vocatione et suo dono contentus vivat, de aliis autem non sit curiosus." This conforms thoroughly, in regard to its *conclusion*, to the definition of traditionalism in the works of Thomas Aquinas (*Secundae secundae* Quest. 118, Art. i):

> Unde necesse est, quod bonum hominis circa ea consistat in quadam mensura, dum scilicet homo . . . quærit habere exteriores divitas, prout sunt necessari' ad vitam ejus secundum suam conditionem. Et ideo in excessu hujus mensuræ consistit peccatum, dum scilicet aliquis supra debitum modum vult eas vel acquirere vel retinere, quod pertinet ad avaritiam.

Thomas grounds the sinfulness of pursuing goods beyond the level of consumption in one's status group in *lex naturae*; this natural law becomes manifest [according to Thomas] through [questions regarding] the *rationality* of the consumer goods. In contrast, Luther grounds this sinfulness in God's judgment. On the relation between faith and the calling in Luther, see also vol. 7, p. 225:

> . . . quando es fidelis, tum placent Deo etiam physica, carnalia, animalia, officia, sive edas, sive bibas, sive vigiles, sive dormias, quæ mere corporalia et animalia sunt. *Tanta res est fides* verum est quidem, placere *Deo etiam in impiis sedulitatem et industriam in officio* (This *activity* in the vocational calling is a virtue *lege naturæ*) sed obstat incredulitas et vana gloria, ne possint opera sua referre ad gloriam Dei (echoing Calvinist ways of speaking). . . . *Merentur* igitur etiam impiorum bona opera in hac quidem vita præmia sua (as distinct from Augustine's 'vitia specie virtutum palliata') sed non numerantur, non colliguntur in altero.

31. This idea is expressed in the *Kirchenpostille* (Erlangen edition, vol. 10, pp. 233, 235–36) in the following manner: "*Everyone* is called into some calling." *This* calling (on p. 236 it is directly a "command") should be heeded, and doing so serves God. The achievement [within the calling] does not please God; rather, the *obedience* to the duties in the given calling pleases God.

32. This statement corresponds to the occasional assertion by modern businesspersons to the effect that (*in contrast to* the statements above on the effect of Pietism on the work habits of female employees) female textile workers, for example, from fundamentalist Lutheran [Pietist], church-going backgrounds commonly *today* (for example, in Westphalia), [continue to] think in the manner of the traditional economic ethic, indeed to an especially high degree. [These businesspersons report that these women] are disinclined to alter their modes of work (even when a transition to the factory system is not involved), despite the temptation of higher earnings. As an explanation, these women then refer to the next world—where all will be, in any case, balanced out in a fair manner. This example indicates that the simple facts of *church membership* and faith are not of any essential significance for the organizing of the believer's entire life. Rather, more important are the more practical *values and ideals* of religious life, for these values and ideals have a direct impact upon the believer. Indeed, their impact played a role in the epoch of capitalism's development. To a lesser degree, they still do.

33. See Tauler, Basel edition [see note 3], pp. 161 f.

34. See the peculiarly emotional sermon of Tauler referred to above [note 3], and chapters 17 and 18 (verse 20) of this work.

35. Because this constitutes, at this point, the single purpose of these comments on Luther, we must be satisfied with this thin, preliminary sketch. If viewed from the standpoint of an evaluation of Luther's achievements, this sketch is not in the least satisfactory. [1920]

36. Although highly influenced by Luther, Zwingli also frequently disagreed with him (especially over the symbolic meaning of communion) [sk].

37. Verses 1532–1540 (bk. 10). See Milton, *Paradise Lost* (London: Folcroft Library Editions, 1972). The two-line emphasis is Weber's [sk].

38. *Ibid.*, verses 1473–1478.

39. This subheading appears in the original table of contents but nowhere in the text. I have inserted it at this point. Weber here turns away from Lutheranism and to more general questions related to the overall "task" of this study [sk].

40. Whoever, of course, shared the Leveller's construction of history would have been in the fortunate circumstance of being able to reduce also [this distinction between Cavaliers and Roundheads] to racial differences. As representatives of the Anglo-Saxons, the Levellers believed it their "birthright" to be able to defend themselves against the descendants of William the Conqueror and the Normans. Until now—and this is quite astonishing—no one has asserted that the plebeian "Roundheads" had "round heads" in the anthropometric sense!

41. English national pride, in particular [cannot be explained by reference to "national character"]. Rather, it results from Magna Carta and the great wars [of the seventeenth century]. The saying so typical today [in Germany] at the sight of a pretty foreign girl—"she looks like an English girl"—is reported as early as the fifteenth century. [1920]

42. These distinctions have, of course, also remained viable in England. Namely, the "squirearchy," to the present, has remained the social carrier of "merrie old England," and the entire era since the Reformation can be understood as a struggle between these two aspects of "the English." I agree on this point with the observations by M. J. Bonn (in the *Frankfurter Zeitung*) on the excellent study by Gerhart von Schulze-Gaevernitz on British imperialism. [See *Britischer Imperialismus und englischer Freihand zu Beginn des 20. Jahrhunderts* (Leipzig, 1906).] See also Hermann Levy [*Soziologische Studien ueber das englische Volk* (Jena, 1920)]. [1920]

43. Precisely these positions—despite this remark and the remarks that follow, which have never been changed and are sufficiently clear, in my opinion—have been, strangely, repeatedly attributed to me. [1920]

44. See Weber's dissertation, "Zur Geschichte der Handelsgesellschaften im Mittelalter," pp. 312–443 in *Gesammelte Aufsätze zur Sozial- und Wirtschaftsgeschichte* (Tübingen: Mohr, 1988). See also Weber, *General Economic History* [sk].

Chapter IV

1. After a short period of expansive domination, Zwinglianism quickly lost its significance. For this reason it will not be treated separately. "Arminianism," whose *dogmatic* uniqueness consisted of the rejection of the predestination dogma in its strict formulation as well as that of "this-worldly asceticism," became established as a sect only in Holland (and the United States). Hence, it is of little interest to us in this chapter. Or, more clearly stated, Arminianism is of interest to us only as a negative case: it was the religion of the merchant elite in Holland (see below). Its dogma was viewed as legitimate in the Anglican Church and in the Methodist denominations. Finally, Arminianism's "Erastian" position (that is, its acknowledgment of the state's sovereignty even in matters regarding the church) was held in common with *all* established authorities with purely political interests: the Long Parliament in England, as well as the Elizabethan monarchy, and the Dutch parliament. Above all, Oldenbarnevelt [see note 12 below] upheld Erastianism.

2. Phillipp Jacob Spener wrote an essay of decisive significance for the expansion of Pietism: *Pia Desideria* [Desired Piety] (Frankfurt: Friedgen, 1676) [sk].

3. A distinguished Pietist, Zinzendorf was a founder of the Herrnhuter Brotherhood (1722) [sk].

4. The Moravian Brethren were founded in 1622 in Bohemia (now in the Czech Republic). They opposed military service, the swearing of oaths, and the owning of private property. Persecuted, in 1722 the Brethren settled in Saxony in the territory of Count Zinzendorf in the village of Herrnhut (north of Zittau in far eastern Germany). One branch emigrated to Pennsylvania and became known as the Church of the Brethren. In the colony, smaller groups split off. In 1946 the major Brethren church merged with the Evangelical Church to form the Evangelical United Brethren Church. This church merged in 1968 with the Methodist Church. Other Brethren churches in Pennsylvania remain independent to this day [sk].

5. See, on the development of the concept of Puritanism, instead of others, John L. Sanford, *Studies and Reflections of the Great Rebellion* (London: J.W. Parker & Son, 1858), p. 65 f. At all times we are using this term in the way that it was used in the everyday language of the seventeenth century, namely, to refer to the religious movements oriented toward asceticism in Holland and England, and without distinctions regarding a church's organizational agenda and dogma. Hence, the term encompasses the "Independents," Congregationalists, Baptists, Mennonites, and Quakers.

6. Casuistic manuals provided believers with exact instruction in regard to all the major activities of life [sk].

7. This distinction has been the subject of hopeless confusion in the literature. Sombart, though also Brentano, continuously cites writers on ethics (generally ones he has become acquainted with through my writings) and their codifications of rules for appropriate conduct. They offer these citations without *ever* asking which of these rules were penetrated by *salvation* rewards. A rule became psychologically effective only if subject to such rewards. [1920]

8. I hardly need to emphasize that this sketch, at those points where it addresses questions of pure dogma, relies at all times on statements from the literature on church history and the literature

that traces the historical development of dogma. Thus, it relies on the secondary literature and, consequently, can hardly claim any *originality.* Of course, to the extent possible, I have sought to become immersed in the primary sources in Reformation history. However, any desire to ignore the in-depth and subtle theological secondary studies of many decades would be extremely presumptuous. Rather, one should (as is entirely unavoidable) allow this research to *guide* one's understanding of the sources.

I can only hope that the necessary brevity of this sketch has not led to incorrect statements, and that I have at least avoided objectively significant misunderstandings. For those familiar with the most important theological literature, this presentation contains something "new" only to the extent that everything here is oriented to the vantage point important for *us.* Many of the highly significant theological investigations are, quite naturally, distant from this vantage point—for example, our concern with the *rational character of asceticism* and its significance for the modern "style of life."

Since this essay originally appeared [1904–05], Ernst Troeltsch's *Social Teachings of the Christian Churches* [New York: Harper & Row, 1960 (1911)] has systematically addressed this theme and in general examined the *sociological* side of the issue. (Troeltsch's *Gerhard und Melanchthon* [1891], as well as numerous reviews in the *Göttingische Gelehrten Anzeige* [Scholar's Review], contained many preliminary studies for this great book.) I have not cited Troeltsch's work below every time I have made use of it (purely for reasons of space); instead, I have made reference *only* to his studies that follow relevant passages in my text or when his works connect directly to it. Not infrequently, I have cited the works of earlier authors, as the vantage points of interest in my study have stood closer to them. The completely inadequate financing of the German libraries has led to a situation in which people in the "provinces" can acquire the most important primary sources and studies only through interlibrary loan from Berlin, or other great libraries, and then only for less than a week. This is, for example, the case for Voët, Baxter, Tyerman, Wesley, and all Methodist, Baptist, and Quaker writers. It is also true for many of the nonmainstream Reformation writers of the early period.

Indispensable for every *thorough* investigation are regular visits to the English and, especially, American libraries. What was available in Germany had, in general of course, to suffice for the following sketch. In America, in recent years, a characteristic and intentional denial of the indigenous *sectarian* past has led to a situation in which the libraries acquire little or nothing of this literature. This very tendency can be seen as a particular manifestation of that general tendency toward *secularization* in American life. In a not-too-distant future, as a result of this tendency, all historical legacies of the general American character will have been dissipated. As this takes place, the meaning of many of that country's foundational institutions will be completely and definitively altered. One must travel to the orthodox, small sectarian colleges in the countryside [to document America's sectarian past].

9. In the following sections we are not interested *mainly* in the ancestry, antecedents, and developmental history of the ascetic movements. Rather, we are taking their ideas as given, namely, as completely developed and as they actually were.

10. On Calvin and Calvinism, in addition to the fundamental work of F. W. Kampschulte [*Johann Calvin, seine Kirche und sein Staat in Genf* (Leipzig: Duncker & Humblot, 1869–99)], the exposition by Erich Marcks is in general among the best. [See his *Gaspard von Coligny: Sein Leben und das Frankreich seiner Zeit* (Stuttgart: Cotta, 1892).] D. Campbell's *The Puritans in Holland, England, and America* (2 vols.) is not always reliable and without bias. A. Pierson's *Studien over Johannes Kalvijn* (Amsterdam: P.N. van Kemper, 1881–91) is a strongly anti-Calvinistic study.

For the development in Holland see (in addition to J. L. Motley) the classical Dutch studies, especially G. Groen van Prinsterer, *Handboek der Geschiedenis van het Vaderland*, [Leiden: Luchtmans, 1841–46]; and *La Hollande et l'influence de Calvin* (Amsterdam: H. Hoveker, 1864). For *modern* Holland see *Le parti anti-révolutionnaire et confessionnel dans l'eglise des Pays-Bas* (Amsterdam: H. Hoveker, 1860). See further, above all, R. J. Fruin's *Tien jaren uit de tachtig jarigen oorlog* [Gravenhage: M. Nijhoff, 1857], and especially, in order to compare, J. Naber, *Calvinist of Libertijntsch* (Utrecht: Beijers, 1884). See also W. J. F. Nuyens, *Geschichte der kerkelijke en politieke geschillen in de Republic der Vereenigde Provincien* (Amsterdam, 1886). For the nineteenth century, see A. Köhler, *Die Niederländische reformierte Kirche* (Erlangen: A Deichert, 1856).

For France, in addition to G. von Polenz, *Geschichte des französischen Calvinismus* (Gotha: F.A. Perthes, 1857–69), see Henry M. Baird, *History of the Rise of the Huguenots in France* (New York: Scribner's Sons, 1879).

For England, in addition to Thomas Carlyle, Thomas B. Macaulay, David Masson, and (last but not least) Leopold von Ranke, see now, above all, the various works of Gardiner and Firth (to be cited later). See also, for example, John James Taylor, *A Retrospect of the Religious Life in England* (London: J. Chapman, 1853), and the excellent book by Hermann Weingarten, *Die Revolutionskirchen Englands* (Leipzig: Breitkopf & Hartel, 1868). Further, see the essay on the English *moralists* by Ernst Troeltsch in the *Realenzyklopädie für protestantische Theologie und Kirche* (3rd ed., 1903), and of course his *Social Teachings of the Christian Churches* (*op. cit.*). Also note Eduard Bernstein's excellent [see note 209] essay, "Kommunistische und demokratisch-sozialistische Strömungen Während der englischen Revolution des 17. Jahrhunderts" in *Geschichte des Sozialismus* (Stuttgart, 1895, vol. 1, sect. 2, pp. 507 ff.). The best bibliography (more than 7,000 titles) is in H. M. Dexter, *The Congregationalism of the Last Three Hundred Years* (New York: B. Franklin, 1920 [1876–79], 1880). Admittedly, this volume concerns mainly, although not exclusively, questions of church *governance.* It is quite superior to Theodore Price, *The History of Protestant Nonconformity in England* (London, 1836–38), to H. S. Skeats, *History of the Free Churches of England, 1688–91* (London: Shepheard Pub., 1891), and to other studies.

For Scotland see, for example, Karl H. Sack, *Die Kirche von Schottland* (1844) and the literature on John Knox.

For the American colonies, a large step above numerous other studies is John Doyle, *The English in America* (London: Longmans, Green, 1887). See further Daniel Wait Howe, *The Puritan Republic of the Massachusetts Bay in New England* (Indianapolis, 1899); John Brown, *The Pilgrim Fathers of New England and Their Puritan Successors* (New York: Revell, 1895). Further references will be given at the appropriate places throughout this chapter.

For differences in respect to *doctrine* the following exposition is indebted especially to Matthias Schneckenburger's lecture series, *Vergleichende Darstellung des lutherischen und reformierten Lehrbegriffs* (Stuttgart, 1855). Albrecht Ritschl's fundamental work, *Die christliche Lehre von der Rechtfertigung und Versöhnung* (3rd ed., Bonn, 1870–74), demonstrates, in closely interweaving historical exposition and value judgments, the unique qualities of its author; despite the author's exceptional conceptual acuity, the reader is not always given complete certainty about Ritschl's *objectivity.* For example, wherever he rejects Schneckenburger's interpretation, I often doubt Ritschl's correctness, even though I do not presume in general to be able to formulate an independent judgment. Moreover, for example, what he establishes out of the great diversity of religious ideas and moods (even in the case of Luther himself) to be *Lutheran* appears often to be defined by his own value judgments. This is so because Ritschl attends to what, for him, is the *eternally valued* in Lutheranism. His Lutheranism is a Lutheranism of what this religion *ought* to be and not what it always *was*. That the studies of Karl Müller, Reinhold Seeberg, and others have *everywhere* been used does not require special mention here.

If I have in the following pages imposed upon the reader (as well as *myself*) a malignant growth of evil endnotes, I had a single decisive hope in doing so: to provide the reader—especially the *non*theologian—with at least the preliminary possibility of independently evaluating the ideas in this essay. The literature noted here can also assist the evaluation of my argument through an investigation of related vantage points.

11. It should be emphasized from the beginning that we are here *not* considering the personal views of Calvin. Rather, our concern is with *Calvinism.* We are concerned, moreover, with Calvinism in *the form* it had developed at the end of the sixteenth century and in the seventeenth century. Finally, we wish to investigate its form in this era in the large territories of its dominant influence that were, simultaneously, carriers of a capitalist culture. Germany must remain for now *completely aside* for the simple reason that pure Calvinism nowhere in Germany *dominated* large territories. "Reformed" is of course by no means identical with "Calvinist." [See Glossary]

12. Oldenbarnevelt was a Dutch diplomat. He negotiated the 1609 armistice with Spain and was executed after conflicts with state authorities [sk].

13. Even though the declaration of the 17th article of the Anglican Confession (the so-called Lambeth Article of 1595, which expressly taught, contrary to the official version, that predestination to eternal death existed) was agreed to by the University of Cambridge and the archbishop of Canterbury, it was not ratified by the queen. The radicals in particular emphasized strongly explicit predestination to death (and not only the *admission* of the condemned, as upheld by the milder doctrine). This was clear from the Hanserd Knollys' confessions. [1920] [Weber is most likely referring to Knollys, William Kiffin, and H. Keach, *London Baptist Confessions* (London: 1689).]

14. *Westminster Confession* (5th official ed., London, 1717). See the Savoy Declaration and the (American [edition of]) Knollys (*ibid.*). On the Huguenots' view of predestination, see, among others, Polenz, *op. cit.*, vol. 1, pp. 545 ff.

15. On Milton's theology see the essay of R. Eibach ("John Milton als Theologe") in the *Theologische Studien und Kritiken,* vol. 5 (1879). See also Thomas Macaulay's essay on it (in *Critical and Miscellaneous Essays* [New York: D. Appleton], vol. 1, 1843), on the occasion of Sumner's translation of the *Doctrina Christiana,* rediscovered in 1823 (Tauchnitz edition, vol. 185, pp. 1 ff.), is superficial. For more detail see the (somewhat too schematic) six-volume English work of David Masson, *The Life of John Milton* (London, 1859–94). See also the German biography of Milton, based on Masson, by Alfred Stern, *Milton und seine Zeit* (1877–99). At an early point, Milton began to grow away from the doctrine of predestination in the form of a double decree. He moved eventually in his advanced years to an entirely unbounded Christianity. He can be compared, in respect to his distance from his own epoch, in a certain sense to Sebastian Franck. Yet Milton's nature was more oriented to the practical, while Franck's was substantially more critical. Milton can be said to be a *Puritan* only in the broader sense of *rationally* orienting his practical life to God's will. This orientation represented Calvinism's lasting legacy to the world. One could call Franck a *Puritan* in an entirely similar manner. As "lonely and isolated figures," both must remain outside our concern.

16. Through his *Confessions* and other works, St. Augustine significantly influenced Christian theology until the mid-thirteenth century [sk].

17. *Hic est fides summus gradus; credere Deum esse clementum, qui tam paucos salvat, justum, qui sua voluntate nos damnabiles facit* is the text of the famous passage in *De servo arbitrio.* [Of observant witnessing]. [This is the highest level of faith. The belief that God is mild is justified; through His will He made us deserving of condemnation, yet He saves the poor.]

18. Melanchthon was closely associated with Luther and author of the first major Lutheran doctrinal statement, the Augsburg Confession (1530) [sk].

19. Both Luther and Calvin basically knew a double God: the revealed, forgiving, and benevolent Father of the New Testament (who ruled the first books of Calvin's *Institutio christianae religionis* [1536; Engl. transl. 1561; London: Wolfe & Harison), and the distant *Deus absconditus* [hidden God], who was a thundering and arbitrary despot. See Ritschl's remarks in *Geschichte des Pietismus* (Bonn, 1880–86) and Köstlin's article "Gott" in *Realenzyklopädie für protestantische Theologie und Kirche* (3rd ed.). The God of the New Testament completely retained the dominant position for Luther. This resulted from his increasing avoidance of *reflection* on the metaphysical realm, which he saw as useless and dangerous. In contrast, the idea of a transcendent Divine power over and above life acquired an increasingly prominent position in Calvin's thinking. Of course, this idea could not be defended and endure with the development of a more popular Calvinism. Nevertheless, the [benevolent] heavenly father of the New Testament did not replace this idea; rather, the [distant and arbitrary] Yahweh of the Old Testament came to the fore as Calvinism developed.

20. Regarding that which follows, see Max Scheibe, *Calvins Prädestinationslehre* (Halle, 1897). On Calvinist theology in general, see Johann Heinrich Heppe, *Dogmatik der evangelisch-reformierten Kirche* (Elberfeld: R.L. Friderichs, 1861).

21. *Corpus Reformatorum* (vol. 77, pp. 186 ff.).

22. The preceding exposition of Calvinist doctrinal concepts can be reviewed in, for example, Hoornbeek's *Theologia practica* (Utrecht, 1663). See the section on predestination (vol. 50, sect. 2,

ch. 1). Characteristically, this discussion comes *directly* after the title: "De Deo" [Of God]. My presentation of these concepts has closely followed Hoornbeek. The first chapter of the Epistle to the Ephesians constitutes the major biblical foundation for his analysis. It is not necessary for us to analyze here the various inconsistent attempts to combine God's predestination and providence with the responsibility of the individual and [thereby] to save the empirical "freedom" of the will (as has been attempted even as early as the first developments of doctrine by Augustine).

23. "The deepest community (with God) is found not in institutions or corporations or churches, but in the secrets of a solitary heart," as Edward Dowden states the pivotal point in his fine book *Puritan and Anglican Studies in Literature* (London: Holt, 1901), p. 234. This deep spiritual loneliness of each believer makes its appearance in the same manner with the Jansenists [see note 153 below] from Port Royal. They also believed in predestination. [Close to Paris, Port Royal was a convent of Cistercian nuns (founded in 1204). It became a center of Jansenism.]

24. "Contra qui huiusmodi coetus tum contemnunt . . . salutis suae certi esse non possunt; et qui in illo contemtu perseverat electus non est." Olevian, *De substantia faederis gratuiti inter Deum et electos* [1558], p. 222. [Those who scorn a church that upholds pure doctrine, the sacraments, and discipline cannot be certain of their salvation; and the person who stubbornly remains disrespectful is not among the saved.]

25. "One says readily that God sent His Son to save the human species. However, that was not his aim. Rather, he wanted to help only a few out of their sinfulness. . . . And I say to you that God died only for the predestined" (sermon preached in 1609 at Broek; found in H. C. Rogge, *Johannes Uytenbogaert*; 1874–76, vol. 2, p. 9; see also Nuyens, *op. cit.,* vol. 2, p. 232). The legitimating foundation for the intermediating role of Christ is also confusing in Hanserd Knollys' confessions [*op. cit.*, note 13]. It is actually universally assumed that God in fact would not have needed this mediation at all. [1920]

26. [This expression is widely believed to be from the German dramatist, historian, and philosopher of aesthetics Friedrich Schiller (1759–1805)] On this process see my Economic Ethics of the World Religions series. [See "Introduction to *The Protestant Ethic*", pp. lviii–lxiv] Even the unusual nature of the ancient Israelite ethic (in contrast to Egyptian and Babylonian ethics, despite their close substantive relationship), and its development since the epoch of the prophets [800–500 BCE], was founded completely upon this fundamental point: this ethic rejected the practice of sacramental magic as a means to acquire salvation. [1920] [As implied in the text, Weber will view this rejection of magic as pivotal for the development of the Western religious tradition. This will become apparent in this volume; see also, for example, *E&S*, pp. 399–634; *The Religion of China*, pp. 226–49; "Social Psychology," in H. H. Gerth and C. W. Mills, eds., *From Max Weber*.]

27. [Because not only Calvinism but *all* the churches and sects of ascetic Protestantism—Puritanism—broadly upheld the predestination doctrine, Weber is broadening out his comments on the influence of this doctrine in the next few pages to Puritanism as a whole.] Similarly, according to the most consistent views, baptism was obligatory (owing to clear regulations) yet not necessary for salvation. *For this reason,* the strict Scottish Puritans and the English Independents sought to put into practice a basic principle: the children of obvious *reprobates* should not be baptized (children of drunkards, for example). The Synod of Edam (1586, Article 32,1) recommended that adults who desired to be baptized but were not yet *ready* to take communion, should be baptized only if their conduct was blameless and if they had placed their desire *sonder superstitie*. [Their wish to be baptized must not be influenced by superstition, cult beliefs, or beliefs in miracles or magic.] [1920]

28. This negative relationship to *all culture that appeals to the senses* is a central constitutive element of Puritanism (as Edward Dowden has explained in elegant fashion; see *op. cit.* [note 23]). [1920]

29. The expression *individualism* encompasses the most heterogeneous phenomena to be imagined. It is to be hoped that what is understood *here* by this term will become clear in the following clarifications. Some (using the term differently) have called Lutheranism "individualistic" because it does *not* involve an ascetic regimentation of life. The term is used in a very different manner by Dietrich Schäfer, for example, when he, in "Zur Beurteilung des Wormser Konkordats" (in *Abhandlung der Berliner Akademie*, 1905), calls the *Middle Ages* the era of "marked individuality." He does so because, for the occurrences *relevant* for the historian, "irrational aspects" [indicating

"individuality"] assumed a significance in the Middle Ages that they no longer possess today. He is correct, but perhaps those who oppose his observations are also correct; varying understandings are apparent here when all concerned speak of "individuality" and "individualism." The ingenious formulations by Jacob Burckhardt [the cultural historian of the Italian Renaissance, 1818–97], are today in part outmoded, and a thorough, historically oriented analysis of individualism would be, especially now, again a highly valuable scientific contribution. The results would be, of course, just the opposite if the playful instincts of certain historians push them, in order simply to be able to stick a label on an historical epoch, to "define" the concept as if it were an advertisement.

30. Similar, although of course less pointed, is the contrast between this pessimistic Puritan individualism and later Catholic doctrine. Pascal's deep pessimism, which likewise rests upon the doctrine of predestination, locates its origin, on the other hand, in Jansenism [see notes 57 and 153 below]. The flight-from-the-world individualism of Pascal, which arose out of his pessimism, does not at all accord with the official Catholic position. See Paul Honigsheim, *Die Staats- und Soziallehren der französischen Jansenisten im 17 Jahrhundert* [Darmstadt: Wissenschaftliche Buchgesellschaft, 1969 (1914)]. [1920]

31. Just like the Jansenists. [See notes 57 and 153 below.]

32. Lewis Bayly, *Praxis pietatis,* German edition (Leipzig, 1724 [orig.: Basel: Johann Brandmuller, 1708]), p. 187. [As clear from its title in English, *The Practice of Piety: Directing a Christian How to Walk That He May Please God* (London: Algonquin Press, 1642), this very popular book in Puritan circles offered the devout practical advice on correct conduct.] Also Spener takes a similar point of view in his *Theologische Bedenken*, 3rd ed. (Halle, 1712): One's friend rarely gives advice grounded in reference to God's honor; rather, his advice usually derives from intentions rooted in physical desires (although not necessarily egoistic motives).

> He the 'knowing man' is blind in no man's cause, but best sighted in his own. He confines himself to the circle of his own affairs and thrusts not his fingers into needless fires. He sees the falseness of it (the world) and therefore learns to trust himself ever, others so far, as not to be damaged by their disappointment.

Thomas Adams philosophizes in this manner (see *Works of the Puritan Divines,* p. 51). [This, and the studies cited below as *Works of the Puritan Divines,* were published in 10 volumes as *Works of the English Puritan Divines* (London: Nelson Publishers, 1845–47).] Bayly (*op. cit.*, p. 176) further recommends that one should imagine, every morning before going out among people, that one is walking into a wild forest full of dangers. Hence, one should pray to God for the "cloak of *caution and justice.*"

This sensibility penetrates, without exception, all the ascetic denominations and leads directly, for many Pietists amidst the world's activities, to a type of solitary life. Even Spangenberg [see note 162 below], in the (Herrnhuter) *Idea fidei fratum* (Leipzig: Weidmanns, 1779, p. 328), emphatically calls attention to Jeremiah 17:5: "Cursed is the man who trusteth in man." One should note also, in order to assess the strange misanthropy of this view of life, Hoornbeek's remarks (*Theologia practica,* vol. 1, p. 882) on the duty to love one's enemy: "Denique hoc magis nos ulcisimur, quo proximum, inultum nobis, tradimus ultori Deo—Quo quis plus se ulscitur, eo minus id pro ipso agit Deus." [In the end, we more likely invite revenge upon us as a result of what we see in a vindictive God and qualities we attribute to Him. Wherever a person takes revenge, however, it is not God who is acting but the person himself.] The same "displacement of revenge" is found here as is found in the post-Exile sections of the Old Testament: a refined intensification and internalization of the feeling of revenge is apparent, in contrast to the ancient maxim "an eye for an eye." On "brotherly love" see also note 43 below.

33. Of course, confession surely not *only* had such an effect. The discussions, for example, by A. Muthmann are all too simple for a psychological problem as highly complicated as confession. See his "Psychiatrisch-theologische Grenzfragen, in *Zeitschrift für Religionspsychologie* (vol. 1, no. 2, 1907), p. 65. [1920]

34. Precisely *this* combination is very important for the ascertainment of the psychological foundation of Calvinist social *organizations*. *All* rest internally upon "individualistic," "means-end rational," or "value-rational" motives. [On these "types of social action," see *E&S*, pp. 24–26]. The indi-

vidual never moves into social organizations on the basis of *feelings*. Such movement is prevented by the orientation to "God's glory" and one's *own* salvation, which continuously hovers *above* one's consciousness. Among those peoples with a Puritan past, this psychological foundation even today imprints the uniqueness of their social organization with certain characteristic traits. [See Weber, "'Churches' and 'Sects' in North America: An Ecclesiastical Socio-Political Sketch," in *Sociological Theory* 3 (1985): 10–11.; reprinted in Peter Baehr and David Wells, eds. and translators, *Max Weber's 'Protestant Ethic and the Spirit of Capitalism': The First Version* (London: Penguin Press, 2001). See also "Sects" below.]

35. The *anti-authoritarian* grounding of the doctrine, which basically devalued, as meaningless, all church and state caretaking responsibility for ethical action and the believer's salvation, led perpetually anew to the prohibition of caretaking initiatives. Such was the situation, for example, in the Dutch parliament. The consequence was clear: the continuous formation of conventicles (as occurred after 1614).

36. On John Bunyan see the biography by James A. Froude, *Bunyan* (London: Macmillan, 1880), in the English Men of Letters series. See also Thomas B. Macaulay's (superficial) sketch on Bunyan in his *Critical and Miscellaneous Essays*, *op. cit.* [note 15], vol. 2 [1860], p. 227. Although a strict Calvinist Baptist, Bunyan is indifferent to the denominational differences within Calvinism.

37. In Italy, Alphonsus of Liguori founded a religious order, the Redemptorists, in 1732. A Catholic reform theologian as well as a church historian, Döllinger was excommunicated because of his challenges to doctrines on the virgin birth and the infallibility of the pope [sk].

38. In citing this passage from Richard Wagner's opera, Weber wishes to convey the warrior's ethos of honor and stoic resignation before death, and to note its clear contrast to the ethos of Christian on the one hand and to the ethos of the citizens of Florence on the other. See Wagner, *Ring of the Nibelung* (New York: Thames & Hudson, 1993), pp. 161, 163 [sk].

39. One might be inclined to explain the *social* character of ascetic Christianity by noting the undoubtedly large importance of the Calvinist idea of an "incorporation into the body of Christ" (Calvin, *Instituto christianae religionis*, vol. 3, sects. 11, 10). In other words, because it is necessary for salvation, there must be admission into a *community* governed by God's prescriptions. For *our* particular vantage point, however, the major issue lies elsewhere.

This dogmatic idea [the importance of an incorporation into the body of Christ] could have been formulated if the church had assumed the character of an institution with membership granted to all; indeed, this type of institution did develop [Catholicism], as is well-known. Yet such a church did not have the psychological power to awaken community-building *initiatives* and to endow them with the sheer strength that Calvinism possessed to do so. In particular, the effects of Calvinism's community-building tendencies played themselves out *beyond* the divinely prescribed church congregation and in the "world." At this point the belief becomes central that the Christian, through activities *in majorem Dei gloriam* [in service to the greater glory of God], testifies to his state of grace (see below).

The sharp condemnation of the deification of human wants and desires and of all clinging to *personal* relationships with others must have directed this energy, imperceptibly, into this pathway of impersonal activity. The Christian, whose entire existence was burdened by the necessity of testifying to his own state of grace, now acted on behalf of *God's* aims. And these could only be *impersonal* aims. Every purely feeling-based *personal* relationship of individuals to one another—that is, relationships not determined by rational aims—now easily fell under suspicion, for Puritanism as well as for every other ascetic ethic, as involving a deification of human wants and desires. The following warning (in addition to what has already been noted) indicates just this tendency clearly enough: "It is an irrational act and not fit for a rational creature to love any one farther than reason will allow us. . . . It very often taketh up men's minds so as to hinder their love of God" (Baxter, *Christian Directory* [London: G. Bell & Sons, 1925 (1673)], vol. 4, p. 253). We will confront such arguments repeatedly.

The Calvinists greeted with enthusiasm the idea that God, in creating the world and also the social order, must have wanted *impersonal and purposive activity* to constitute a means for the glorification of His reputation. He did not create, the Calvinists realized, human beings for their own sake, simply for the fulfillment of the physical needs of the body. Rather, He created a world in which the physical being would be *ordered* under His will. Liberated by the doctrine of predestination, the fervid activity of the chosen could now flow entirely into a striving to make the world rational (*Rationalisierung der Welt*). More precisely, the idea that the "public" good (or, as Baxter says, "the good of the many"; see, with its rather strained citation to Romans 9:3, p. 262 of his *Christian Directory*, vol. 4, p. 262), which was formulated in the same manner entirely as the later liberal rationalism [Classical Economics], is to be given preference over the "personal" or "private" prosperity of each person, followed for Puritanism (even though not a new idea as such) from the rejection of all glorification of human wants and desires. The long-standing American deprecation of those who *carry out* the personal commands of others, although it must be viewed in combination with many other causes that derive from "democratic" sentiments, nonetheless goes together (in an indirect manner) with this opposition to the deification of wants and desires.

This rejection of all human glorification is likewise related to the *relatively* high degree of immunity to authoritarianism possessed by peoples influenced by Puritanism. Furthermore, this rejection is related, in general, to the internally less inhibited posture of the English vis-à-vis their great statesmen (and their greater capacity to criticize them). This posture contrasts to some of our experiences in Germany from 1878 to the present (both positively and negatively) in respect to our statesmen. The posture of the English is characterized by a tendency, on the one hand, to acknowledge leadership in distinguished persons. It is marked, on the other hand, despite this acknowledgment, by a further proclivity to reject all hysterical idolization of leaders.

Finally, the tendency to oppose a naive idea is also apparent in Puritanism; namely, that one can render a person duty-bound, out of a sense of "thankfulness," to obey political authorities [as in Germany]. On the sinfulness of the belief in authority, see Baxter, *Christian Directory*, 2nd ed. (1678, vol. 1, p. 56). He makes it clear that a belief in authority is permissible only if the authority is *impersonal*; that is, the belief is oriented to the content of a written [statute or regulation in a] document. Likewise, an exaggerated respect for even the most holy and wonderful person is sinful. The great danger exists, in attributing both authority and respect, that eventually the obedience to *God* will thereby be endangered.

A discussion of what the rejection of the "deification of human wants and desires" meant *politically,* as well as the principle that (first in the church and then in the end also in life as a whole) only God should "rule," does not belong in this context.

40. The relationship between dogmatic and practical-psychological "consequences" will be often discussed. It scarcely needs to be remarked that these two types of consequences are not identical. [1920]

41. "Social," of course, without any echo of the modern sense of the word. [Weber wants to steer his German audience away from the (modern) nineteenth- and early twentieth-century use of "social" in Germany in certain religious groupings and political parties; it referred to the obligations of major societal institutions (the state, churches, etc.) to the welfare of all.] [For the Calvinist,] the term merely implies being active in political or church groups, or other organizations that build community.

42. Good works for *any* purpose other than to serve the honor *of God* are *sinful.* See Hanserd Knollys' confession, *op. cit.* [note 13], chapter 16. [1920]

43. What such a rendering of the "love thy neighbor" commandment as "impersonal," resulting from the exclusive relating of one's life to God, meant for the believer's own realm—the life of the religious community—can be very well depicted by a glance at the conduct of the "China Inland Mission" and the "International Missionaries' Alliance." See Warneck, *Geschichte der protestantischen Missionären* (1899, pp. 99, 111). At enormous cost, a huge squad of missionaries (for example, approximately 1,000 for China alone) was equipped in order "to offer" the gospel in a strictly literal sense, through itinerant preachers, to all heathens. It was necessary to do so because Christ had commanded this activity and had made his second coming dependent upon it. Whether those preached to in this manner were converted to Christianity, and hence became among the saved, and whether they *understood* the language of the missionary, even grammatically—all this is in principle a thoroughly secondary matter and a concern of God alone (who of course exclusively decides such issues). According to Hudson Taylor (see Warneck), China has approximately 50 mil-

lion families. A thousand missionaries could "reach" 50 families per day (!). Thus, in 1,000 days, or less than three years, the gospel could be "offered" to all Chinese.

As is apparent from Calvinist church discipline, for example, Calvinism operated exactly according to this model. The goal was *not* the salvation of those subject to church discipline. That remained true for the simple reason that the believer's salvation fate was to be decided in the end by God (and, in actual practice, by believers themselves). This fate could not be influenced in any way by the disciplinary measures available to the church. The aim of such measures was instead to increase the glory of God.

Calvinism as such is not responsible for the achievements of the modern missions, for the simple reason that the mission is based upon an interdenominational foundation. (Calvin himself rejected the duty of missionizing to the heathens; to him, the further expansion of the church was *unius Dei opus* [the work of the single Christian God].) Nevertheless, the missions originate apparently out of the circle of ideas (extending throughout the Puritan ethic) that argue in favor of viewing the commandment to love one's neighbor as one loves oneself as adequately practiced if believers fulfill it for the sake of God's glory. In this way one's neighbor is given his due, and everything else is God's concern alone. The "humanity" of the relations to "one's neighbor" has, so to speak, died out. This is apparent in the most diverse situations.

For example, if we wish to note a further basic aspect of the Calvinist milieu, giving to charity by ascetic Protestants could be discussed. In a certain sense such giving is justifiably famous. Even in the twentieth century, the orphans of Amsterdam, with their skirts and pants vertically divided into black and red or red and green halves, are led in parades to church. Dressed in this sort of fool's costume, the orphans were, for the sensibilities of the past, surely a highly delightful show. Moreover, and precisely to the extent that a show took place, the children served the glory of God: as the entertainment proceeded, all personal "human" sensibilities had to feel insulted. And, as we shall see, the effects of this dulling of human sensibilities then extended into personal relationships in all aspects of one's private occupational activities.

Of course, this example depicts only a *tendency*. We will later have to define certain qualifications. However, this tendency, *as* one element (and indeed a very important one) of ascetic devoutness, must be pointed out here.

44. The problem of theodicy refers to the enduring existence of evil despite the existence of an all-knowing, all-powerful, and fundamentally benevolent God [sk].

45. In all these ways the ethic of Port Royal [see note 23, above] which was determined by predestination, diverged. As a result of its mystical and *other*-worldly (and hence, to the same degree, Catholic) orientation, this ethic was entirely different. See Paul Honigsheim, *op. cit.* [note 30]. [1920]

46. Karl Bernhard Hundeshagen (see *Beiträge zur Kirchenverfassungsgeschichte und Kirchenpolitik, insbesonders des Protestantismus* [Wiesbaden, 1864], vol. 1, p. 37) defends the position (which has been often repeated) that the doctrine of predestination came from the teachings of theologians rather than from the people. This view is correct, however, only if one identifies the concept "people" (*Volk*) with the uneducated *masses* of the lower strata. And even then this argument holds only to a highly limited extent. In the 1840s, Köhler (*op. cit.*) found that just these "masses" (he refers to the lower middle-class in Holland) were strict followers of the idea of predestination. To them, any person who denied the double decree was a heretic and among the condemned. Even Köhler was asked about the *particular time* of his rebirth (in the sense of its predestined determination).

Moreover, the [seventeenth-century] da Costa and de Kock independence revolts were highly influenced by the idea of predestination. Not only Cromwell, whom Zeller has already viewed as exemplifying the effect of the doctrine (see *Das Theologische System Zwinglis* [1853], p. 17), but also his troops, knew full well what was involved. The canons on predestination issued by the Dordrecht and Westminster synods were major national events. Cromwell's tryers and ejectors [who examined candidates for the ministry] admitted only those who believed in predestination, and Baxter (*Life,* vol. 1, p. 72), although otherwise its opponent, judged the effect of predestination upon the quality of the clergy as significant. It is quite impossible that the doctrine was unclear to the Reformed Pietists (the participants in the English and Dutch conventicles). On the contrary, it was precisely *predestination* that drew this group together to search for the *certitudo salutis*. Wherever predestination was a teaching *of theologians*, its significance (or lack thereof) can be indicated by a glance at orthodox Catholicism, where it was by no means unknown (in precarious forms) as an esoteric teaching. (What was decisive—the view that the *person* must *consider* himself as among the predestined and testify to this elect status through conduct—was continuously omitted.) On Catholic doctrine see, for example, Adolf Van Wyck, *Tract. de praedestinatione* [Cologne, 1708]. The extent to which [the Catholic] Pascal's belief in predestination was correct cannot be investigated here.

Hundeshagen, to whom the doctrine is unappealing, acquired his impressions of it apparently predominantly from the German circumstances. All of his hostility is rooted in an opinion, acquired through pure deduction, that predestination must necessarily lead to moral fatalism and antinomianism. Zeller has already refuted this opinion (see *op. cit.*). Nevertheless, the *possibility* of such an interpretation cannot be denied. Both Melanchthon and Wesley discuss it. It is characteristic for both, however, that the doctrine is combined with a *feeling*-based "faith." Hence, in this context, given the absence of the rational idea of *testifying to belief through conduct*, this result—moral fatalism and antinomianism—in fact lies at the essence of the matter.

These fatalistic results appear in *Islam.* But for what reason? Because the prior decision making in Islam referred to a *predetermination* (not a predestination) of the believer's religious destiny in *this* world, and not to an *other-worldly* salvation. Consequently, that which is ethically decisive—a testifying by the believer, through conduct, that he belongs among the predestined elect—plays no role in Islam. Hence, only the warrior's fearlessness (as with *moira* [the idea that death in battle was in God's hands]), rather than a *methodical ordering* of the believer's life (because the religious "reward" was absent), could follow from Islam's ideas of predestination. See the study by F. Ullrich, *Die Vorherbestimmungslehre im Islam und Christenheit* (Heidelberg University, School of Theology [diss.], 1912). [1920]

The doctrine of predestination was not substantially weakened as long as the idea remained uncontested that God's decision took place in respect to a *particular* individual and his *testing*. (The later alterations by Baxter, for example, addressed difficulties encountered by ministers when they sought, on the basis of the *doctrine's* tenets, to provide pastoral care to believers). Above all, all the great figures of Puritanism (in the broadest sense of the term) ultimately located their journey's point of departure in the doctrine of predestination. Its melancholy seriousness influenced the development of their youth. This was true for Milton, just as for Baxter (although, admittedly, less effectively) and even later for the very freethinking Franklin. Their later emancipation from a strict interpretation of the doctrine corresponded entirely to the development, even in its details and direction, of the religious movement as a whole. Nevertheless, *all* great church revivals—at least in Holland and usually also in England—connected directly and continuously to the doctrine of predestination.

47. This question repeatedly, and in so powerful a manner, formulates the basic mood in John Bunyan's *Pilgrim's Progress* [London: Penguin, 1965 (1676–84)].

48. This *question* was already more distant to the Lutheran epigone (and without regard to the predestination doctrine) than to the Calvinists. A putatively lesser interest on the part of Lutherans in the salvation of their souls was not the issue here. Rather, this question was more distant because the development taken by the Lutheran Church placed the character of the church—as an institution that *offers salvation*—in the forefront. Hence, the single believer became an object of the church's activity and felt cared for by the church. Characteristically, Pietism first awakened this problem of how the faithful could become certain of their salvation in Lutheranism. However, the question of the *certitudo salutis itself* was absolutely central for every religion based in non-sacramental salvation, whether Buddhism, Jainism, or any other. This point should not be mistaken. From *this* question arose all psychological motivations of a purely *religious* character. [The last three sentences were added in 1920.]

49. As directly stated in the letter to Bucer, *Corp. Ref.* (vol. 29, pp. 883 f.). See, in this regard, again Scheibe (*op. cit.*, p. 30).

50. The Westminster Confession (vol. 18, pt. 2) holds out to the chosen the prospect of an *undeceiving certainty* of grace, even though we remain, despite our constant activity, "useless servants"

(vol. 16, pt. 2). Moreover, the struggle against evil lasts our entire life long (vol. 18, pt. 3). Even the chosen often must struggle for a very long time in order to acquire the *certitudo salutis* that provides their consciousness with a sense of having done their duty. The believer is never completely robbed of this consciousness.

51. For example, Olevian, *De substantia faederis gratuiti inter Deum et electos* (1585, p. 257); Heidegger, *Corpus theologiae Christianae*, vol. 24 (Tiguri: 1732), p. 87; see also further passages in Heppe, *op cit.* [note 20], p. 425.

52. Genuine Calvinist doctrine referred to both *faith* and a consciousness of a community with God as acquired through the sacraments. This doctrine viewed the "other fruits of the spirit" as secondary. See the passages in Heppe (*op. cit.,* p. 425). Calvin himself strongly emphasized good works, even though they were for him, as for the Lutherans, outgrowths of belief rather than *signs,* to those who performed them, of God's favor (Calvin, *Instituto christianae religionis*, vol. 3, pts. 2, 37, 38). The practical turn to the notion of good works as themselves testifying to the believer's faith, which is characteristic of *asceticism*, develops parallel with a gradual transformation of Calvin's teachings. As with Luther, according to Calvin, the true church was *primarily,* at its origin, designated by pure doctrine and sacraments, and later by the elevation of *disciplina* [church discipline] to a position of equal importance. This development can be traced, for example, in passages in Heppe (*op. cit.,* pp. 194–95). It is also apparent in the manner in which, even at the end of the sixteenth century, membership in a religious congregation was acquired in Holland. (An explicit, contract-based submission to church *discipline* constituted a central condition.)

53. See the remarks by Schneckenburger (*op. cit.,* p. 48) on this point.

54. For example, the distinction between a "mortal" and a "venial" sin appears again (entirely in the manner of Catholicism) in Baxter's works. A mortal sin constitutes a sign that the state of grace is absent (or, at any rate, not felt by the believer). In this case, only a "conversion" of the entire person can testify to the possession of this state of grace. It is not to be acquired in the case of a venial sin.

55. In various shadings, this idea can be found in Baxter, Bayly, Sedgwick, and Hoornbeek. See also the examples given by Schneckenburger (*op. cit.*, p. 262).

56. The view of the "state of grace" as a sort of social *status* (similar, for example, to that of the state of asceticism in the old church) is to be found often, among others, in Wilhelmus Schortinghuis. See his *Het innige Christendom* [Groningen: Jurjen Spandaur, 1752]. (This volume was *banned* by the Dutch parliament!)

57. As will be discussed later, this is apparent in innumerable places in Baxter's *Christian Directory* [*op. cit.* (note 39)], as well as in its concluding passage. This recommendation to work in a calling, as a mechanism of distracting oneself from the anxiety that results from perceived moral inferiority, reminds one of Pascal's psychological interpretations of the drive to pursue money and of vocational asceticism. Both represented to him self-invented mechanisms believers used to delude themselves regarding their own moral worthlessness. Moreover, for Pascal, precisely the belief in predestination, together with the conviction (owing to original sin) that everything having to do with the body is worthless, is placed completely in the service of a renunciation of the world and a recommendation to practice contemplation. Renunciation and contemplation are the single means both for the believer's relief from the oppression of a sense of sinfulness and for the acquisition of the certainty of salvation.

In his fine dissertation, Paul Honigsheim has offered cogent remarks on the correct Catholic and Jansenist formulation of the concept of vocation. The Jansenists omit every trace of a linkage between the quest for a certainty of salvation and this-worldly *activity*. Their conception of a "calling," far more than in Lutheranism and even more than in orthodox Catholicism, clearly possesses the sense of an *acceptance* of one's situation in life as given. This Jansenist conception was ordained not only (as in Catholicism) by the social order, but also by the voice of one's own conscience. (Honigsheim, *op. cit.* [note 30], pp. 139 ff.; this is part of a larger work that will be, one hopes, pursued). [1920] [On Jansenism see also note 153 below.]

58. Schneckenbuerger's point of view is also pursued by P. Lobstein in his very lucidly written sketch. See "Zum evangelischen Lebensideal in seiner lutherischen und reformierten Ausprägung," in *Theologische Abhandlungen für H. J. Holtzmann* (Tübingen: Mohr, 1902). Lobstein's work can

be compared with the following paragraphs. Others have criticized his work for placing too strong an emphasis on the guiding idea of *certitudo salutis*.

Just at this point a distinction must be made between the theology of Calvin and *Calvinism*, and between the theological system and the necessities of pastoral care. *All* religious movements that encompass broad strata depart from the question: How can I become *certain* of my salvation? As noted, this question plays a central role not only in Calvinism but also in the history of religion generally (for example, also in India). How could it actually be otherwise? [The last two sentences were inserted in 1920.]

59. Nevertheless, it is not to be denied that the *full* development of this *concept* came to the fore first in the *late* Lutheran epoch (Prætorius, Nicolai, Meisner). (The *unio mystica* exists also in the works of [the hymnist] Johann Gerhard, indeed in a manner in complete conformity with its usage here.) For this reason Ritschl, in book 4 of his *Geschichte des Pietismus* (*op. cit.* [note 10], vol. 2, pp. 3 f.), claims that the introduction of the concept of *unio mystica* into Lutheranism constituted a renaissance, or borrowing, from Catholic piety. He agrees (p. 10) that the problem of the individual's sense of certainty of his salvation was the same for Luther and the Catholic mystics. Nevertheless, he believes they offer polar opposite solutions.

I should certainly not trust myself to offer an independent judgment on this point. However, every person perceives of course that the mood penetrating Luther's *On the Freedom of a Christian* is different from the contrived sweet flirtation with the "childlike and loving Jesus" of the later Lutheran writers on the one hand, and [the mystic] Tauler's religious mood on the other hand. Moreover, similarly, the maintenance of a mystical-magical component in the Lutheran teachings on communion certainly has different religious motives from that "Bernardian" piety (as in the mood of the Song of Solomon) which Ritschl repeatedly sees as cultivating [mystical] interactions with a Christ figure. [Bernard of Clairvaux (1090–1153) was a mystic and founder of the Cistercian Order.] Nevertheless, should not the teachings of Luther himself on communion have, among other things, also *co-favored* the rejuvenation of a religion of mystical devotion?

Moreover, it is by no means adequate (see Ritschl, *ibid.*, p. 11) to argue that the freedom of the mystic existed simply in his *withdrawal* from the world. Tauler, in particular, in analyses of great interest to the psychology of religion, has understood *order* as a *practical* effect of nighttime contemplation (which he recommends for insomnia). Order is then, he argues, through contemplation, brought into this-worldly work in a calling (which shares with contemplation a related way of thinking):

> Only in this way—through the mystical unifying with God in the evening before sleeping—is *reason purified and, thereby, the mind strengthened.* This spiritual exercise allows persons to live their days in a more peaceful and providential manner, and truly to unify themselves with God. At this point all of the believer's activities will be *ordered*. Hence, if persons have admonished themselves (that is, prepared themselves) and decided beforehand to stand on the side of *virtue*, and only then commence their everyday activities, these activities will be carried out in a *virtuous* and divine manner. (*Predigten* [sermons], brochure 318)

At any rate, we can see (and we will return to this point) that mystical contemplation and a rational view of the calling *do not exclude each other*. They do so only at that point where religious belief acquires a clearly hysterical character. Neither for all mystics nor, especially, for all Pietists was this the case.

60. On this point see my essay, "The Social Psychology of the World Religions," in *From Max Weber*, edited and translated by H. H. Gerth and C. Wright Mills (New York: Oxford University Press, 1946). This essay is the introduction to my Economic Ethics of the World Religions series.

61. In respect to this position, Calvinism comes into contact with orthodox Catholicism. However, while the necessity of confession resulted from this position for Catholicism, the result for Calvinism was the necessity for a practical *testifying* to belief through activities in the everyday world.

62. See, for example, as early as Theodor Beza, *De praedestinationis doctrina et vero usu tractatio (. . .) ex (. . .) praelectionibus in nonum Epistolae ad Romanos caput, a Raphaele Eglino (. . .) excerpta* (Geneva, 1582), p. 133:

> Just as we are offered the gift of salvation from the performance of good works and then, from salvation, ascend to faith, so do we acquire from actions, if ones of continuity, not merely a random calling but an effective calling. From this calling we then attain, through Christ, the gift of predestination. It has come to us from the effective connection, which is as unmovable as the throne of God, between activity and principles. [This is a translation of the Latin passage Weber offers.]

One had to be cautious only about the signs of one's *damnation*, for on these depended one's *final* condition. (The first group to think otherwise on this point were Puritans.) See, further, the detailed discussions by Schneckenburger (*op. cit.*), who admittedly cites only a demarcated category of studies.

This feature—the signs of one's salvation—comes to the fore repeatedly throughout the entire Puritan literature. Bunyan states: "It will not be said, did you believe?—but: were you Doers or Talkers only?" Faith is, according to Baxter (*The Saints' Everlasting Rest* [Welwyn, UK: Evangelical Press, 1651/1978], ch. 12), who teaches the mildest form of predestination, the submission in heart and *in deeds* to Christ. "Do what you are able first, and then complain of God for denying you grace if *you have cause*." This was his answer to the objection that the human will is not free and it is God alone who possesses the capacity to bestow salvation. See *Works of the Puritan Divines* (vol. 4, p. 155). Fuller, the church historian, limited his investigation to the specific question of the practical testifying believers could give and the believer's self-demonstration of his state of grace through conduct. Howe makes the same point (*op. cit.* [note 10]). Every scrutiny of the *Works of the Puritan Divines* also provides regular evidence on this point. Not infrequently, it was the *Catholic* writings on asceticism that had the effect of "converting" believers to *Puritanism,* as a Jesuit tract did in the case of Baxter.

If compared to Calvin's own teachings, these conceptions were not completely new. See *Institutio christianae religionis* (original edition of 1536; ch. 1, pp. 97, 113). For Calvin himself, however, the certainty of salvation could not be acquired in this manner (see p. 147). Normally, one referred to 1 John 3:5 and similar passages. The demand for a *fides efficax* was (to note at the outset) not an exclusive demand of the Calvinists. *Baptist* confessions of faith addressed this demand in their statutes on predestination, and they discussed also the fruits of faith: "Proper evidence of its regeneration appears in the holy fruits of repentance and faith and *newness of life*." See Article 7 of J. N. Brown, D.D., *The Baptist Church Manual* (Philadelphia: American Baptist Publications Society, 1876–99). (This document concerns printed confessions.) A *Mennonite*-influenced tract begins in the same way. See *Olijf-Tacxken,* which the Harlem Synod adopted in 1649. It begins (p. 1) with the question of how the children of God are to be *recognized,* and answers (p. 10): "Nu al is't dat dasdanigh *vruchtbare* ghelove alleene zii het seker fondamentale kennteeken . . . om de conscientien der gelovigen in het nieuwe verbondt der genade Gods te versekeren." [Only such *visible fruits* of belief offer the certain and absolutely reliable sign that *certifies* to the consciousness of believers their belonging among the saved.] [1920]

63. A few observations on the significance of *this* for the substantive content of the social ethic were noted above. Our concern now is not the *content* but the *motivation* toward ethical *action.*

64. How this idea must have promoted the penetration of Puritanism by the Jewish spirit of the Old Testament is apparent.

65. This is stated in the Savoy Declaration about the members of the *ecclesia pura* [true church]: they are "saints by *effectual* calling, *visibly manifested* by their profession *and walking.*" [1920]

66. Stephen Charnock [1628–80], "A Principle of Goodness," in *Works of the Puritan Divines* (p. 175).

67. As Sedgwick occasionally expresses it, a conversion has "the exact same sound as the decree of predestination." And, as Bayly [*op. cit.*] teaches, those who are chosen are also called to obey *and rendered capable of obeying. Only* those *God* has called to believe (as becomes manifest in their conduct) are actually believers, not simply "temporary believers." This doctrine is taught by the (Baptist) Hanserd Knollys [see note 13].

68. One could compare the conclusion to Baxter's *Christian Directory* [see note 39].

69. See, for example, Stephen Charnock, "Self-Examination" in *Works of the Puritan Divines* (p. 183), on the refutation of the Catholic doctrine of *dubitatio* [doubt].

70. This argument recurs again and again, for example, in John Hoornbeek, *Theologia practica (op. cit.)*. See, for example, vol. 2, pp. 70, 72, 182; vol. 1, p. 160.

71. For example, as stated in the *Confessio Helvetica,* vol. 16: "et improprie his (the works) *salus adtribuitur*" [works bestow health].

72. On all the above, see Schneckenburger (*op. cit.*, pp. 80 ff).

73. Allegedly, as early as Augustine, this was already noted: "Si non es prædestinatus, fac ut præstineris." [If you have not determined the matter beforehand, make sure that you are able the next time to determine the matter beforehand.]

74. One is reminded of the maxim from Goethe that carries, in essence, the same meaning: "How can a person know himself or herself? Never through pondering, but surely through activity. Attempt to fulfill your obligations, and then you will immediately know yourself. But what are your obligations? The demands of the day." [See *Maximen und Reflexionen,* ed. by Max Hecker (Weimar, 1907), nos. 442, 443; see also Weber, "Science as a Vocation" in Gerth and Mills, *op. cit.*, p. 156.]

75. Even though Calvin himself argued that *saintliness* must be apparent in one's *outward appearance* (see *Institutio christianae religionis,* vol. 4, p. 1, pars. 2, 7, 9), human knowledge could not grasp the boundary between the elect and the nonelect. We have to believe that in those places where the word of God is announced in pure form—in churches organized and administered according to His law—the elect are present also (even if unrecognizable to us).

76. Calvinist piety offers one of the many examples in the history of religion in which *logical* and *psychological* consequences for practical religious *behavior* have been mediated from certain religious ideas. Viewed *logically*, fatalism would naturally follow [see note 46 above], as a deduction, from the idea of predestination. However, as a consequence of the insertion of the idea of "conduct as testifying to one's belief," the *psychological effect* was exactly the opposite. (For reasons in principle the same, the followers of Nietzsche, as is well-known, have claimed that actual ethical significance must be bestowed upon the idea of eternal rebirth. In this case, however, the responsibility for the future life is in no way connected, through a continuity of consciousness, to the acting person. For the Puritan, on the contrary, this connection was *tua res agitur* [your affairs will be done].)

Hoornbeek (see *Theol. pract.* [see note 22], vol. 1, p. 159) offers a fine analysis of the relationship between predestination and action. He does so in the language of the period. To him, the chosen are simply, on the basis of their selection, inoculated against fatalism. Indeed, they testify to their chosen status precisely in the act of turning away from the fatalistic consequences of the idea of predestination; *Quos ipsa electio sollicitos reddit et diligentes officiorum* [The predestination choice itself awakens persons and makes them conscientious about their duties]. The entanglement of *practical* interests cuts off the conclusion—fatalism—that can be *logically* drawn (which, by the way, in spite of all occasionally actually appeared).

On the other hand, the content of the *ideas* of a religion (as Calvinism is demonstrating to us) are of *far* greater significance than, for example, William James is inclined to concede. See *The Varieties of Religious Experience* [New York: Penguin American Classics, 1985 (1902)], pp. 444 f. The very significance of the rational element in religious metaphysics is demonstrated, in a classical manner, in the grandiose effects that precisely the structure of *thought* comprising the Calvinist concept of God exercised on life. If the God of the Puritans has influenced history unlike any other God before or after Him, this influence resulted mainly from those attributes that the power of *thinking* bestowed upon Him. (By the way, the "pragmatic" evaluation by James of the significance of religious ideas—namely, according to the extent to which the believer's life testifies to them—is itself a true legacy of that world of ideas in the Puritan homeland of this excellent scholar.)

As is true of *every* experience, the religious experience as such is obviously irrational. In its highest mystical form it is exactly *that* inner experience [that is singular and extraordinary]. As so beautifully analyzed by James, it is distinguished by its absolute incommunicability. This inner experience possesses a *specific* character and appears to us as if it were *knowledge*, even though the tools given to us by language and concepts do not allow us to capture it adequately. Moreover, it is also correct that *every* religious experience, whenever one attempts to formulate it *rationally,* immediately loses part of its content—and loses all the more the greater the development of the conceptual formulation. Here lies the reason for the tragic conflicts in all rational theology, as the baptizing sects knew even in the seventeenth century.

This irrationality, however (which, by the way, does *not at all* hold *exclusively* for the *religious* "experience," but—although with varying meanings and to varying degrees—for *every* experience), does not call into question one important matter: the particular *type of idea* system, which takes for itself what is directly "experienced" as religious and (so-to-speak) confiscates it, directing it into its pathways, is of the highest importance for practical activity. For, *according to this directing* (in those eras of intense influence of the church on life and of a stronger development, within it, of dogmatic interests), most of the differences among the world's various religions with respect to ethical consequences have unfolded. These differences have been very important for practical action.

Everyone who knows the historical sources is aware how unbelievably intense (when measured by today's standards) was the interest in dogma in the era of the great religious struggles [the sixteenth and seventeenth centuries]. One can see a parallel between that interest and the (basically even superstitious) idea among the proletariat today regarding that which "science" can accomplish and prove. [This paragraph is from 1920, as are several earlier sentences in this note.]

77. In *The Saints' Everlasting Rest* (vol. 1, p. 6), Baxter answers the question: "Whether to make salvation our end be not mercenary or legal? It is properly mercenary when we expect it as *wages* for work done. . . . Otherwise it is only such a mercenarism as Christ commandeth . . . and if seeking Christ be mercenary, I desire to be so mercenary." Actually, a collapse back to the practice of an entirely crass "salvation through good works" was not lacking among many who were viewed as orthodox Calvinists. According to Bayly, the giving of alms constituted a means of preventing *a temporal* punishment (see *Praxis pietatis, op. cit.* [note 32], p. 262). Other theologians recommended the performance of good works to the *damned.* They argued that damnation would then become, perhaps, more bearable. To the elect, however, the performance of good works was recommended for a different reason: God would then love them not only without reasons but *ob causam* [for a cause]. And surely this love would somehow lead to benefits. The apologists also made certain silent concessions about the significance of good works for the extent of one's salvation. See Schneckenburger (*op. cit.*, p. 101).

78. It is indispensable also here, in order to isolate the characteristic differences, to discuss these matters in the language of "ideal-type" concepts. Doing so implies, in a certain sense, doing violence to historical reality. If this procedure were abandoned, however, qualifying clauses would have to be inserted incessantly, and thus a clear formulation would be fully impossible. The contrasts noted here have been drawn as sharply as possible. Yet the extent to which, on the one hand, they actually hold in empirical reality, or, on the other hand, the degree to which the contrasts are only relative, will have to be discussed separately. [See Weber, " 'Objectivity' in Social Science and Social Policy," in *The Methodology of the Social Sciences,* translated and edited by Edward A. Shils and Henry A. Finch (New York: Free Press, 1949), pp. 89–111; *E&S,* pp. 19–22. See also John Drysdale, "How Are Social-Scientific Concepts Formed?" *Sociological Theory* 14 (March, 1996): 71–88.

It is self-evident that official Catholic *doctrine*, as early as the Middle Ages, for its part also formulated an ideal of a systematic striving for salvation that engaged the believer's *entire life.* Nevertheless, it remains just as doubtless that (a) the everyday practices of the church, owing precisely to its most effective disciplinary mechanism (confession), facilitated the learning of an "unsystematic" organization of life. Moreover, (b) it is likewise doubtless that the Calvinists' underlying mood of strictness and cold distance, and their complete, self-reliant isolation, had to be perpetually lacking in medieval lay Catholicism.

79. As already noted, the absolutely central significance of *this* theme will gradually come to the fore only in the Economic Ethics of the World Religions essays. [1920]

80. And, to a certain extent, *also* to the Lutheran. Luther did not *want* to strike down this last residual of sacramental magic. [1920]

81. See, for example, Sedgwick, *Buss- und Gnadenlehre* (German translation by Röscher, 1689). The penitent person has "a firm rule," which he strictly holds to. He orients and transforms his entire life according to it (p. 591). He lives, according to the rule, in an intelligent, awake, and cautious manner (p. 596). *Only* a lasting alteration of the *entire* person can, because a consequence of predestination, bring about this way of living (p. 852). Actual repentance is expressed continuously in conduct (p. 361). The difference between good works, which are only "moral," and the *opera spiritualia* [spiritual task], is apparent (a) in that the latter is the consequence of life's rebirth (as Hoornbeek explains; see *op. cit.,* vol. 1, pt. 9, ch. 2), and (b) in that a perpetual progress in regard to the *opera spiritualia* is perceptible (see vol. 1, p. 160). As concerns a transformation of conduct, this progress can be attained only as a result of the supernatural influence of God's grace (p. 150). Salvation implies a metamorphosis of the *entire* person, and this results from God's grace (pp. 190 f.).

These are ideas common to all Protestantism. They are found also, of course, in the highest ideals of Catholicism. *However,* they could first demonstrate consequences for the world when manifest in the *this*-worldly asceticism of the Puritan denominations. Above all, these ideas became endowed with a sufficiently strong psychological *reward* only in these denominations.

82. Although, in Holland, "Precisians" stem from the "fine" among the devout who led their lives precisely according to the *Bible*'s statutes (as Voët notes). Occasionally, by the way, "Methodists" is used in the seventeenth century to refer to the Puritans.

83. For, as the Puritan preachers emphasize (Bunyan, for example, in "The Pharisee and the Publican," *Works of the Puritan Divines,* p. 126), *every* single sin destroys *all* that could be accumulated as *service,* through good works, in the course of an entire lifetime. Yet they also emphasized how fully inconceivable it is that human beings could be at all capable of achieving anything God would then be compelled to *attribute* to them as service. Similarly, it remains inconceivable to these preachers that anyone could live permanently without sin. For them, there simply does not exist, unlike in Catholicism, a sort of bank account book and then balancing-out procedures [for sins and confessions]. (This image was common even in antiquity.) Rather, for the Puritans, a harsh either-or prevailed; damnation or grace. On this bank account image, see note 115 below.

84. This is the difference compared to simple *Legality* and *Civility,* which Bunyan depicts as fellow travelers who live with Mr. "Worldly-Wise-Man" (who is depicted as "Morality") in the city. [See *The Pilgrim's Progress* (note 47).]

85. Stephen Charnock, "Self-Examination" (*Works of the Puritan Divines*): "*Reflection* and knowledge of self is a prerogative of a *rational* nature" (p. 172). See the accompanying footnote: "*Cogito, ergo sum* is the first principle of the new philosophy."

86. This is not the appropriate occasion to discuss the relationship of certain streams of ideas in ascetic Protestantism to the [Scholastic] theology of [the Franciscan] Duns Scotus [1266–1308]. (This theology never became dominant; generally only tolerated, it was occasionally considered heresy.) The later animosity of the Pietists to Aristotelian philosophy was shared by Calvin (and, although in a somewhat different manner, by Luther), who stood consciously opposed, on this point, to Catholicism (see *Institutio christianae religionis,* vol. 2, ch. 12, par. 4; vol. 4, ch. 17, par. 24). In the words of Wilhelm Kahl, the "primacy of the will" is common to all these denominations. [See *Die Lehre vom Primat des Willens* (Strasbourg: Trubner, 1886).] [1920]

87. St. Benedict founded a monastic order in Italy in 529. The Benedictine abbey at Cluny in France, founded in 910, became a center of monastic reform in the tenth and eleventh centuries. The Cistercian Order was founded in France in 1098 by Benedictine reformers. St. Ignatius of Loyola founded the Society of Jesus (Jesuits) in 1534 [sk].

88. For example, the article "asceticism" in the Catholic *Church Lexicon* defines the word in just this way. This definition accords completely with the highest form of its historical manifestation. Likewise, Seeberg; see *Realenzyklopädie für protestantische Theologie und Kirche*). For the purposes of this discussion, the use of *asceticism* in this manner must be permitted. It is well-known to me that the term can be defined differently, both more broadly and more narrowly (and usually the attempt is made to do so).

89. The Puritans, in Samuel Butler's *Hudibras* [London: Oxford/Clarendon Press, 1967 (1664–78)], are compared to barefoot monks. A report of the ambassador from Geneva, Fieschi, calls Cromwell's army an assembly of "monks." [1920]

90. In light of this entirely direct assertion of mine regarding the internal continuity between the other-worldly asceticism of monks and the this-worldly asceticism of the vocational calling, I am surprised to discover Brentano's recommendation to me that I note the asceticism oriented toward work in *monks* (see *op. cit.* [ch. 1, note 15], p. 134 and *passim*)! His entire *excursis* against me culminates in this point. However, just such a continuity (as everyone can see) is a foundational assumption of my entire discussion: the Reformation carried rational Christian asceticism and the methodicalness of life out of the monastery and into the life of work in a calling. See the following, unrevised analyses. [1920]

91. As apparent in the many, and often repeated, reports on the trials of Puritan heretics. See Daniel Neal, *The History of the Puritans* [London: D.R. Hett, 1732–38] and Thomas Crosby, *The History of the English Baptists* [London, 1738–40].

92. Sanford already (*op. cit.* [note 5]; and before and after him many others) has traced the origin of the ideal of "[social] distance" back to Puritanism. On this ideal, see, for example, also the observations by James Bryce on the American college (*American Commonwealth* [New York: Macmillan, 1888], vol. 2). The ascetic principle of "self-control" also renders Puritanism one of the fathers of modern *military discipline.* On Maurice of Orange, as the founder of the modern army, see G. Roloff, *Preussisches Jahrbuch,* vol. 3 (1903): 255. Cromwell's "Ironsides" [soldiers], striding forth toward the enemy at a brisk pace with cocked pistols in their hands, yet without shooting, were not superior to the "Cavaliers" because of a fanatic passion; rather, the dispassionate self-control of Cromwell's men (which remained perpetually in the hands of their leader) proved decisive. The knightly, boisterous, and impetuous style of attack of the Cavaliers dissolved their troops every time into single fighters. On this theme see Charles Firth, *Cromwell's Army* [London: Greenhill Books, 1992 (1902)].

93. See Wilhelm Windelband, *Üeber Willensfreiheit* (Tübingen: Mohr, 1904), pp. 77 ff.

94. Yet not in such a straightforward manner in Catholic monasticism. The procedures of contemplation, occasionally bound together with a foundation based on feeling, are intertwined in monasticism with these rational elements in multiple ways. Just for this reason, contemplation is further *methodically* regulated.

95. According to Richard Baxter, *sinful* is *everything* that stands against "reason." Reason is created in us by God and given by Him as a norm for our action. In other words, not simply passions, because of their content as such, are sinful. Rather, all meaningless or unrestrained affects *as such* are sinful—because they destroy the "countenance." [Weber has here used the English word.] Moreover, as processes purely of the realm of physical desires, they turn us away from the rational relationship with God that all of our activity and sensibility should cultivate. As such, these emotions insult God. See, for example, what is said about the sinfulness of moodiness (Baxter, *Christian Directory,* 2nd ed., 1698, vol. 1, p. 285; Tauler is cited on this subject on p. 287). On the sinfulness of *anxiety,* see p. 287. If our *appetite* becomes "the rule or measure of eating," then idolatry, it is emphasized, is apparent (pp. 310, 316, and *passim*). Baxter frequently cites mainly, as the opportunity presents itself, Proverbs; however, he also cites other treatises, such as Plutarch's *De tranquillitate animi* [On the tranquil spirit]. Not infrequently, he also calls attention to the writings of the Middle Ages on asceticism (St. Bernhard, St. Bonaventura, and others).

The contrast to the way of life represented by "who does not love wine, women, and song. . ." could scarcely be more sharply formulated than through the expansion of the concept of idolatry to encompass *all* pleasures of the senses—*as long as* they are not justified for *hygienic* reasons. If they are, these pleasures are allowed (as are, within these boundaries, sports, and also other "recreations"). This theme will be addressed further below [see ch. 5].

We wish here only to note that the sources cited here and elsewhere are neither dogmatic nor edifying works; rather, they grew out of the daily practice of pastoral care. Hence, these sources offer a good picture of the direction in which they had an *effect.*

96. In passing, I would find it regrettable if an *evaluation* of any sort would be read out of this presentation, whether regarding one or the other form of religious devotion. Such an evaluation lies distant from our concern here. The *effect* of specific important features of this devotion on practical *behavior* is the only concern here (however comparatively peripheral such a concern may be for those looking for a pure evaluation, according to religious standards, of this behavior). [1920]

97. Although this title may refer to a compilation of diverse writings, it more likely refers to a volume written by Thomas à Kempis (1380–1471; from Kempen, Holland). Kempis possessed an enormous knowledge of the Bible and wrote many inspirational works, ranging from treatises on the practical piety of daily life to the mystical experience [sk].

98. On this point in particular see the article "Moralisten, englische" by Ernst Troeltsch, in the *Realenzyklopädie* [see note 10], vol. 13.

99. The great extent to which *entirely matter-of-fact* religious ideas and situations, which appear to be "historical accidents," have had an effect is revealed with unusual clarity in [two examples]: (a) those circles of Pietism arising out of a Reformed foundation occasionally directly *regretted,* for example, the absence of a monastery; and (b) the "communist" experiments of Labadie, among others, were in the end a surrogate (*Surrogat*) for the monastic life. [Jean de Labadie (1610–74), originally a Jesuit, was a major representative of mysticism-oriented French Spiritualism. He later became a Calvinist and then a Mennonite. His writings influenced Spener.]

100. Because of his unorthodox views of Christianity, Franck became defined as an opponent of the Reformation [sk].

101. Indeed, this idea was in some denominations of the Reformation period itself. Even Ritschl (see *Pietismus, op. cit.* [note 19]; vol. 1, pp. 258 f.), although he sees the later development as a degeneration of Reformation ideas, does not contest that "the Reformed Church was characterized by completely empirical features and that believers could not be counted as members of this true church *without the sign of ethical activity*" (see, for example, *Confessio Gallicana* [1559] 25, 26; *Confessio Belgica* [1562] 29; and *Confessio Helvetica posterior* [1562] 17).

102. "Bless God that we are not of the many" (Thomas Adams, *Works of the Puritan Divines,* p. 138).

103. The historically so important idea of "birthright" thus received in England a significant bolstering: "The firstborn which are written in heaven. . . . As the firstborn is not to be defeated in his inheritance, and the enrolled names are never to be obliterated, so certainly they shall inherit eternal life" (Thomas Adams, *Works of the Puritan Divines,* p. 14).

104. The Lutheran feeling of penitent *contrition* is not internally foreign to developed Calvinist asceticism in theory. In practice, however, it surely is. To this Calvinism, such contrition is ethically worthless and of no use to the damned. To the person who is more certain of his election, his own sins (which are acknowledged to some extent) constitute a symptom of backward development and incomplete striving toward elect status. Instead of showing contrition for the sin, the Calvinist *hates* it and endeavors to overcome it through activity on behalf of God's glory. See the analysis by Howe (who was Cromwell's chaplain from 1656 to 1658) in "Of Men's Enmity Against God" and "Of Reconciliation Between God and Man" (*Works of the Puritan Divines*): "The carnal mind is *enmity* against God. It is the mind, therefore, not as speculative merely, but as practical and active that must be renewed" (p. 237). Moreover, "Reconciliation . . . must begin in (a) a deep conviction . . . of your former *enmity* . . . [and awareness that you] have been *alienated* from God . . ." (p. 246), [and] (b) "A clear and lively apprehension of the monstrous iniquity and wickedness thereof [must occur]" (p. 251).

A hatred of sin alone is spoken of here, rather than a hatred of the sinner. Yet the famous letter of the Duchess Renate d'Este (Leonore's mother) to Calvin already indicates that sins are being transferred to persons. Here, among other subjects, she writes of the *hatred* she would carry for her father and husband *if* she became convinced they belonged among the damned. Above I spoke about the separation of the individual internally, as a result of the doctrine of predestination, from the ties to communities established through a "natural" feeling (see pp. 61–62). This letter offers an example of this separation and, simultaneously, of its transference to relationships with specific persons.

105. The "Independents" (founded 1581 in England) wanted the full independence of each congregation from the Anglican Church. American branches were instrumental in the founding of Harvard and Yale universities [sk].

106. Owen, the Independent-Calvinist vice-chancellor of Oxford University under Cromwell, formulated the principle thus: "None but those who give evidence of being *regenerated or holy* persons ought to be received or counted fit members of visible churches. Where this is wanting, *the*

very essence of a church is lost" *(Investigation into the Origin of Evangelical Christianity)*. On this theme, see further "The Protestant Sects" essay below.

107. Founded by Donatus, a bishop from Carthage, the Donatist Church existed in northern Africa in the fourth to seventh centuries. Donatus advocated that churches impose extreme disciplinary measures upon members [sk].

108. See "The Protestant Sects" essay below.

109. *Catéchisme genevois,* p. 149. Bayly, *Praxis pietatis* [see note 32], p. 125: "In life we should act as though no one but Moses had authority over us."

110. "The law is a favorable presence in the minds of the Reformed Christians, constituting an ideal norm. On the other hand, to the Lutherans, because an unreachable norm, the Law disheartens and crushes them." In Lutheranism, in order to awaken the necessary *humility,* the law stands *at the beginning* of the catechism and before the gospel, whereas, in the Reformed catechism, the law stands commonly *behind* the gospel. The Reformed churches reproached the Lutherans for having a "true fear of becoming holy" (Möhler), while the Lutherans criticized the Reformists for their "slavish servitude to the Law" and their arrogance.

111. *Studies and Reflections of the Great Rebellion, op. cit.* [note 5], pp. 79 f.

112. The Song of Solomon, in particular, should not be forgotten. Entirely ignored by the Puritans, its Oriental eroticism influenced, for example, the development of the notion of piety in St. Bernard's writings.

113. On the necessity for this self-discipline, see, for example, the sermon already noted [see note 85] by Charnock on 2 Cor. 13:5, *Works of the Puritan Divines,* pp. 161 f.

114. Most moral theologians advised in favor of such procedures. Also Baxter; see *Christian Directory, op. cit.*, vol. 2, pp. 77 ff. He does not, however, conceal its "dangers."

115. Bookkeeping, as concerns one's ethical conduct, has of course also been widespread elsewhere. The *accent* placed upon it, however, was heretofore missing. Bookkeeping now becomes the single means of *knowing* the decision made for eternity regarding one's elect or condemned status. Hence, also missing earlier was a psychological *reward.* When placed upon the diligence and attentiveness of this "calculation," this reward became decisive. [1920]

116. *This* was the decisive distinction vis-à-vis other, externally similar, types of behavior. [1920]

117. Baxter also (*Saints' Everlasting Rest,* ch. 12) explains God's *invisibility*: just as it is possible to carry out a profitable trade with an unseen foreigner through written correspondence, it is also possible, through "holy commerce" with an invisible God, to acquire the "one expensive pearl." These commercial similes, instead of the forensic similes common in the writings of the earlier moralists and in Lutheranism, are highly characteristic of Puritanism. In effect, Puritanism allowed people "to acquire through bargaining" their own salvation. See also, for example, the following passage from a sermon: "We reckon the value of a thing by that which a wise man will give for it, who is not ignorant of it nor under necessity. Christ, the Wisdom of God, gave Himself, His own precious blood, to redeem souls, and He knew what they were and had no need of them" (Matthew Henry, "The Worth of the Soul," in *Works of the Puritan Divines,* p. 313).

118. On Knollys, see note 13 [sk].

119. In contrast, Luther himself said, "Crying goes before all the tasks that we undertake, and suffering is more noble than all of our initiative-taking."

120. "Complete transcendence" refers to the Puritan's Old Testament God. Because He is distant from believers, all-mighty and omniscient, His motives remain completely unknowable by mere earthly mortals. One might easily conclude that such an unfathomable Deity would be dismissed and ignored. Weber argues just the opposite here, however, namely, because the doctrine of predestination linked even this God to His children, and even in an intense manner ("with absolute determinism"). Once this linkage had been established, His norms—owing to His omnipotence and omniscience—became "unconditionally valid" [sk].

121. Weber has succinctly summarized his "yardstick" usage of the "ideal type" in the above few lines. Once formulated, a model (ideal type) is used as a point of orientation for empirical investigations. Particular cases are then "measured" against the model. Once their "deviation" from the model becomes demarcated, empirical cases are then clearly defined. See Weber, "Objectivity"

and *E&S* (see note 78 above). See also S. Kalberg, *Max Weber's Comparative-Historical Sociology* (Chicago: University of Chicago Press, 1994), pp. 81–142 [sk].

122. This is also demonstrated most clearly in the development of Lutheran ethical theory. On this subject see G. Hoennicke, *Studien zur altprotestantischen Ethik* (Berlin, 1902). See also Ernst Troeltsch's informative review in *Göttinger Gelehrter Anzeige* (1902, no. 8). The movement of Lutheran doctrine in the direction of the older *orthodox*-Calvinist doctrine in particular was often, in form, quite significant. The different religious orientation, however, again and again became manifest.

[Luther's advisor] Melanchthon placed the concept of *penitence* in the forefront in order to provide a firm base for the connection of morality to faith. Penitence, which arose out of the believer's relationship to the commandments, must precede faith, but good works must follow faith. Otherwise, the believer's faith (formulated almost in a Puritan manner) could not be the true faith—namely, the faith on the basis of which salvation is justified.

To Melanchthon, a certain degree of (relative) perfection could be attained also on earth. Indeed, he even taught originally that a sense of justification that one is saved was awarded to persons in order to render them capable of good works. Moreover, the increasing perfection of the faithful itself implies at least that degree of this-worldly salvation that faith is capable of providing. And the later Lutheran dogmatists also developed the idea that good works were the necessary *fruits* of faith, and that faith could call forth a new life. This idea was externally entirely similar to ideas developed by the Reformed churches.

The question of what "good works" are was answered as early as Melanchthon (and even more so among the later Lutherans) increasingly by reference to the commandments. There remained, as a legacy of Luther's original ideas, only the lesser seriousness accorded to Bible learning and, in particular, to an orientation toward the particular norms of the Old Testament. Essentially, only the Decalogue remained. It codified the most important principles of the *natural* moral law and hence was viewed as offering norms for action. *However,* no secure linkage led from the statutory validity of the Decalogue to justification through *faith*, which was more and more emphasized by Lutherans as of exclusive significance for salvation. This linkage was absent simply because Lutheran faith had a completely different psychological character—see above—from that of faith in Calvinism.

The orthodox Lutheran standpoint of the first period was abandoned. This had to occur because Lutheranism now took the form of a church that considered itself an institution for the saving of souls (*Heilsanstalt*) [See *E&S*, pp. 557–63]. Lutheranism, however, abandoned the old without having formulated a new standpoint. In particular, one could not introduce (for fear of losing the dogmatic *sola fide* foundation) the notion of an ascetic rationalization of the entire life as the ethical task of each believer. Missing was just the motivation that would allow the idea of a *testifying* by believers to grow to the significance it attained, through the effect of the doctrine of predestination, in Calvinism. In addition, and taking place in harmony with the absence of this doctrine, the interpretation of the sacraments in Lutheranism as being based on magic (which occurred once the notion of a *regeneratio* [regeneration of one's hopes for salvation], at least in its early forms, became transferred into the practice of *baptism*) must have had the effect, assuming the *universalism* of grace, of working against the development of a methodical morality [as in Calvinism]. This followed as well because the magical interpretation of the sacraments in Lutheranism must also have weakened the contrast between the *status naturalis* and the state of grace—all the more owing to the strong Lutheran emphasis on original sin.

Yet any development in the direction of a methodical morality was weakened even more in Lutheranism by a factor of no less significance: Lutheranism's *exclusively forensic* interpretation of the act of justification. This interpretation assumed the changeability of God's decisions as a consequence of the converted sinner's *specific* act of penitence. Just this effect was increasingly emphasized by Melanchthon. This entire alteration of his teaching, which comes to the fore in the increasing weight he gives to *penitence,* in fact internally develops together with his professions on the *freedom of the will.*

All this determined the *un*methodical character of the Lutheran organization of life. Simply as a consequence of the continuation of the confessional, *specific* acts of grace in exchange for specific sins must have constituted the content of salvation for the average Lutheran. The development of an aristocracy of elect saints, who themselves created the certainty of their own salvation, did not characterize Lutheranism. Neither a development in the direction of a morality *without* God's law, nor a movement toward a rational *asceticism* oriented toward this law, could occur. Instead, God's law remained in Lutheranism, as a statute and an ideal claim, side-by-side with *faith,* yet organically unconnected to it. Furthermore, because a rigorous study of the Bible was rejected (for it implied salvation through good works), the law remained quite uncertain, imprecise, and, above all, unsystematic in terms of its exact content.

As Troeltsch has written (*op. cit.*), the life of the Lutheran, from the perspective of ethical theory, remained a "sum of mere beginnings, never entirely successful," and a piecing together of fragmented and uncertain maxims. None had the effect of directing life "toward a coherently organized unity." Rather, and fully in accord with the route that Luther himself had already taken, life became oriented toward a resignation to the existing situation, large or small.

The "resignation" of the Germans to the influence of foreign cultures and their more rapid change of nationality than other peoples (which is so often complained about in Germany) is *also,* essentially, to be explained by this development (*together* with certain political destinies of the nation). Even today this general posture of resignation has an impact on all of our relationships. The individual's absorption of culture in Germany, *because* it occurred essentially along the pathway of passive reception of what was offered in an "authoritarian" manner, remained weak.

123. On these matters, see, for example, the book that set off a great deal of conversational chatter, August Tholuck's *Vorgeschichte des Rationalismus* (Halle: Eduard Anton, 1853–1862).

124. Largely owing to Prussian-based stereotypes formed in the aftermath of World Wars I and II, Germans today are often viewed differently [sk].

125. On the entirely different effect of the *Islamic* doctrine of predestination (or better: *predetermination* [see note 46]) and its causes, see F. Ullrich, *op. cit.* [note 46]. On the predestination doctrine of the Jansenists, see P. Honigsheim, *op. cit.* [note 30]. [1920]

126. See "The Protestant Sects" essay [below]. [1920]

127. In his *Geschichte des Pietismus* (*op. cit.* [note 19], vol. 1, p. 152), Ritschl seeks, for the period before Labadie (and, by the way, only on the basis of examples from the Netherlands), to define these boundaries in the following ways: (a) the Pietists formed conventicles; (b) they cultivated the idea of the "worthlessness of physical and bodily existence" in a "manner that opposed the Protestant interest in salvation"; and (c) they sought, "in a tender relationship with the Lord Jesus, the certainty of grace" in a manner opposed to the Reformist tradition.

[Yet there are many problems with Ritschl's criteria.] For this earlier period, the last criterion is correct only for *one* of the representatives of Pietism he discusses. Moreover, the notion of a "worthlessness of physical and bodily existence" was an indigenous, true product of the Calvinist spirit, and this notion directed Calvinism out of Protestantism's normal line of development only in those instances where the "worthlessness of the human desires" led to an actual flight from the world. Finally, the conventicles (to a certain degree and, in particular, for reasons concerning the catechism) had been established by the synods of Dordrecht themselves [and hence related not only to Pietism].

Only some of the features of Pietist piety analyzed by Ritschl's study are relevant to us here: (a) the greater "precision" with which, in all "external aspects" of life, chapter and verse of the Bible were followed, even in a servile manner (as occasionally with Gisbert Voët); (b) the treatment of the justification before God and reconciliation with Him not as ends in themselves but simply as *means* toward the holy, ascetic life (as is perhaps to be found in Lodensteyn but as also suggested by Melanchthon; see note 121 above); (c) the high evaluation of the "penitence struggle" as a sign of genuine rebirth (as was first taught by W. Teellinck); (d) the abstinence from participation in communion by persons who have not been reborn (as will be discussed later in a different context) and the related formation of conventicles once "prophecy" had been revived—that is, the exegesis of texts also by nontheologians, even women (Anna Maria Schürman), became permitted (although this transgressed the boundaries of the Dordrecht canons).

All of the above points involve Pietist deviations—at times to a significant extent—from the doctrine and practice of the Reformed churches. Nevertheless, and in contrast to the denominations Ritschl has not included in his study (especially the English Puritans), all of the putatively distinguishing features he notes (except for point "c" [the Pietists sought, "in a tender relationship with the Lord Jesus, the certainty of grace"]) represent actually only an intensification of tendencies within the entire line of development of Reformist piety.

The even-handedness of Ritschl's analysis is weakened in a specific manner: this great scholar brings into his study his own value judgments in respect to church-political or (perhaps, better stated) religious policy debates. In particular, his hostility to all ascetic devoutness leads him to interpret all developments toward asceticism as reversions to "Catholicism." The old Protestantism, however, just as is true of Catholicism, refers to "all sorts and conditions of men" [Sir Walter Besant]. *Certainly* the Catholic *Church*, in its Jansenist [reform] manifestation, [still] rejected the rigor of this-worldly asceticism, just as Pietism [which inclined toward contemplation] opposed the Catholic Quietism of the seventeenth century.

At any rate, for our particular investigation, Pietism began to diverge qualitatively (not simply in degree) from Calvinism when the intensified anxiety of Pietist believers, in the face of "worldly" tasks, led to a flight away from one's vocational life in the private economy. Namely, this flight led Pietists to form conventicles anchored in a monastic-communistic foundation (as Labadie advocated). It also led, as contemporaries reported regarding some extreme Pietists, to the intentional *neglect*, in favor of contemplation, of this-worldly work in a vocational calling.

This turn naturally appeared with particular frequency wherever contemplation began to acquire that feature referred to by Ritschl as "Bernardianism" (because echoes of it first appeared in Bernard's exegesis of the Song of Solomon): a mystical religion of devotional mood that strives for the *unio mystica*, which is secretly tinged with sexuality. Even from the point of view of a psychology of religion, the *unio mystica* undoubtedly presents an *aliud* [different vantage point] antagonistic to Reformist piety, yet one "also" opposed to Calvinism's *ascetic* form as exemplified by Voët. Ritschl, however, seeks continuously to couple this [mystic] Quietism with Pietist *asceticism,* and thus to render the latter asceticism subject to [his usual] criticisms. He attempts to do this by putting his finger on every citation to be found in the Pietist literature that comes from Catholic mysticism or asceticism. Yet even English and Dutch moral theologians entirely "above suspicion" cite [the mystics] Bernard, Bonaventura, and Thomas à Kempis [as antagonistic to asceticism].

For all Reformed churches, the relationship to the Catholic past was a very complex one. According to the vantage point that one places in the forefront, first one feature of Calvinism, then the other appears as standing more closely to Catholicism (or certain features of it).

128. The highly informative article "Pietism" by K. M. Mirbt (*Realenzyklopädie für protestantische Theologie und Kirche*, 3rd ed.) addresses the origin of Pietism. His omission of its Reformist antecedents and his concern exclusively with the personal religious experience of Spener strike one as rather strange. The description by Gustav Freytag in the *Bildern aus der deutschen Vergangenheit* series offers even today an introduction to Pietism that is well worth reading. For the beginnings of English Pietism as it was viewed at the time, see W. Whitaker, *Prima Institutio disciplinaque pietatis* (1570).

129. As is well-known, this view had enabled Pietism to become one of the major social carriers of the idea of *tolerance.* This opportunity should be taken to insert a few points on this theme. If we leave aside for the moment the Humanist-Enlightenment idea of *indifference,* the idea of tolerance in the West had the following major sources: (a) purely political *Staatsraison* [reasons of state] (as represented by William of Orange); (b) mercantilism (for example, as particularly apparent in the city of Amsterdam and the numerous cities, lords of manors, and monarchs who supported sect members as important social carriers of economic progress); and (c) Calvinist piety in its radical manifestation. [Before turning to a further source of the idea of tolerance in the West, several remarks must be offered regarding the manner in which Calvinist piety constituted an important source for this idea.]

The idea of predestination basically prevented the state, through its intolerance, from actually promoting religion. In light of this idea, the state's intolerance did not enable it to save a single soul; only the idea of *God's honor* induced the church to request the state's assistance in suppressing heresy. However, the more the emphasis was placed on the necessity for the minister and all participants in communion to be members of the elect, all the more unacceptable was (a) every instance of the state's intervention in processes to appoint new clergy, (b) every appointment to the ministry of students from the university made simply on the basis of completed theological training (which might include someone who perhaps did not belong among the elect), and in general (3) every intervention in the congregation's concerns by the political powers (whose conduct was often not above reproach).

Reformed Pietism strengthened this opposition to external intervention by devaluing dogmatic correctness and by gradually loosening the axiom *extra ecclesiam nulla salus* [no salvation outside the church]. To Calvin, the *subjection* of all, including the damned, under the church's divine guidance was alone consistent with God's glory. Nonetheless, in New England the attempt was made to establish the church as an aristocracy of the chosen. As early as the radical Independents, however, every intervention of civic groups, as well as any hierarchical powers, in the process of monitoring the devout's testifying to belief (which was possible only inside the *particular* congregation) was rejected. The idea that God's glory required a bringing of even the damned under the church's discipline became subjugated to a different idea (present from the beginning, but then gradually more and more passionately emphasized): if one whom God had condemned were allowed to participate in communion, God's glory would be violated. This idea had to lead to voluntarism, it was argued, for it would lead to a "believer's church," namely, to a religious community that encompassed only the elect.

Calvinist Baptism (to which, for example, Praisegod Barebone, the leader of the "parliament of the saints" belonged) drew the consequences from this line of thought with greater consistency than did other congregations. Cromwell's army upheld freedom of conscience, and the "parliament of saints" supported even the separation of church and state, *because* its members were devout Pietists. That is, religious reasons *were effective* in providing their motivation to uphold the freedom of conscience and, hence, the idea of tolerance.

[Now let us turn to a fourth major source of the idea of tolerance in the West.] (d) From the beginning of their existence, the *baptizing sects* (which will be discussed later) have continuously upheld the basic principle that only the elect can be taken into the community of the church. (They have done so more forcefully and with greater internal consistency than the other ascetic Protestant congregations.) For this reason, they (a) repudiated the idea of the church as an institution (*Anstalt*) offering salvation to all [see *E&S,* pp. 557–63], and (b) opposed every intervention by secular powers. Hence, it was an *effective religious* reason also in this case that produced the demand for unconditional tolerance.

The first who, for these reasons upheld an unconditional tolerance *and* the separation of church and state was surely [the English theologian and opponent of the Anglican Church] Robert Browne [1550–1633]. He was almost a generation before the Baptists and two generations before Roger Williams [1628–80], the Puritan founder of the colony of Rhode Island and pioneer of religious liberty. The first declaration of a church community in this regard appears to have been the resolution of the English Baptists in Amsterdam in 1612 or 1613: "The magistrate is not to meddle with religion or matters of conscience . . . because Christ is the King and lawgiver of the Church and conscience." The first official document of a church community that demanded the *effective* protection of freedom of conscience from the state as *a right* was surely Article 44 of the Confession of the (Particular) Baptists of 1644.

It should once again be emphasized that the view occasionally found—that tolerance *as such* favored capitalism—is of course completely wrong. Religious tolerance is not specifically modern, nor is it unique to the West. It dominated in China, in India, in the great empires of the Near East in the Hellenic era, in the Roman Empire, and the Islamic empires. It ruled for longer epochs, circumscribed only for reasons connected to the state itself (*Staatsraison*) (and these reasons even today define the limits of its expanse). This degree of tolerance, however, was nowhere in the world to be found in the sixteenth and seventeenth centuries. It was least to be found in those regions where Puritanism *dominated,* as, for example, in Holland and Zeeland [the Dutch island province off the coast of Denmark] in the era of political-economic expansion, or in Puritan England or New England. Clearly characteristic of the West (after the Reformation, as well as prior to it, and similar to, for example, the Sassanian dynasty [of Persia, 226–651], was *religious intolerance,* as had reigned also in China, Japan, and India during particular epochs (although mostly for political reasons). It follows that tolerance as such certainly has not the slightest thing to do with capitalism. It depended on *who was favored by it.* The consequences of the requirement for religious tolerance in the "believer's church" will be discussed further [in "The Protestant Sects" essay] below. [The last two paragraphs were added in 1920.]

130. The practical application of this idea appeared, for example, among the Cromwellian "tryers," who were the examiners of candidates for the ministry. They attempted to ascertain the individual state of grace of candidates more than they sought to assess their theological knowledge. See also the ["Protestant Sects"] essay below.

131. Pietism's characteristic mistrust of Aristotle, and of classical philosophy in general, is already stated in an early form in Calvin (see *Institutio christianae religionis*, vol. 2, ch. 2, sect. 4; vol. 3, ch. 23, sect. 5; vol. 4, ch. 17, sect. 24). In Luther's writings, as is well-known, this mistrust was no less intense. The antagonism in Luther, however, is pushed to the side by the influence of humanism (mainly through Melanchthon) and compelling circumstances related to apologetics and the educational training of ministers. What is *necessary* for salvation, also for the uneducated, is contained in the scriptures in a clear manner. Of course, the Westminster Confession also taught this and did so in a manner in conformity with Protestant traditions (see ch. 1, pt. 7). [1920]

132. The official churches protested against this development in Pietism. See, for example, even the (shorter) catechism of the Scottish Presbyterian Church of 1648 (sect. 7). Participation of *non*family members in family prayers is viewed, by the official churches, as an infringement upon the authority of the church *office* and prohibited. Pietism also, as occurred with the formation of every ascetic congregation, loosened the ties of the individual to all family patriarchalism (which always had an interest in the prestige of established offices). [1920]

133. For good reasons, we are here intentionally omitting a discussion of the "psychological" relationships (in the sense of the scientific and *technical* usage of the term) between the substantive elements in this religious consciousness. Even the use of the corresponding terminology is avoided where possible. The accepted and reliable conceptual armament of psychology, and also of *psychiatry,* does not extend far enough at present to be used directly for the purposes of historical research in the area of our themes—at least not without casting doubt on whether historical judgments have been formed in an unprejudiced manner. The use of the terminology of psychology would in the end create the temptation to drape a veil, comprised of the scholarly obfuscation that follows from the dilettante's fondness for obscure and strange words, around the easily understandable and often quite trivial facts of the given case. The result would be to produce an illusion of increased conceptual precision.

Unfortunately, the writings, for example, of Karl Lamprecht [1856–1913, the cultural and economic historian, and founder of the Department of Culture and Universal History at the University of Leipzig] are typical in this regard. Some approaches to the application of psychopathological concepts for the understanding of certain historical collective action can be taken more seriously. See chapter 12 of W. Hellpach's, *Grundlinien einer Psychologie der Hysterie* [Leipzig: W. Engelmann, 1904] and his *Nervosität und Kultur* [Berlin: J. Rade, 1902]. In my view, even this versatile author has been adversely influenced by certain theories of Lamprecht (although I cannot here attempt to confront this issue). Even those acquainted only with the introductory literature on Pietism know full well how completely worthless Lamprecht's schematic remarks on Pietism are compared to the older studies (see vol. 7 of his *Deutsche Geschichte* [Berlin: Weidman, 1909–20, 12 vols.]).

134. As, for example, occurred with the adherents of "Spiritual Christianity" led by Schortinghuis [see note 56]. In the history of religion, this idea can be traced back to the verse about the servant of God in Isaiah [53] and the 22nd Psalm.

135. As appeared occasionally in Dutch Pietism and then later under influences stemming from *Spinoza.*

136. See Labadie, [the hymnist, mystic, and psychologist Gerhard] Teersteegen, etc.

137. Francke founded schools for orphans and homeless children that practiced a severe discipline designed to strengthen independence and religious devotion [1697–1769]. See note 2 above on Spener and notes 3 and 4 on Zinzendorf [sk].

138. Perhaps this train of thought appears most clearly when Spener (one thinks: Spener!) protests against the competence of the ruling power to control the conventicles (except in cases of dis-

order and abuse). To him, the issue here concerns the *basic rights* of Christians, which are guaranteed by apostolic decree (see *Theologische Bedenken,* vol. 2, pp. 81 f.). In principle, this is exactly the Puritan standpoint in respect to the extent and validity of the rights of each person, namely, they follow *ex jure divino* [from divine law] and are therefore inalienable.

Neither this heresy [from the point of view of Lutheranism] nor the one mentioned later in Bayly's text has eluded Ritschl (see his *Pietismus, op. cit.* [note 19], pp. 115, 157). Ritschl's positivistic criticism of the idea of "basic human rights" is highly unhistorical (not to mention philistine). We owe not much less than *everything* to the idea of basic human rights, and today even the most "reactionary" person values it as basic to his sphere of individual freedom. Nonetheless, we must of course completely agree with Ritschl that, regarding both the extent and validity of the rights of each person, an organic connection to this idea is missing from Spener's thinking, which remains at this point Lutheran. [On Weber on "basic human rights," see, e.g., *E&S,* p. 1403; "Prospects for Democracy in Tsarist Russia," in *Weber: Selections in Translation,* edited by W. G. Runciman (New York: Cambridge University Press, 1978), pp 282–83.]

The conventicles (*collegia pietatis*) themselves, which became theoretically grounded in Spener's famous *Pia desideria* [see note 2] and which were in practice founded by him, basically corresponded to the English "prophesyings." The latter appeared first in Johannes of Lasco's Bible study groups in London (1547). Since then, they have belonged among the permanent inventory of forms of Puritan piety utilized against church authority. Finally, as is well-known, Spener legitimized his rejection of church discipline (as defined in Geneva) by arguing that its designated social carrier, the "third estate" (namely, the *status oeconomicus:* the lay Christians) is *not*, in the Lutheran Church, integrated into the church's organization. On the other hand, a typical instance of Lutheranism's weakness is apparent in the discussion of excommunication: the landed gentry, who were appointed as secular members of the governing court body, were recognized as representatives of the "third estate."

139. What was characteristic, according to the views of contemporaries, is visible even in the *name* "Pietism" (which appeared first in Lutheran regions); namely, that a methodical business *company* was produced out of *pietas.*

140. Admittedly, while this motivation fit extremely well with Calvinism, it did not *only* fit with this denomination. It can be found with particular frequency in the *oldest* Lutheran church statutes.

141. In the sense of Hebrews 5:13, 14. See Spener, *Theologische Bedenken,* vol. 1, p. 306.

142. Alongside Bayly and Baxter (see Spener, *Consilia et judicia theologica latina* [Frankfurt: Jungi, 1709], vol. 3, ch. 6, pt. 1, pars. 1, 47; ch. 6, pt. 1, pars. 3, 6), Spener was especially fond of Thomas à Kempis, and, above all, Tauler (whose writings he did not entirely understand; *ibid.,* vol. 3, ch. 1, pt. 1, par. 1). For detailed discussion of Tauler, see *op. cit.,* vol. 1, ch. 1, par. 1, no. 7. According to Spener, Luther's thinking is derived directly from Tauler.

143. See Ritschl, *op. cit.,* vol. 2, p. 113. Spener rejected the "penitence struggle" of the later Pietists (and of Luther) as the *single* decisive indication of a true conversion (Spener, *Theologische Bedenken,* vol. 3, p. 476). On the striving toward salvation as the result of thankfulness that stems from faith in reconciliation (a specifically Lutheran formulation; see ch. 3, note 7 above), see passages cited in Ritschl, *op. cit.,* p. 115, note 2. On the *certitudo salutis* see, on the one hand, *Theologische Bedenken* (vol. 1, p. 324): the true faith will not so much be *perceived as based on feeling* as it will be *recognized* by its *fruits* (love and obedience to God). On the other hand (see *Theologische Bedenken,* vol. 1, pp. 335 f.): "As concerns your anxiety regarding how you should become certain of your state of grace, it is more secure if you are guided by our"—that is, the Lutheran—"books rather than by the English writings." Spener agrees, however, with the English on the nature of the striving toward salvation.

144. The religious diaries, as recommended by A. H. Francke, were also here the external signs of one's state of grace. The methodical practice and *habit* of striving toward salvation should produce growth in this direction and the *separation* of good persons from evil persons. This is, approximately, the basic theme of Francke's book, *Von des Christen Vollkommenheit.*

145. Characteristically, the deviation of this rational, Pietist belief in predestination from its orthodox meaning came to the fore in the famous debate between the Pietists in Halle and Löscher, the representative of Lutheran orthodoxy. In his *Timotheus Verinus,* Löscher goes so far as to argue

that everything attained through *human* activity can be set against the decrees of predestination. Francke's position, which became increasingly firm, stood against Löscher: every lightning flash of clarity regarding what should occur—and these insights resulted only from patient *waiting* for God's decision—must be considered as "God's hint." All this takes place in a manner fully analogous to Quaker psychology and corresponds to a general notion in asceticism: the believer becomes closer to God through the pathway of rational *methodicalness*. Of course, Zinzendorf, who in one of his most important decisions, submitted the destiny of his community to a lottery, stands far removed from Francke's belief in predestination. In *Theologische Bedenken* (vol. 1, p. 314), Spener, in examining the Christian "calm tranquility and resignation," and then concluding that believers should be left to God's acts and, thus, that they should not undertake hasty, self-reliant activity, referred back to [the mystic] Tauler. This was, in essence, also Francke's position.

Compared to Puritanism, the essentially weakened activity of Pietist devotion, which sought (this-worldly) peace, appeared everywhere clear enough to see. A leading Baptist (G. White, in a lecture that will be cited later) formulated the ethical agenda for his denomination in 1904 in opposition to this Pietist devotion: "First righteousness, then peace." See *Baptist Handbook* (1904, p. 107).

146. *Lectiones paraeneticae,* vol. 4, p. 271.

147. Ritschl's criticism is oriented primarily against this recurring idea. Francke's *Von des Christen Vollkommenheit* contains this teaching.

148. It is found also among the English Pietists who did *not* uphold predestination; Goodwin, for example. On him and others, see Heppe, *Geschichte des Pietismus und der Mystik in der reformierten Kirche* [in Holland] (Leiden: E.J. Brill, 1879). Despite Ritschl's standard work, Heppe's book is not yet out of date for England or (occasionally) Holland. Köhler was often asked, even in the nineteenth century, in Holland about the *exact time* of his rebirth. See his *Die Niederländische reformierte Kirche, op. cit.* [note 9].

149. In this way one sought to confront the lax consequences of the Lutheran teaching regarding the reacquisition of grace (and especially to counteract the common "conversion" *in extremis* [in extreme circumstances, such as immediately prior to death]).

150. In opposition to the necessity of knowing the day and hour of the "conversion" (which was connected to this penitence and breakthrough), as an *unconditional* sign of its authenticity, see Spener, *Theologische Bedenken,* vol. 2, pt. 6, par. 1, p. 197. A "penitence struggle" was as unknown to him as Luther's *terrores conscienti* was to Melanchthon.

151. Of course, the anti-authoritarian interpretation of the "universal priesthood," specific to all asceticism, also played a related part. It was occasionally recommended to the minister to postpone absolution until a "testifying" to genuine contrition was forthcoming. Ritschl characterizes this practice correctly as Calvinist in principle.

152. The points essential for us are most accessible in H. Plitt, *Zinzendorf's Theologie* (3 vols., Gotha, 1869 f.), vol. 1, pp. 325, 345, 381, 412, 429, 433 f., 444, 448; vol. 2, pp. 372, 381, 385, 409 f.; vol. 3, pp. 131, 167, 176. See also Bernhard Becker, *Zinzendorf und sein Christentum* (Leipzig: F. Jansa, 1900), bk. 3, ch. 3.

153. Cornelius Otto Jansen (1585–1638), a Dutch and French theologian, founded Jansenism. This movement inside the Catholic Church in Holland and France opposed the Jesuits. It advocated a great moral rigorism and a return to the teachings of St. Augustine's ancient Christianity, especially its indifference to the world. Jansenists were persecuted in eighteenth-century France by the church as unorthodox [sk].

154. Admittedly, Zinzendorf held the Augsburg Confession to be a suitable document of the Lutheran-Christian faith only if a "scalding sore" were poured over it (as he expressed it in his repulsive terminology). Because his language, which dissolves ideas in a sloppy brew, has an even worse effect than the "christo-turpentine" so wretched in the writing of F. Thomas Vischer (see his polemics on the Munich "christo-turpentines"), to read him is an act of penitence.

155. See note 4 above [sk].

156. "No religion recognizes as brothers those who have not been, through the sprinkling with holy water, bathed in the blood of Christ. These believers are *thoroughly changed,* and this becomes manifest in the manner in which their striving for the salvation of the spirit *is continued.* We

recognize no evident (visible) congregation of Christ. This congregation comes into being only where the word of God is taught in an authentic and candid manner, and only where members of the congregation, as the children of God, *also live* the *holy life according to* God's word." Admittedly, the last sentence is taken from Luther's "small" catechism [which was addressed to ministers for instruction of lay believers rather than to theologians (the "large" catechism)]. Yet, as Ritschl has already emphasized, it serves *there* as an answer to the query of how the name of *God* can be made holy. *Here* it serves, in contrast, to demarcate the church of the *elect saints.*

157. See Plitt, *op. cit.* (vol. 1, p. 346). Even more decisive is the answer, quoted in Plitt (p. 381), to the question of whether "good works are necessary for salvation." "They are," Zinzendorf answers, "unnecessary and harmful for the acquisition of holiness. However, after salvation has been attained, they are so necessary that those who fail to perform them must be said not actually to be saved." Hence, it is also clear here that, for Zinzendorf, good works are not the cause of salvation; rather, they are the means—and the *single* means!—of recognizing it.

158. See note 4 [sk].

159. For example, in those caricatures of "Christian freedom" (which Ritschl lashes out against; see *op. cit.,* vol. 3, p. 381).

160. They did so primarily through an intensified emphasis on the idea of retributive punishment in the doctrine of salvation. After the rejection of his missionary attempts by the American sects, Zinzendorf made this idea the foundation of his salvation-striving methodology. From this point onward, he places the maintenance of *childlikeness* and the virtues of a humble modesty in the foreground as the aim of Herrnhuter asceticism. Doing so places Zinzendorf in sharp opposition to tendencies in his community clearly analogous to Puritan asceticism.

161. His impact, however, had its limits. For this reason alone it is incorrect to attempt to incorporate Zinzendorf's teachings in a *social*-psychological developmental stage model [along with the other Protestant sects and churches], as Lambrecht does. Moreover, Zinzendorf's entire religious outlook is influenced by nothing more strongly than one circumstance: he was a *count* with fundamentally feudal instincts. Precisely the *element* of *feeling* in these instincts would fit, from the point of view of "social psychology," just as well into the epoch of chivalry's sentimental decadence as into the epoch of religious "experience." The opposition of the element of feeling in this experience to Western European rationalism, if at all to be understood "social-psychologically," can be best comprehended by reference [to the forms of organization and rulership] in the German eastern territories [such as Prussia and Bohemia], that have remained entirely unsevered from patriarchalism.

162. The controversies of Zinzendorf with Dippel lead to the same conclusion, as do statements from the Synod of 1764 (after Zinzendorf's death). These indicate clearly that Herrnhuter congregations had the character of salvation *institutions* [of open membership rather than as sects with exclusive membership; see *E&S,* pp. 557–63]. See Ritschl's criticism (*op. cit.*, vol. 3, p. 443 f.).

163. Spangenberg was a bishop in the German Brethren Congregation and Zinzendorf's successor. He was sent by Zinzendorf to found a church in Pennsylvania (the United Brethren) [sk].

164. See, for example, paragraphs 151, 153, 160. That it is possible to exclude striving for salvation, *in spite of* true contrition and the forgiveness of sins, derives in particular from statements on p. 311. This view corresponds to the Lutheran doctrine on salvation and contradicts Calvinism (and Methodism also).

165. See Zinzendorf's statements (cited in Plitt, *op. cit.,* vol. 2, p. 345). Similarly, see Spangenberg, *Idea Fidei Fratrum,* p. 325.

166. See, for example, Zinzendorf's remark on Matthew 20:28 as cited by Plitt, *op. cit.,* vol. 3, p. 131:

> When I see a person to whom God has given a fine talent, I am delighted and share in the talent with pleasure. However, if I note that this person is not content with his talent, and instead wants to render it manifest in something more beautiful, then I see here the beginning of the ruin of this person.

Hence, and especially in his discussion with John Wesley (1743), Zinzendorf denied *progress* in striving for salvation. He does so because on the one hand he identifies such striving with [Luther's emphasis upon] justification of salvation through faith; he does so because on the other hand he remains in a relationship to Christ that has been acquired *exclusively* through the *feelings* (Plitt, *op. cit.*, vol. 1, p. 413). In place of the feeling of being an *instrument of God* there appears a feeling of a *possession* by the Divine. In other words, mysticism replaces asceticism (as discussed in my "Social Psychology of the World Religions" essay [H. H. Gerth and C. W. Mills, eds., *From Max Weber, op. cit.*, pp. 285, 289–92; see also, in Gerth and Mills, "Religious Rejections of the World," pp. 324–30]). As examined in the "Social Psychology" essay, the Puritan is also of course *really* striving for a present, *this-worldly* disposition (*Habitus*). Yet this disposition, which he interprets to be the *certitudo salutis* [certainty of salvation], involves a *feeling* of being an active *instrument* of God's Will. [The last four sentences were added in 1920.]

167. On account of this derivation, however, work in a calling here was not consistently grounded in ethics. Zinzendorf rejects Luther's idea of the calling as a "service to God" and this service as the *decisive* aspect for loyalty to a calling. Rather, for Zinzendorf, loyalty to a calling is more *a payback* to Christ for "Christ's loyalty to his trade" (Plitt, vol. 2, p. 411). [Zinzendorf's meaning is also metaphorical, as Weber knows the German will imply to readers: our loyalty to our calling is a form of thankfulness to Christ for having sacrificed himself for our sins.]

168. His maxim from his essay on Socrates is well-known: "A reasonable person should not be without belief and a believer should not be unreasonable." In other words, as he notes also in this essay: "The reasonable person should be able to reveal with candor not only various unknown basic truths, but also contested basic truths" (1725). Well-known also is his partiality for writers such as [the French opponent of systematic philosophy, Pierre] Bayle [1647–1707].

169. The distinct predilection of Protestant asceticism for an empiricism that is rationalized through the application of mathematics is familiar to us and need not be discussed here. On the turn of the sciences toward a mathematical-rationalized, "exact" form of research, see Wilhelm Windelband, *Lehrbuch der Geschichte der Philosophie* [Tübingen: Mohr, 1980 (1892)], pp. 305–7 [*A History of Philosophy* (New York: Harper, 1958)]. Windelband [1848–1915] examines the philosophical motivations behind this turn and the contrasting position held by Bacon. See in particular the comments appropriately rejecting the idea that the modern natural sciences can be comprehended as a *product* of material-technological interests (p. 305). Highly important relationships of this sort are naturally present, but the issue is far more complex. See also Windelband, *Geschichte der neueren Philosophie* ([Leipzig: Breitkopf and Hertel, 1878–1880], vol. 1, pp. 40 ff.).

The *point of view* decisive for the position of ascetic Protestantism, as surely appears in its clearest form in Spener's *Theologische Bedenken* (vol. 1, p. 232; vol. 3, p. 260), was certainly that, just as one could know the Christian by the *fruits* of his beliefs, so one could know God and His intentions only out of knowledge of His *deeds*. Accordingly, the favorite scientific field of all Puritan, baptizing, and Pietist Christianity was physics. Other disciplines that utilized the methodologies of similar mathematical and natural sciences were the next choices. Quite simply, one believed, starting from the *empirical* comprehension of the divine laws of nature, that one was able to ascend to knowledge of the "meaning" of the world. As a result of the fragmentary character of divine revelation (a Calvinist idea), this meaning could surely never be known through the avenue of conceptual speculation.

The empiricism of the seventeenth century was the mechanism for asceticism to seek "God in nature." [See "Science as a Vocation" in Gerth and Mills, *op. cit.,* pp. 142–43.] *Empiricism* appeared to lead *toward* God, and philosophical speculation appeared to lead away from God. Aristotelian philosophy in particular has been a fundamental detriment to Christianity, according to Spener. *Every* other philosophy would be better, especially "Plato's." See Spener's *Consilia Theologica* [note 141] (vol. 3, ch. 6, pt. 1, par. 2, no. 13). Further, see the following passage, which is characteristic:

> Unde pro Cartesio quid dicam non habeo (he had not read him), semper tamen optavi et opto, ut Deus viros excitet, qui veram philosophiam vel tandem oculis sisterent in qua nullius hominis attenderetur auctoritas, sed sana tantum magistri nescia ratio [I have always very much wished for Descartes (he had not read him), and continue to do so, that God would be able to frighten men into recognizing the true philosophy as one comprehended with the eyes

and not with human cognition. A healthy power of understanding should be oriented in this direction, which is so unknown to teachers]. (Spener, vol. 2, ch. 5, no. 2)

The significance of these views of ascetic Protestantism for the development of education (especially for those courses of studies oriented more toward the acquisition of practical skills and technical knowledge) is known. The educational agenda of ascetic Protestantism became formulated once these views had combined with its position [versus Catholicism] on *fides implicita*. [Namely, while recognizing that the devout believe (even as individuals) in the revelation of God, the Catholic Church reserved the right to give instructions to the faithful regarding correct belief and to require that believers support the authority of the church. This position was denounced strongly by both Lutheranism and Calvinism.]

170. "That type of person seeks his happiness in roughly four ways. . . : (1) to be lowly, despised, and ill-spoken of; (2) to neglect . . . all senses not needed in order to serve his God. . . ; (3) to either have nothing or to give away all that he receives. . . ; and (4) to work on the basis of a *daily wage,* and to do so not in order to earn the wage, *but on behalf of a calling* and a service to God and his neighbors" (Zinzendorf, *Religiöse-Reden*, vol. 2, p. 180; see Plitt, *op. cit.*, vol. 1, p. 449). *Not all* could or should become "disciples"; rather, only those called by God. However, according to Zinzendorf's own confession, difficulties still remain because the Sermon on the Mount is addressed formally to *all* (see Plitt, *op. cit.,* vol. 1, p. 449). The affinity of this "free, acosmic love" with the old Anabaptist ideals is obvious. [On the Reformation's "radicals," the Anabaptists, from which the Baptists, Quakers, and Mennonites [see pp. 93 ff. below] trace their roots, see notes 194 and 214 below.]

171. For the internalization (*Verinnerlichung*) of piety on the basis of feelings was actually by no means foreign to Lutheranism. This holds even for its later period of weak leadership. Rather, the fundamental difference *here* involved the *ascetic* dimension. Lutherans viewed asceticism with suspicion as a regimentation of life with overtones of "good works."

172. For Spener, a "strong dose of anxiety" constituted a better sign of one's salvation than did "security." See his *Theologische Bedenken* (*op. cit.,* vol. 1, p. 324). We find, of course, strong warnings against a "false certainty" also in Puritan writers. Nonetheless, at least the doctrine of predestination had the opposite effect, to the extent that its influence determined the nature of the pastoral care believers received,

173. For the *psychological* effect of confession was everywhere to *unburden* individuals of their own responsibility for their conduct. Indeed, this effect is why confession was sought. It relieves the rigorous consequences of asceticism's demands. [Lutheranism offers in principle to each the possibility of confession. In practice, however, believers stated their sins to God in silence before taking communion.]

174. The strong role played, in the process, by purely *political* forces—even for the *type* of Pietist piety—has already been suggested by Ritschl in his presentation of Pietism in Württemberg. See his volume 3 (*op. cit.* [note 19]).

175. See Zinzendorf's statement (quoted in note 169 above).

176. Of course Calvinism (at least the genuine version) is also "patriarchal." And the connection to success is clearly visible in Baxter's autobiography (for example, in his activity in Kidderminster, which had a cottage industry). See the passage quoted in *Works of the Puritan Divines:* "The town liveth upon the weaving of Kidderminster stuffs, and as they stand in their loom, they can set a book before them, or edify each other" (p. 38). Nevertheless, patriarchalism rooted in the Calvinist ethic, and especially when anchored in the ethic of the baptizing congregations, is constituted differently from what is found on the soil of Pietism. This problem can be addressed only in a different context.

177. See his *Lehre von der Rechtfertigung und Versöhnung* ([see note 10], vol. 1, p. 598). The description of Pietism by Frederick William I [1648–1740]—a religion that offers beliefs suitable to persons of independent means—clearly tells us more about this king than about the Pietism of Spener and Francke. Moreover, the king knew well why he opened, through his edict on tolerance, his territories to Pietism. [Weber here alludes to Frederick William's knowledge of the Pietists as conscientious and obedient workers, and his need for such a population.]

178. The article by Friedrich Loofs offers an excellent introductory overview to Methodism. See "Methodismus," in the *Realenzyklopädie für protestantische Theologie und Kirche* (3rd ed.). The studies by L. Jacoby (especially the *Handbuch des Methodismus*), Kolde, Jüngst, and Southey are useful [Robert Southey, *The Life of Wesley* (New York: Harper & Brothers, 1847)]. On Wesley, Luke Tyerman's *Life and Times of the Rev. John Wesley* is popular [New York: Harper, 1872]. Northwestern University in Evanston (near Chicago) has one of the best libraries on the history of Methodism. The religious [psalmist and hymnist] Isaac Watts [1674–1748] has built a chain of sorts from classical Puritanism to Methodism. He was a friend of Oliver Cromwell's chaplain (Howe), and then of Richard Cromwell. Presumably, Whitefield sought his advice (see Skeats, *History of the Free Churches of England, 1688–1891* [*op. cit.* (see note 10)], pp. 254 f.).

179. This affinity (if the personal influences of the Wesleys are left aside) results historically from, on the one hand, the dying out of the dogma of predestination and, on the other hand, the powerful reawakening among the founders of the idea of *sola fide.* This affinity, however, was primarily motivated by Methodism's specifically *missionary* character. This missionary component introduced a (transforming) rejuvenation of certain medieval methods stemming from "awakening" preaching, and these methods then combined with Pietist forms.

Methodism's systematic organization of life, with the aim of attaining the *certitudo salutis,* certainly does not belong in a *general* line of development toward "individualism." On the contrary, in this respect, this systematic organization of life can be seen to be not only prior to Pietism but also prior to the Bernhardian piety of the Middle Ages.

180. A bench in the Methodist church set aside for those suffering particular internal turmoil as a result of uncertainty regarding their state of salvation. The open expression of fear and anxiety is here permitted [sk].

181. Wesley himself occasionally characterized the effect of Methodist belief in this way. The affinity with the "blessedness" (*Glückseligkeit*) of Zinzendorf is apparent.

182. The same point is made, for example, in Watson's *Life of Wesley* (German edition), p. 331.

183. Matthias Schneckenburger, *Vorlesungen über die Lehrbegriffe der kleinen protestantischen Kirchenparteien,* ed. by K. B. Hundeshagen (Frankfurt: H.L. Bonner, 1863), p. 147.

184. Whitefield, the leader of the group upholding predestination (which disbanded, owing to disorganization, after his death), essentially rejected Wesley's doctrine of "perfection." Actually, this doctrine is only a *surrogate* for Calvinism's idea of conduct as testifying to belief.

185. Schneckenburger (*ibid.,* p. 145). Loofs takes a slightly different position. See *op. cit.* Both outcomes are typical of all similar devoutness.

186. As in the case of the conference of 1770. The first conference of 1744 had already recognized that the words of the Bible skirted "within a hair" of Calvinism on the one hand and Antinomianism on the other. Given this unclarity, and as long as the Bible's validity as a *practical* norm remained firm, doctrinal differences [it was believed] should not lead to a separation. [Followers of Antinomianism argued that Christians, through God's grace, are not obligated to adhere to the commandments. Obedience as such was rejected as legalistic, for life must be guided by the Holy Spirit within.]

187. On the one hand, the Methodists were separated from the Herrnhuter by the former's doctrine on the possibility of sinless perfection. Zinzendorf [a Herrnhuter founder], in particular, also rejected this teaching. On the other hand, Wesley perceived the element of *feeling* in Herrnhuter devoutness to be "mysticism." Furthermore, he characterized Luther's position on "God's law" as "blasphemy." One can see here the barrier that unavoidably remained between every type of *rational* organization of life and Lutheranism.

188. John Wesley occasionally points out that everywhere—for the Quakers, the Presbyterians, and the Anglican Church—dogma must be believed. This did not hold only in the case of the Methodists, he contends. Compare also the (admittedly rather summary) discussion in Skeats, *op. cit.,* to the above paragraphs.

189. See, for example, Dexter, *The Congregationalism of the Last 300 Years* (*op. cit.* [note 10]), pp. 455 ff.

190. Of course, however, it *can* detract from the rational character of the organization of life, as occurs today with the American Negroes. The frequently pathological character, by the way, of Methodist emotionalism, in contrast to the relatively mild orientation to the feelings characteristic of Pietism, *perhaps* also (in addition to purely historical reasons and the publicity of the procedure) goes closely together with a stronger *ascetic* penetration of life in the regions where Methodism is widespread. A decision on this point, however, belongs to the domain of the neurologist.

191. See chapter 5, below [sk].

192. Loofs (*op. cit.*, p. 750) emphasizes strongly that Methodism distinguishes itself from other ascetic movements in that it appeared *after* the period of the English Enlightenment [in the seventeenth century]. He then places Methodism in a parallel relationship to the renaissance of Pietism in the first third [of the nineteenth century] in Germany. Although, as Loofs admits, Pietism was a much weaker movement, the parallel can stand. (Loofs is following Ritschl's *Lehre von der Rechtfertigung* [see note 10], vol. 1, pp. 568 f.) It holds even for Zinzendorf's version of Pietism, which, in contrast to the Pietism of Spener and Francke, *also,* like Methodism, reacted against the English Enlightenment. Nevertheless, this reaction in Methodism (as we saw) indeed took a very different direction from that of the Herrnhuter, at least to the degree that the latter were influenced by Zinzendorf.

193. Methodism, however, developed this idea of a calling (as the passage above from John Wesley indicates) in the same manner, and with the exact same effect, as the other ascetic denominations. [1920]

194. This section concerns *das Täufertum*, namely, "the baptizing sects" (Mennonites, Baptists, and Quakers; see next paragr. in the text) rather than "the Baptist sect," as the translation by Parsons implies. Central to all was the baptism of adult believers (even if they had been baptized as children), namely, when the "age of reason" had been attained. This maturity, it was argued, enabled believers to reach a conscious decision regarding their beliefs. Baptism (by full immersion) then constituted the external sign of an inner experience of adulthood: the spirit's rebirth. (See "The Protestant Sects" essay below for Weber's observations on the social significance of baptism in 1904 in the United States.) Following Weber, the terms *baptizers, baptizing sects, baptizing communities, baptizing congregations, baptizing denominations,* and *the baptist movement* are used synonymously [sk].

195. And, as shown, *weakened forms* of the consistent ascetic ethic of Puritanism. If one wished, following the more preferred [Marxist] manner, to interpret these religious conceptions only as "manifestations" or "reflections" of the development of capitalism, then *precisely the opposite* of such a weakening would have occurred. [1920]

196. Among the Baptists, only the "General Baptists" [Christ died for all and not only for an elect] can be traced back to the old Anabaptists [of the early-to-mid sixteenth century, the Reformation's left-wing radicals]. As already noted, the "Particular Baptists" were Calvinists who, in principle, restricted church membership to the elect (or at least to those who had made a "personal" confession of belief). Hence, this group stayed, in principle, voluntaristic and remained an opponent of all state churches. Admittedly, in practice, under Cromwell they did not always hold consistently to this position. Nonetheless, the Particular Baptists, although also the General Baptists, however important historically they were as the carriers of the baptizing tradition, fail to offer to us adequate reason to undertake here a special analysis of their dogma. Formally, the Quakers were a new creation by George Fox and his compatriots. However, when scrutinized in terms of their basic ideas, they must unquestionably be seen in the end as a group that continued the Anabaptist tradition. [A few bibliographical sources should be noted.]

The best introduction to the history of the Quakers, and simultaneously to their relationship to the Baptists and Mennonites, is by Robert Barclay. See his *The Inner Life of the Religious Societies of the Commonwealth* [London: Hodder & Stoughton, 1876].

On the history of the Baptists, see, among others, H. M. Dexter, *The True Story of John Smyth, as Told by Himself and His Contemporaries* (Boston: Lee & Shepard, 1881); on this volume, see J. C. Lang in *The Baptist Quarterly Review* (1883, p. 1). See also J. Murch, *A History of the Presbyterian and General Baptist Church in the West of England* (London: Hunter Pub., 1835); A. H. Newman, *A History of the Baptist Church in the United States* (New York: Christian Literature,

1894) (American Church History Series, vol. 2); Henry Clay Vedder, *A Short History of the Baptists* (London, 1897 [Philadelphia: American Baptist Publication Society, 1952 (1907)]); Ernest Belfort Bax, *Rise and Fall of the Anabaptists* (New York: American Scholar Publications, 1966 [1903]); George Lorimer, *The Baptists in History* [Boston: Silver, Burdett, 1893]; Joseph Augustus Seiss, *The Baptist System Examined* (Lutheran Publication Society, 1902).

See also the material in the *Baptist Handbook* (London, 1896 ff.); *Baptist Manuals* (Paris, 1891–93); *The Baptist Quarterly Review;* and the *Bibliotheca Sacra* (Oberlin, 1900). The best Baptist library seems to be found at Colgate College in the State of New York.

The collection in Devonshire House in London (which I have not used) is considered the best for the history of the Quakers. The official, modern volume on Quaker orthodoxy is the *American Friend,* edited by Professor Rufus Jones [1894 ff.]. The best Quaker history is that of Rowntree. In addition, see: Rufus B. Jones, *George Fox, an Autobiography* [New York: Harper & Brothers, 1930 (1903)]; Alton C. Thomas, *A History of the Society of Friends in America* (Philadelphia, 1895); Edward Grubbe, *Social Aspects of the Quaker Faith,* (London: Headley Brothers, 1899). See also the large and very good *biographical* literature. [1920]

197. Karl Müller's *Kirchengeschichte* (Tübingen: Mohr, 1892–1919 [3 vols.]) makes many contributions. Among them is his awarding to the Anabaptists (a movement great in its own way, although outwardly barely visible) the position they deserve. Like no other religious grouping, the Anabaptists suffered from relentless persecution by *all* churches—simply because they *wanted* to be, in the specific sense of the term, a *sect.* As a result of the catastrophe suffered in Münster by the branch that unfolded in an eschatological direction, the sects still remain, after five generations, discredited throughout the entire world (in England, for example). [See notes 213 and 214 below.] Above all, oppressed repeatedly and chased underground, the Anabaptists achieved a coherent formulation of their religious *ideas* only long after their period of origin.

Hence, they produced *even* less "theology" than would have been consistent with their principles, which were at any rate antagonistic to the technical managing of the belief in God as if it were a "science." [Weber is saying that theology often does just this.] This situation induced the older specialist theology (even in its own period) to show little sympathy for the Anabaptists and to remain unimpressed by them. Yet even many later theological schools were equally unimpressed. Ritschl (see *Pietismus* [note 19], vol. 1, pp. 22 f.) treats the "Re-Baptizers" with many preconceptions; indeed, he addresses them with scorn and in a condescending manner. In reading him, the reader feels as if spoken to from the point of view of a theological "bourgeoisie." This remains the case even though the excellent study by Cornelius was published several decades before Ritschl's volumes. See *Geschichte des Münsterschen Aufruhrs* (1853–60, 2 vols.).

In this analysis, Ritschl constructs the notion of Anabaptism's general collapse (viewed from his vantage point) into "the Catholic." He suspects here the direct influence of the Franciscans (including their more strict wing, the Spiritualist Franciscans). However, even if demonstrable in regard to particulars, the evidence would still be very thin. Moreover, and above all, the historical circumstances were different. On the one hand, the orthodox Catholic Church treated the *this*-worldly asceticism of the laity with great mistrust as soon as it began to form conventicles. The church then sought to direct this asceticism toward the formation of a religious order—hence, to push it *out* of the world. On the other hand, the church also deliberately attempted to integrate lay asceticism into the existing monasteries, but only with second-class status. In this manner the church sought to bring this new asceticism under its control. Wherever this attempt failed, it saw again the danger that the cultivation of an individualistic, ascetic morality would lead to a denial of authority and to heresy. The Anglican Church under Elizabeth I [1558–1603] took just such a posture of antagonism—with the same line of justification—against the "prophesyings," namely, against the half-Pietist Bible conventicles (even in those cases where this group assumed an entirely correct position in respect to "conformism"). Under the Stuarts [1603–1714] this conflict became expressed in their Book of Sports (see below, pp. 112–13).

The history of numerous heretical movements offers evidence for this argument, though the history of, for example, the Humiliati [northern Italian wool workers who, amidst poverty, became a monastic brotherhood in 1170] and the Beguins [f. 1200, pious women who lived in voluntary poverty and chastity, mainly in Holland and Germany] does so as well, as does the fate of St. Francis.

The preachings of mendicant friars, especially the Franciscans, helped in many ways to prepare the path for the ascetic lay morality of the Reformist-Anabaptist Protestantism. However, the massive elements of affinity between asceticism inside religious orders in the West and the ascetic organization of life in Protestantism—which will be repeatedly emphasized as highly instructive precisely for the themes addressed here—derive their ultimate legitimation not so much from the preachings of friars. Rather, they are rooted otherwise, namely, in the circumstance that, of course, *every* asceticism standing on the foundation of biblical Christianity *must* necessarily have certain important common features. To be more specific, *every* such asceticism, regardless of its denominational heritage, requires specific tried and proven mechanisms that *subdue* the desires of the body.

Still to note is the brevity of the following sketch. Its shorter length must be ascribed to the circumstance that the ethic of the baptizing communities is of only very limited significance for the particular problem to be discussed in *this* study: the development of the religious foundation of the idea of a *calling* shared by a "middle class." This ethic did not add anything qualitatively new to this idea. The far more important social side of the baptizing movement will be left aside for the moment. [See "The Protestant Sects" essay below.] Of the substantive historical issues surrounding the *older* Anabaptist movement, we can discuss, as a result of our definition of the particular problem, *only* those issues that influenced the uniqueness of the baptizing sects in the foreground here: the Baptists, the Quakers, and (less directly) the Mennonites.

198. See above [note 106].

199. On their origin and changes, see A. Ritschl in his *Gesammelte Aufsätze*, vol. 1 (Freiburg, 1893), pp. 68 ff.

200. Of course, the baptizers continually rejected other Christians' characterization of them as "sects." They were, in the sense of the Epistle to the Ephesians (5:27), *the* church. For *our* terminology, however, they were sects *not only* because they renounced every relationship to the state. Admittedly, the relationship between church and state in ancient Christianity was their ideal, even for the Quakers (see Barclay, *op. cit.*), because to them (as for some Pietists; see Tersteegen [note 136]) *only* the purity of the early churches was without suspicion. Yet, if oppressed under a *secular* state, or even under a theocracy, then [not only the baptizing movement] but also the Calvinists had to be in favor (for want of something better) of a separation of state and church (similar to, in the same situation, even the Catholic Church). [Therefore, this reason—their renunciation of every relationship to the state—cannot be decisive in defining the baptizing congregations as sects.] Moreover, the baptizers are defined as a sect not *because* the entry into church membership *de facto* followed from an induction contract between the congregation and the candidate. This was true *formally*, for example, also in the Dutch Calvinist congregations (as a result of the original political situation), according to the old church constitution (see H. von Hoffmann *Kirchenverfassungsrecht der niederlandischen Reformierten* (Leipzig, 1902).

Rather, the baptizing congregations are defined as a sect because, to them, the religious community *can only* be organized voluntaristically, namely, as a sect (and not as a church, in the way that a large institution is organized) if it wants to exclude the unsaved from membership and, thereby, to follow the ideal of the earliest Christian community [which was a community of the elect]. To the baptizing communities, the *concept* "church" included this voluntaristic organization. For the Reformists, on the other hand, the church, as a large institution that allowed membership to [include] the unsaved, already existed as an actual condition. Admittedly, very definite religious motives pushed even the Calvinists toward a "believer's, voluntaristic church," as has been already suggested.

See "The Protestant Sects" essay below for more detail on "church" and "sect." As used here, the concept "sect" overlaps in part with and (I assume) deviates from Kattenbusch's usage. See the article "Sects" in the *Realenzyklopädie für protestantische Theologie und Kirche* [1906, vol. 18, pp. 157–166]. Troeltsch accepts my definition, and discusses it in more detail, in his *Social Teachings* (*op. cit.* [note 8]). See also the introduction to my essays in the Economic Ethics of the World Religions series ["The Social Psychology of the World Religions," in Gerth and Mills, *op. cit.*] [See, finally, *E&S*, pp. 1204–10; *Gesammelte Aufsätze zur Soziologie und Sozialpoltik* (Tübingen: Mohr: 1924), pp. 442–46.]

201. How important this symbol was historically, for the preservation of the community of churches (because it created for them an unambiguous and unmistakable identifying characteristic), has been examined by Cornelius in a very clear manner (see *op. cit.* [note 197]).

202. Certain approximations to this orthodox dogma in the Mennonite doctrine of justification can be omitted here.

203. The fourth-century Pneumatics believed that God's will could be understood through natural reason, angels and demons, and the human soul. This sect was viewed as a predecessor to the "awakening" movements of ascetic Protestantism [sk].

204. On this idea rests perhaps the religious interest in the questions of how the incarnation of Christ and his relationship to the Virgin Mary are to be understood. Often as the *single* purely dogmatic component, they appear quite peculiar, even in the oldest documents of the Anabaptists (for example, in the "confessions" printed in Cornelius, *op. cit.,* appendix to vol. 2; see also, among others, Karl Müller, *Kirchengeschichte* [note 197], vol. 2, pt. 1, p. 330). Similar religious interests lay at the foundation of the difference in the christologies of the Reformists and the Lutherans (as concerns the doctrine of the so-called *communicatio idiomatum*). [Weber refers here to Calvin's view that the unity between God and human beings did not result from Christ's divinity, but owing to his possession of both divine and human features.]

205. It became expressed in particular in the (originally) strict avoidance of the excommunicated, even in interaction in middle-class economic activities. In this regard, even the Calvinists, who held the view that religious censors in principle should not interfere with middle-class economic activity, made strong concessions. See "The Protestant Sects" essay [below].

206. We know how this principle was expressed among the Quakers in the apparently unimportant external aspects of life (the refusal to remove the hat, to kneel down, to bow, to use the formal form of speech ["vous" in French]). However, the *basic* idea is indigenous to *every* asceticism to a certain degree. For this reason, in its *authentic* form, asceticism is always "hostile to authority." This hostility became manifest in Calvinism in the principle that only *Christ* should rule in the *church.* As concerns Pietism on the other hand, one thinks of Spener's efforts to justify, by reference to the Bible, the *use of titles. Catholic* asceticism, in regard to matters concerning rulership in the *church,* did not share this hostility to authority. Instead, through the oath of obedience, it interpreted *obedience* itself as ascetic.

The "inverting" of this principle by Protestant asceticism is the historical foundation for the uniqueness, even today, of the *democracy* among peoples influenced by Puritanism. It is also the foundation for the differences between this democracy and the democracies that flowed out of the "Latin spirit." This hostility to authority among Protestants is also constitutive for that "lack of respect" at the foundation of American behavior. Some view this feature of American life as offensive, while others view it as refreshing. [Weber is here referring to widespread prejudices (hence the quotation marks) among many Germans who viewed Americans as rude, boisterous, and unruly, and not showing adequate respect for high status and authority. Other Germans experienced the American "lack of respect" for authority as relief from a German climate of widespread and unquestioned respect for authority, which they perceived as oppressive. For a discussion of differences on this point (and others) that remain to this day, see S. Kalberg, "West German and American Interaction Forms: One Level of Structured Misunderstanding" (*Theory, Culture and Society* 4 [Oct. 1987]: 602–18).

207. Admittedly, this holds for the baptizing sects, from their beginnings in Anabaptism, essentially only for the *New* Testament. It cannot be said for the Old Testament in the same way. As a social-ethical program, the Sermon on the Mount in particular enjoyed, in all denominations, a clear prestige.

208. Condemned by Luther (1540), Schwenckfeld had sought to mediate between conflicting parties during the early Reformation. Some of his followers emigrated to Pennsylvania in the eighteenth century [sk].

209. Even Schwenckfeld saw the external performance of the sacraments as an *Adiaphoron* [a matter of indifference in the eyes of the church]. The "General Baptists" [see note 195] and the Mennonites, however, continued to uphold strictly infant christening and communion. The Mennonites also practiced the bathing of feet. Among all denominations that upheld predestination, how-

ever, the downplaying of the sacraments was very apparent (one could even, with the exception of communion, speak of *suspicion*). See "The Protestant Sects" essay below.

210. At this point the baptizing denominations, especially the Quakers, referred to Calvin's statement. See Robert Barclay, *Apology for the True Christian Divinity* (London, 1701, 4th ed., made available to me through the gracious assistance of [the prominent German socialist and member of the Reichstag] Eduard Bernstein); see Calvin's *Institutio christianae religionis* [note 19], vol. 3, p. 2. Indeed, quite unmistakable approximations to the doctrine of the baptizing communities are found here. Even the older *distinction* regarding the dignity of "God's word" (as words that God had revealed to the patriarchs, prophets, and apostles) and the "holy scriptures" (as what of God's word had been *written down* by the patriarchs, prophets, and apostles) related internally, although a historical context was lacking, to the view of the baptizers on the essence of the revelation.

The mechanical doctrine of inspiration [according to which God had decreed that the Bible is to be understood literally as the Word of God], and hence the strict Bible learning of the Calvinists, likewise arose only as a product of a development (which had begun in the course of the sixteenth century) that unfolded in a particular direction. Similarly, the Quaker doctrine regarding an "inner light" (which rested upon an Anabaptist foundation) was the result of a development in the exactly opposite direction. The sharp separation was actually here also in part a consequence of a continuous confrontation.

211. This was emphasized sharply against certain tendencies of the Socinians [a northern Italian brotherhood of the sixteenth century, a precursor to English and American Unitarianism]. "Natural" reason knows *nothing at all* of God (Barclay, *op. cit.,* p. 102). Thus, the position that *lex naturae* [natural law] otherwise held in Protestantism was once again altered. "General rules" and a moral *code,* in principle, could not exist, for now the "calling," which every person has and which is *particular* to every person, reveals God to each—through the *conscience.* We should *not* do "the good" (as known to us in the form of a generalizing concept called natural reason); rather, we should do *God's Will,* as it is now—in a new contract with God—written in our hearts and expressed in our conscience (Barclay, *op. cit.,* pp. 73 f., 76).

This *irrationality* of morality [in the sense of being now particular to each person rather than a general code], which follows out of the accentuated contrast [in ascetic Protestantism] between the Divine and the mortal human being, becomes manifest in tenets foundational to the Quaker ethic: "What a man does contrary to his faith, *though his faith may be wrong,* is in no way acceptable to God—*though the thing might have been lawful to another*" (Barclay, *op. cit.*, p. 487). Of course, in daily life this standard could not be upheld. The "moral and perpetual statutes acknowledged by all Christians" are, for example for Barclay, actually the demarcation lines for *tolerance* [rather than the individual conscience]. In practice, the contemporaries understood their ethic (with a few exceptions) to be the same as that of the Reformist Pietists. Spener repeatedly emphasizes that "everything that is good in the church is suspected of being Quakerism." Hence, he would like the Quakers, on account of their reputations, to be envied (see *Cons. Theol.* [note 141], vol. 3, pt. 6, sect. 1, par. 2, no. 64). The rejection of taking an oath on account of a passage from the Bible demonstrates that an actual emancipation from the Bible had scarcely occurred. We cannot here address the *social*-ethical meaning of that principle viewed by some Quakers as the essence of the *entire* Christian ethic: "Do unto others as you would have them do unto you."

212. Barclay legitimizes the necessity for the acceptance of this *possibility* by arguing that, without it, "there should never be a place known by the Saints wherein they might be free of doubting and despair, which *is most absurd.*" One can see that the *certitudo salutis* connects to this passage. This is clear in Barclay (*op. cit.,* p. 20).

213. Eschatology is concerned with religious beliefs about the end of the world and events associated with it. Chiliasm is the belief that a new society, in which only the just and good live, will exist at the end of time [sk].

214. Weber is referring to the victory of the radical Anabaptist sect in the city of Münster in northwestern Germany in 1534 and the religious fanaticism, chiliasm, polygamy, collective ownership of property, and terror that followed. The brutal defeat they suffered in 1535 marked the end of Anabaptist radicalism [sk].

215. Hence, a difference in accent between the Calvinist and the Quaker rationalization of life continues to exist. However, Baxter's formulation—for the Quakers, "reason" should have an effect on the soul as it has on a corpse, whereas for Reformists (characteristically formulated) "reason and spirit are conjunct principles" (*Christian Directory* [see note 39], vol. 2, p. 76)—fails to recognize that this difference, for all practical purposes, ceases to exist in *this* form for Baxter's own time.

216. Weber added the following sentences in his 1920 revisions. I have taken them out of the text because they express a new idea and hence disrupt the flow of his argument [sk].

> The radical elimination of magic from the world's occurrences indigenously [see pp. 60, 70] did not allow a pathway of development other than one leading to this-worldly asceticism. However, these baptizing groups were pushed in the direction of work in a vocation not only by this development; an external factor was also important: their unwillingness to have anything to do with the political powers-that-be, and their machinations, also pushed them in this direction.

217. See the very careful articles "Menno" and "Mennoniten" by S. Cramer in the *Realenzyklopädie für Protestantische Theologie und Kirche* (esp. p. 604). Although these articles are very good, the article "Baptisten" in the same encyclopedia is not very compelling and is, in some respects, completely imprecise. Its author is not familiar with, for example, the Publications of the Hanserd Knollys Society series. These articles remain indispensable for the history of the Baptists.

218. The Dunkers were founded in Germany (in Hesse) by Alexander Mack and soon thereafter emigrated to Pennsylvania. Today they are allied with the Church of the Brethren [sk].

219. Hence, Barclay (*op. cit.,* p. 404) explains that eating, drinking, and the *acquisition of goods* are *natural*, rather than spiritual, acts that can be pursued without a special call from God. His explanation is an answer to the (characteristic) criticism: if (as the Quakers teach) one is not allowed to pray without a special "motion of the spirit," then one would not even be allowed, without such a special motivation bestowed by God, to plow the fields.

It is also characteristic (even if such ideas are also occasionally found in the other denominations, even among the Calvinists) that Quakers advise, even in modern resolutions of the Quaker synods, one to withdraw from making a living after one has earned a sufficient fortune. One should withdraw in order, in the peacefulness outside the world's hustle and bustle, to be able to live fully in the kingdom of God. It becomes apparent, in this advice, that the adoption of a middle-class vocational ethic by its social carriers constituted the this-worldly turn of an originally world-*fleeing* asceticism. [Weber refers to the asceticism of medieval Catholicism within monasteries (see the end of this chapter); he sees the Quaker advice as a manifestation of asceticism because it assumes the believer had remained focussed upon God's will despite the acquisition of (corrupting) material goods.]

220. The excellent studies by Eduard Bernstein should here again be emphasized (*op. cit.* [see note 10]). An opportunity will be available at another time to address Kautsky's extremely schematic presentation of the Anabaptist movement and his theory of "heretical communism" in general.

221. In his stimulating book, *The Theory of Business Enterprise* [New York: Scribner, 1904], Thorstein Veblen is of the opinion that this maxim belongs exclusively to the epoch of "early capitalism." Yet economic "supermen," who have stood beyond good and evil, have always existed [and did not follow this policy of honesty]. Indeed, the "captains of industry" today are no different from these supermen. This maxim—"honesty is the best policy"—is valid even today for the broad stratum, exhibiting capitalist conduct, just below these heroic figures.

222. [From *Maximen und Reflexionen,* edited by Max Hecker (Weimar, 1907, no. 207).] "In civil actions it is good to be *as the many,* in religious, to be as the best," as, for example, Thomas Adams notes (*Works of the Puritan Divines,* p. 138). Admittedly, this advice sounds somewhat more far-reaching than is actually meant. It implies that the Puritan candor constitutes a sort of *formalistic legality,* as does the claim gladly made by peoples with a Puritan heritage that "truthfulness" or "uprightness" is a national virtue. It is entirely *different,* re-fashioned in a formalistic and cognitive manner, from the German "honesty." Some good remarks on this theme, from the point

of view of an educator, can be found in the *Preussische Jahrbuch,* vol. 112 (1903): 226. [See also Henry James, *The Europeans* (New York: Penguin Books, 1974 (1878).] For its part, the *formalism* of the Puritan ethic is the entirely expected consequence of its tie to *God's law.*

223. Which will be somewhat examined in "The Protestant Sects" essay [that follows].

224. *Here* is to be found the reason for the acute effect upon economic action of (ascetic) Protestant (but not Catholic) *minority status.* [1920] [See chapter 1.]

225. The grounding of dogma, which varied widely, could be unified through a decisive interest in "testifying" to belief. The *ultimate* reason why this could occur is to be located in Christianity's religious-historical particular features in general. This reason is still to be discussed. [1920]

226. "Since God hath gathered us to be a people," as, for example, Barclay also states (*op. cit.*, p. 357). The Quaker sermon that I myself heard at Haverford College [Pennsylvania] placed the emphasis entirely upon the "saints" as separate from other believers.

Chapter V

1. For later examples, see the "Protestant Sects" essay below [sk].

2. These terms refer to Catholic Church documents that recorded the multiple ways in which guidance was offered by the church [sk].

3. Throughout this chapter, as well as earlier, Weber generally places this term in quotation marks in order to signify that national character must be understood as constructed from social forces (and religious forces in particular) rather than as a genetic predisposition. Weber's position stood in opposition to views in his time widespread in the political arena, as well as to major schools of scholarship. See the concluding pages of the "Prefatory Remarks" essay below [sk].

4. See the fine characterization of Baxter in Edward Dowden [*Puritan and Anglican* (ch. 4, note 23). His various works are reprinted in the Works of the Puritan Divines series [see note 6]. The introduction to them examines Baxter's theology in a reasonably satisfactory manner. Written by Jenkyn, it is oriented to his thinking after his gradual movement away from a strict belief in the "double decree."

Baxter's attempt to combine universal redemption and personal election had not pleased anyone. For our purposes it is only important *that* he nonetheless retained a belief in *personal* election. In other words, he held to the ethically crucial point in the predestination doctrine. On the other hand, because it indicates a certain convergence with the baptizing groups, his downplaying of the *forensic* conception of exculpation is important.

5. On St. Bartholomew's Day (August 24, 1572), which followed the marriage of the Protestant Henry of Navarre (later Henry IV) to a Catholic princess, thousands of French Protestants (Huguenots) were persecuted and murdered [sk].

6. Tracts and sermons by Thomas Adams, John Howe, Matthew Henry, J. Janeway, Stephen Charnock, Baxter, and Bunyan have been collected in the 10 volumes of the Works of the Puritan Divines (London: Nelson Publ., 1845–47). The selection is often somewhat arbitrary. Editions used of the works by Bayly, Sedgwick, and Hoornbeek have been noted above.

7. Works by Voët or other continental representative of this-worldly asceticism could have just as well been utilized. Brentano's view[*op. cit.*, ch. 1, note 15]—this development occurred "only among the Anglo-Saxons"—is completely erroneous. [1920]

The selection rests upon the wish to give expression, not exclusively but as much as possible, to the ascetic movement of the second half of the seventeenth century directly *before its turn into utilitarianism.* In light of the focus of this sketch, the stimulating task of illuminating the ascetic Protestant style of life in a further manner, namely through biographies, unfortunately must be abandoned. Exploring the case of the Quakers in particular, because relatively unknown in Germany, would be particularly worthwhile.

8. One could just as well take the writings of Gisbert Voët or the proceedings of the Huguenot synods or the literature from the Baptist movement in Holland. In a very unfortunate manner, Sombart and Brentano have emphasized precisely that "ebionitic" component [see note 10] in Baxter's writings (which I stressed myself) in order to confront my thesis with the undoubtedly

(capitalist) "backwardness" of his *doctrines*. However, one must *know* this entire literature very thoroughly in order to use it correctly. Furthermore, one should not overlook that I sought to demonstrate how, *despite doctrines* opposed to mammonism, the spirit of this ascetic *religious devotion* gave birth, just as in the businesses run by cloisters, to *economic rationalism*. This religious devotion did so because it *placed a psychological reward* upon what was crucial: rational *motivations* conditioned by asceticism. This alone mattered, and this is precisely the point of my entire essay. [1920]

9. This held in the same way for Calvin, who was certainly no enthusiast of middle class wealth. (See his sharp attacks on Venice and Antwerp; in *Jes. Opp.,* vol. 3, 140a, 308a.) [1920]

10. The Ebionite sect was founded in the first century in Jerusalem, with lineage tracing back to the apostles. Members believed that Judaic law was binding on Christians. As in the original Christian community, they idealized the poor and scorned wealth [sk].

11. *Saints' Everlasting Rest* [see ch. 4, note 62], chs. 10, 12. See Bayly (*Praxis pietatis, op. cit.* [ch. 4, note 32], p. 182) or Matthew Henry: "Those that are eager in pursuit of worldly wealth despise their Soul, not only because the Soul is neglected and the body preferred before it, but because it is employed in these pursuits"; see Ps. 127:2 ("The Worth of the Soul," in *Works of the Puritan Divines*, p. 319). (However, the remark on the sinfulness of the squandering of time, especially on recreations, is found on the *same page*; this remark will be cited later.) Similar commentaries are found throughout this literature, especially in English-Dutch Puritanism. See, for example, Hoornbeek's tirade against *avarice (op. cit.* [ch. 4, note 22], vol. 50, no. 10, chs. 18 and 19). (It should be noted that, in Hoornbeek's works, sentimental-Pietistic influences enter into his analysis; see his praise of the *tranquillitas animi* [silent soul] as more pleasing to God than the *sollicitudo* [activities] of the mundane world.) The same idea is apparent in Bayly when he remarks, paraphrasing the familiar passage from the Bible, "it is not easy for a rich man to become saved" (*op. cit.,* p. 182). The *Methodist* catechism also warns against "gathering treasures in this life." This idea is completely self-evident to Pietism, as it is for the Quakers. As Barclay states, ". . . and therefore beware of such temptations as to use their callings and engine *to be richer*" (*op. cit.* [ch. 4, note 210], p. 517).

12. Not only riches, but also the *obsessive pursuit of profit* (or what passes for it) was similarly severely condemned. This position became clear in the response to a question posed at the South Holland Synod of 1574: although the charging of interest for loans was legally permitted, its practitioners, the bankers from Lombardy, should not be allowed to attend communion. The Deventer Provincial Synod of 1598 (Article 24) expanded the decision to include the employees of the Lombard bankers, and the Synod of Gorichem in 1606 passed statutes according to which severe and humiliating conditions accompanied the admission of the wives of "usurers" to communion. Whether the Lombard bankers should be allowed to participate in communion was still discussed in 1644 and 1657. (This latter point contradicts Brentano, who offers the case of his Catholic ancestors as evidence for his argument, even though foreign-born traders and bankers have existed in the entire European-Asian world for millennia.) Even Gisbert Voët wanted to exclude the "Trapezites" (the bankers from Lombardy and Piedmont) from communion (see "De usuris," in *Selectae disputationes theologicae* [1667], p. 665). The Huguenot Synods took the same position. *These* types of capitalist strata were not at all the typical carriers of the frame of mind and organization of life of concern to this investigation. Moreover, these strata were, compared to the ancient and medieval worlds, not at all *new.* [1920]

13. This point is developed in the *Saints' Everlasting Rest* (ch. 10):

> He who should seek to rest in the 'shelter' of possessions which God gives, God strikes even in this life. A self-satisfied enjoyment of wealth already gained is almost always a symptom of moral degradation. If we had everything which we *could* have in this world, would that be all we hoped for? *Complete satisfaction of desires* is not attainable on earth because God's will has decreed it *should* not be so.

14. *Christian Directory, op. cit.* [ch. 4, note 39], vol. 1, pp. 375–76:

> It is for *action* that God maintaineth us and our activities; work is the moral as well as the natural *end of power*. . . . It is *action* that God is most served and honored by. . . . *The public welfare or the good of the many* is to be valued above our own.

Just at this point the point of departure for the transformation from the will of God to the purely utilitarian perspectives (see note 7) of classical [early nineteenth-century English] Liberalism becomes apparent. On the religious sources of Utilitarianism see below in the text and above (ch. 4, note 169).

15. The commandment of silence has been, beginning with the biblical threat of punishment for "every unnecessary word," namely, since the [Benedictine] monks of Cluny [981], a proven ascetic means of socialization toward self-control. Even Baxter goes into detail on the sinfulness of unnecessary speech. The significance of this development for the development of character has already been noted by Sanford (*op. cit.* [see ch. 4, note 5], pp. 90 ff.).

The "melancholy" and "moroseness" of the Puritans, so clearly perceived by contemporaries, was actually a consequence of the displacement of the *spontaneity* inherent to the *status naturalis.* The prohibition upon thoughtless speech served this purpose. Washington Irving in *Bracebridge Hall* (New York: Putnam, 1865) discovers the reason for this melancholy and moroseness in part in capitalism's "calculating spirit" and in part in the effect of political freedom, which leads to self-responsibility (ch. 30). It must be noted, however, that this melancholy and moroseness did not appear among the peoples of the Mediterranean [where a calculating, "practical rationalism" is widespread; see pp. 36–37]. The situation for the English was clearly different: (1) Puritanism enabled its adherents to develop free institutions and, nonetheless, to become a world power, and (2) Puritanism transformed that "calculatedness") (called by Sombart a "spirit"), which indeed is definitive for capitalism, from an instrument utilized in economic transactions into a *principle* for the entire organization of life.

16. Baxter, *op. cit.*, vol. 1, p. 111.

17. Baxter, *op. cit.*, vol. 1, pp. 383 f.

18. Similarly on the preciousness of time, see Barclay, *op. cit.,* p. 14.

19. Baxter, *op. cit.,* vol. 1, p. 79:

> Keep up a high esteem of time and be every day more careful that you lose none of your time, than you are that you lose none of your gold and silver. And if vain recreation, dressings, feastings, idle talk, unprofitable company, or sleep be any of them temptations to rob you of any of your time, accordingly heighten your watchfulness.

"Those that are prodigal of their time despise their own souls" says Matthew Henry ("Worth of the Soul," *Works of the Puritan Divines*, p. 315). Protestant asceticism is moving also here in its old tried and proven pathway. Today we are accustomed to observe that the modern professional "has no time" and to measure (as did even Goethe in his *Wilhelm Meister's Years of Travel*) the degree of capitalist development according to whether the *clocks* strike every quarter hour (as Sombart notes in his *Der moderne Kapitalismus*). We should not forget, however, that the first person who (in the Middle Ages) lived according to a *differentiated notion of time* was the *monk.* The church bells originally had to serve *his* need to measure time.

20. See Baxter's discussion of the calling (*Christian Directory, op. cit.*, vol. 1, pp. 108 ff.). These pages include the following passage:

> Question: But may I not cast off the world that I may only think of my salvation? Answer: You may cast off all such excess of worldly cares or business as unnecessarily hinder you in spiritual things. But you may not cast off all bodily employment and mental labor in which *you may serve the common good*. Everyone as a member of Church or Commonwealth must employ their parts to the utmost for the good of the Church and the Commonwealth. To neglect this and say: I will pray and meditate, is as if your servant should refuse his *greatest* work and tie himself to some lesser, easier part. And *God hath commanded* you some way or other to *labor for your daily bread and not to live as drones off of the sweat of others only*.

God's commandment to Adam—"in the sweat of your face you shall eat bread" [Gen. 3:19]—and the admonition of St. Paul ("If anyone will not work, let him not eat" [2 Thess. 3:10]) were also quoted. It has always been known that the Quakers always sent sons, and even those from the most wealthy families, to learn a vocation. (They did so for ethical reasons rather than, as Alberti recommends, for utilitarian reasons.) [1920; last par. only]

21. Pietism, on account of its *feeling* character, deviates from these points. Although Spener emphasizes, fully in keeping with the Lutheran meaning, that work in a calling is a *service to God*, he nonetheless contends (and even this is Lutheran) that the *commotion* in places of business has the effect of distracting the faithful from their orientation to God (see *Theologische Bedenken,* vol. 3, *op. cit.* [ch. 4, note 32], p. 445). This idea constitutes a highly characteristic contrast to Puritanism.

22. Baxter, *Chr. Dir.*, p. 242. "It's they that are lazy in their callings that can find no time for holy duties." This is the origin of the opinion that primarily the *cities*—the location of a middle class oriented to rational acquisition—are the location of the ascetic virtues. Accordingly, in his autobiography, Baxter says of his hand-loom weavers in Kidderminster: "And their constant *converse and traffic with London* doth much to promote civility and piety among tradesmen . . ." (selections in *Works of the Puritan Divines,* p. 38). The notion that proximity to a large city ought to have a positive influence upon virtue will be a great surprise to the clergy today, at least to the German clergy. Yet similar views are apparent even in Pietism, as is clear in Spener's occasional letters to a young colleague:

> At any rate, it is apparent that, although most inhabitants in cities of large populations are completely wicked, persons of good spiritual natures can occasionally be found. These persons can be depended upon to do good. In villages, in contrast, it is frequently the case that scarcely anything involving good spiritual activity can be found. (*Theologische Bedenken,* vol. I, sect. 66, *op. cit.,* p. 303)

Peasants are actually poorly suited for the ascetic and rationally organized life; their *ethical* glorification is quite modern. We cannot here examine the significance of this comment, as well as similar statements, in respect to the question of the extent to which asceticism is conditioned by *class*.

23. One could take, for example, the following passages:

> Be wholly taken up in diligent business of your lawful callings when you are not exercised in the more immediate service of God. Labor hard in your callings.
>
> See that you have a calling which will find you employment for all the time which God's immediate service spareth." (Baxter, *op. cit.,* pp. 336 f.)

24. That the specifically ethical valuation of work and its "dignity" was not one of the ideas that *originally* belonged to Christianity, or was even specific to Christianity, has been again recently emphasized sharply by [the theologian Adolf von] Harnack. See *Mitteilungen des Evangelischen-sozialen Kongresses*, vol. 14 (1905), no. 3/4, pp. 48 f.

25. It is the same also in Pietism (see Spener, *op. cit.,* vol. 3, pp. 429–30). For Pietism, characteristically, loyalty to a vocational calling, which has been imposed upon us on account of original sin, serves to *kill* the believer's own *will.* Work in a vocation is, as a service that expresses love of one's neighbor, a duty performed out of gratitude to God for his grace (a Lutheran idea!). For this reason God is not pleased when it is offered unwillingly and reluctantly (*op. cit.,* vol. 3, p. 272). Thus, the Christian should show himself "to be industrious in his work as any person engaged actively in the world" (*op. cit.,* vol. 3, p. 278). This Pietist motivation to work is clearly less developed than the Puritan outlook.

26. Only a far more comprehensive investigation would be able to explore the foundation upon which *this* important contrast rests. It exists apparently since the Benedictine dictum [Ora et labora (prayer and work)]. [1920]

27. According to Baxter, its purpose is "a sober procreation of children" (Gen. 9:1). [The Pietist] Spener is similar, although he makes concessions to the coarse Lutheran view according to which the avoidance of immorality is a secondary matter (and, in any case, for Luther immorality cannot be suppressed). Concupiscence, which is inherent to impregnation, even in marriage, is sinful. According to the view, for example, of Spener, concupiscence is a *consequence* of original sin, which transformed a natural and God-ordained process into something unavoidably interwoven with sinful sensations and hence into shamefulness. The highest form of Christian marriage, according to the view of some Pietist groups, preserves virginity. Ranking second is the type of marriage in which sexual intercourse serves exclusively to produce children. On the other end of the spectrum stands the marriage that occurs for purely erotic or purely external reasons—which, viewed ethically, constitutes concubinage. At these lower levels the marriage that exists for purely external rea-

sons (because, at any rate, such marriages arise out of *rational* considerations) is preferred over the marriage entered into for erotic considerations.

The theory and practice of the Herrnhuter should not be considered here. The rationalist philosophy ([of the philosopher and legal scholar] Christian Wolff [1679–1754]) adopted the ascetic theory, according to which what is ordained as *means* to an end—concupiscence and its satisfaction—should not be turned into an end *in itself*. The turn into a purely hygienic [health-oriented] utilitarianism has occurred already with Franklin, who took approximately the same ethical standpoint as the modern physician. Franklin defines "virtue" as the limitation of sexual intercourse to that which is desired *for health*. As is well-known, he even offered theoretical advice on the question of "how?" As soon as these matters are in general made the object of purely "rational" considerations, this turn into a hygienic utilitarianism everywhere began. The Puritan and the hygienic sexual-rationalist, who move along very different pathways, "comprehend each other immediately" on this particular point. [For example], in a lecture on the regulation of houses of prostitution, a zealous representative of "hygienic prostitution" defended the moral permissibility of "extra-marital sexual intercourse" (which was interpreted as *hygienically* useful) by noting its literary glorification in [Goethe's characters] *Faust and Margaret*. The treatment of Margaret as a prostitute and the equating of the powerful rule of human passions with sexual intercourse on behalf of one's health—all this corresponds *thoroughly* to the Puritan position.

This connection to the Puritan point of view is also evident, for example, in the genuinely specialist viewpoint occasionally upheld by very prominent physicians. They argue, namely, that the question of the significance of sexual abstinence, which penetrates into the most subtle problems of the personality and cultural milieu, belongs "exclusively" in a forum of physicians (as the *specialists* on this subject). While the moral person was the "specialist" for the Puritans [those who work in vocational callings], he has now become the hygienic [medical] theorist. However, it should be noted that the resolution of questions and issues by reference to the principle of specialized "competence," which appears to us today rather provincial, is common to both cases (although the direction has been reversed [in the one case toward the moral, in the other toward the utilitarian]).

Yet, and despite its developed prudery, the powerful idealism of the Puritan view could demonstrate favorable results. This is the case if Puritanism is viewed from the perspective of the preservation of the boundaries of races and if examined purely in terms of the "hygiene" it introduced. On the other hand, the modern sexual hygiene movement, on account of the call for a "lack of prejudice" which it must make, runs the risk of destroying the very foundation [the moral] on which it rests.

How, in the end, a refinement of the marital relationship, its penetration by a spiritual-ethical dimension, and a blossoming of matrimonial chivalry indeed arose out of this rational understanding of sexual relations among those peoples influenced by Puritanism must be omitted here. This development stands in contrast to the patriarchal bluster in Germany that has expanded, even in the form of frequently perceptible residues, into circles of the intellectual elite. This theme likewise cannot be considered here. (Influences from the baptizing groups have played a role in the "emancipation" of women. The protection of women's *freedom of conscience* and the extension of the "universal priesthood" idea to include women were in these groups the first breakthroughs against patriarchalism.)

28. This idea appears repeatedly in Baxter. Support in the Bible is regularly found either in those passages well-known to us from Franklin (Prov. 22:29) or the praise of work in Proverbs (31:16). See Baxter, *op. cit.*, vol. 1, pp. 377, 382, *et passim*.

29. Even Zinzendorf says occasionally: "One doesn't work alone in order to live; rather, one lives owing to the wish to work. If one must work no longer, then one suffers or dies." (Plitt, vol. 1, *op. cit.*, p. 428).

30. [2 Thess. 3:10] Even a symbol of the Mormons closes (according to quotations) with the words: "But a lazy or indolent man cannot be a Christian and be saved. He is destined to be struck down and cast from the hive." Nevertheless, it was in this case primarily the grandiose discipline, which held a middle position between the cloister and the factory, that presented the person with the choice to either work or perish. It was this discipline, *bound up* of course with religious enthusiasm

and made possible *only through it*, that brought forth the amazing economic achievements of these sects.

31. Hence, its manifestations are carefully analyzed by Baxter (*Chr. Dir.*, vol. I, *op. cit.*, p. 380). "Sloth" and "idleness" are *therefore* such burdensome sins because they have the character of being continuous. Baxter sees them as the "destroyers of one's state of grace" (vol. 1, *op. cit.*, pp. 279–80). They are the diametrical opposite of the *methodical* life.

32. See above, ch. 3, note 6.

33. Baxter, *Chr. Dir.*, vol. 1, *op. cit.*, pp. 108 ff. The following passage strikes one immediately. "Question: But will not wealth excuse us? Answer: It may excuse you from some sordid sort of work by making you more serviceable to another, but you are no more excused from the service of work . . . than the poorest man." Also: "Though they [the rich] have no outward want to urge them, they have as great a necessity to obey God. . . . God hath strictly commanded it (labor) to all" (vol. 1, *op. cit.*, p. 376). See ch. 4, note 57.

34. Similarly, Spener (vol. 3, *op. cit.*), pp. 338, 425. For this reason, he opposes as morally troubling the tendency of persons to retire early. Moreover, he emphasizes (in rejecting an objection to the legality of taking interest, namely, that living off interest leads to laziness) that even those able to live off interest are nonetheless, according to God's commandment, *obligated* to work.

35. Including Pietism. Spener takes the position, as concerns the question of a *change* of vocation, that, once work in a particular vocation has commenced, a continuation of and devotion to it is a duty of obedience vis-à-vis God's predestination.

36. On Scholasticism, see ch. 3, note 9.

37. With what high pathos, which dominates the entire organization of life, the salvation doctrine of India [Hinduism] connects vocational traditionalism with prospects for a favorable rebirth, is explored in the essays in the Economic Ethics of the World Religions series [see *The Religion of India* (New York: Free Press, 1958)]. Precisely through such an example one can become acquainted with the difference between merely an ethical, *doctrinal* concept and the creation, through religion, of psychological *motivations* of a specific type. The pious Hindu could acquire favorable rebirth prospects *only* through a strict, *traditional* fulfillment of the duties associated with the caste into which he was born. This constituted the most rigid religious anchoring of economic traditionalism that can be conceived. In fact, in this respect the ethic of India is actually the most consistent antithesis to the Puritan ethic, just as it is, in a different respect (status traditionalism) the most consistent antithesis to Judaism. [1920]

38. Baxter, *Chr. Dir.*, vol. 1, *op. cit.*, p. 377.

39. But this does not imply that the utilitarian motivation can be historically derived out of these points of view. On the contrary, more so manifest is an entirely central Calvinist idea: the cosmos of the "world" serves the majesty of God and his self-glorification. The utilitarian turn, namely, that the economic cosmos should serve the common good (good of the many, etc.), was a result of the idea that every other interpretation would lead to the deification of human wants and desires (an idea closely associated with the aristocracy) or, at any rate, to a serving of human "cultural ends" [everything that is created by and for human beings] rather than God's glory. However, God's will, as expressed in the purposeful formation of the economic cosmos (see ch. 4, note 43), can only be, at least to the extent that *this*-worldly ends at all come into consideration, the well-being of the "whole community"; that is, *im*personal "usefulness." Hence, as noted earlier, [classical] utilitarianism is a result of the *im*personal formulation of the "love thy neighbor" commandment and the rejection of all glorification of this world that followed from the Puritan's exclusive earthly purpose: *in majorem Dei gloriam* [to serve the greater glory of God].

That every glorification of human nature violates God's glory and is therefore unconditionally reprehensible is an idea that dominates all of ascetic Protestantism. Just how intensively it does so is revealed overtly in the hesitation and pain experienced even by Spener, a man surely without "democratic" proclivities, as he maintained usage of *titles* ἀδι ἄφορον [because he saw this issue as matter of indifference to the church] in the face of numerous objections. In the end he comforted himself with the knowledge that even in the Bible [Porcius] Festus [the procurator of Judea, 60–62], was given the title κράτιστος [Excellency] by the apostles. [The use of titles, Weber is noting, in calling attention to persons, involves to ascetic Protestants self-glorification (see above paragr.) and hence in sublimated form a deification of the human species.] The *political* side of this issue does not belong in this context.

40. "The *inconstant* man is a stranger in his own house," is said also by Thomas Adams (*Works of the Puritan Divines,* p. 77).

41. On this theme see, in particular, George Fox's remarks in the *Friends' Library,* edited by W. & Thomas Evans, vol. 1 (Philadelphia, 1837), p. 130.

42. Clearly, this turn of the religious ethic of course cannot be seen as a reflection of the actual economic conditions. Vocational specialization was far further developed in Italy than in England in the Middle Ages. [1920]

43. For God, as is frequently emphasized in the Puritan literature, nowhere ordered that one's neighbor should be loved *more* than oneself. Rather, he commanded the love of one's neighbor *as* one loves oneself. Hence, the *duty* to love oneself is apparent. Whoever knows, for example, how to utilize his property in a more efficient manner than his neighbor, and thus in a way that better serves God's honor, is not duty-bound, owing to his love of his neighbor, to convey this useful knowledge to him.

44. Spener's thinking also comes close to this position. Nonetheless, he remains, even in the example of a change from the vocation of businessman (which is morally especially dangerous) to the vocation of theologian, quite hesitant and generally opposed (see *Theologische Bedenken,* vol. 3, *op. cit.,* pp. 435, 443; vol. 1, p. 524). The frequent appearance of the answer to precisely *this* question (regarding the permissibility of changing one's vocation) in Spener's unsurprisingly tendentious writing on this theme shows, by the way, how the various interpretations of 1 Corinthians 7 were eminently *practical*, relating directly to everyday circumstances.

45. These ideas, at least in their writings, are *not* found in the leading continental Pietists. The position of Spener in regard to "profit" vacillates between Lutheran (the "livelihood" standpoint) and mercantilist arguments on the usefulness of, for example, the *Flors der Commerzien* [prosperity of commerce] (see vol. 3, *op. cit.,* pp. 330, 332; vol. 1, p. 418). The *cultivation of tobacco* brings money into the country and is *therefore* useful; that is, *hence*, not sinful (see vol. 3, pp. 426–27, 429, 434)! However, his writings do not fail to note that, as is apparent from the example of the Quakers and Mennonites, one can make profits and still remain pious—and that especially large profits (as we will have occasion later to note) can be a direct *consequence* of pious uprightness (*op. cit.,* p. 435).

46. These views of Baxter are *not* merely a reflection of the economic milieu in which he lived. His autobiography stresses the *opposite*: the success of his domestic missionary work was in part owing to the fact that the merchants who lived in [his home town] Kidderminster were *not* wealthy (rather, they earned only "food and raiment") and that the master craftsmen had to live, in a manner no better than their workers, "from hand to mouth." "It is *the poor* who receive the glad tidings of the Gospel."

Thomas Adams remarks on the striving for profit: "He (the knowing man) knows . . . that money may make a man richer, not better, and thereupon chooseth rather to sleep with a good conscience than a full purse . . . therefore desires no more wealth *than an honest man may bear away.*" Yet *he does want this amount* (Adams, *Works of the Puritan Divines,* vol. 51). And this means that every formally *honest* earning is also *legitimate.*

47. Thus Baxter (*Chr. Dir.*, vol. 1, *op. cit.,* ch. 10, pt. 1, ch. 9, par. 24: "Weary thyself not to be rich" (vol. 1, p. 378, column 2; see Prov. 23:4) means only "riches for our fleshly ends must not ultimately be intended." Possession, in the feudal-seigneurial form of *use*, is actually what is odious (see the remark on the "debauched part of the gentry"; vol. 1, *op. cit.,* p. 380), not possession *as such.* Milton, in his first *Defensio pro populo Anglicano* [Defense of the Anglican Peoples], upheld the well-known theory that only the "middle stratum" (*Mittelstand*) can be a social carrier of *virtue.* It must be noted that he here means a middle stratum in the sense of a "class oriented to work and business" (*bürgerliche Klasse*), and he is contrasting this group to the "aristocracy." His explanation clarifies that he is referring to just this distinction, namely, when he notes that both "luxury" [the aristocracy] and "necessity" [the destitute] hinder the exercise of virtue.

48. *This* is what is pivotal. To this statement should be added, once again, the general comment: whatever theology-oriented ethical theory developed conceptually is naturally for us not the important matter. Rather, central here is the question of what morality was *valid* in the *practical* life of believers. In other words, our concern involves the question of *how* believers' religious orientation exercised a practical *effect* upon their vocational ethic. One can read, at least occasionally, discussions in Catholicism's casuistic literature (namely, the Jesuit) that sound similar to the many casuistic discussions in the Protestant literature (for example, on the question of the permissibility of usury, which we cannot address here). Indeed, in respect to that which is understood as "allowed" or "probable," the Protestants appear to have moved beyond the Catholic positions. (The Puritan position was frequently criticized later on as basically the same as the Jesuit ethic.) Just as Calvinists were concerned to cite Catholic moral theologians, and not only Thomas of Aquinas, Bernhard von Clairvaux [*ca.* 1090–1153], and Bonaventure [1221–74], but also their contemporaries, so also Catholic casuistic thinkers regularly attended to the heretical ethic's development (though this as well cannot be further examined here).

Nonetheless, leaving aside the central placing of religious *rewards*, by ascetic Protestants, upon an ascetic life for the *laity*, a massive distinction is apparent even in theory: in Catholicism these latitudinal [broad and liberal] views were a product of especially *lax* ethical theories not approved by church authorities and from which the most sincere and strict adherents of the church distanced themselves. The Protestant idea of a vocational calling, on the other hand, placed the striving for success of precisely the *most sincere* adherents of the ascetic life in the service of a capitalist earning of one's livelihood. That which in the one case could be conditionally *allowed*, appeared in the other case as a positive moral *good*. These foundational differences in the two ethics, which were very important for the *practical* life of believers, have been conclusively defined, even for the modern period, since the controversy over Jansenism [1641–1705; ch. 4, note 153] and the Bull *Unigenitus* [of 1713 against Jansenism].

49. "You may labor in that manner as tendeth most to your success and lawful gain. You are *bound* to improve all your talents." This passage [from Baxter] follows the passage cited in the text above [see note 47]. For a discussion that draws a direct parallel between the striving for riches in God's kingdom and the striving after success in an earthly vocation, see, for example, James Janeway, *Heaven upon Earth* (in *Works of the Puritan Divines,* p. 275).

50. A protest against the *oath* of poverty is rendered already in the (Lutheran) confession of Duke Christopher of Württemberg [1515–1568], which was submitted to the Council of Trent [1545–1563]: those who are poor according to their stratum should tolerate their situation; however, for the poor to vow to *remain* poor is the same as vowing to be continuously sick or to have a *bad reputation.*

51. This is clear in Baxter and also in Duke Christopher's confession. Further, see passages such as: ". . . the vagrant rogues whose lives are nothing but an exorbitant course; the main begging," etc. (Thomas Adams, *Works of the Puritan Divines,* p. 259).

Already Calvin strictly prohibited begging, and the Dutch Synods declaimed against begging letters and certificates for begging purposes. [These letters allowed itinerant preachers to offer sermons in the churches of a specific region. Afterwards, donations would be requested. The preacher was permitted to retain these funds for his organization (perhaps a monastery). Because those who donated were in turn offered salvation, the begging-letter system worked quite well. However, the work ethic of the Puritans diametrically opposed this mode of raising funds.] During the reign of the Stuarts, and especially the regime of [William] Laud under Charles I [1635–44; see note 122], when the principle of public support for the poor and of governmental allocation of work to the unemployed was systematically formulated, the battle-cry of the Puritans was: "Giving alms is no charity." (This became the title of a later well-known work by Daniel Defoe.) The deterrent system, the "workhouses" for the unemployed, developed out of this precedent near the end of the seventeenth century. See E. M. Leonard, *Early History of English Poor Relief* (Cambridge, 1900 [London: Frank Cass, 1965]) and Hermann Levy, *Die Grundlagen des ökonomischen Liberalismus in der Geschichte der englischen Volkswirtschaft* (Jena, 1912), pp. 69 ff., *op. cit.* [ch. 3, note 17]. [1920]

52. In his inaugural address before the assembly in London in 1903, the President of the Baptist Union of Great Britain and Ireland, G. White, emphasized: "The best men on the roll of our Puritan Churches were *men of affairs*, who believed that religion should permeate the whole of life" (*Baptist Handbook,* 1904, p. 104).

53. [Weber used the English expression "self-made man."] Just *at this point* the characteristic contrast to all outlooks rooted in feudalism becomes apparent. According to the feudal conception of things, the benefits of the parvenu's (political or social) success and sacred blood can be reaped only by the descendants. (This is characteristically expressed in the Spanish *Hidalgo [parvenu]* = *hijo d'algo* = *filius de aliquo;* the *aliquid* refers directly to *wealth* that is inherited from ancestors.)

In the United States today, in view of the rapid transformation and Europeanization of the American "national character," these distinctions are rapidly fading. Nonetheless, the specifically middle-class outlook *diametrically opposed* to feudalism is still today occasionally apparent. This outlook glorifies business *success* and *acquisition* as a symptom of spiritual *achievement* and cannot muster respect for mere (inherited) *wealth* as such. In contrast, in Europe money can in effect purchase almost every social honor (as James Bryce [the author of *The American Commonwealth*, 1888], already once remarked)—if only its owner has not *himself* stood behind the counter and the necessary metamorphosis of his wealth is executed (through the formation of trusts, etc.). *Against* the feudal view that the *blood* bond is an honorable one, see, for example, Thomas Adams, *Works of the Puritan Divines* (*op. cit.*), p. 216.

54. This held, for example, already for the founder of the Familist sect, Hendrik Nicklaes [*ca* 1501–1580], who was a merchant. See Barclay, *Inner Life of the Religious Societies of the Commonwealth, op. cit* [ch. 4, note 22], p. 34. [Members of the Familist sect (f. in 1530 in Amsterdam) believed themselves to be the true children of God who have overcome sin; direct predecessors of the Quakers]

55. Weber is here alluding to a wrathful, vengeful, distant God, all-knowing and omnipotent [sk].

56. Hoornbeek, for example, firmly draws this conclusion because also Matt. 5:5 and 1 Tim. 4:8 made promises for the saints that concerned purely earthly matters (see vol. 1, *op. cit.* [ch. 4, note 22], p. 193). Everything is a product of God's providence. Yet he especially cares for His saints: "Super alios autem summa cura et modis singularissimis versatur Dei providentia circa fideles" [Above and beyond the others is to be found God's providence, offering the greatest care, and in an unusual manner, to believers] (*ibid.*, p. 192).

There then follows the explanation of how one can recognize that a fortunate occurrence derives from this special care *and not* from a *communis providentia* [common ordering of the world]. Bayly also refers to God's predestination to explain success in one's vocational work (*op. cit.* [ch. 4, note 32], p. 191). And the notion that prosperity "often" is the reward for a godly life is perpetually found in the writings of the *Quakers*. See, for example, such passages even as late as 1848 in *Selection from the Christian Advices,* issued by the yearly meeting of the Society of Friends in London, 6th ed. (London, 1851), p. 209. The connection to Quaker ethics will be returned to later.

57. Thomas Adams's analysis of the conflict between Jacob and Esau can serve as an example of this orientation to the Old Testament patriarchs. It is equally characteristic of the Puritan view of life: "His (Esau's) folly may be argued from the base estimation of the birthright that he would so lightly pass from it and on *so easy condition* as a pottage [thick soup]."(*Works of the Puritan Divines,* p. 235; the passage is also important for the development of the idea of birthright, which will be noted later). However, that Esau then wished to call the sale invalid, on account of fraud, was perfidious. Rather, he is "a cunning hunter, a man of the fields," and a person living irrationally and without civility. Jacob, on the other hand, represents "a plain man, dwelling in tents" and the "man of grace."

The sense of an inner relationship between Puritanism and Judaism, as expressed as late as the well-known writings of Theodore Roosevelt [see *Economy and Society*, p. 923], was discovered by Köhler to be widespread in Holland even among peasants (*op. cit.* [ch. 4, note 10]). On the other hand Puritanism, in regard to its practical dogma, was well aware of its *opposition* to Jewish ethics [see *Economy and Society*, pp. 615–23]. This is clearly demonstrated in the essay by Prynne against the Jews (on the occasion of the Cromwellian proposals for tolerance). See note 124 below. [1920]

58. Those books in the Greek and Latin versions of the Old Testament that were not originally written in Hebrew. Not considered genuine by the Jews, they were also denigrated by early Reformation theologians. Translations of the Bible influenced by ascetic Protestantism (the King James Version of 1611, the American Standard Version of 1901, and the Revised Standard Version of 1952) omitted these books (unlike the translation by Luther) [sk].

59. A rural Thuringian pastor published *Zur bäuerlichen Glaubens- und Sittenlehre* [On Peasant Beliefs and Moral Teachings], 2nd ed. (Gotha, 1890), p. 16. The peasants depicted in this volume are, in a characteristic manner, products of the *Lutheran* Church. I have repeatedly written "Lutheran" in its margins where the excellent author assumed a general "peasant" devoutness.

60. Compare, for example, the passage cited in Ritschl, *Pietismus,* vol. 2 (*op. cit.* [ch. 4, note 19]), p. 158. Spener likewise bases his objections to a change of vocational calling and to the pursuit of profit *partly* on passages from Jesus Sirach. *Theologische Bedenken,* vol. 3 (*op. cit.* [ch. 4, note 32]), p. 426.

61. Of course, nonetheless, Bayly, for example, recommends its reading. He does quote from the Apocrypha, at least here and there, although rarely of course. I cannot (perhaps accidentally) recall any such quotation from Jesus Sirach.

62. When the obviously condemned are then allotted external success, the Calvinist comforts himself (according to Hoornbeek, for example), in accordance with the "theory of hardening," with the certainty that God allows this success to come to them in order to harden them and hence to condemn them with all the more certainty.

63. In this context we cannot examine this point in more detail. Of interest here is only the formalistic character of Puritan "legal correctness." There is a great deal in [Ernst] Troeltsch's "social teachings" on the significance of the Old Testament ethics for *lex naturae* [*The Social Teachings of the Christian Churches* (New York: Harper, 1960/1911)].

64. The obligatory character of the Bible's ethical norms is so encompassing in nature that, according to Baxter, they must be seen (1) as a "transcript" of the law of nature or (2) as actually carrying the "express character of universality and perpetuity". See *Christian Directory,* vol. 3 *op. cit.* [ch. 4, note 39], pp. 173 f.)

65. Dowden, for example (with reference to Bunyan). [See the later edition, *op. cit.* (ch. 4, note 23), pp. 26–34.]

66. On the economic ethic of Judaism, see Max Weber, *Economy and Society*, pp. 611–23; and *Ancient Judaism* (New York: Free Press, 1952). Weber is here opposing in particular Sombart's argument that the Jews were the driving force behind the development of modern capitalism. See pp. xxiii above and Sombart, *The Jews and Modern Capitalism* (New York: Burt Franklin, 1969) [sk].

67. More details are offered on this point in my Economic Ethics of the World Religions series [see pp. lviii–lxiv]. The vast influence of these norms, and of the *second commandment* in particular ("thou shalt not make unto thee a graven image") on, for example, the characterological development of Judaism—its rational character foreign to all culture oriented to the senses—cannot be analyzed here. Nonetheless, perhaps as characteristic, it may be noted that one of the leaders of the "Educational Alliance" in the United States—an organization that furthers the Americanization of Jewish immigrants with amazing success and munificent resources—described the primary purpose of its cultural acquisition program (*Kulturmenschwerdung*) to me, which is pursued through all manner of artistic and social instruction, as the "emancipation from the second commandment." The tabooing of all anthropomorphic rendering of God in human form among the Israelites corresponds to Puritanism's prohibition upon all deification of human wants and desires; although somewhat different, the effect is nonetheless in a related direction.

As concerns Talmudic Judaism, even principal features of Puritan morality are certainly related. The Talmud emphasizes, for example (as noted by August Wünsche, *Babylonische Talmud, 1886–89,* vol. 2, p. 34), that it is better, and more rewarded by God, if one does something good because of a *duty* to God's law than if one performs a good deed *not* obligated by God's law. In other words, loveless fulfillment of duty stands ethically higher than emotion-infused philanthropy. And, in essence, Puritan ethics would accept this. Kant, as well, who descended from Scots and whose socialization was strongly influenced by Pietism, would in the end come close to these passages. (Many of his formulations tie in directly to ideas of ascetic Protestantism—but this cannot be discussed here.) Talmudic ethics were, however, also once deeply immersed in the traditionalism of the Middle East. As R. Tanchum said to Ben Chanilai: "A person never changes a custom" (Gemara to Mischna; vol. 7, pt. i, sect. 86b, no. 93; cited in Wünsche, *ibid.*; the context concerns the boarding costs of day laborers). This maxim was not valid in relationships with persons outside one's own blood group. However, the Puritan conception of "legal correctness" as a means of *testifying* to sincere belief provided, when compared to the Jewish obligation simply to fulfill the commandment, visibly stronger motives for *activity*.

Of course, the idea that one's success revealed God's blessing is not totally foreign to Judaism. Yet the variation in fundamental religious-ethical meaning that success assumed in Judaism as a consequence of its ethical dualism (according to which relations with non-Jews were not bound to the same ethical standards as relations with Jews) prevented, in regard to this decisive point, a similarity of effects. What was *permitted* in regard to the "outsider" was *prohibited* in regard to one's "brother." It was impossible (for this reason alone) for success in the arena of the "not commanded" but "permitted" to become a sign that testified to *religious* belief. Hence, a motivation for the methodical formation of life in every respect, as occurred with the Puritans, could not arise. On this entire problem, which Sombart has in many ways incorrectly addressed in his *The Jews and Modern Capitalism* [New York: Burt Franklin, 1969/1911], see [the Economic Ethics of the World Religions series]. As strange as it first sounds, Judaism's economic ethic remained very strongly traditionalistic. [1920]

Christianity implied a massive alteration of the believer's inner posture toward the world. This change occurred through the Christian version of the ideas of "grace" and "salvation." In peculiar ways, the seed for *new* possibilities of development was continuously borne within these ideas. Likewise, this theme cannot yet be explored. See also, for example, Albrecht Ritschl on Old Testament "legal correctness," *Die christliche Lehre von der Rechtfertigung und Versöhnung,* vol. 2 [Bonn: A. Marcus, 1870–74], p. 265.

The Jews, to the English Puritans, represented that type of capitalism oriented to war, government subsidy programs, state monopolies, the speculative promotion of companies, and the construction and finance projects of princes. Just these sorts of business activities were roundly condemned by the Puritans. Indeed, if we keep constantly in mind the unavoidable qualifications, the general difference can be formulated in this manner: Jewish capitalism was a speculative, *pariah*-capitalism, while Puritan capitalism involved the organization of work by a middle class. [1920] [See *Economy and Society*, pp. 615–23.]

68. For Baxter, the *truth* of Holy Scripture follows ultimately from the "wonderful difference of the godly and ungodly," the absolute difference of the "renewed man" from others, and the evident, entirely unusual care of God for the salvation of the soul of His people (which naturally *can* be expressed in *testing*). See *Christian Directory,* vol. 1 (*op. cit.*), p. 165, col. 2.

69. What characterizes this mood of life can be seen if only we read Bunyan's account of his inner torture when reconciling himself to the parable of the Pharisee and the publican [collector of customs] (see the sermon *The Pharisee and the Publican, op. cit.* [ch. 4, note 83], pp. 100 f.). Even with Bunyan there can occasionally be found an approximation to Luther's mood in Luther's *Freiheit eines Christenmenschen*; see, for example, Bunyan's "Of the Law and a Christian" in *Works of the Puritan Divines,* p. 254).

Why is the Pharisee condemned? He does not truly uphold God's commandments; rather, as clearly a *sectarian*, he is concerned only with ceremonies and external matters of little significance (p. 107). Most importantly, he is condemned because he attributes merit to himself but still thanks God for his virtue. He does so "as the Quakers do," by misusing God's name. In sinful ways, he relies on the value of his virtue (p. 126) and thus implicitly rejects *God's predestination* (p. 139). His prayer, therefore, involves a deification of human nature, and this constitutes its sinfulness.

On the other hand, as the sincerity of his confession demonstrates, the publican is spiritually reborn, for—as expressed in a manner that reveals the characteristic Puritan weakening of the Lutheran feeling of sin—"to a right and sincere conviction of sin there must be a conviction of the *probability* of mercy" (p. 209).

70. Printed, for example, in S. R. Gardiner's *Constitutional Documents.* One may draw parallels between this struggle against (anti-authoritarian) asceticism to, for example, Louis XIV's persecution of the Port Royal settlement and the Jansenists [see ch. 4, notes 23 and 153].

71. In this respect the standpoint of *Calvin* was significantly milder, at least to the extent that the finer aristocratic forms of enjoying life were considered. The only limitation is the Bible. The person who stays oriented to it and maintains a good conscience is not required to be suspicious, amidst anxiety, of every stirring in himself to enjoy life. The discussions, which belong here, in chapter 10 of Calvin's *Institio christianae religionis* (for example, "nec fugere ea quoque possumus quæ videntur oblectatione magis quam necessitate inservire" [we cannot flee from those things that clearly serve pleasure more than necessity]), might have alone been able to open the floodgates to a very lax praxis. Nonetheless, the distinction between Calvin and Puritanism at this point becomes clear. In addition to an increasing anxiety among the Puritans in regard to the *certitudo salutis* question, it is also the case that, as we will appreciate fully elsewhere, members of the lower *middle-class* became the social carriers of the ethical development of Calvinism in the *ecclesia militans* [militant church] regions.

72. As was common in the German scholarship of his day, Weber here (in contrast to the Anglo-Saxon division between the humanities and the natural sciences) includes in "science," in addition to the natural sciences, literature, history, and languages (the "humanities") [sk].

73. Thomas Adams (*Works of the Puritan Divines,* p. 3) begins a sermon on the "three divine sisters" ("but love is the greatest of these") with the remark that even Paris gave the golden apple to Aphrodite!

74. Novels and the like, considered as "wastetimes," should not be read (Baxter, *Christian Directory,* vol. 1, p. 51). The decline of lyric poetry and folk music, and not only drama, after the Elizabethan Age in England is well-known. Puritanism did not discover all that much to oppress in the realm of the visual arts. Striking, however, is the decline, from a very good level of musical talent (the role of England in the history of music was not insignificant), to that absolute nothingness in respect to musical giftedness that we later observe among the Anglo-Saxon peoples, and even today. In America, except for the singing in the Negro churches and for the professional singers, who the churches now hire as "attractions" (for $8,000 annually in 1904 in Trinity Church in Boston), one hears mostly "congregational singing"—a noise that is intolerable to German ears. (*Partly* analogous developments appeared also in Holland.)

75. As the proceedings of the synods make clear, the same occurred in Holland. See the resolutions on the may pole in the Reitsma'schen Collection, vol. 6, pt. 78, ch. 139. [J. Reitsma and S.D. van Veen, *Acta der Provinciale en Particuliere Synoden, 1572–1620*, 8 vols. (Groningen, 1892–99); the may pole celebration involved a tall, fixed pole. Dancers on May Day, each holding a ribbon attached to the top of the pole, danced around the pole, weaving the ribbons.]

76. It is apparent that the "Renaissance of the Old Testament" and the Pietist orientation to certain Christian sensibilities in art antagonistic to beauty, which in the last analysis refer back to Isaiah [Verse 53] and the 22nd Psalm, must have contributed to making *ugliness* more of a possible object of art. It is also evident that, in regard to this development, the Puritan rejection of the deification of human wants and desires played a part. All details, however, appear uncertain. Entirely different motives (demagogical) in the Catholic church brought about developments that, although externally related, led artistically to an entirely different conclusion. Whoever stands in front of Rembrandt's "Saul and David" (in the Mauritshuis museum) believes he directly experiences the powerful effect of the Puritan sensibility. The inspired analysis of Dutch cultural influences in Karl Neumann's *Rembrandt* (Berlin and Stuttgart, [1924] 1902) probably demarcates the extent to which one *can*, as of today, know the extent to which creative effects in the realm of art can be attributed to ascetic Protestantism.

77. In Holland, a diverse number of pivotal causes (which are impossible to delve into here) were decisive for a comparatively lesser penetration of the Calvinist ethic into everyday life and for a weakening of the ascetic spirit. This situation was visible as early as the beginning of the seventeenth century (the English Congregationalists who fled to Holland in 1608 believed the Dutch sabbath to inadequately uphold the "day of rest" decree); however, it became widely apparent under

the [provincial military governor] Friedrich Heinrich [1584–1640]. This decline of the ascetic spirit weakened the expansionary thrust of Dutch Puritanism generally.

The causes for this decline must be located in part in the political constitution (a decentralized federalism of cities and states) and in part in Holland's far lesser development of military forces. (The War of Independence [against Spain, 1568–1648] was early on, for the most part, fought with *money* from Amsterdam and by mercenary soldiers; English preachers illustrated the confusion of tongues among the Babylonians by reference to the Dutch army.) The result was clear: the fervor surrounding the conflict over religious belief was, to a great degree, shifted onto others. As a consequence, however, the chance for participation in political power was flittered away. In contrast, Cromwell's army, although in part conscripted, felt itself to be an army of *citizens*. (To be sure, even more characteristic is that *precisely this* army abolished conscription—because one should fight only for the glory of God and for a cause recognized by the conscience, and not to satisfy the moods of princes. Hence, that English military referred to, according to traditional German views, as possessing an "unethical" constitution, had *historically* very ethical motives at its beginning. Their implementation was demanded by soldiers who had never lost a battle. The ethical values of these soldiers were placed into service in the interest of the Crown only after the Restoration [after 1665].)

As visible in the paintings of [Frans] Hals [1580–1666], the Dutch *schutterijen* [militia], the social carriers of Calvinism in the period of the Great War [1568–1648], appear scarcely "ascetic" as early as one-half generation after the Dordrecht Synod [1574]. Protests in the synods against the organized lives of the *schutterijen* are found repeatedly. The Dutch notion of stiff, haughty formality [*deftigheid*—Weber used a German amalgam: *Deftigkeit*] is a mixture of middle class, rational "respectability" and patrician consciousness of status. This aristocratic character of the Dutch church is evident even today in the allocation of church pews according to class.

The endurance of the city economy in Holland inhibited the development of industry, which expanded only when a new wave of refugees appeared—and therefore only sporadically. Nevertheless, the this-worldly asceticism of Calvinism and Pietism proved effective also in Holland, and in entirely the same direction as elsewhere (even in the sense of an "ascetic compulsion to save," as will be discussed immediately and as G. Groen van Prinsterer demonstrated; see the passage referred to in note 97). The almost entire absence of a belletristic literature in Calvinist Holland is naturally not accidental. [1920]

On Holland see, for example, C. Busken-Huet, *Het Land van Rembrandt*; see also von der Ropp, *Rembrandts Heimat* (Leipzig, 1886–1987).

The understanding of Dutch religious devoutness as involving an "ascetic compulsion to save" is quite apparent even in the eighteenth century; see, for example, the drawings of Albertus Haller. On the characteristic features of Dutch evaluations of art and the motives behind its production, see, for example, the autobiographical remarks of Constantine Huyghens (written 1629–31) in *Oud Holland* (1891). (The work of Groen van Prinsterer, *La Hollande et l'influence de Calvin,* [1864], offers for *our* problem nothing pivotal.) The New-Netherlands colony in [New York] involved, viewed in terms of its social composition, a quasi-feudal rulership by "patrons," namely, businessmen who were money-lenders. In contrast to New England, it proved difficult to persuade those near the bottom to emigrate to this region. [1920]

78. It should be remembered that the Puritan city officials closed the Stratford-on-Avon-theater even during Shakespeare's time and even when he was, in his later years, still living in Stratford. (His hatred and contempt for the Puritans comes to the surface at every opportunity.) Even in 1777 the city of Birmingham refused to license a theater, arguing that it would promote "slothfulness" and thus adversely influence commerce. See W. J. Ashley, *Birmingham Industry and Commerce* (London, 1913), pp. 7–8. [1920]

79. It is decisive that, for the Puritans, also in this case only an either-or alternative existed: either God's will or the vanity of the flesh. Thus, there could not be, for them, an "Adiaphora" situation [of indifference]. Calvin, as mentioned, in this regard took a different position: as long as an enslavement of the soul under the power of the desires does not take place, what one eats, wears, etc. is a matter of indifference. Freedom from the "world" should be expressed, as for the Jesuits, in indifference; that is, for Calvin, in an undiscriminating, uncovetous usage of whatever goods

earthly life offered (see Calvin, *Institutio christianae religionis*, 1st ed. (*op. cit.* [ch. 4, note 19]), p. 409. This position evidently stood closer to Lutheranism than to the precisionism of Calvin's epigones.

80. The behavior of the Quakers is well-known in this regard. Even as early as the beginning of the seventeenth century tumultuous crowds of pious believers thronged the streets in Amsterdam for a decade in protest against the fashionable hats and apparel of a preacher's wife. (See Dexter's *op. cit.* [ch. 4, note 10], for a charming description). Sanford (*op. cit.* [ch. 4, note 5]) already noted that the male haircut of today is that of the often-mocked "Roundheads." He also observes that the similarly mocked male *apparel* of the Puritans is essentially the same as apparel today, at least in terms of the *principle* at its foundation.

81. See again on this point Veblen's *Theory of Business Enterprise*, *op. cit.* [ch. 4, note 221].

82. We will return continuously to this vantage point. Statements such as the following are explained by reference to it: "Every penny which is paid upon yourselves and children and friends must be done as by God's own appointment and to serve and please Him. Watch narrowly, or else that thievish, carnal self will leave God nothing" (Baxter, *Chr. Dir., op. cit.*, vol. 1, p. 108). This is decisive: Whatever is turned toward one's *personal* purposes is *withdrawn* from service to God's glory.

83. One is correctly in the habit of remembering (as does Dowden, *op. cit.* [note 4]), for example, that Cromwell saved Raphael's drawings and [Andrea] Mantegna's [1431–1506] *Triumph of Cæsar* from extinction while Charles II attempted to sell them. Restoration court society stood either entirely distant or directly in opposition to England's national literature; instead, among the aristocracy the influence of Versailles was everywhere dominant.

Puritanism uprooted believers from an unreflected enjoyment of everyday life. To analyze in detail the impact of this uprooting on the intellect of the highest types of Puritanism and on those persons influenced by it is a task that cannot be undertaken in the context of this sketch. Washington Irving formulates this influence in the familiar English terms: "It (he means political freedom where we would say Puritanism) evinces less play of the fancy, but more power of the imagination" (*Bracebridge Hall, op. cit.*). One needs only to think of the position of the *Scots* in England in science, literature, technical innovation, and business life in order to sense that this observation strikes the right chord, even though somewhat too narrowly formulated.

We cannot here address the significance of Puritanism for the development of technology and the empirical sciences. The relationship itself between Puritanism and science appears overtly and comprehensively even in daily life [see Robert K. Merton, "Puritanism, Pietism, and Science," in *Social Theory and Social Structure* (New York: Free Press, 1968); F. H. Tenbruck, "Max Weber and the Sociology of Science: A Case Reopened," *Zeitschrift für Soziologie* 3 (1974): 312–20; " 'Science as a Vocation'—Revisited," *Standorte im Zeitstrom*, ed. by Ernst Forsthoff and Reinhard Hörstel, eds. (Frankfurt: Athenäum Verlag, 1974)]. Permitted "recreations" for the Quakers, according to Barclay, are, for example: the visiting of friends, the reading of history, carrying out of experiments in *mathematics and physics*, gardening, the discussion of business and other practical proceedings, etc. The cause of this relationship is that which has been explained earlier.

84. Excellently and beautifully already analyzed in Karl Neumann's *Rembrandt* (*op. cit.*). His analysis should be compared in general with the above remarks.

85. According to Baxter. See the passages cited above [p. 109 and note 49] and *Chr. Dir., op. cit.*, vol. 1, p. 108.

86. See, for example, the well-known description of Colonel Hutchinson (which is often quoted, for example, in Sanford, *op. cit.*, [ch. 4, note 5], p. 57) in the biography written by his widow. After a presentation of all of his chivalrous virtues and his nature inclined toward cheerfulness and an enjoyment of life, she continues: "He was wonderfully neat, cleanly, and genteel in his habit, and had a very good fancy in it; but he left off very early the wearing of anything that was costly." According to the description in Baxter's funeral oration for Mary Hammer, the ideal of this cosmopolitan and well-educated Puritan woman is quite similar. However, she is thrifty in regard to time and expenditures for "pomp" and pleasure. See Baxter, *Works of the Puritan Divines* (*op. cit.* [note 6]), p. 533.

87. In addition to *many* other examples, I remember one in particular. A manufacturer, who had been unusually successful in business and had become very wealthy in his later years, suffered from a stubborn digestive disorder. His physician advised him to enjoy daily a few oysters—yet he complied only after great resistance. That here the issue involved a residual of an "ascetic" disposition (and not simply something related to "stinginess") suspicious of all personal *enjoyment* of wealth becomes apparent *in the end* when one notes that this same manufacturer had made very significant philanthropic contributions throughout his lifetime and had always shown an "open hand" to those in need.

88. The *separation* of workshop, office, and "business" in general from the private residence, of business firm and one's own name, of business capital and private wealth, and the tendency to define the "business" as a *corpus mysticum* [mystical organization] (at least in the case of corporate assets)—all of these developments go back to the Middle Ages. See my *Handelsgesellschaften im Mittelalter* [in *Gesammelte Aufsätze zur Sozial- und Wirtschaftsgeschichte,* (Tübingen: Mohr, 1924/1889), pp. 312–443].

89. In his *Der moderne Kapitalismus*, 1st ed. (Leipzig: Duncker & Humblot, 1902), Sombart has cogently referred occasionally to this characteristic phenomenon. It should be noted, however, that the accumulation of wealth derives psychologically from two very different sources.

One such source extends far back into the nebulous periods of antiquity and becomes manifest in foundations, family fortunes, trusts, etc. It is just as apparent in these ways, or even in a far more pure and clear form than in the same kind of pursuit, namely, at once to die weighted down with one's own massive accumulation of material possessions and, above all, to insure the continued viability of one's "business," even when doing so violates the personal interests of the majority of the inheriting children. In *these* cases the issue involves, in addition to the wish to lead an ideal life beyond death on the basis of personal achievements that maintain the "splendor familiae," a vanity that takes, so to speak, the expanded personality of the founder as its point of reference. Hence, fundamentally egocentric goals are here apparent.

It is different when one considers the "middle class" motives with which *we* are here concerned. The maxim of asceticism—"renounce, you should renounce"—holds here and becomes turned toward capitalist activity: "earn, you should earn." And this maxim, with its irrationality, now stands before us plain and pure as a sort of categorical imperative. Only God's glory and one's own duty, not the vanity of human beings, was the motivating force for the Puritans—and *today only* the duty to one's "vocational calling" constitutes one's motivation.

Whoever derives pleasure from illustrating an idea by looking at its extreme consequences will remember, for example, that theory of certain American millionaires: their earned millions should *not* be left to the children. Doing so would only deny to them the moral task of having to work and earn for themselves. Of course *today* this idea is only "theoretical" bubble-blowing.

90. As must be emphasized repeatedly, *this* is the final, decisive religious motive (in addition to the purely ascetic points of view on the mortification of the flesh). It comes to the forefront especially clearly with the Quakers.

91. Baxter (see *Saints' Everlasting Rest, op. cit.* [ch. 4, note 62], p. 12) completely repudiates this position by reference to the common motive, which is also found normally among the Jesuits: the body must be able to acquire what it needs. Otherwise, one becomes its slave.

92. This ideal, particularly in Quakerism, already clearly existed even in the first period of its development, as has been demonstrated in respect to important points by Hermann Weingarten. See his *Englishe Revolutionskirchen* (*op. cit.* [ch. 4, note 10]). Barclay's detailed discussions also illustrate this point very clearly (*op. cit.* [ch. 4, note 10], pp. 519 ff., 533). To be avoided are bodily vanity, thus all ostentation, and sparkling trinkets. This includes the use of things that have no *practical* purpose or that are valued only on account of their rarity (hence, for vanity's sake). Also to be avoided is all unconscientious use of possessions. This takes place when spending occurs, to a *disproportionate degree*, for less necessary needs instead of for the indispensable needs of life and the provision for the future.

The Quaker life, which was organized according to a living "law of marginal utility," so to speak, exemplified these maxims. "Moderate use of the creature" is completely permitted; *namely*, an emphasis may be placed upon the quality and solidity, etc., of the material used only as long as doing so does not lead to "vanity." On all these matters, see *Morgenblatt für gebildete Leser* (1846), no. 216 ff. (In particular, on the comfort and solidity of materials among the Quakers, see Matthias Schneckenburger, *Vorlesungen, op. cit.* [ch. 4, note 183] (1863), pp. 96 f.

93. Weber is here playing on the words of Goethe's Mephistopheles, who characterizes himself as "that power which always intends evil, and always creates good" (see *Faust*, Act 1, lines 1336–37) [sk].

94. As already mentioned, the question of the determination of the religious movements' social class cannot be addressed *here* (on this theme see the Economic Ethics of the World Religions essays). However, in order to see that Baxter, for example, who is referred to more than others in this investigation, does not view matters through the eyes of the "bourgeoisie" of his period, it suffices only to note his rank ordering of the vocations pleasing to God: after the teaching vocations, there follows husbandman, and only *then*, in a colorful mix, mariners, retailers of clothing, booksellers, tailors, etc. Even the (characteristically enough) "mariners" are probably at least just as likely thought of as fishermen as ship owners.

In this regard, many statements in the *Talmud* express a different notion. For example, see the, admittedly, not unchallenged sayings of Rabbi Eleasor. All imply that business is better than agriculture. See A. Wünsche, *Babylonische Talmud,* vol. 2, *op. cit.* [note 6], pp. 20–21. Several later sayings are milder. Here he offers advice for the investing of capital: one-third in land, one-third in merchandise, and one-third in cash (see Wünsche, vol. 2, p. 68).

For those whose conscience remains troubled whenever an economic (or "materialistic" as one, unfortunately, says even today) interpretation is omitted from discussions on causality, let it be noted here that I find the influence of economic development on the destiny of the formation of religious ideas very significant. I will later seek to demonstrate how, in our cases, mutually interacting adaptive processes and relationships produced both economic development on the one hand and religious ideas on the other. [See the Economic Ethic of the World Religions series and pp. lviii–lxiv above.] Nonetheless, by no means can the content of religious ideas be *deduced* from "economic" forces. These ideas are, and nothing can change this, actually, *for their part*, the most powerful elements shaping "national character"; they carry purely within themselves an autonomous momentum, lawful capacity (*Eigengesetzlichkeit*), and coercive power. Moreover, the *most important* differences—those between Lutheranism and Calvinism—are predominantly, to the extent that non-religious forces play a part, conditioned by *political* forces.

95. Eduard Bernstein is thinking of this compulsive saving when he says:"Asceticism is a middle-class virtue" (*op. cit.* [ch. 4, note 10], p. 681; see also p. 625). His discussions *are the first* to have suggested these important connections. However, the association is a far more comprehensive one than he suspects. Decisive was not merely capital accumulation; rather, central was the ascetic rationalization of the entire vocational life.

In the case of the American colonies, the contrast between the American North and South was emphasized as early as John Doyle (*The English in America, op. cit.* [ch. 4, note 10]. As a consequence of the "ascetic compulsion to save," capital continuously existed in the Puritan north that needed to be invested. Conditions were quite different in the South. [1920]

96. See Doyle (*ibid.*, vol. 2, ch. 1.) The existence of iron works companies (1643) and weaving (1659) for the market (and, by the way, the great prospering of handicrafts) in [northern] New England in the first generation after the founding of the colonies are anachronisms if examined from an economic point of view. These developments stand in striking contrast both to conditions in the South and in Rhode Island. In this non-Calvinist state, which enjoyed full freedom of conscience and despite an excellent harbor, a shortage of merchants existed. According to a 1686 report by the "governor and council": "The great obstruction concerning trade is the want of merchants and men of considerable estates amongst us" (S. G. Arnold, *History of the State of Rhode Island,* [Newport, RI: John P. Sanborn & Co., 1876], p. 490.) It can scarcely be doubted that the compulsion repeatedly to invest savings, which resulted from the Puritanical limitation placed upon consumption, played a role here. Church discipline was also important. The role of this factor cannot yet be discussed.

97. The discussion by Busken-Huets indicates that these circles, however, quickly declined in numbers (*op. cit.* [note 77], vol. 2, chs. 3, 4).

Nevertheless, Groen van Prinsterer notes: "De Nederlanders verkoopen veel en verbruiken wenig" [The Dutch sell much and need little], even in the period *after* the Peace of Westphalia [1648]. See his *Handboek der Geschiedenis* [History] *van het Vaderland,* 3rd ed. (p. 254n.). [1920]

98. The petition, for example, of a Royalist aristocrat presented after the entry of Charles II into London [1660] advocated a legal prohibition upon the acquisition of landed estates using business capital. The aim was to force the owners of this capital to invest it in trade (quoted in Leopold von Ranke, *Englische Geschichte,* vol. 4 [Leipzig: Duncker & Humblot, 1861], p. 197).

The stratum of Dutch "regents" [governors] separated itself as a "status group" from the wealthy, old-family patrician merchants in the cities *through* the purchase of old feudal manors. (In 1652 many complaints were heard that the regents had become landlords and were no longer merchants; cited by Robert Fruin, *Tien jaren uit den tachtigjarigen oorlog* [Ten Years after the Eighty Years' War].) Admittedly, these circles were never spiritually sincerely Calvinist. And the notorious pursuit of titles and entry into the nobility across broad circles of the Dutch middle class in the second half of the seventeenth century itself indicates that for *this* epoch, at any rate, such a contrast [as indicated in the text] between English and Dutch conditions can be accepted only with caution. In this case the superior power of inherited wealth broke the ascetic spirit.

99. The great epoch of English agricultural prosperity [in the eighteenth century] followed upon the period of widespread purchase of English landed estates by middle-class persons with business capital.

100. Even into [the twentieth] century Anglican landlords have not infrequently refused to rent land to the Nonconformists. (At present, both religious parties are of approximately equal numerical strength, whereas earlier the Nonconformists were perpetually in the minority.) [1920]

101. Hermann Levy correctly observes that the "character disposition" of the English, which can be compiled from their numerous features, is one *less* disposed than that of other peoples to adopt an ascetic ethos and middle-class, business-oriented virtues (see "Studien über das englische Volk," in *Archiv für Sozialwissenschaft und Sozialpolitik* 46 [1918–19]: 636–90). A basic feature of the English was (and is) a robust and raw enjoyment of life. The power of Puritan asceticism in the era of its dominance is demonstrated overtly in the amazing extent to which this character trait was *tempered* among Puritanism's adherents. [1920]

102. This polarity appears time and again in the exposition by John Doyle [*op. cit.*, ch. 4, note 10]. In the positions taken by the Puritans, religious motivations were continuously a decisive influence (of course not always *exclusively* decisive). The New England colony (under the leadership of [Governor John] Winthrop) was inclined to permit the settlement of [English] Gentlemen in Massachusetts, and even an upper house in which nobles would pass on their seats to their descendants, *if only* the Gentlemen would agree to join the *church*. On account of *church* discipline it was decided to retain a *closed* settlement. (Anglican merchants of great wealth, who created large stock-raising plantations, colonized New Hampshire and Maine; only a much smaller social connection to Puritanism existed in these colonies.) Complaints about the strong "greed for profit" of the New Englanders were heard as early as 1632; see, for example, W. Weeden, *Economic and Social History of New England, 1620–1789*, vol. 1 [Boston: Houghton Mifflin, 1890], p. 125). [1920]

103. The literal translation of Weber's term here, *Wirtschaftsmenschen*, "persons oriented to economic activity," better conveys his thought. He is seeing, with modernity, an "elevation" of economic activity in people's lives to a position of heretofore unknown salience [sk].

104. This point is emphasized by Sir William Petty. See *Political Arithmetick, op. cit.* [ch. 1, note 13], vol. 1, p. 262. Without exception, all contemporary sources speak especially of the Puritan *sectarians*; the Baptists, Quakers, and Mennonites are noted as belonging partly to a group without means and partly to a stratum of *small*-scale capitalists (*kleinkapitalistische Schicht*). They are then portrayed as standing in opposition to both the aristocracy of large-scale merchants and financiers engaged in adventurous and speculative enterprises. That which was *characteristic* of Western capitalism—a middle-class, private-ownership organization of industrial work—originated, however, out of just this stratum of *small*-scale capitalists and *not* out of the hands of the great financial magnates: monopolists, government contractors, those who financed the state, colonial entrepreneurs, promoters, and the like (see G. Unwin, *Industrial Organization in the Sixteenth and Seventeenth Centuries* [London: Clarendon Press, 1904], pp. 196 ff.). This opposition was familiar already to

contemporaries themselves; see [William] Parker's *Discourse Concerning Puritans* [London: Robert Bostock, 1641]. Here, similarly, the contrast between those engaged in projects and those engaged in court society is also stressed. [1920]

105. On the way in which this became expressed in Pennsylvania's politics in the eighteenth century, and especially in the American Revolution, see I. Sharpless, *A Quaker Experiment in Government* [Philadelphia: Ferris, 1898].

106. Quoted in Robert Southey, *Life of Wesley* , 2nd ed., vol. 2 [New York: Harper & Brothers, 1847], ch. 29. I received this reference, which I did not know, in a letter from Professor W. J. Ashley (1913). Ernst Troeltsch (to whom I communicated it for the purpose) has already occasionally cited it [see his *Social Teachings, op. cit.* (note 63)]. [1920]

107. This passage should be recommended to be read by all those today who wish to be better informed and more intelligent in regard to these matters than the leaders and contemporaries of this religious movement *themselves*. As one can see, these leaders knew very precisely what they were doing and what presented a risk to their activities. It is really not acceptable, as some of my critics unfortunately have done, to call into question so lightly matters that have been entirely uncontested and have remained until now unchallenged by anyone. I simply investigated these matters in the end more in terms of their internal driving forces than have others. Not a single person in the seventeenth century doubted these interrelationships. See further Thomas Manley, *Usury of 6% Examined* [London: Thomas Ratcliffe, 1669], p. 137.) They have been treated as obvious by, in addition to the modern writers earlier cited, poets such as Heinrich Heine and John Keats, representatives of science such as Macaulay, Cunningham, and Rogers, or writers such as Matthew Arnold. From the most recent literature, see W. J. Ashley, *Birmingham Industry and Commerce, op. cit.* [note 78]. Ashley has just now expressed to me his complete agreement, also by letter. On this entire problem see the essay by Hermann Levy (*op. cit.* [note 101]). [1920]

108. Exactly the same connections were obvious even to the Puritans of the classical period. Perhaps this cannot be more clearly demonstrated than by reference to Bunyan. His Mr. Money-Love argues: "By becoming religious he may mend his market. . . . To become religious is a virtue, by what means soever a man becomes so. . . . Nor is it unlawful to get a rich wife or more custom[ers] to my shop . . . or a good gain . . . to become religious to get all these is a good and profitable design" (*Pilgrim's Progress* [Middlesex, UK: Penguin, 1965], pp. 141–42). [1920]

109. [The author of *Robinson Crusoe*, Daniel] Defoe was a zealous Nonconformist opponent of Puritanism.

110. According to this adage, the good conscience, like a soft pillow, is soothing and allows deep sleep [sk].

111. This distinction between social change that originates from religious forces and social change that originates from laws can be found frequently throughout Weber's sociology [sk].

112. [Again: "The merchant cannot be pleasing to God."] Although Spener also considers the businessman's vocation to be one of temptations and pitfalls, he nonetheless, in response to a query, explains:

> It is pleasing to me that my dear friend does not hesitate to become engaged in business and instead recognizes this commercial activity as a legitimate way of life, as it is. A great deal is offered by business that is useful to the human species; hence, *love* is exercised through such activity and this accords with God's will. (see *Theologische Bedenken, op. cit.* [ch. 4, note 32], pp. 426, 429, 432 ff.)

This idea is more fully defended by arguments in favor of mercantilism in various other passages. Spener occasionally, in a fully Lutheran manner, depicts the lust to become rich as the main pitfall and as to be unconditionally rejected (in keeping with 1 Tim. 6:8–9 and by reference to the Book of Jesus Sirach; see above!); he then upholds the [Lutheran] "basic sustenance" position (*ibid.,* vol. 3, p. 435). However, he then reverses himself by referring to the sectarians—who are prosperous and at the same time live with God's blessing (see note 45 above). Moreover, as an *effect* of industrious work in a vocation, wealth is to him without suspicion. As a consequence of Lutheran influences on his thinking, his position is less consistent than Baxter's.

113. Baxter warns against the hiring of "heavy, flegmatic, sluggish, fleshly, slothful persons" as "servants" and recommends that preference be given to "godly" servants. He does so not only because "ungodly" servants would be merely "eye-servants," but above all because "a truly godly servant will do all your service in obedience to God, as if God Himself had bid him do it." In contrast, ungodly servants are inclined "to make no great matter of conscience of it." Moreover, it is not the external allegiance to a religion that constitutes a sign of holiness among workers, but the "conscience to do their duty" (*Chr. Dir.*, vol. 2, p. 16). One sees that the interests of God and the interests of employers here suspiciously interweave one with another. Even Spener, who otherwise urgently warns the faithful to allow *time* for meditation on God, assumes as self-evident that workers must be satisfied with a bare minimum of free time (even on Sundays) (*Theologische Bedenken,* vol. 3, *op. cit.* [ch. 4, note 22], p. 272).

English writers have correctly called the Protestant immigrates the "pioneers of skilled labor." See also the convincing demonstration of this in a discussion by H. Levy, *Die Grundlagen des ökonomischen Liberalismus in der Geschichte der englischen Volkswirtschaft, op. cit.* [ch. 4, note 51], p. 53. [1920]

114. The analogy between the "unjust," according to human standards, predestination of only a few and the similarly unjust distribution of goods (ordained by God as much as is the predestination of the few)—this is an infinitely tight connection. It is noted, for example, in Hoornbeek, vol. 1, *op. cit.* [ch. 4, note 22], p. 153. Furthermore, according to Baxter, poverty is very often a symptom of sinful laziness (*Chr. Dir, op. cit.* [ch. 4, n.39], vol. 1, p. 380).

115. According to Thomas Adams, God presumably allows so many to remain poor because He knows that many will not be able to withstand the temptations that come from wealth—for riches all too frequently drive religion out of persons (*Works of the Puritan Divines*, p. 158).

116. The text at this point includes the following passage:

> In the mendicant orders, medieval Catholicism had not only tolerated begging, but actually glorified it. Moreover, because they offered to the wealthy the opportunity for good works (the giving of alms), secular beggars were occasionally depicted as a "status group"—and valued, accordingly, more positively. This position appeared as late as the Anglican social ethic of the Stuarts [1615–1644], which stood spiritually very close to it. A formulation of severe laws on the treatment of the poor awaited the participation of the Puritans, who then fundamentally changed the old laws. This could occur because the Protestant sects and the strict Puritanical communities actually *did not know* begging in their midst. (See above note 51 and H. Levy, *English Economic Liberalism, op. cit.* [note 51]; all descriptions emphasize this same point; see for example Manley on the Huguenots, *op. cit.* [note 107])

Because this passage, which was added in 1920, severely disrupts the flow of Weber's argument, I have rendered it as an endnote [sk].

117. Similar developments were not missing in England. Belonging together with them are, for example, also that Pietism which, tied to W. Law's *Serious Call* (1728), preached *poverty*, chastity, and, originally, even isolation from the world.

118. Baxter's great success in his Kidderminster community, which had declined into absolute rack and ruin by the time of his arrival, is almost without precedent in the history of pastoral care. His accomplishments can serve as a typical example of *how* asceticism socialized the masses to work, or in Marxist terms, to produce "surplus value." In doing so, asceticism *first made possible* the utilization of the masses in the capitalist workplace (such as in cottage industries, textile factories, etc.). The causal relationship lies largely in this direction.

Viewed from Baxter's perspective, he understood the adaptation of his flock to the machinery of capitalism as occurring in the service of his religious-ethical interests. Viewed from the perspective of the development of capitalism, his religious-ethical interests entered into the service of the development of the capitalist spirit.

119. And one more point: a notion that one so often works with today may well be questioned, namely, the assumption that the medieval craftsman's "enjoyment" of "that which he produced himself" was quite strong. One must ask to what extent this enjoyment played a substantial role as a psychological motivating force. Undoubtedly, something important is touched upon here. At any

rate, [with the arrival of Puritanism] asceticism *stripped away* from work all this-worldly appeal—which today has been destroyed by capitalism for eternity—and oriented work toward the next world. Work in a vocational calling *as such* was desired by God. In other words, the impersonal character of work today, which offers little enjoyment and is meaningless when considered from the point of view of each person, was at that time still transfigured and glorified by religion because desired by God. In the period of its origin capitalism required workers who stood available, for the sake of the *conscience*, to be economically exploited. Capitalism today sits in the saddle and is capable, without any other-worldly reward, of coercing a willingness to work. [The last sentence was added in 1920]

120. Weber here implies that the greater quantitative productivity of work under capitalism should not be viewed as an unequivocal blessing. Viewed from particular vantage points, it may have unintended, negative consequences. In this respect, see the last few pages of this volume [sk].

121. See *Political Arithmetick, op. cit.* [ch. 1, note 13] [sk].

122. Laud was a central figure in the seventeenth-century Anglican Church. He used his power effectively to suppress the Puritans [sk].

123. On these oppositions and developments, see H. Levy, *op. cit.* [note 51]. The very powerful posture opposed to monopolies, which is characteristic for public opinion in England, originated historically in the seventeenth century from a linking of *political* power struggles against the Crown (the Long Parliament [1640–53] excluded the monopolists as Members) with the ethical motives of Puritanism and the economic interests of small- and middle-scale capitalists against the financial magnates. The declaration of the Army on August 2, 1652 and, similarly, the petition of the Levellers on January 28, 1653 demanded, in addition to the removal of excise, customs, and indirect taxes, the introduction of a single tax on all estates and, above all, "free trade." This latter demand involved the removal of all monopolistic barriers to trade, both internally and externally, for such obstacles were viewed as violating human rights. The "Great Remonstrance" [presented as a statement of grievances by the House of Commons to the Crown in 1641] placed similar demands. [1920]

124. A controversial Puritan, Prynne's writings, especially on the theater, brought him into conflict with the Anglican Church and the English monarchy. He attacked the *Book of Sports*. Nevertheless, he later defended the monarchy, criticized Cromwell, and advocated a subjection of the clergy to the Crown. A moderate reformer, Parker became an archbishop in the Anglican Church and the subject of considerable criticism by the Puritans [sk].

125. See Levy, *op. cit.* [note 51] [1920]

126. That even the components here (which have not yet been traced back to their religious roots)—namely, the maxim honesty is the best policy (Franklin's discussion of *credit*)—are also of Puritan origins is a theme that belongs in a somewhat different context (see the "Protestant Sects" essay below). Only the following observation of J. S. Rowntree (*Quakerism, Past and Present* [London: Smith, Elder and Co., 1859], pp. 95–96), to which Eduard Bernstein called my attention, needs to be repeated:

> Is it merely a *coincidence*, or is it a *consequence*, that the lofty profession of spirituality made by the Friends has gone hand in hand with shrewdness and tact in the transaction of mundane affairs? Real piety favors the success of a trader by insuring his integrity and fostering habits of prudence and forethought. [These are] important items in obtaining that standing and credit in the commercial world which are requisites for the steady accumulation of wealth (see the "Protestant Sects" essay).

"Honest as a Huguenot" was as proverbial in the seventeenth century as the respect for law of the Dutch (which Sir W. Temple admired) and, a century later, that of the English. The peoples of the European continent, in contrast, had not moved through this ethical schooling. [1920]

127. This theme is analyzed well in Albert Bielschowsky's *Goethe: sein Leben und seine Werke*, 3rd ed., vol. 2 (Munich: C. H. Beck, 1902–04), ch. 18. A related idea is articulated in regard to the development of the *scientific* "cosmos" by Windelband at the end of his *Blütezeit der deutschen Philosophie* (vol. 2 of his *Geschichte der neueren Philosophie* [Leipzig: Breitkopf und Hartel, 1899], pp. 428 ff.).

128. *Saints' Everlasting Rest*, *op. cit.* [ch. 4, note 62], p. 310. [The text varies slightly from Weber's quote. It reads: "Keep these things loose about thee like thy upper garments, that thou mayest lay them by whenever there is need."]

129. Translated by Parsons as "iron cage," this phrase has acquired near-mythical status in sociology. Weber elaborates upon its meaning in several passages in his "Parliament and Government in Germany" essay, which was taken by the editors of *Economy and Society* from the corpus of his political writings and incorporated into this analytic treatise (see pp. 1400-03), and in "Prospects for Liberal Democracy in Tsarist Russia" (see *Weber: Selections in Translation*, ed. by W. G. Runciman [Cambridge, UK: Cambridge University Press, 1978], pp. 157–58). Parallel German expressions are translated in these passages as "housing," "shell of bondage," and "casing."

There are many reasons that speak in favor of "steel-hard casing." Not least, it is a literal rendering of the German. Had Weber wished to convey an "iron cage" to his German readership he could easily have done so by employing a commonly used phrase, *eisener Käfig* (or even *eisenes Gefängnis* [iron prison]; see Stephen Kent, "Weber, Goethe, and the Nietzschean Allusion," *Sociological Analysis* 44 (1983): pp. 297–320 (esp. at pp. 299–300). Let us turn first to the adjective.

Weber's choice of *stahlhart* appropriately conveys (even more than *eisen*) the "hardness" of the constraining casing, as emphasized in the mechanistic images utilized in this passage to describe this new "powerful cosmos." This same image of hardness, however, is visible also in the "lightweight coat" metaphor above: once supple, it has now hardened itself into something (the power of material goods over the individual) that encases persons and cannot be thrown off. Appropriately, because ascetic Protestantism constitutes to Weber a direct precursor to this cosmos, the same adjective is used to describe the Puritan merchant (see p. 66). This lineage is apparent, he argues, even though the dimension foremost for this "merchant saint"—the ethical—has today vanished and left, unforeseeably, in its wake instrumental (or "mechanical") modes of action devoid of genuine brotherhood and resistant to ethical regulation (see, again, the images above and below; see also *E&S*, pp. 346, 585–86, 600, 635–40, 1186–87; "Religious Rejections of the World," in Gerth and Mills [*op. cit.*], pp. 331–40). Finally, although not directly apparent in this passage, "steel-hard" conveys a related theme crucial to Weber (as well as Marx and Simmel): the massively impersonal, coldly formal, harsh, and machine-like character of modern public sphere relationships whenever they remain uninfluenced by either traditions or values (see, e.g., "Science as a Vocation," in *ibid.*, pp. 155–56).

Now let us turn to the noun. There are substantive reasons also to prefer "casing" over "cage." Almost without exception, the secondary literature has argued that *stahlhartes Gehäuse* is a phrase intended to call attention to a bleak future inevitably on the horizon. Once in place, this commentary asserts, according to Weber, a nightmare society is putatively permanent. He is then characterized as a dour prophet of doom who, heroically, performs the worthy service of analyzing in a realistic manner a civilization on its deathbed. However, through conditional terms such as "if," "perhaps," "might," "would," "potentially," and "possibly," the usages of this and similar expressions in Weber's other works (as noted above) stress that such a cosmos arises from a series of identifiable economic, religious, political, historical, etc., forces that have become juxtaposed in a unique manner, rather than from an unstoppable unfolding of "bureaucratization and rationalization." In other words, if a *stahlhartes Gehäuse* does appear, it must be seen, Weber insists, as a contingent occurrence with, as other occurrences, a period of development and a period of decline.

In my view, this interpretation conforms to the overall tenor of Weber's sociology—a body of work that attends on the one hand to configurations of forces and their contexts rather than to linear historical change and, on the other hand, sees change, conflict, dynamism, and upheaval nearly universally (see *E&S* and Kalberg, *Max Weber's Comparative-Historical Sociology* [*op. cit.*], pp. 71–78, 98–117, 168–77, 189–92). Of course, Weber notes that a few civilizations have been quite ossified, such as China for 1500 years and ancient Egypt. Yet their closed character did not result from an "inevitable development" or "evolutionary historical laws" (see above, pp. l, lviii, 35–37, 48–49, 73). Rather, their rigidity must be understood as a consequence of an identifiable constellation of historical, political, etc., forces. (See also the paragraph below on "new prophets . . . ideas and ideals.") "Cage" implies great inflexibility and hence does not convey as effectively as "casing" (which, under certain circumstances, can become less restrictive and even peeled off) this contingency aspect.

In general, in regard to *stahlhartes Gehäuse*, the commentary has vastly exaggerated the importance of this metaphorical image in Weber's works, in the process transforming him from a rigorous comparative-historical sociologist into a social philosopher of modernity (see Lawrence A. Scaff, *Fleeing the Iron Cage* [Berkeley: The University of California Press, 1989)]. Notably, *stahlhartes Gehäuse*, and its equivalents, appear in Weber's works either at the end of an empirical study, where he cannot resist the temptation to offer more general speculations (this volume and this volume only), or in his political writings ("Prospects" and "Parliament and Government"), but only once in the body of his sociology; see above (p. 18). Not a single entry can be found in the detailed index to *E&S*, for example, nor in the comprehensive index to the German edition. On the "steel-hard cage" theme generally, see Kalberg, "The Modern World as a Monolithic Iron Cage? Utilizing Max Weber to Define the Internal Dynamics of the American Political Culture Today," in *Max Weber Studies* 1, 2 (2001): 45–60 [sk].

130. "Couldn't the old man be satisfied with his $75,000 a year and retire? No! The frontage of the store must be widened to 400 feet. Why? That beats everything, he says. Evenings, when his wife and daughter read together, he longs for bed. Sundays, in order to know when the day will be over, he checks his watch every five minutes. What a miserable existence!" In this manner the son-in-law (who had emigrated from Germany) of this prosperous dry-goods-man from a city on the Ohio River offered his judgment. Such a judgment would surely appear to the "old man" as completely incomprehensible. It could be easily dismissed as a symptom of the lack of energy of the Germans.

131. This phrase (*letzte Menschen*) is from Friedrich Nietzsche. It could as well be translated as "last people." It is normally rendered as "last men." See *Ecce Homo* (New York: Vintage Books; transl. by Walter Kaufmann, 1967), p. 330; see also *Thus Spoke Zarathustra* (New York: Penguin; transl. by R. J. Hollingdale, 1961), pp. 275–79, 296–311. The "last humans," to Nietzsche, are repulsive figures without emotion. Through their "little pleasures" they render everything small—yet they claim to have "invented happiness." Weber uses this phrase also in "Science as a Vocation." See *From Max Weber*, ed. by H. H. Gerth and C. Wright Mills (New York: Oxford, 1946), pp. 143 [sk].

132. Despite thorough investigations by several generations of Weber scholars, the source of this quotation has remained unidentified. Although it appears not to be directly from Nietzsche, as often believed, it is clearly formulated from the tenor of *Thus Spoke Zarathustra* (*ibid.*) In full accord with the common usage in academic circles in his time, Weber is using the term Geist here to denote a thinker's "multidimensional" capacity to unify and integrate diverse ideas and concepts. This vital capacity was lamented as lacking among specialists (*Fachmenschen*). This passage links back to the above paragraph on Goethe [sk].

133. This term is a synonym for "ascetic Protestantism" and "spirit of asceticism" [sk].

134. This remark (which remains here unchanged) might have indicated to Brentano [*Die Anfänge des modernen Kapitalismus, op. cit.* (ch. 1, note 15)] that I never doubted the *independent* significance of humanistic rationalism. That even Humanism was not *pure* "rationalism" has been strongly emphasized recently again. See Karl Borinski, "Die Wiedergeburtsidee in den neueren Zeiten," in *Abhandlungen der Münchener Akademie der Wissenschaft* (1919). [1920] [Humanistic rationalism, which Weber is here contrasting to his subject, ascetic rationalism, refers to Humanism generally as it arose out of the Renaissance and the Reformation.]

135. This phrase (*geistige Kulturgüter*) refers to the entire spectrum of "products of the mind," ranging from mathematical ideas and philosophical theories to interpretations of art and history. In Weber's time, they were more frequently referred to as "cultural ideas" (*Kulturideen*) or, simply, "ideas" (*Ideen*) [sk].

136. Namely, the relationship between religious belief and economic activity [sk].

137. The university lecture by Georg von Below, *Die Ursachen der Reformation* [Munich: Oldenbourg, 1917], is not concerned with this problem, but with the Reformation in general, especially with Luther. For the theme addressed *here*, and in particular the controversies that have tied

into this study, the book from Heinrich Hermelink should be noted finally. See *Reformation und Gegenreformation (Tübingen: Mohr*, 1911). Nonetheless this investigation primarily addresses other problems. [1920]

138. The sketch above has intentionally taken up only the relationships in which an influence of religious ideas on "material" life is actually beyond doubt. It would have been a simple matter to move beyond this theme to a conventional "construction," according to which *all* that is "characteristic" of modern civilization is logically *deduced* out of Protestant rationalism. However, this sort of construction is better left to that type of dilettante who believes in the "unity" (*Einheitlichkeit*) of the "social psyche" and its reducibility to *one* formula. It should only further be noted that naturally the period of capitalist development *before* the development we have considered was *comprehensively co*-determined by Christian influences, both inhibiting and promoting. What type of influences these were belongs in a later chapter.

Whether, by the way, of those further problems outlined above, one or another can be discussed in the pages of *this* journal remains, in light of its particular tasks, uncertain. [Weber was an editor of *Das Archiv*.] I for one am not at all inclined to write large treatises that rest upon, as would occur if these "further problems" were to be pursued, unfamiliar (theological and historical) investigations. (I am allowing [1920] these sentences to stand unchanged [despite Weber's authorship over a decade-long period of a three-volume treatise, *E&S*, and the three-volume EEWR series].)

On the *tension* between life-ideals and reality in the "early capitalist" period before the Reformation, see now Jakob Strieder, *Studien zur Geschichte kapitalistischer Organisationformen*, vol. 2 (Munich: Duncker & Humblot, 1914). (This study stands against the earlier cited work of Franz Keller, which Sombart used [see ch. 1, note 24; ch. 2, note 31].) [1920]

139. I would have believed that this sentence and the directly preceding observations [in the text] and endnotes might well have sufficed to exclude every misunderstanding regarding what this investigation *wanted* to achieve—and I find *no occasion for any sort of supplement*. Instead of pursuing the originally intended, direct continuation of this study, in the sense of the *agenda* outlined above, I have decided to follow a different course. This conclusion was arrived at in part owing to accident (especially the publication of Ernst Troeltsch's *The Social Teachings of the Christian Churches* [*op. cit.*], which comes to conclusions on subjects I would have taken up; yet, as a non-theologian, I could not have addressed them adequately), and in part as a consequence of a decision to strip this study on the Protestant ethic of its isolation and to place it in relation to the entirety of civilizational development. In order to do so I decided at the time to write down first of all the results of several comparative studies on the *universal*-historical relationships between religion and society. [See Weber, *The Religion of China*, *The Religion of India*, *Ancient Judaism*, and the "Prefatory Remarks" to these studies below (pp. 149–64).]

There follows now only a short, informal essay (*Gelegenheitsaufsatz*) that seeks to clarify the concept of "sect," as it was used above. This essay [pp. 127–48] simultaneously attempts to offer an explanation for the significance of the Puritan conception of *churches* for the capitalist spirit of the modern period. [1920]

Notes for 'The Protestant Sects and the Spirit of Capitalism'

Note: Certain footnotes in this article have been placed in the text.

1. This is a new and greatly enlarged draft of an article published in the *Frankfurter Zeitung*, Eastern 1906, then somewhat enlarged in the *Christliche Welt*, 1906, pp. 558 ff., 577 ff., under the title, "Churches and Sects." I have repeatedly referred to this article as supplementing *The Protestant Ethic and the Spirit of Capitalism*. The present rewriting [1920] is motivated by the fact that the concept of sect as worked out by myself (as a contrasting conception to "church") has, in the meanwhile and to my joy, been taken over and treated thoroughly by Troeltsch in his *Soziallehren der christlichen Kirchen* [*The Social Teachings of the Christian Churches*, trans. by O. Wyon, 2 vols., London, 1931]. Hence, conceptual discussions can the more easily be omitted as

what is necessary has been said already in *The Protestant Ethic and the Spirit of Capitalism*, pp. 221, note 200. This essay contains only the barest data supplementing that essay.

2. Details are of no interest here. Reference should be made to respective volumes of the American Church History Series—a work of uneven value.

3. The organization of the religious congregation during the immigration to New England often preceded the political societalization (in the fashion of the well-known pact of the Pilgrim Fathers). Thus, the Dorchester Immigrants of 1619 first bound themselves together by organizing a church congregation *before* emigrating, and they elected a parson and a teacher. In the colony of Massachusetts the church was formally a completely autonomous corporation, which admitted, however, only citizens for membership, and affiliation with which, on the other hand, was a prerequisite of citizenship. Likewise, at first, church membership and good conduct (meaning admission to the Lord's Supper) were prerequisites of citizenship in New Haven (before it was incorporated in Connecticut township was obliged to maintain the church) (a defection from the strict principles of Independentism to Presbyterianism).

This at once meant a somewhat laxer practice, for after the incorporation of New Haven the church there was restricted to giving out certificates stating that the respective person was religiously inoffensive and of sufficient means. Even during the seventeenth century, on the occasion of the incorporation of Maine and New Hampshire, Massachusetts had to depart from the full strictness of the religious qualification of political rights. On the question of church membership compromises had also to be made, the most famous of which is the Half-way Covenant of 1657. In addition, those who could not prove themselves to be regenerate were nevertheless admitted to membership. But, until the beginning of the eighteenth century, they were not admitted to communion.

4. Some references from the older literature which is not very well known in Germany may be listed. A sketch of Baptist history is present in: Vedder, *A Short History of the Baptists* (Second ed. London, 1897). Concerning Hanserd Knollys: Culross, *Hanserd Knollys*, vol. II of the Baptist Manuals edited by P. Gould (London, 1891).

For the history of Anabaptism: E. B. Bax, *Rise and Fall of the Anabaptists* (New York, 1902). Concerning Smyth: Henry M. Dexter, *The True Story of John Smyth, the Re-Baptist*, as told by himself and his contemporaries (Boston, 1881). The important publications of the Hanserd Knollys Society (printed for the Society by J. Hadden, Castle Street, Finsbury, 1846–54) have been cited already. Further official documents in *The Baptist Church Manual* by J. Newton Brown, D.D. (Philadelphia, American Baptist Publishing Society, 30 S. Arch Street). Concerning the Quakers, besides the cited work of Sharpless: A. C. Applegarth, *The Quakers in Pennsylvania*, ser. X, vol. VIII, IX of the Johns Hopkins University Studies in History and Political Science. G. Lorimer, *Baptists in History* (New York, 1902), J. A. Seiss, *Baptist System Examined* (Lutheran Publication Society, 1902).

Concerning New England (besides Doyle): The Massachusetts Historical Collections; furthermore, Weeden, *Economic and Social History of New England*, 1620–1789, 2 vols. Daniel W. Howe, *The Puritan Republic* (Indianapolis, Bobbs-Merrill Co.).

Concerning the development of the "Covenant" idea in older Presbyterianism, its church discipline, and its relation to the official church, on the one hand, and to Congregationalists and sectarians on the other hand, see: Burrage, *The Church Covenant Idea* (1904), and *The Early English Dissenters* (1912). Furthermore, W. M. Macphail, *The Presbyterian Church* (1918). J. Brown, *The English Puritans* (1910). Important documents in Usher, *The Presbyterian Movement*, 1584–89 (Com. Soc., 1905). We give here only an extremely provisional list of what is relevant for us.

5. During the seventeenth century this was so much taken for granted that Bunyan, as mentioned previously, makes "Mr. Money-Love" argue that one may even become pious *in order* to get rich, especially in order to add to one's patronage; for it should be irrelevant for what reason one had become pious. (*Pilgrim's Progress*, Tauchnitz ed., p.114.)

6. Thomas Clarkson, *Portraiture of the Christian Profession and Practice of the Society of Friends*. Third edition (London, 1867), p. 276. (The first edition appeared around 1830.)

7. Sources are Zwingli's statements, Füssli I, p. 228, cf. also pp. 243, 253, 263, and his *Elenchus contra catabaptistas, Werke III*, pp. 357, 362. In his own congregation, Zwingli characteristically had much trouble with Antipedobaptists [opposed to infant baptism]. The Antipedobaptists, in turn,

viewed the Baptist "separation," hence voluntarism, as objectionable according to the Scriptures. A Brownist petition of 1603 to King James I demanded the exclusion of all "wicked liars" from the church and only the admission of the "faithful" and their children. But the (Presbyterian) Directory of Church Government of (probably) 1584 (published from the original for the first time in the Heidelberg Ph.D. thesis of A. F. Scott Pearson, 1912) demanded in article 37 that only people who had submitted to the disciplinary code, or *literas testimoniales idoneas aliunde attuleriut* [had furnished testimonial letters from elsewhere] be admitted to communion.

8. The problematic nature of the sectarian voluntarist principle follows logically from the demand for the *ecclesia pira* by the reformed (Calvinist) church. This dogmatic principle, as opposed to the sect principle, is strikingly evident in modern times in A. Kuyper (the well-known later Premier minister). The dogmatic position in his final programmatic essay is especially obvious: *Separatie en doleantie* (Amsterdam, 1890). He sees the problem as due to the absence of the infallible doctrinal office among non-Catholic Christianity. This doctrine asserts that the *Corpus* of the visible church cannot be the *Corpus Christi* of the old Reformed Church, but that it must rather remain divided in time and space, and the shortcomings of human nature must remain peculiar to it. A visible church originates solely through *an act of will* on the part of the believers and by virtue of the authority given them by Christ. Hence the *potestas ecclesiastica* may be vested neither in Christ himself, nor in the *ministri*, but only in the believing congregation. (In this Kuyper follows Voët.) The greater community originates through the legal and voluntary association of the congregations.

This association, however, must be a religious obligation. The Roman principle, according to which a church member is *eo ipso* a member of the parish of his local community, is to be rejected. Baptism makes him a mere passive *membrum incompletum* and grants no rights. Not baptism, but only *belijdenis en stipulatie* (confession of faith and profession of good will) gives membership in the congregation, in the legal sense. Membership alone is identical with subordination to the *disciplina ecclesiae* (again following Voët). Church law is believed to deal with the man-made rules of the visible church, which, though bound to God's order, do not represent God's order itself. (Cf. Voët *Pol. Eccles.* vol. I, pp. I and II.)

All these ideas are Independentist variants of the genuine constitutional law of the reformed churches and imply an active participation of the *congregation*, hence of the laity, in the admission of new members. (Von Rieker has described this law especially well.) The co-operatine participation of the whole congregation also constituted the program of the Brownist Independents in New England. They adhered to it in constant struggle against the successfully advancing "Johnsonist" faction which advocated church government by the "ruling elders." It goes without saying that only "Regenerates" were to be admitted (according to Baillie "only one out of forty"). During the nineteenth century the church theory of the Scotch Independents similarly demanded that admission be granted only by special resolution (Sack, *loc. cit.*). However, Kuyper's church theory *per se* is, of course, *not* "congregationalist" in character.

According to Kuyper, individual congregations are religiously obliged to affiliate with and to belong to the church as a whole. There can be only one legitimate church in one place. This obligation to affiliate is only dropped, and the obligation of *separatie* emerges only when *doleantie* has failed; that is, an attempt must have been made to improve the wicked church as a whole through active protest and passive obstruction (*doleeren*, meaning to protest, occurs as a technical term in the seventeenth century). And finally, if all means have been exhausted and if the attempt has proved to be in vain, and force has prevailed, then separation is obligatory. In that case, of course, an independent constitution is obligatory, since there are no "subjects" in the church and since the believers *per se* hold a God-given office. Revolution can be a duty to God. (Kuyper, *De conflict gekomen*, pp. 30–31). Kuyper (like Voët) takes the old independent view that only those who participate in the *communion of the Lord's Supper* by admission are full members of the church. And only the latter are able to assume the trusteeship of their children during baptism. A believer, in the *theological* sense, is one who is inwardly converted; in the legal sense a believer is only one who is *admitted* to the Lord's Supper.

9. The fundamental prerequisite for Kuyper is that it is a sin not to purge the sacramental communion of non-believers. (*Dreigend Conflict*, 1886, p. 41; reference is made to 1 Cor. 11:26–27, 29; 1 Tim. 5:22; Apoc. 18:4.) Yet according to him the church never has judged the state of grace "before God"—in contrast to the "Labadists" (radical Pietists). But for admission to the Lord's Supper

only belief and *conduct* are decisive. The transactions of the Netherlands Synods of the sixteenth and seventeenth centuries are filled with discussions of the prerequisites of admission to the Lord's Supper. For example, the Southern Dutch Synod of 1574 agreed that the Lord's Supper should not be given if no organized congregation existed. The elders and deacons were to be careful that no unworthy person be admitted. The Synod of Rotterdam of 1575 resolved that all those who led an obviously offensive life should not be admitted. (The elders of the congregation, not the preachers alone, decided admissions, and it is almost always the congregation which raises such objections—often against the more lax policy of the preachers. Cf. for instance, the case cited by Reitsma [vol. II, p. 231].)

The question of admission to the Lord's Supper included the following cases: whether the husband of an Anabaptist could be admitted to the Lord's Supper was decided at the Synod at Leyden in 1619, article 114; whether a Lombard's servant should be admitted, Provincial Synod at Deventer, 1595, article 24; whether men who declared their bankruptcy, Synod of Alkmaar, 1599, article II, similarly of 1605, article 28, and men who had settled an accord, Northern Holland Synod of Enkhuizen of 1618, Grav. Class. Amstel. No. 16, should be admitted. The latter question is answered in the affirmative in case the *consistorium* finds the list of properties sufficient and judges the reservations for food and clothing made therein adequate for the debtor and his family. But the decision is especially affirmative when the creditors state themselves to be satisfied by the accord and when the failing debtor makes a confession of guilt. Concerning non-admission of Lombards, see above. Exclusion of spouses in case of quarrelsomeness, Reitsma III, p. 91. The reconciliation of parties to a legal dispute is a prerequisite for admission. For the duration of the dispute they must stay away from communion. There is conditional admission of a person who has lost a libel suit and has appealed the case. *Ibid.* III, p. 176.

Calvin may well have been the first to have forced through in the Strassborg congregation of French emigrants the exclusion of the person from the Lord's Supper whose outcome in the examination of worthiness was unsatisfactory. (But then the minister, not the congregation, made the decision.) According to Calvin's genuine doctrine (Inst. Chr. Rel. IV, chap. 12, p. 4) excommunications should legitimately apply only to reprobates. (At the quoted place excommunication is called the promulgation of the *divine* sentence.) But in the same place (cf. p. 5) it is also treated as a means of "improvement."

In America, nowadays, among the Baptists formal excommunication, at least in metropolitan areas, is very rare. In practice it is replaced by "dropping," in which case the name of the person is simply and discreetly stricken from the record. Among the sects and Independents, laymen have always been the typical bearers of discipline; whereas the original Calvinist-Presbyterian church discipline expressly and systematically strove for domination over state and church. However, even the "Directory" of the English Presbyterians of 1584 (p. 14, note 2) summoned an equal number of lay elders and ministers to the classes and to the higher offices of the church government.

The mutual relation of the elders and the congregation has been occasionally ordered in different ways. Just as the (Presbyterian) Long Parliament placed the decision of exclusion from the Lord's Supper into the hands of the (lay) elders, so the Cambridge Platform did likewise about 1647 in New England. Up to the middle of the nineteenth century the Scotch Independents, however, used to transmit notice of misconduct to a commission. After the commission's report the whole congregation decided about the exclusion, in correspondence with the stricter view of the joint responsibility of all individuals. This absolutely corresponded with the Brownist confession quoted above, which was submitted to King James I in 1603 (Dexter, *loc. cit.*, p. 303) whereas the "Johnsonists" considered the sovereignty of the (elected) elders to be Biblical. The elders should be able to excommunicate even against the decision of the congregation (occasion for Ainsworth's secession). Concerning the corresponding conditions among the early English Presbyterians, see the literature quoted in note 4, above, and the Ph.D. thesis of Pearson quoted in note 7, above.

10. The Dutch Pietists, by the way, believed in the same principle. Lodensteijn, for instance, held to the point of view that one must not commune with non-regenerates; and the latter are for him expressly those who do not bear the *signs* of regeneration. He even went so far as to advise against saying the Lord's Prayer with children since they had not as yet become "children of the

Lord." In the Netherlands, Kahler still occasionally found the view that the regenerate does not sin at all. Calvinist orthodoxy and an astonishing knowledge of the Bible was found precisely among the petty lower middle class masses. Also here it was the very orthodox who, distrusting theological education and faced with the church regulation of 1852, complained of the insufficient representation of laymen in the Synod (besides the lack of a sufficiently strict *"censura morum"*). Certainly no orthodox Lutheran church party in Germany would have thought of that at the time.

11. Quoted in Dexter, *Congregationalism of the Last Three Hundred Years as Seen in its Literature* (New York, 1880), p. 97.

12. During the seventeenth century, letters of recommendation from non-resident Baptists of the local congregations were a prerequisite for admission to the Lord's Supper. Non-Baptists could only be admitted after having been examined and approved by the congregation. (Appendix to the edition of the Hanserd Knollys Confession of 1689, West Church, Pa., 1817). Participation in the Lord's Supper was *compulsory* for the qualified member. Failure to affiliate with the legitimately constituted congregation of one's place of residence was viewed as schism. With regard to the obligatory community with other congregations, the Baptist point of view resembled that of Kuyper (cf. above, note 8). However *all* jurisdictional authority *higher* than that of the individual church was rejected. Concerning the *litterae testimoniales* [testimonial letters] among the Covenanters and early English presbyterians, see note 7 and the literature quoted in note 4.

13. Shaw, *Church History under the Commonwealth*, vol. II, pp. 152–65; Gardiner, *Commonwealth*, vol. III, p. 231.

14. This principle was expressed, for instance, in resolutions like the one of the Synod of Edam, 1585 (in the Collection of Reitsma, p. 139).

15. Baxter, *Eccles. Dir.*, vol. II, p. 108, discusses in detail the shying away of doubtful members from the Lord's Supper at the congregation (because of article 25 of the Church of England).

16. The doctrine of Predestination also represents here the purest type. Its relevance and great practical importance is evidenced in nothing so clearly as the bitter struggle over the question whether children of reprobates should be admitted to baptism after having proved themselves to be worthy. The practical significance of the doctrine of Predestination has been, however, again and again unjustly doubted. Three of the four Amsterdam Refugee congregations were in favor of admitting the children (at the beginning of the seventeenth century); but in New England only the "Half-way Covenant" of 1657 brought a relaxation of this point. For Holland see also note 9.

17. Loc. cit. vol. II, p. 110.

18. Already at the beginning of the seventeenth century the prohibition of the conventicles (*Slijkgeuzen*) caused a general *Kulturkampf* in Holland. Elizabeth proceeded against the conventicles with frightful harshness (in 1593 with threat of capital punishment). The reason behind this was the anti-authoritarian character of asceticist religiosity or, better in this case, the competitive relationship between the religious and secular authority (Cartwright had expressly demanded that excommunication of princes also be permitted). As a matter of fact the example of Scotland, the classic soil of Presbyterian church discipline and clerical domination against the king, had to have a deterrent effect.

19. In order to escape the religious pressure of orthodox preachers, liberal Amsterdam citizens had sent their children to neighboring congregations for their confirmation lessons. The Kerkraad [church council] of the Amsterdam congregation refused (in 1886) to acknowledge certificates of the moral conduct of the communicants made out by such ministers. The communicants were excluded from the Lord's Supper because the communion had to remain pure and because the Lord, rather than man, must be obeyed. When the synodal commission approved of the objection against this deviation, the church council refused to obey and adopted new rules. In accordance with the latter, suspension of the church council gave the council exclusive disposition over the church. It rejected community with the synod and the now suspended (lay) elders, T. Rutgers and Kuyper, seized by the ruse the Nieuwe Kerk [New Church] in spite of the watchmen who had been hired. (Cf. Hogerfeil, *De kerkelijke strijd te Amsterdam*, 1886, and Kuyper's publications mentioned above.)

During the 1820s the predestinarian movement had already begun under the leadership of Bilderdijk and his disciples, Isaac da Costa and Abraham Capadose (two baptized Jews). (*Because* of the doctrine of predestination it rejected, for example, the abolition of Negro slavery as "an interference with Providence" just as it rejected vaccination!) They zealously fought the laxity of church discipline and the imparting of sacraments to unworthy persons. The movement led to separations. The synod of the "Afgeschiedenen gereformeerten Geemeente" [Separated reformed congregation] of Amsterdam in 1840 accepted the Dordrecht Canouns and rejected any kind of domination (*gezag*) "within or above the church." Groen van Prinsterer was one of Bilderdijk's disciples.

20. Classical formulations are found in the "Amsterdam Confession" of 1611 (Publ. of the Hanserd Knollys Society, vol. X). Thus, article 16 states: "That the members of every church and congregation *ought to know one another* . . . therefore a church ought not to consist of such a multitude as cannot have practical knowledge one of another. Hence any synodal rule and any establishment of central church authorities were considered in the last instance as principled apostasy. This happened in Massachusetts and likewise in England under Cromwell. The rules, at that time, established by Parliament in 1641, allowed every congregation to provide itself with an orthodox minister and to organize lectures. This measure was the signal for the influx of Baptists and radical Independents. The early Presbyterian Dedham Protocols, published by Usher, also presuppose the individual congregation (actually, at that time, in all probability, the individual minister) to be the bearer of church discipline. Admission by ballot, as evidenced by the protocol of 22 October 1582, states: "That none be brought in as one of this company without the general consent of the whole." But as early as 1586 these Puritans declared their opposition to the Brownists, who went in the direction of Congregationalism.

21. The "classes" of the Methodists, as the foundation of the co-operative cure of soul, were the very backbone of the whole organization. Every twelve persons were to be organized into a "class." The leader of the class was to visit each member weekly, either at home or at the class meeting, during which there was usually a general confession of sins. The leader was to keep a record of the member's conduct. Among other things, this book-keeping was the basis for the writing of certificates for members who went away from the local community. By now, and for a long time, this organization has been disintegrating everywhere, including the U.S.A. The manner in which church discipline functioned in early Puritanism may be judged from the above-quoted Dedham Protocol, according to which "admonition" was to be given in the conventicle "if any things have been observed *or espied* by the brethren."

22. In the Lutheran territories, especially those of Germany, either church discipline was notoriously undeveloped or else church discipline completely decayed at an early date. Church discipline was also of little influence in the reformed churches of Germany, except in Julich-Cleve and other Rhenish areas. This was due to the influence of the Lutheran surroundings *and* to the jealousy between the state power and the competing and autonomous hierocratic forces. This jealousy had existed everywhere, but the state had remained overpowering in Germany. (Traces of church discipline are nevertheless found up to the nineteenth century. The last excommunication in the palatinate took place in 1855. However, the church rules of 1563 were there handled in an actually Erastian way from an early date.)

Only the Mennonites, and later the Pietists, created effective means of discipline and disciplinary organizations. (For Menno a "visible church" existed *only* where church discipline existed. And excommunication because of misconduct or mixed marriage was a self-understood element of such discipline. The Rynsburg Collegiants had no dogmas whatever and recognized "conduct" alone.) Among the Huguenots, church discipline *per se* was very strict, but again and again it was relaxed through unavoidable considerations of the nobility which were politically indispensable.

The adherents of Puritan church discipline in England were found especially among the bourgeois capitalist middle class, thus, for instance, in the City of London. The city was not afraid of the domination of the clergy, but intended to use church discipline as a means of mass domestication. The strata of artisan craftsmen also adhered firmly to church discipline. The political authorities were the opponents to church discipline. Hence, in England the opponents included Parliament. Not "class interests" but, as every glimpse into the documents shows, *primarily* religious, and, in addition, political interests and convictions played their part in these questions. The harshness not only of New England but also of the genuinely Puritan church discipline in Europe is known. Among Cromwell's major-generals and commissioners, his agents for enforcing church discipline, the proposal to exile all "idle, debauched, and profane persons" emerges repeatedly.

Among the Methodists the dropping of novices during the periods of probation was permissible without further ado. Full members were to be dropped after an investigation by a commission. The church discipline of the *Huguenots* (who for a long time actually existed as a "sect") is evidenced in synodal protocols. These indicate, among other things, censure of adulteration of commodities and of dishonesty in business. Sixth Synod (Avert. Gen. XIV). Thus sumptuary laws are frequently found, and slave ownership and slave trading are *permitted*, Twenty-Seventh Synod; a rather lax practice toward fiscal demands prevails (the fiscus is a tyrant), Sixth Synod, cas de conc. dec, XIV; usury, *ibid.*. XV (cf. Second Synod, Gen. 17; Eleventh Synod, Gen. 42). Toward the end of the sixteenth century, the English Presbyterians were designated as "disciplinarians" in official correspondence (Quotations to be found in Pearson, *loc. cit.*).

23. In the "Apologetical Narration" of the five (Independent) "dissenting brethren" of the Westminster Synod the separation from the "casuall and formall Christians" is placed in the foreground. This means, at first, only voluntaristic separatism, not renunciation of commercium. But Robinson, a strict Calvinist and advocate of the Dordrecht Synod (about him cf. Dexter, *Congregationalism*, p. 402) had originally held the opinion which he later softened, that the independent separatists must not have social intercourse with the others, even should they be *electi*, which was considered conceivable. However, most sects have avoided committing themselves overtly to this principle, and some have expressly rejected it, at least as a principle. Baxter, *Christian Directory*, vol. II, p. 100 (at the bottom of column 2), opines that, should not oneself but the housefather and parson assume the responsibility, then one might acquiesce to praying together with an ungodly person. However, this is un-Puritan. The *mijdinge* [middle things] played a very important part in the radical Baptist sects in Holland during the seventeenth century.

24. This became strikingly obvious even in the discussions and struggles within the Amsterdam Refugee congregation at the beginning of the seventeenth century. Likewise in Lancashire the rejection of a *ministerial* church discipline, the demand for a lay rule in the church and for a church discipline enforced by laymen were decisive for the attitudes in the internal church struggles of Cromwell's times.

25. The appointment of the elders was the object of prolonged controversies in the Independent and Baptist communities, which will not concern us here.

26. The ordinance of the Long Parliament of 31 December 1646 was directed against this. It was intended as a stroke against the Independents. On the other hand, the principle of the liberty of prophesying had also been vindicated in literary form by Robinson. From the Episcopalian standpoint Jeremy Taylor, *The Liberty of Prophesying* (1647), made concessions to it. Cromwell's "tryers' requested that permission to prophesy depend on the certificate of six admitted members of the congregation, among whom were four laymen. During the early period of the English Reformation the "exercises" and "prophesyings" had not only been frequently tolerated by ardent Anglican bishops, but had been encouraged by them. In Scotland these were (in 1560) constituent elements of church activities; in 1571 they were introduced in Northampton. Other places were soon to follow. But Elizabeth persisted in suppressing them as a result of her proclamation of 1573 against Cartwright.

27. The charismatic revolutions of the sectarians (of the type of Fox and similar leaders) in the congregations always began with the fight against the office-holding prebendaries as "hirelings" and with the fight for the apostolic principle of free preaching without remuneration for the speaker who is moved by the spirit. Heated disputes in Parliament took place between Goodwin, the congregationalist, and Prynne, who reproached him that, against his alleged principle, he had accepted a "living," whereas Goodwin declared acceptance only of what was given voluntarily. The principle that only *voluntary* contributions for the maintenance of ministers should be permissible is expressed in the petition of the Brownists to James I, in 1603 (point 71: hence the protest against "Popish livings" and "Jewish tithes").

28. In 1793 Methodism abolished differences between ordained and non-ordained preachers. Therewith, the non-ordained traveling preachers, and hence, the missionaries, who were the charac-

teristic bearers of Methodism, were placed on an equal footing with the preachers still ordained by the Anglican church. But at the same time the monopoly of preaching in the whole circuit and of administering sacraments was reserved to the traveling preachers alone. (The autonomous administration of sacraments was then principally carried through, but still at hours different from those of the official church to which membership was still pretended now as before.) As, ever since 1768, preachers were forbidden to engage in ordinary middle class occupations, a new "clergy" emerged. Since 1836 formal ordination has taken place. Opposite the circuit preachers were the lay-recruited local preachers who took up preaching as a minor vocation. They had no right to administer sacraments and they had only local jurisdiction. None among these two categories of preachers donned an official garb.

29. Actually, in England at least, most of the "circuits" have become little parishes and the travel of the preacher has become a fiction. Nevertheless, up to the very present, it has been upheld that the same minister must not serve the same circuit for more than three years. They were *professional* preachers. The "local preachers," from among whom the traveling preachers were recruited, were, however, people with a middle class occupation and with a license to preach, which (originally) was given for one year at a time. Their existence was necessary because of the abundance of services and of chapels. But above all, they were the backbone of the "class"—organization and its curing of souls. Hence, they were actually the central organ of church discipline.

30. Among other things Cromwell's opposition to the "Parliament of the Saints" became acute on the question of the universities (which with the radical elimination of all tithes and prebends would have collapsed). Cromwell could not decide to destroy these cultural institutions, which, however, then were meant especially to be institutions for the education of theologians.

31. An example is given by Gardiner, *Fall of the Monarchy*, vol. I, p. 380.

32. The Westminster Confession also (XXVI, I) establishes the principle of *inner and external* obligation to help one another. The respective rules are numerous among all sects.

33. Every case of failure to pay in early Methodism was investigated by a commission of brethren. To incur debts without the certain prospect of being able to pay them back was cause for exclusion—hence, the credit rating. Cf. the resolution of the Dutch synods quoted in note 9. The obligation to help one's brother in emergencies is determined, for example, in the Baptist Hanserd Knollys Confession (c. 28) with the characteristic reservation that this should not prejudice the sanctity of property. Occasionally, and with great harshness (as in the Cambridge platform of 1647, edition of 1653, 7, no. VI) the elders are reminded of their duty to proceed against members who live *"without a calling"* or conduct themselves *"idly in their calling."*

34. Among the Methodists these certificates of conduct originally had to be renewed every three months. The old Independents, as noted above, gave the Lord's Supper only to holders of tickets. Among the Baptists a newcomer to the community could be admitted to the congregation only upon a letter of recommendation from his former congregation: cf. the appendix to the edition of the Hanserd Knollys Confession of 1689 (West Chester, Pa., 1827). Even the three Amsterdam Baptist Communities at the beginning of the sixteenth century had the same system, which since then recurs everywhere. In Massachusetts since 1669, a certificate from the preacher and the select men concerning orthodoxy and *conduct* has been the attestation that the holder is qualified for acquiring political citizenship. This certificate replaced the admission to the Lord's Supper, which had originally been required.

35. Again we should like to stress emphatically this absolutely decisive point of the first of these two essays. (*The Protestant Ethic and the Spirit of Capitalism.*) It has been the fundamental mistake of my critics not to have taken notice of this very fact. In the discussion of the Ancient Hebrew Ethics in relation to the *doctrines* of Egyptian, Phoenician, and Babylonian ethical systems we shall hit upon a very similar state of affairs.

36. Cf. among others the statement p. 166 in the *Protestant Ethic and the Spirit of Capitalism*. The formation of congregations among ancient Jewry, just as among early Christians, worked, each in its own way, in the same direction (among Jewry the decline of the social significance of the *sib*, as we shall see, is conditioned thereby, and Christianity during the early Middle Ages has had similar effects).

37. Cf. The *Livre des Métiers* of the Prévôt Étienne de Boileau of 1268 (éd. Lespinasse & Bonnardot in the *Histoire générale de Paris*) pp. 211, sect. 8; 215, sect. 4. These examples may stand for many others.

38. Here, in passing, we cannot analyze this rather involved causal relationship.

Notes for 'Prefatory Remarks' to Collected Essays in the Sociology of Religion (1920)

1. Stemming originally from the German polymath Johann Gottfried von Herder (1744–1803), "universal history" (*Universalgeschichte*) came to refer in the nineteenth century to a mode of German historiography that avoided specialist studies and instead attempted to offer a synthesizing portrait of an entire historical epoch or area of culture. See, for example, Theodor Mommsen on ancient Rome, Jacob Burckhardt on the Italian Renaissance, and Ernst Troeltsch on Christianity. The term does not imply "world history" [sk].

2. Thucydides of ancient Greece is best known for his history of the Peloponnesian War (431–404 BCE). Weber refers to his attempt to record events and occurrences as they empirically took place; hence he interviewed direct observers, avoided speculative interpretations and reference to supernatural forces ("the will of the gods"), and sought to offer an "objective" account. He was the first historian to do so [sk].

3. "Rational" here implies to Weber "rigor" and a "systematic aspect" (as also in the next paragraph and throughout). The term does not imply "better." See Kalberg, "Max Weber's Concept of Rationality," in *American Journal of Sociology* 85 (1980): 1145–79 [sk].

4. A religious-philosophical school in India that developed out of the pre-Hindu Vedas (seventh century BCE). It emphasized that salvation could be attained though the performance of certain ritualized good works [sk].

5. "Major third" (*harmonische Terz*) refers to the distance on the piano keyboard from note "c" to "e." Use of these notes together formed a harmonious sound that was used frequently in classical composition [sk].

6. "Rationalization" can be equated with "systematization." See the article cited in note 3 [sk].

7. A succinct translation of these German and Latin phrases does not capture that which Weber wishes to convey here, namely, the manner in which the Western *Ständestaat* involved, uniquely, a precarious balancing of powers between the ruler, a cohesive aristocracy, and powerful municipally based political actors. Hence, it implied temporary alliances and a rudimentary division of powers, an arrangement that was a precursor to the division of powers in the modern constitutional state. See *Economy and Society*, pp. 1085-87 [sk].

8. The German editor, Johannes Winckelmann, attributes this phrase to the progressive English social critic, novelist, biographer, urban historian, and philanthropist, Sir Walter Besant (1836–1901) [sk].

9. As in regard to a number of other points, I am here also taking a position in opposition to our honorable master, Lujo Brentano [see *Die Anfänge des modernen Kapitalismus* (Munich: Akademie der Wissenschaften, 1916)]. We disagree primarily on terms, though also on substantive matters. It does not seem to me helpful to bring together under the same category heterogeneous factors, such as earning a living through seizing booty and earning a living through managing a factory. It appears to me even less helpful to designate every striving to acquire *money* (in contrast to other forms of acquisition) as a "spirit" of capitalism. If one refers to this "spirit" in this manner, the concept loses all precision; if one brings heterogeneous factors together under one category, it becomes impossible to clarify what is specific to Western capitalism vis-à-vis other forms of capitalism.

"The money economy" and "capitalism" are also placed far too closely together in Georg Simmel's *Philosophie des Geldes* (1900) [*The Philosophy of Money*, translated by Tom Bottomore and David Frisby (London: Routledge & Kegan Paul, 1978)], to the detriment also of the substantive analysis. That which is *specific* to the West—the rational organization of work—moves strongly into the background in Werner Sombart's writings, above all in the more recent edition of his fine major work, *Der moderne Kapitalismus* [Leipzig: Duncker & Humblot (2nd edition), 1916–17]. Instead, placed in the foreground are development forces that have been effective throughout the world and not only in the West.

10. The sea loan, which originated in Mediterranean antiquity and became used widely in the Western Middle Ages, was a response to the unusually high danger of shipping by sea and the attempt by borrowers (who had purchased the goods on credit) and creditors to distribute the risk of total loss: the borrower agreed to pay to the creditor an extremely high interest rate (perhaps 30 percent) in exchange for which the creditor assumed liability for the goods in the event of loss. See Weber, *General Economic History* (New Brunswick: Transaction Books, 1981), pp. 204–06 [sk].

11. A type of company that limits liability for owners in respect to both damage caused by faulty products and injuries suffered by employees [sk].

12. In contrast to barter [sk].

13. Again, Weber is using "rational" in the sense of a systematic, organized, disciplined, and economically-efficient manner of organizing work [sk].

14. *Ergasteria* are shops, separate from the private residence, where workers perform their labor. They vary widely, from the bazaar, which combines the place of work and the place of sale, to the factory. Central in all cases is that an entrepreneur prescribes the conditions of work and pays wages. See Weber, *General Economic History* (*ibid.*), pp. 119, 162 [sk].

15. Of course the contrast should not be understood as absolute. Rational, *permanent* businesses grew out of politically-oriented (above all tax farming-based [see ch. 2, note 16]) capitalism as early as antiquity in the Mediterranean and Middle East regions, although also in China and India. Moreover, their accounting, which is known to us only in miserable fragments, may have had a "rational" character. Finally, politically oriented "adventure" capitalism has been closely connected to rational, industrial capitalism with respect to the historical origin of modern *banks*, which for the most part originated out of businesses that were motivated by *political* and military considerations, even as late as the Bank of England [in 1694]. For example, the contrast of the individualism of [its founder William] Paterson, for example, a typical "promoter," to the individualism of members of this Bank's board of trustees (which provided the distinguishing imprint on its long-term policies—the Bank very quickly became known as The Puritan Usurers of Grocers' Hall) is characteristic of the close connection between politically oriented adventure capitalism and rational, industrial capitalism. Just as illustrative is the collapse, on the occasion of the South Sea Bubble [1720; *General Economic History, ibid.*, pp. 289–90], of the policies of this "most solid" Bank.

In sum, the contrast between adventure and rational capitalism is of course a fluid one. Yet it is *there*. A rational organization of *work* was created as little by the titan promoters and financiers as—again, in general and with specific exceptions—by the typical carriers of finance and political capitalism: the Jews. Rather, the rational organization of *work* was created by an entirely different group of people. [See above, pp. 103 ff.]

16. Rodbertus created the term *oikos* for antiquity's large-scale household economies. To him, all economies of the ancient Mediterranean were *oikos* economies. See Weber, *E&S*, pp. 381–84; *Agrarian Sociology of Ancient Civilizations* (London: NLB, 1976), pp. 42–43 [sk].

17. Weber discusses the inefficiencies of slave labor elsewhere. See, for example, *The Agrarian Sociology, ibid.*, (see above note), pp. 202–09 [sk].

18. This sentence is central to Weber's entire argument. It succinctly captures the theme he has been developing over the last few pages: Major historical developments must be understood as occurring in reference to a series of causal forces, and the effect of single factors—such as economic interests—can be ascertained only after an investigation of how they are situated within a context of forces (above referred to as a "social order"). On the "contextual" and "conjunctural" character of causal analysis in Weber's comparative-historical sociology, see Kalberg, *Max Weber's Comparative-Historical Sociology* (Chicago: The University of Chicago Press, 1994), pp. 98–102, 151–92 [sk].

19. Weber adds at this point in the text: "As the later analyses will repeatedly make clear." This is a reference to the volumes that follow this essay in the German edition: *PE*, *The Religion of China* (New York: The Free Press, 1951), *The Religion of India* (New York: The Free Press, 1958),

and *Ancient Judaism* (New York: The Free Press, 1952). Interspersed between these studies are also two central essays, both of which relate to the "rationalism" theme: "The Social Psychology of the World Religions" and "Religious Rejections of the World" [See H. H. Gerth and C. Wright Mills, eds., *From Max Weber* (New York: Oxford University Press, 1946)]. See above, pp. lviii–lxiv [sk].

20. By "other realms of life" Weber has in mind, for example, the arenas of the economy or politics. Because "activity in the world" is valued as worthwhile and meaningful in these realms, the mystic's withdrawal through contemplation is seen as meaningless, or "irrational." See "Religious Rejections of the World" (see above note), pp. 325–26; *E&S*, pp. 541–51 [sk].

21. Weber's use of the expression "circles of cultural life" is not intended to refer to "high," "low," or "popular" culture, as it would today in the United States. Instead, this term (*Kulturkreisen*) in his time refers to various arenas of life, such as the political, economic, religious, scientific, artistic, etc. See the "Religious Rejections of the World" essay (see note 19) [sk].

22. In the volumes that follow in the German edition (see note 19), Weber will refer repeatedly to, for example, "Chinese rationalism," "the rationalism of India," and "the rationalism of the Middle Ages" [sk].

23. Weber is referring to the German edition. *PE* and "The Protestant Sects" essay are placed at the beginning of the three-volume study [sk].

24. Namely, the side of the causal relationship involving the influence of "internal factors," that is, ideas and values [sk].

25. Namely, the "other" side of the causal relationship, that is, in Weber's terms the causal role of "interests," or "external factors." Hence Weber's famous formulation: "ideas and interests." See, for example, "The Social Psychology of the World Religions" (see note 19), p. 280; "Religious Rejections of the World" (see note 19), pp. 325–26 [sk].

26. Weber did not live to write a systematic volume on this subject. Innumerable short statements that compare the development of the West to that of China and India are found throughout his substantive works. See, for example, *E&S*, pp. 551–56, 809–38, 1064–69, 1108–09, 1192–93, 1236–65; *General Economic History* (see note 10), pp. 315–37; "Prospects for Democracy in Tsarist Russia," in *Weber: Selections in Translation*, ed. by W. G. Runciman (Cambridge, UK: Cambridge University Press, 1978), pp. 282–83; *The Religion of China* (see note 19), pp. 226–49; *The Religion of India* (see note 19), pp. 33–44, 329–43. See also Kalberg, *Max Weber's Sociology of Civilizations* (forthcoming) [sk].

27. Also the remains of my knowledge of Hebrew are entirely unreliable.

28. See "Science as a Vocation" (in Gerth and Mills; see note 19), p. 138.

29. I need not note that attempts such as those on the one hand by Karl Jaspers, in his book *Psychology of World Views* [Berlin: Springer, 1919], or on the other hand by Ludwig Klages [see *Charakterkunde*, (Leipzig, 1910)] and similar studies, do not fall into this category. These investigations can all be distinguished from what is here attempted by reference to their differing point of departure. This is not the place for a critical confrontation.

30. For Weber's more succinct formulations of the tasks and limits of science, see "Science as a Vocation" (in Gerth and Mills; see note 19), pp. 138–39, 145–48, 150–51 [sk].

31. Weber contends here that those who wish to pursue social science (as he does) must not come too close to the object under investigation. "Intuition" does not provide the appropriate distance [sk].

32. Weber did so in his chapter "Sociology of Religion" in *E&S* (pp. 399–634) [sk].

33. Many years ago an excellent psychiatrist expressed the same opinion to me. ✦

NAME INDEX

SUBJECT INDEX

X, Y, Z